MARX, REASON, AND THE ART OF FREEDOM

Foreword by
Marx W. Wartofsky

MARX, REASON,
AND THE ART
OF FREEDOM

Second Edition

KEVIN M. BRIEN

Humanity
Books

an imprint of Prometheus Books
59 John Glenn Drive, Amherst, New York 14228-2197

Published 2006 by Humanity Books, an imprint of Prometheus Books

Inquiries should be addressed to
Prometheus Books
59 John Glenn Drive
Amherst, New York 14228–2197
VOICE: 716–691–0133, ext. 207
FAX: 716–564–2711
WWW.PROMETHEUSBOOKS.COM

10 09 08 07 06   5 4 3 2 1

Library of Congress Cataloging-in-Publication Data

Brien, Kevin M.
  Marx, reason, and the art of freedom / Kevin M. Brien.–2nd ed.
      p. cm.
  Originally published: Philadelphia: Temple University Press, 1987.
  Includes bibliographical references (p.) and index.
  ISBN 1–59102–366–1 (alk. paper)
  1. Marx, Karl, 1818–1883. 2. Liberty. I Title.

B3305.M74B73 2005
123'.5'092—dc22

                                                                        2005052725

Printed in the United States of America on acid-free paper

In memory of
Karl Marx,
Social-Scientist—Philosopher
(1818–1883)
&
Marx W. Wartofsky,
Philosopher—Artist
(1928—1997)

Contents

Contents

Foreword

by Marx W. Wartofsky

An appropriate subtitle of Kevin Brien's book on Marx might well be "Taking Marx Seriously." In this extraordinarily rich and systematic study, Professor Brien makes it clear that Marx is neither to be taken piecemeal, nor is he to be taken to have had the last word. Now this takes Marx very seriously indeed; for it insists on taking Marx whole, in two senses: first, in attempting to understand any given aspect of Marx's thought, or any part of the body of his work, in relation to a larger and systematic framework of thought and method of inquiry (which Brien reconstructs); second, in showing that Marx himself thought of his project in these terms, that is, that he was a philosophically systematic thinker. Thus, in his presentation of Marx's thought, Brien brings different aspects, different subject matters, different periods of Marx's work into connection with each other, in order to clarify and deepen our understanding of these parts. But he does not propose that there is some finished "totality," some unchanging essence or structure standing behind the currents and shifts in Marx's thought. Rather, Brien sees the corpus of Marx's work as a dialectical unity, as a developing set of views and analyses through which there runs a red thread (if one is permitted to say so) of method.

Brien takes Marx seriously also in another way: he regards the project of Marx's thought as open-ended and incomplete. Therefore, Brien offers us what I would characterize as an *empathetic reconstruction* of Marx, and a projection of what ought to follow from what Marx *did* say, about what Marx did *not* say, but *would* have said concerning a number of important issues.

Marx's thought has not been treated kindly, either by its enemies or by its friends. What has emerged, in the century since Marx's death, is a series of largely antithetical readings of Marx, made plausible only by the radical measure of bisecting the Marxian corpus, into "two Marx-isms": "early" and "late"; "humanist" and "positivist"; "Feuerbachian" and "scientific"; "radical democrat" and "Prussian authoritarian"; "rigid determinist" and "voluntarist"; "reductionist" and "emergentist." One view of relatively recent vintage has it that *all* of these diverse elements are "in" Marx, and that just as the devil can quote scripture, there are many devils who can quote Marx. Another, older view has it that Marx's views changed radically at a certain juncture (e.g., with the *Theses on Feuerbach* of 1845, or with *Capital* in 1867) and that this accounts for the two Marxisms. The difficulty has been that Marx seems to use very different categories, even a different philosophical and technical vocabulary and linguistic framework, at different stages of his thought, and that certain fundamental ideas seem to change, or indeed vanish in his later work.

Professor Brien takes the hard road: he proposes that there is a deep unity and continuity through all of Marx's thought. But that leaves him with the problem of showing that there is coherence where others have seen divergence, or where Marx seems to be at cross-purposes with himself. Brien acknowledges the difficulties, and goes back to the texts for his arguments. What he attempts to show is that the bifurcated Marx is the product of misreading and misinterpretation, *or* that, where Marx has left a question undiscussed, there is a plausible reconstruction of what one could say, within the Marxian project, that avoids or refutes the rejected reading.

All this lends itself to some lively criticism, as well as appreciative appropriation of various contemporary writers on Marx and Marxism. The surge of Marx scholarship in the two decades, 1960-80, (and since) comes under Brien's scrutiny; names one would expect: Ollman, Baran and Sweezy, Althusser, Marcuse, Mészáros, Gould, Rader, among others; Popper, of course, for his misreading of Marx's "Historicism." But then, names one would not expect: Blanshard on internal relations and on concrete universals (and in footnotes, E. Nagel's criticism of Blanshard); a critique of the Oppenheim–Putnam "Unity of Science" essay; and an appropriation and extension of Bohm's interpretation of quantum-theory. Strikingly, also, Brien devotes a long and important discussion to Marx's (and Marxism's) view on the social relation between men and women, in the light of the feminist literature of the recent period, (e.g., Firestone, Chodorow, Harding, Reed).

All of this lies before the reader. But what is most important is Brien's view of Marx's thought as principally, and systematically, a discourse on human freedom, or better yet, an elaborated philosophical-scientific theory of freedom. This is the framework of Brien's work, and within it, he attempts to show how, for Marx, the political economy and the philosophical anthropology, the metaphysics and the empirical research, the theory of history and the aesthetics of free creative activity are all related to each other in deeply systematic ways.

This is a book generous in intellect and in temperament, ambitious in its project, provocative in its serious assessment of the greatness and complexity of Marx's thought. It deserves a hard and critical reading. For taking Marx seriously, Brien deserves to be taken seriously.

Introduction to the Second Edition

What English-speaking person is not familiar with the following famed verse?

O' say does that star spangled banner yet wave
O'er the land of the free and the home of the brave?

How many, though, ever dwell on the ambiguity of the term "free" that has come to be enveloped here in the aura of the sacred? Think of the differing connotations of these phrases: *being free from, being free to, being free for*, and *being free at*. Think, for example, of situations like the following: being free *from* the power of a dictator to oppressively determine one's life; being free *to* speak one's mind, or practice one's religion; being *potentially* free *for* individual development along whatever lines one might choose; and being *actually* free *at* some creative activity that actualizes one's powers.

But think, too, of the possibilities of one person or group seeking to be free in ways that might dynamically interfere with other people also being "free" in some way. Could it be that the complicated skein of meanings of the term "free" as currently understood is such that in some situations, the freedom of one person or group might actually be based on a diminution in the freedom of another person or group? Could it be that the sacred aura that hovers around the notion of "the land of the free" might actually cloak an unconscious allegiance to a social agenda that makes it impossible for everyone to be free, while simultaneously promising and then offering certain kinds of compensatory wish-fulfillment?

While such issues would in themselves be reason enough to undertake a philosophical exploration of the meaning of freedom, more compelling reasons for such an exploration begin to emerge as one considers the political atmosphere that envelopes planet Earth at this juncture in history. Consider just a few of the major factors that have deeply shaped the current political atmosphere: (a) the break up of the Soviet bloc, together with the disappearance of the Soviet Union as a superpower; (b) the subsequent emergence of the United States as the sole world superpower on the threshold of the twenty-first century; (c) the surge of religious fundamentalism throughout the world—including Muslim fundamentalism in the Middle East and elsewhere, Hindu fundamentalism in India, and Christian fundamentalism in the United States; (d) the recourse to terrorism by militant fundamentalist groups in a vast panoply of incidents throughout the world, and the development of world-wide terrorist networks; and (e) an ever mushrooming military-industrial complex in the United States, and throughout the world.

Then add to this volatile mixture other factors, such as the widening gap between the richer and poorer segments of the populations of the various nations; egregious corporate scandals in the United States and elsewhere; the global spread of the ethos of materialism and consumerism; a burgeoning world population; growing environmental degradation; a host of lingering and mounting tensions in hot spots throughout the world; and, of course, the arms trade, together with the development of ever more sophisticated weaponry as well as the political willingness to use it; and finally the ongoing development of militarism around the world.

One can only conclude that we who are now alive, standing as we do on the threshold of the twenty-first century, live in times that are fraught with peril. The threats to freedom in *some* of its various meanings, and often in *all* of them, loom over all of us in one way or another—no matter where we might live; for our global economic and social village becomes increasingly mired in deepening trouble. Is there any realistic course of remedial action that could be effective in *humanely* coping with such problems? More importantly perhaps, is there any worthy cultural horizon toward which to orient such action?

Now I do not share any utopian belief that there is some kind of effective panacea that would enable humankind to adequately cope with *all* the serious threats that face it at this juncture in its history. However, while recognizing the immense practical difficulties involved, I do argue in what follows that it is theoretically possible, *nonetheless*, for a gradual shift toward a more advanced stage of cultural evolution to become established—a stage which would be much more humanely effective in addressing such a daunting array of cultural problems as those just indicated above. I argue, too, that for such a shift to come about a widespread transformation of consciousness amounting to a sort of spiritual revolution would be required. My arguments are presented from within a humanistic Marxist philosophical/scientific paradigm; for it is within this paradigm and its intricate web of philosophical presuppositions that I comprehend the possibilities for development toward a new stage of cultural evolution. So in what follows I have also been especially concerned to lay out as clearly as possible the main lines of what I have come to construe as a *humanistic Marxist multidimensional perspective on "Reality."*

Here let me indicate that I am mindful of the fact that in the aftermath of the breakup of the Soviet Union and the Soviet bloc there seems to be a strong tendency in many quarters to dismiss Marx's philosophy as passé or irrelevant—even basically erroneous—since presumably it has been refuted by history. In my view, though, what has really been refuted is not Marx's philosophy as such, but rather some seriously misguided attempts to implement various radically flawed versions of his philosophy. So then, I invite my readers to explore with me a way of looking with new eyes at Marx.

In 1987 I published the first edition of this book because of my belief that Marx's scientific/philosophical paradigm, when seen in the appropriate way, stands as the most viable currently available perspective for understanding human cultural evolution; and also because of my belief that Marx's paradigm, when properly understood, provides extremely fruitful guidance for nurturing a development toward a new plateau of human culture and of human freedom. In undertaking to publish this second edition after the break up of the Soviet Union, and now well into the twenty-first century, these beliefs still function as my basic motivation.

My primary concern in what follows is to articulate the philosophical dimensions of Marx's paradigm—and with a central focus on the problem of freedom. But I do not thereby mean to suggest in any way that there is an essential dichotomy between the philosophical and scientific dimensions of Marx's paradigm. Indeed I believe that the projection of such an essential dichotomy radically distorts both the philosophical and the scientific dimensions of his thought. To be sure the scientific dimension of Marx's thought is vastly important—so much so that I personally consider Marx to be the Newton of social science. But his kind of social science does not float on some kind of positivist raft; rather it is rooted in a philosophical background which must inform the interpretation of all the foreground concepts of the scientific dimension. A major problem, though, is that Marx himself never gave us a systematic articulation of his philosophical paradigm. My objective in what follows, then, is to bring this philosophical background into the foreground by articulating its most essential aspects.

In the work that is carried out here, I attempted to project myself in imagination into the perspective of the mature Marx; and I set myself the task of developing an analysis of the philosophical problem of freedom from this perspective. But the analysis to come, although having a primary focus on the philosophical problem of freedom in Marx, also gives developed attention to the themes of theoretical and practical reason in Marx. For, after all, there is a deep conceptual connection between a given philosopher's view of freedom and that philosopher's understanding of theoretical and practical reason.

This is a work of philosophical reconstruction that draws on the full chronological spectrum of Marx's writings. The analysis is structured in keeping with Marx's level-by-level method of dialectical explanation as it obtains in its most developed form in the three volumes of his scientific magnum opus, *Capital*. In the philosophical reconstruction of Marx that I present in keeping with this method, much attention is given to the explicit analysis of various philosophical presuppositions implicitly adopted by Marx. The reconstruction also involves various dialectical extensions of Marx's thinking suggested by his method; and it involves the filling in of various conceptual gaps that stand as "research problems" for Marx's theoretical perspective. Sometimes, too, this philosophical reconstruction involves "critical departures" from Marx's stated positions on certain issues—and "critical appropriations" of earlier positions from the mature perspective.

Chapter 1 sketches the main lines of Marx's conception of human reality. My discussion begins with the notion of being-in-the-world. I note, though, that my use of the phrase "being-in-the-world" throughout this work is not the use of a Heideggerian *concept*, but simply the use of an apt phrase to which I give a very different meaning than the one given to it by Heidegger. Nor do I intend to insinuate any connections with Heidegger's concerns by using this phrase. Rather my concern is to stress that human beings are natural beings existing within a wider natural world that by and large exists independently of humankind—but also that they are natural beings who shape and reshape their subjectivity over time by their changing activity in and upon the natural world. Thus I reject the conflation of the ontological into the phenomenological that we find in Heidegger, while also recognizing that Marxist-humanist ontology gives full recognition to human subjectivity and to its historicity. The particular conception of being-in-the-world I explain comes directly from Marx himself, though Marx himself does not use the phrase.

Also it is methodologically significant that my exploration of freedom in Marx begins with this notion. For, when seen in the light of Marx's dialectical method of explanation, I hold that this notion is the most appropriate beginning for a *level-by-level dialectical explanation* of the nature of freedom as seen from within Marx's perspective. Among other things, my readers will come to see that Marx's conception of being-in-the-world can *itself* only be adequately comprehended in a level-by-level explanatory movement. Also, they will come to see that it constitutes a kind of structured matrix that is oriented toward more fully developed levels of elaboration. Moreover, such a beginning will provide my readers with an outlook that will enable them to envision how this notion is conceptually interwoven with the thesis of historical materialism which figures so centrally in Marx's thought. Importantly, too, it will give them an early sense of the way Marx's thesis of historical materialism can *only* be properly understood if it too is conceptually situated in a level-by-level explanatory movement that implicitly points to its more concrete elaborations.

Chapter 2 offers an analysis of Marx's mature level-by-level method of dialectical explanation. This analysis, while building on other thinkers who have brought out the significance of internal relations in Marx's thinking, also goes beyond them by bringing out the crucial role of the *concrete universal* in understanding Marx's level-by-level method of dialectical explanation. I see this method as a *nondeductive dialectical-empirical* method of explanation—a method that essentially involves the concrete universal as a basic canon of interpretation as the explanatory movement is played out from more abstract to more concrete levels. No other treatment of Marx's method of explanation that I know about brings out the role of this canon of interpretation; but it is a canon that significantly changes everything in subtle ways when it is systematically brought into play in a dialectical explanatory movement.

Here let me enter a caveat for my readers. My application of Marx's method of explanation throughout this book calls for my readers to make a methodological shift in the direction toward which they must orient themselves if they are to see how the justification of some of the claims that I make about Marx is to be properly assessed. In fact, the methodological peculiarities of the explanatory movement that is applied in the philosophical reconstruction of Marx that I offer conceptually mandate a shift in the direction in which justification of claims is to be sought. In this context I point out that much of what I say is initially likely to be regarded as controversial—especially by those who have already developed their own settled interpretation of Marx before coming to my book. However, an openness on the part of my readers to consider the methodological shift to which I refer will go a long way toward dissipating the aura of controversy.

Perhaps a metaphor and then an example will help here. Think of a three-dimensional pyramid made of stones. The vertex of the pyramid is not self-supporting. Rather it is supported by the configuration of stones laid out on the base, as well as by the configurations of stones laid out on the various levels of stone built upon the base. Just so, the concepts I project and the claims that I make *on the more abstract levels* of the explanatory movement are not self-supporting; but find their support, and their justification in relation to the much more complexly structured elaborations provided later on at the more concrete levels.

As an example let me point to the category of "freedom as transcendence" that I bring into focus at the very beginning of Chapter 3 (although I give it preliminary treatment toward the end of Chapter 1). My projection of this category goes like this: "Human beings are always more than antecedent conditions may have made them be, by virtue of their capacity to make what they become by their own activity." Nowhere in his works does Marx himself articulate this category in this specific way. However this category is projected as a philosophical postulate that I have abstracted out of the vast array of rich-textured discussions bearing on the issue of human freedom that Marx *does* give in various places over the course of his life's work. Let me stress that I have abstracted it only after many, many years of careful exploration of Marx's texts—and I have projected it because I believe it serves as a methodologically viable matrix for carrying out the philosophical reconstruction of Marx that I envision.

What then about the justification for using the category of "freedom-as-transcendence"? If I may use that old cliché still again, I suggest that the proof of the pudding is in the eating. The justification for projecting this category is really a practical one—namely the actual success of the subsequent elaboration of the various dimensions of Marx's thought bearing on the issue of human freedom that is carried out within the projected matrix of this category. This elaboration is coherently and systematically presented in accordance with a nondeductive explanatory movement moving from abstract to concrete, and in a way that is tied to a host of specific passages in Marx as the explanatory movement is carried out. *Thus, it is the complexly structured concrete elaboration that provides the theoretical justification for the abstractly projected claims.*

Before turning to some introductory remarks on other chapters, I note that this methodological chapter is a philosophically important one because, in my view, the established interpretations of Marx all fail (in one way or another) to come to adequate grips with Marx's mature method of explanation. This is especially true of those interpretations that project a sharp dichotomy between the early and late Marx. However, although this is an important chapter, it is not methodologically significant that it is placed in the text where it is. In any case, this chapter is a demanding one for the reader. I urge most readers to read the later chapters before reading this one. Among other things, this would allow readers to develop a sense of Marx's dialectical method *via its usage* in the course of the discussion undertaken in the various chapters. This, in turn, would make for easier going over the very abstract terrain of Chapter 2.

The bulk of my presentation is given in Chapters 3, 4, 5, and 6—and Marx's dialectical method is in play throughout. These chapters explore the problem of freedom under three main categories of freedom that I distinguish: (a) freedom-as-transcendence; (b) freedom-as-a-mode-of-being; and (c) freedom-as-spontaneity.

Chapters 3 and 4 are developed under the category of "freedom as transcendence." Marx's thesis of historical materialism is seen to be central for understanding how this category is to be interpreted within Marx's framework. Among other things, I provide critical remarks concerning some of the dominant ways of construing historical materialism; and I go on to bring out that the thesis of historical materialism, when properly seen in connection with Marx's level-by-level method of dialectical explanation, really constitutes a conceptual matrix for a theory of cultural evolution that must be understood in relation to more concrete articulations that take into account complicating factors that Marx himself did not explicitly address. Then I articulate some laws of cultural development—i.e., laws construed in terms of dynamic structural tendencies. In the course of the discussion I go on to situate male-female social relations within the level-by-level articulation. Also I explore some key structural tendencies of capitalism; and in addition I address the issue of a potential transcending agency.

Chapter 5 is carried out under the category of "freedom-as-a-mode-of-being." The primary concern of this chapter is to give a developed account of what an unalienated mode of being might look like as interpreted from within Marx's philosophical perspective. This analysis is carried out against the contrasting background of Marx's positions concerning alienated modes of being. In the ongoing discussion I give developed positions on unalienated social relationships, unalienated production, unalienated activity, and unalienated modes of reason and of sensuousness.

Chapter 6 is carried out under the category of "freedom-as-spontaneity." I bring out that fully understanding Marx's scientific/philosophical paradigm requires a recognition of an important philosophical presupposition he makes to the effect that there is a margin of freedom from antecedent causal conditioning in the social world, and in nature at large. I note that in his doctoral dissertation he explicitly indicates his belief in some sort of real indeterminacy in nature, and also suggests some real indeterminacy in the domain of human events. Then, for my part, I take the position that running through all of Marx's later work is his philosophical presupposition that there is some degree of indeterminacy in the domain of human events.

I develop these themes by contrasting an analysis of the *classical* conception of the unity of science on the one hand, with a tentative analysis of a *dialectical* conception of the unity of science on the other hand. Then I go on to address the question of a dialectics of nature. In this connection I explore Engels' views concerning purported "laws of dialectics." In doing so, though, I show how Engels' formulations would have to be critically appropriated if they are to harmonize with Marx's own dialectical method of explanation.

In passing, I should indicate that I nowhere *attribute* a dialectical nonreductive theory of the unity of science to Marx himself. Rather I construct a metascientific interpretation of such a view of science that would be fully in keeping with Marx's dialectical method of explanation as I have presented it. My intent is to provide a tentative exposition of a dialectical theory of the unity of science as a speculative extension of Marx's philosophic/scientific paradigm. Among other things, this brings out the potential fruitfulness and explanatory power of his method for science in general. Of course, just how fruitful my construction of a dialectical nonreductive theory of the unity of science might be as speculative extension of Marx's paradigm is something that remains to be seen.

Following this brief indication of the content of the various chapters, I venture to relate my book to the general literature on Marx. I do this by referring to Alvin Gouldner's book, *The Two Marxisms*.[1] This book reflects a tension in the existing literature about Marx concerning two major dimensions of his thought. These dimensions seem to conflict with, and even contradict, each other. The "two Marxisms" that Gouldner speaks about are "critical Marxism" and "scientific Marxism." As characterized by Gouldner: "critical Marxism" emphasizes the continuity with Hegel, as well as the continuity between the early and late Marx. It focuses on "praxis," alienation, and the new human being. It advocates a voluntaristic attitude toward social action. And it is antipositivist in tone. (However, it generally superimposes a positivist interpretation on the scientific dimension of Marx's thought—as with the Frankfurt School, for example.[2]) According to Gouldner: "scientific Marxism," in turn, emphasizes the discontinuity with Hegel, and holds to a split between the early and late Marx. It focuses on deterministic laws that somehow ensure the inevitability of socialism. It is much more passive in its attitude toward social action; and it has a decidedly positivist character.

Now, I do not dispute with Gouldner that the existing literature bears witness to an alleged conceptual conflict between the two dimensions of Marx's thought. Nor do I dispute that partisans of each dimension have been pitted against partisans of the other in their respective interpretations of Marx. But I hold that there is no such conflict in Marx's own intricately worked-out analysis. Once Marx's mature method of dialectical explanation is understood, the claim that there is a fundamental philosophical conflict between the critical and scientific dimensions of his thought can readily be seen to be illusory.

For what we have in the work of the mature Marx is a "critical science," in which the critical and scientific dimensions must be seen as being harmoniously integrated. The alleged conflict rests on a positivist interpretation of the scientific dimension of Marx's thought that systematically distorts what he is actually doing. Moreover, we have, in the artful level-by-level method of dialectical explanation at play in the mature Marx, an instrument for making clear the essential philosophical continuity of the early and late Marx, as well as the philosophical harmony of the critical and scientific dimensions—and an instrument for doing so from the perspective of the mature Marx.

This said, let me relate my book to the literature on Marx in still another way. Just as I disagree with those interpretations that project a sharp dichotomy between the early and the late Marx—or between the critical and scientific dimensions of his thought—so do I disagree with those interpretations that project a sharp philosophical dichotomy between Marx and Engels. To say this does not mean I take them to be seamlessly related, though. In fact I do not even take the various stages of Marx's thought to be seamlessly related. For one can find contradictions between isolated comments Marx makes at one stage of his development as a thinker, and those he makes at other stages. Moreover, even some of the things Marx says at a given stage contradict other things he says at the *same* stage.

In any case, contradictions do obtain between Marx and Engels on some things; and of course there are many differences of emphasis in their respective writings. One of the main differences is Engels' emphasis on dialectical development in nature at large, versus Marx's emphasis on dialectical development in human cultural, social, and economic contexts. Not only that, but there are some significant differences between the specific way that Engels presents and explains his view of a dialectics of nature, and the way that I present a dialectics of nature *as it might be seen* in terms of Marx's dialectical explanatory movement when one critically appropriates Engels.

Before leaving this context, a few words on orthodox Marxism. While it might be true that orthodox Marxism views Marx and Engels as being seamlessly related, I reject both the sharp split between the early and late Marx that orthodox Marxism projects, and also the reading of Engels that is associated with orthodox Marxism. My bringing Engels and Marx together in the way I do (but *not* in a way that is *seamless*) implies my abandoning the orthodox Marxist interpretations of both Marx and Engels. Both of them have fallen prey to persistent positivist distortions of their work. In fact, I submit that much of the positivist distortion of Marx has its historical roots in the positivist distortion of Engels. Positivism was easily foisted onto Engels, and rubbed off him onto Marx. I shall try to break away from some of the distortions of Engels when I bring him on the scene at various points in the discussion ahead.

Next, let me say something about the relation of this book to my sources. To begin with, I want to stress that the writings of Marx stand as my primary source. My major concern has been to present a philosophically systematic interpretation of freedom from Marx's mature perspective—and one which draws on the full chronological spectrum of his thought. However, I also want to acknowledge an enormous intellectual debt to all the secondary sources I have explored. Without the stimulation of these works, and my internal dialogue with, and reflection upon them, this book would not have been possible. But while I try to celebrate as much as possible the many thinkers with whom I have internally dialogued about Marx in advancing my own interpretation of Marx, it has not really been possible to do justice to the various secondary works that have been cited; nor was there any attempt on my part to address *all* the various interpretations of Marx's thought that have become available. When I do refer to secondary works, it is often to adopt clear formulations, already provided by various authors, on themes that are also essential for my own analysis. But often, too, I give sharp criticisms of certain positions taken by various authors when they provided a convenient counterpoint to bring out my own position. This helps me to differentiate my own position and to advance the interpretation of Marx that I propose, but there is no intent to diminish the overall importance of the contributions to the understanding of Marx made in these works.

If I were asked what I take to be novel about my project, I would point first to its structure—although I believe there are novel elements throughout it as well. For what I most particularly take to be novel is the way in which the various aspects of my dialectical presentation of the categories of freedom in Marx are synthesized in a level-by-level philosophical reconstruction and extension of Marx's paradigm carried out in accordance with Marx's mature method of dialectical explanation. Then, also, there is my developed articulation and analysis of this method of explanation in a way that brings out the crucial role of the "concrete universal"—a notion that does not come into play in any other treatment of Marx's method of explanation I know about; and it is a notion that significantly changes everything in subtle ways when it is systematically brought into play in a dialectical explanatory movement.

Next, a comment on the style of presentation in what follows. My concern throughout was to provide as clear a sense of the theoretical structures of Marx's philosophical perspective on freedom and reason as was possible. To this end, I have used language in a way that would bring these structures into full relief with maximum clarity. Although I have adopted the "we" mode of speech as a literary device throughout the text, there is no wish to be authoritarian in what is said. The "we" can be taken as a spokesperson for Marx's dialectical-humanist perspective whose task it is to bring the theoretical structures of the position into full relief. But this "we" is intended as a "socialist we"—not a "royal we." Thus the particular positions this spokesperson assumes are everywhere intended to be provisional, open to further elaboration, and subject to modification in the light of further study and further critical dialogue. I do not take myself as trying to give any final word on anything about Marx.

Finally, I want to make some personal acknowledgments. First, my mentors, Robert S. Cohen and Marx W. Wartofsky. Without their inspiration as philosophers, as scholars, and as deep humanists, this work would not have been possible. Without their rigorous standards, which I accepted and tried to meet, this work would not have been possible. Without their hard criticism of earlier versions of the various chapters, this work would not have been possible. But the book owes more to them still, since it is a work which is rooted in their work, and which stands within the tradition of interpretation of Marx with which they associate themselves. However, the "we" mode of speech that I use in the text does not imply that my mentors would necessarily agree with everything I say on every issue.

I also want to express my deep gratitude to a number of other people who encountered my manuscript at various stages of its development, and who shared many encouraging critical comments ranging over the whole work or just sections of it. They include Alasdair MacIntyre, Karsten Harries, Loyd D. Easton, John Lachs, Ronald E. Santoni, Joseph Margolis, Carol C. Gould, Bertell Ollman, Iris Young, Michael Howard, Sandra Harding, James Lawler, Joseph L. Walsh, Howard L. Parsons, J. David Newell, Robert Anderson, Peter Tapke, Janusz Kuczynski, Albert Anderson, Jerzy Hubert, Kusum Jain, Jane Cullen, Jazmine Gabriel, Ann O'Hear, and Diane Shields. Moreover, Daniel Little, Marilyn Nissim-Sabat, Chris Sciabarra, Hugh Wilder, Sean Sayers, and John W. Murphy all published appreciative and helpful critical reviews of the first edition. Also I am grateful for support from the Boston Philosophy of Science Association. Last, I want to acknowledge the important role that many of my students have played over the years in the generation of this book, including the new material. Their attentive listening to rough preliminary formulations, their careful reading of earlier versions of the various chapters, their appreciative comments, as well as their challenging questions, were all significant factors in developing the book, including all the new material.

In addition to this new introduction, this second edition also includes an extended *Postscript* that did not appear in the first edition. The first part of it is a response to some issues raised in various published critical reviews of my book. My intention is to respond briefly to some of the main criticisms that came up in these reviews that I have not already addressed in my new introduction. For it seems to me that many of my new readers are quite likely to be concerned with some of the very same issues as were brought up by these reviewers. Hopefully the responses I give to their comments in what follows will clarify a number of these issues for my new readers. But I note that a completely developed response to some of them must await another occasion.

I believe the most important issues that are addressed in this part concern my interpretation of Marx's dialectical method of explanation. Among other things, I try to parry an attempt by one reviewer to construe Marx's method of explanation as a traditional empirical method that is *not* dialectical at all. In doing so my aim is to clarify the way in which I take Marx's method of explanation to be a *dialectical empirical* method. Furthermore, and most importantly, I show how the *specific form* of Marx's dialectical method of explanation that I have elaborated and applied in the main body of my text is one that *can subsume under itself* some of the variant competing interpretations of Marx's method of explanation that are now current—especially the "logic of institutions" model of explanation and the "functional" model of explanation associated with the tradition of analytic Marxism.

While these competing interpretations are significant so far as they go, I believe they do not go nearly far enough in capturing the many dimensions of Marx's method—especially the many philosophical dimensions of his thought. Nor do they bring out the full explanatory power of his method—especially as it concerns the integration of the philosophical and scientific dimensions of his paradigm. However, I hold that what they do capture can be readily encompassed within the broader methodological framework of the interpretation I have elaborated. Thus I argue that a *dialectical* "logic of institutions" model of explanation is actually embedded within Marx's dialectical-empirical method of explanation; and further, that the functional model of explanation as it might apply to Marx can be fully integrated into the dialectical method of explanation that I have presented.

The second part of the *Postscript* presents an interpretation of the spiritual dimension in keeping with Marx's paradigm—and thereby addresses what I personally take to be the main philosophical lacuna of the first edition. Also, I believe that my manner of presenting the spiritual dimension in Marx is methodologically significant. For it amounts to a kind of *dialectical extrapolation* from much of what Marx himself explicitly says about changing human nature throughout the whole range of his thought—an extrapolation carried out in accordance with my understanding of Marx's mature method of dialectical explanation. As such it systematically integrates the spiritual dimension with the theory of historical materialism, as well as with the overall philosophical reconstruction of Marx that I offer; and thereby brings out that what I say about the spiritual dimension notion is not artificially grafted onto Marx. Furthermore, my manner of presentation helps to more fully draw out the explanatory power of Marx's method of explanation by extending it in new directions, and displaying its potential fruitfulness in so doing. Last, it helps to address the serious problem of identifying a potential revolutionizing agency in the context of the twenty-first century—that is, a transcending agency that could have the potential to foster a development toward a new plateau of human cultural evolution.

In the main body of my text I argue that transforming male-female social relations in holistic ways is crucially important for transcending the crisis of the human person in which we are all enmeshed. But this is just part of what needs to happen! In my addendum on the spiritual dimension, I go on to add that going beyond the terrible racist modes of being with which human cultures have been so sadly riven for so many ages is also crucially important. Furthermore, as I see things, transforming both racist and male-female social relations *requires building holistic coalitions* between and among the various specialized groups focused on confronting sexism, racism, economic-class problems, environmental degradation, etc.—and holistic coalitions not only within the capitalist countries themselves, but between those countries and other countries throughout the world wherever oppressed, exploited, marginalized, alienated, and neglected people suffer. But, one might ask, how could this ever happen? It is my deep belief that a nondogmatic, nonsectarian, *this-world* oriented attitude concerning the spiritual dimension holds great promise for building such transcending holistic coalitions that could nurture developments toward a new plateau of cultural evolution—while acknowledging and even cultivating diversity.

Finally, I note that this second edition also includes an addendum on Marxism and Buddhism. This addendum is important to the themes of this book for many reasons. Among other things, it provides a concentrated distillation of the main dimensions of humanistic Marxism explored throughout this book. Thereby it serves to clearly distinguish humanistic Marxism from orthodox Marxism—especially the version of it that was dominant in the former Soviet Union—and from other distortions of Marx. Furthermore, it also highlights the essential role that the spiritual dimension of human reality would play in a transition from capitalism to a genuine socialism.

In this addendum I also argue that, despite some significant differences, the core of humanistic Marxism and the core of Buddhism mutually complement one another, and that these perspectives converge on the same basic values. My argument serves to bring out the viability of the projection of a spiritual dimension that does not invoke a creator god or a substantial soul such as I find in Marx inasmuch as Buddhism while being recognized as one of the great world religions, has never subscribed to a creator god or a substantial soul. My argument in this addendum also strengthens the philosophical case I make in the book as a whole for a potential transcending social agency in the contemporary historical juncture. By showing how there is a convergence of values between humanistic Marxism and Buddhism, and therefore how there is a genuine moral basis for common social action among adherents of these perspectives, I also point to the pathway for establishing holistic coalitions among various specialized groups focused on confronting sexism, racism, economic class problems, environmental degradation, etc.

MARX,
REASON,
AND
THE ART
OF
FREEDOM

1

Being-in-the-World

In the first chapter we shall sketch in broad strokes the main lines of Marx's view of human reality. To accomplish this it will help to employ the concept of being-in-the-world as a central concept around which to gather the various elements that in their interrelatedness constitute Marx's concept of human reality. But first, a word on terminology.

The phrase "being-in-the-world" is perhaps most frequently associated with Martin Heidegger's phenomenological analysis of human reality in *Being and Time*.[1] Because of this association it is necessary to stress that the usage of the phrase "being-in-the-world" in the discussion that follows is very different from Heidegger's usage of the same phrase. Heidegger's conception of being-in-the-world is a phenomenological one which would conflate the ontological into the phenomenological. However, the conception of being-in-the-world introduced here is projected as an ontological conception that would resist conflation into the phenomenological. It is a much broader conception than Heidegger's phenomenological conception. For, although it takes account of phenomena, it is also concerned to get at the essential structures of reality on the basis of which the phenomena come to be the phenomena. It can be considered as a fundamental ontological postulate concerning the relation between mind and body, and between other minds and bodies. And it is a postulate of both theoretical and practical reason as interpreted in a dialectical–humanist universe of discourse.

The methodological significance of beginning this work on human freedom with the concept of being-in-the-world will only become apparent following the discussion of Marx's method of analysis undertaken in Chapter 2. That discussion will make clear that the conception of being-in-the-world at play in what follows is an abstract schema that can serve as a proper starting point for the explanation of freedom to

1

follow. It will also make clear that this conception of being-in-the-world is intentionally oriented toward more concrete elaborations in relation to which it is to be more fully comprehended. The rationale for using the phrase "being-in-the-world" will stand out as the discussion proceeds.

Being-in-the-World

Being-in-the-world is the most general characteristic of human reality for Marx. It is the basic ontological structure of human existence and of human consciousness. This holds across the board no matter what society and what period of human development might be considered. But what does it mean to say that being-in-the-world is the basic ontological structure of human existence?[2]

It means first that the relationship in which the human being stands to the natural world, and to other people in the natural world, is constitutive of human existence itself. It means this both in the sense of the very existence of the human subject and in the sense of the particular constellation of ideas, needs, drives, activities, and the like, that characterize human existence at any point in the history of human development. And it means in addition that the natural world is absolutely necessary for the formation, exercise, and confirmation of human powers.

Consider first being-in-the-world in the sense that the very existence of the human subject is constituted by the human being's relationship to the natural world. To say that the human being is a being-in-the-world in this sense is meant to affirm that the relationship between consciousness and the natural world is an internal relationship. Without the natural world there would be no human existence, no human consciousness. The so-called independent subject that confronts the natural world as object is not at all independent of that world, but is only given as a function of the dynamic interrelationship obtaining between the human organism and its environment.[3] Thus the human being is not just in the world. There is a necessary internal connection between the human being and the natural world. The human being is a subject that has its dimension as an object, as well as an object that has its dimension as a subject.[4] Human existence, human being, human consciousness, is essentially and internally related to the natural world.

This internal relationship between human reality and the natural world is already there before people begin to inquire into the nature of this relationship. And this separates Marx's view of human reality from all forms of dualism that postulate a subject which stands in a mere external relationship to the natural world, or which is ontologically real independently of the natural world.

So far the concept of being-in-the-world has been considered at a level on which abstraction was made from the specific contents of human existence. But properly speaking, there is, for Marx, no real being-in-the-world—there is no real human existence—that is not at the same time a being-in-the-world with specific contents. Human existence, the human subject–object, is constituted by its specific contents, its specific activities. It is constituted by specific interacting processes within the natural world, to begin with those processes that constitute the brain and body; and in every case human existence is made up of specific contents, specific activities, and specific modes of consciousness. Moreover, comprehension of these factors requires reference to those interacting processes within the natural world that constitute specific social, political, and economic conditions.

To clarify things here, it would be well to draw attention to the *general form* of being-in-the-world—a general form characterizing human existence wherever it is found.[5] For Marx, the general form of being-in-the-world is *conscious activity that is transformative of the natural world, as well as formative and transformative of human existence itself*.[6] Here is the core meaning of the notion of "praxis," which has figured so centrally in international discussions about Marx in the last two decades.

In working toward a more adequate understanding of this general form of being-in-the-world, let us focus first on the following passage from the "Theses on Feuerbach":

> The chief defect of all hitherto existing materialism—that of Feuerbach included—is that the thing, reality, sensuousness, is conceived only in the form of the object or of *contemplation*, but not as *human sensuous activity, practice*, not subjectively. . . . Feuerbach wants sensuous objects, really distinct from thought objects, but he does not conceive human activity itself as objective activity.[7]

The forms of materialism Marx criticizes have in common the fact that they do not construe objects subjectively, or more properly, that they do not construe objects subjectively insofar as they have been acted upon by man. But what does it mean to construe objects subjectively? For Marx at any rate, the meaning is something like this. Objects that have been acted upon by man are imbued with human activity. In the state in which they stand transformed by human activity, they are such that their very being is partially constituted by human activity.[8] The being of objects that have been acted upon by man is not the same as the being of those same objects prior to such action. The human activity that went into transforming these objects is internally related to the being that these objects now have. And what is internally related to any being is partially constitutive of that very being. To maintain that objects that have been acted upon by man must be conceived subjectively is just to maintain that such objects cannot be comprehended unless human activity is understood as entering into their very being.[9]

Now the conception of objects as subjective in the sense described above, and the conception of human activity as objective activity, are two conceptions which are conceptually interdependent. Materialism could not conceive objects that have been acted upon by man subjectively, as long as it failed to conceive human activity as objective activity. And it could not conceive human activity as objective activity as long as it conceived objects "only in the form of the object." The two conceptions go hand in hand.

The concept of being-in-the-world presupposes that the natural world is absolutely necessary for the formation, exercise, and confirmation of human powers. For Marx, it is absolutely necessary for human beings to objectify themselves in the natural world, to externalize themselves.[10] In other words, wherever you have human beings—and this is true at any stage in human history—you have beings who objectify themselves in the natural world, beings who express their powers, and who do so only by acting in and upon the natural world, thereby making them real powers. Man's subjective powers are at the same time objective powers.[11] They are actualized only by virtue of action in and upon the objective natural world, and in relation to other people in the natural world.

> To say that man is a *corporeal*, living, real, sensuous, objective being full of natural vigor is to say that he has *real, sensuous objects* as the objects of his being or of his life, or that he can only *express* his life in real, sensuous objects. *To be* objective, natural and sensuous, and at the same time to have object, nature and sense outside oneself . . . is one and the same thing.[12]

Self-Creation and Changing Human Nature

In the very process through which human beings objectify themselves—and constitute their powers as real powers by acting in and upon the natural world, and in relation to other people in the natural world—human beings make themselves.[13] The history of humanity is the history of the self-creation of human beings. However, it is a self-creation conditioned in definite ways by the past self-creative activity of human beings. Because human beings make themselves they can go beyond or transcend the ways in which they have made themselves in the past by making themselves in new ways. But the scope and character of man's transcending activity is always shaped by the summed-up results of man's past activity, as these results condition the transcending activity that takes place in the present.

Now consider any individuals, in any society, and at any point in the development of that society. Those individuals will be related to the natural world in certain definite ways. Those individuals will be active in the world in certain definite ways. In consequence those individuals will have established, by means of their real activity in the world, certain definite activities that are real for them, and which actually characterize them. Which of their potential powers become actual will be constituted and established by the definite and specific ways in which those individuals are active in the world. Thus the particular constellation of ideas, drives, needs, activities, and the like, which actually characterizes human existence at any point in time, will be determined and constituted by the particular ways in which individuals are related to the world in terms of their activity in and upon it, including of course their social activity.

This must be seen in interconnection with one of the fundamental tenets of Marx's view of man to the effect that human existence, human nature if you will, is subject to change, and in fact has been quite different at different stages in human history.[14] The change in human nature is so profound that it reaches down into the driving forces and very needs of man—even into those relatively fixed needs associated with physiological imperatives, as well as other less fixed needs.[15] But what factors are responsible for the changes in human existence? What lies behind these changes in human nature?

The initial direction in which this answer is to be found should be apparent. Though it has already been indicated that the general form of being-in-the-world is conscious activity that is transformative of the world and formative and transformative of the self, this does not mean that the succession of particular concrete forms of human existence is generated out of this general form. Rather, it is man's particular concrete conscious-activity-in-the-world that shapes human existence. Thus changes in the modes of human existence must be due to changes in the modes of man's conscious-activity-in-the-world. The problem of the change in human nature is the problem of the change in man's mode of conscious-activity-in-the-world. The history of human existence is the history of man's conscious-activity-in-the-world. Thus it must be asked: "What underlies the changes in man's mode of conscious-activity-in-the-world?"

Preliminaries on Historical Materialism

As a point of departure for answering this question, we point to the concrete requirement that any mode of conscious-activity-in-the-world must fulfill if it is to continue in existence. This concrete requirement is the satisfaction of those needs which, if not satisfied, would preclude the survival of the human organism.[16] In addition there is the requirement of satisfying new needs generated in the course of the productive activity aimed at satisfying the first needs.[17] In contrast to animals who satisfy their needs without productive activity, men "themselves begin to distinguish themselves from animals as soon as they begin to *produce* their means of subsistence".[18] This concrete requirement of production for the satisfaction of needs has the consequence that particular modes of man's conscious-activity-in-the-world are shaped by particular modes of the productive activity through which the satisfaction of needs is brought about. And this in turn means that attention must be shifted to the mode of production and the factors operative in it. To get at them, consider the following passage from *The German Ideology*.

> The way in which men produce their means of subsistence depends first of all on the nature of the actual means of subsistence they find in existence and have to reproduce. This mode of production must not be considered simply as being the reproduction of the physical existence of the individuals. Rather it is a definite form of activity of these in-dividuals, a definite form of expressing their life, a definite *mode of life* on their part. As individuals express their life, so they are. What they are, coincides with their production, both with *what* they produce and with *how* they produce. The nature of individuals thus depends on the material conditions determining their production.[19]

If one can distinguish the chief factors operative in determining "what they produce" and "how they produce," then one can understand the chief conditions determining man's mode of conscious-activity-in-the-world, and therefore the chief conditions determining man's mode of being-in-the-world. And in understanding the conditions determin-ing man's mode of conscious-activity-in-the-world, one will be able to understand the development of human nature in history. For the development of human nature through history can be read in terms of the development of these determining conditions. What then are these conditions? And what is the pattern of their development?[20]

The first group of factors,[21] which in their interplay dynamically condition "what they produce" and "how they produce," are usually collectively referred to as the "forces of production." Human (a) *labor power* guided by certain (b) *skills, techniques, and knowledge* and employing specific (c) *tools and instruments* of production shapes and transforms (d) *matter* for the satisfaction of (e) human *needs*. In addi-tion, men and women, in the conscious activity of producing in order to satisfy needs, enter into specific forms of association with one another. The "forces of production" are set in motion within the context of specific forms of human interrelation, that is, specific "social relations of production," the specific form of which must be adapted to the forces of production that obtain.

Arising on the dynamic basis of a given complex of forces of production and social relations of production, a corresponding complex of ideas and social institutions comes into being.[22] This complex reinforces and stabilizes the given complex of forces of production and social relations of production. The total complex constituted by the two dynamically interrelated complexes just distinguished is only relatively stable, however. For the forces of production are continually developing over time as new needs come into play, as new knowledge and technical skills are acquired, as new tools and instruments of production are created. As the forces of production develop, a steadily increasing conflict builds up between the developed stage of the forces of production and the old social relations of production. These relations become increasingly less well adapted to the developing forces of production.

This increasing conflict does not immediately issue in a transformation of social relations of production because there is a resistance against such a transformation that is grounded in the continued widespread adherence to the established ideology and the established social institutions. This adherence practically reinforces the established social relations and actively blocks a transformation to a new set of social relations. However, the increasing conflict between the forces of production and the social relations of production continues to mount. The conflict becomes so great that widespread adherence to the established ideology and social institutions gradually diminishes and is replaced by a growing predominance of new ideas and new concepts of social organization. In the meantime, these have been arising on the basis of the developing forces of production, leading in turn to a change to a new set of social relations better adapted to the developed stage of the forces of production.[23]

In considering the dynamic interplay between the forces of production and the social relations of production, we emphasize in passing that neither of these exists as something apart from conscious-activity-in-the-world. The dynamic interactions, tensions, and conflicts that obtain among them are interactions, tensions, and conflicts within the development of conscious-activity-in-the-world. The development of conscious-activity-in-the-world under both aspects is also the development of man himself. This development of conscious-activity-in-the-world is not the Hegelian development of the Idea where the concrete particular forms are generated out of the abstract Idea. It is instead a development *in* the concrete-real. And it is a development *of* the concrete succession of particular forms of conscious-activity-in-the-world together with the ideas and social institutions that evolve out of these concrete particular forms of conscious-activity-in-the-world. This development is the concrete development of different modes of being-in-the-world.

In this concrete development of being-in-the-world, another critically important factor that must be considered is the development of the social relationships between men and women, including the various

modes of the human family. As Marx puts it in *The German Ideology:*
A key

> circumstance which, from the very outset, enters into historical develop-
> ment, is that men, who daily remake their own life, begin to make other
> men, to propagate their kind: the relation between man and woman,
> parents and children, the *family*. The family, which to begin with is the
> only social relationship, becomes later, when increased needs create new
> social relationships and the increased population new needs, a subor-
> dinate one . . . and must be treated and analysed according to the existing
> empirical data.[24]

Here a distinction should be made between "the social relations of
economic production and reproduction" and "the social relations between men and women in the family." Among other things, Marx is
suggesting in the above passage that historical shifts have taken place
in the relative weight of "the social relations between men and women
in the family" vis-à-vis "economic social relations" in shaping human
development. Marx speculates that in early human history social relations between men and women had a relative parity with economic
social relations in shaping social life, inasmuch as economic social
relations were coextensive with the family then. But the development
of the earliest forms of "private wealth in the means of production"
upset this relative parity. And with the emergence of private wealth in
the means of production, the social relations of economic production
took on a relative primacy over male–female relations in the family in
shaping ongoing human development. This relative primacy has persisted ever since throughout the succession of the various social formations in human history. However, as the analysis of Chapter 4 will
disclose, there are circumstances in which activity aimed at developing
a new form of male–female relations could take on a relative primacy
in shaping the future course of human development.

Preliminaries on Alienated and Unalienated Modes of Being

By now it should be clear that it is basic to Marx's view of human
nature that man's particular mode of being-in-the-world is different at
different stages in man's development; and thus that human nature
changes throughout history. In this section two particular modes of
being-in-the-world that are crucial for an understanding of Marx's view
of human reality will be introduced. These two modes of being-in-the-
world are the alienated mode that Marx associates with capitalism,[25] and
the unalienated mode that he associates with genuine socialism. In view
of the fact that neither of these two modes of being-in-the-world can be
properly understood without reference to the other, let us provide some
initial comment on their interrelation.

In characterizing the alienated mode of being-in-the-world, Marx speaks of man as being alienated from his essence.[26] Now the essence of humankind as understood by Marx is to be construed, and can only properly be construed, as a particular mode of being-in-the-world. When Marx says that man is alienated from his essence, this means that man is alienated from a particular mode of being-in-the-world that is potentially his. (Before proceeding we make a brief comment on the usage of the term "man" in this context, and in others. For the most part, we use the term in its generic sense to mean "humankind" or "the collectivity of male and female human beings." Moreover, we hold that, for the most part, the term "man" also has this meaning when it occurs in the various citations from Marx given hereafter. However, there are a few contexts in which we use the term "man" in a nongeneric way—and a few citations in which Marx does too. On such occasions the nongeneric usage should be clear by virtue of an *explicit* conjunction with, or contrast to, the term "woman.") What, then, is this particular mode of being-in-the-world from which man is said to be alienated? To eventually arrive at a clear understanding of these matters we set out from the following passage from the *Economic and Philosophic Manuscripts of 1844:*

> The whole character of a species—its species character—is contained in the character of its life activity; and free, conscious activity is man's species character.[27]

In this passage Marx is talking about what he regards as the essence of man. The essence of man, for Marx, consists in free conscious activity. Such activity would be constitutive of a particular mode of being-in-the-world—although *not* a presently existing one. Thus, the general form of being-in-the-world is not itself to be construed as the essence of human being. Such an interpretation would render senseless all Marx's talk about the alienation of man from his essence. For if the general form of being-in-the-world characterizes man wherever he is found, then, under the interpretation that this general form is the essence of man, it would be a logical contradiction to say that man was alienated from his essence at any time at all.

That there is no contradiction should become clear when it is realized that the general form of being-in-the-world on the one hand, and the essence of man as here understood on the other hand, are categories employed at different levels of analysis, that is, different levels of abstraction. The general form of being-in-the-world is the general form of all human conscious existence, just because it can be abstracted at any point in the development of human conscious existence. From the abstract level of analysis of the general form of being-in-the-world one cannot grasp the qualitative differences manifest in successive stages of this development. These can be comprehended only on a lower level of analysis, one which can grasp the more fine-textured structures of concrete human reality from which, in turn, the general form of being-in-the-world has itself been abstracted. And it is essential to understand that, when Marx refers to free conscious activity as the essence of man, he is operating on a level of analysis concerned with the comprehension of the qualitative differences that have characterized different stages in the development of human conscious existence.

With these considerations in mind one can transcribe all talk about the alienation of man from his essence into the following kind of language. To say that the human being, in the past as well as the present, has been and is still alienated from his essence means that the particular modes of being-in-the-world that have characterized human existence up to now are *not* modes of being-in-the-world in which the human being's conscious activity has been free. In addition it means that a mode of being-in-the-world in which conscious activity is free is a real possibility for humankind.

The paradoxical aura of this claim will be dispelled if it is recognized that Marx is operating with a dialectical and historical conception of essence.[28] The fully developed essence of a thing is projected here in relation to the concrete process of development that precedes its full realization. While in one sense the essence of something is its whole process of development—including its fully developed stage—in another sense the essence refers to a stage of mature development projected as possible on the basis of a comprehension of the past history and laws of development of the process in question. The projection of such a possibility on such a basis can be thought of as a real possibility, as opposed to an abstract logical possibility.[29] (As we proceed now to a more specific treatment of the alienated and unalienated modes of being-in-the-world, it should be kept in mind that the full analysis will only be forthcoming in Chapter 5.)

In a previous section it was indicated that a human being's particular mode of being-in-the-world was determined, among other things, by other people and their modes of interrelation. Clearly then the alienated mode of being-in-the-world involves other people. Even stronger, alienation as conceived by Marx cannot be understood unless it is understood as a social phenomenon. As Marx puts it:

> The proposition that man's species nature [i.e., free conscious activity] is estranged from him means that one man is estranged from the other, as each of them is from man's essential nature. The estrangement of man, and in fact every relationship in which man stands to himself, is first realized and expressed in the relationship in which a man stands to other men.[30]

The alienated mode of being-in-the-world is partially constituted by (and therefore has as one of its aspects) an alienated mode of interrelationship with other people. Thus we can conveniently approach the alienated mode of being-in-the-world by first considering the "relationship in which a man stands to other men" in the alienated mode of interrelating with other people.

As a textual basis on which to anchor the discussion, consider the following. In the alienated mode of interrelation with other people,

> [a]ctual man is recognized only in the form of an egoistic individual.[31]

> Speaking exactly . . . the members of civil society are not atoms. . . . The atom has no needs. . . . Every activity and property of his [i.e., the egoistic individual's] being, every one of his vital urges becomes a need, a necessity which his self seeking transforms into seeking for other things, and human beings outside him.[32]

> The only bond between men is natural necessity, need and private interest, the maintenance of their property and egoistic persons.[33]

> [E]very individual is a totality of needs and only exists for the other person, as the other person exists for him, in so far as each becomes a means for the other.[34]

The interrelations between human beings are dominated by private interest and egotism. Men are so related that each treats the other as a means for securing his own private ends. The immediate consequence of this is that men are related in segmental ways, and not as whole persons. If the other person is regarded as a means for securing my own private ends—if the other person is used as a tool for attaining ends that are my ends and not ends belonging to that person—then as far as my practice is concerned, I deny the other as an end in himself, and cut myself off from those aspects of his being which do not enter into the purpose for which I use that person. As far as my practice is concerned the other is not a whole person. My conscious-activity-in-the-world is conscious activity in which the other is recognized only in a segmental way, as well as in a way useful to me.[35]

In turn the other in his conscious activity recognizes me only in a segmental way, and in a way useful to him. Each is cut off from the other as a whole person. "Individuals have become so separated and isolated that they establish contact only when they can use each other as means to particular ends: bonds between human beings are supplanted by useful associations not of whole persons but of particularized individuals."[36]

And in virtue of the fact that each regards the other as a means to his own ends, each regards the other as essentially threatening and hostile. There is a "war of all against all"—sometimes covert, sometimes open—always war. Each sees the other as an object to be manipulated, and as an object from which manipulation is projected. Each closes him- or herself off from the other who stands in a position of threat.

The alienated mode of being-in-the-world is one in which each is cut off from the fullness of the other, sees the other as hostile, regards the other as means.

At this point one might interject and ask what bearing alienation from others has on self-alienation. To be sure, people are alienated from other people. But how does this go hand in hand with self-alienation? The answer to this is close at hand. Man's mode of being-in-the-world is shaped by his interrelation with others. This interrelation with others is not an abstract interrelation, but is a "real practical relationship."[37] It has a real practical outcome in the distribution of power, privilege, wealth, and property. The real practical outcome of the real practical interrelation between individuals in capitalist society generates, and regenerates, class divisions, in which power, privilege, wealth, and property are so divided that the lack of all these is concentrated in the working class, while the full presence of these is concentrated in the capitalist class.

Thus, in capitalist society, the alienated mode of being-in-the-world embraces the alienated mode of being-in-the-world of the capitalist class on the one hand, but also the alienated mode of being-in-the-world of the working class on the other. Most importantly, these two alienated modes of being-in-the-world are dynamically interconnected with one another, so that each is constituted to be what it is by virtue of its internal relation to the other.[38] The capitalist and the worker are alienated from each other, to be sure, but both of them are self-alienated as well. The self-alienation of each is a function of the concrete practical interconnection that they bear to the other.

In order more fully to understand this it would be well to focus on the characteristic activity of both. The characteristic activity of the worker is "forced" productive activity (although not direct forced labor as in slavery) performed under the dominion of the capitalist.[39] The characteristic activity of the capitalist is appropriative activity that maintains dominion over the worker in its quest to augment profits. For both the worker and the capitalist, their characteristic activity is a failure to realize that kind of free conscious activity which is constitutive of an unalienated mode of being-in-the-world.

The worker's activity is forced activity imposed upon the worker "by *external* and accidental necessity and *not* by an *internal* and *determined* necessity."[40] The worker's activity is "activity performed in the service, under the dominion, the coercion, and the yoke of another man."[41] It is activity in which the worker objectifies himself in such a way that the product in which his productive activity has been embodied is appropriated not by himself, but by the capitalist—and in a manner that ensures the prolongation of the worker's activity as a "forced activity."

In turn the activity of the capitalist is appropriative activity in which the capitalist takes "possession of alien objective essence,"[42] namely, the product in which the worker has objectified himself through his productive activity. The "alien objective essence" that the capitalist appropriates is alien vis-à-vis the worker, because it is taken from the worker—even though it is the summary expression of the worker's productive activity. But it is also alien vis-à-vis the capitalist because it is not a product in which the capitalist has objectified his own being through his own productive activity, even though he appropriates it as his own in order to amass profits.[43] The appropriative activity of the capitalist generates the capitalist as the alien being who maintains dominion over the worker. "If the product of labor does not belong to the worker, if it confronts him as an alien power, then this can only be because it belongs to some *other man than the worker.* . . . Not the gods, not nature, but only man himself can be this alien power over man."[44]

Here it should be emphasized that private property is the practical medium through which the characteristic activities of worker and capitalist come to be what they are.[45] This means that the supersession of private property is required in order to realize the human essence—that is, in order for human activity to become free conscious activity. In speaking of private property in this context, though, it should be stressed that Marx does not mean private property of any sort what-soever, but only private property in the means of production, that is, private property understood as an exploitative social relation.[46] "Private property, as the material, summary expression of alienated labor, embraces both relations—the relation of the worker to work and to the product of his labor and to the non-worker, and the relation of the non-worker to the worker and to the product of his labor."[47]

The working class as well as the capitalist class is each defined in terms of their respective relationships to the material factors of produc-tion, including raw materials, instruments of production, and finished products. The alienated modes of being-in-the-world of the capitalist class, and the working class, are constituted as what they are by virtue of the conflicting ways in which capitalist and worker interrelate through the medium of the material factors of production. Private property is constituted as private property, through the conflicting ways in which capitalist and worker interrelate with one another in relation to these material factors of production.

The supersession of private property is required for "the real ap-propriation of the human essence by and for man"[48]—that is, for the realization of free conscious activity. This is to say that the supersession of the characteristic activity of both the alienated worker and the capitalist is required in order for human activity to become conscious activity that is free. If this is so, and if therefore the activity of both worker and capitalist is the activity of self-alienation, how is one to understand what Marx means by "free conscious activity"? The following preliminary sketch of free conscious activity brings out in a first approximation what is at issue.

In free conscious activity the bifurcation—of objectification as it occurs in the characteristic activity of the alienated worker, and appropriation as it occurs in the characteristic activity of the capitalist—is dialectically overcome through the establishment of a harmonious union of human objectification–appropriation. Free conscious activity is activity in which objectification and appropriation are undertaken in a way that does not imply dominion *over* the other, and which does not imply dominion by the other. Free conscious activity is thus activity that does not dominate the other, and is not dominated by the other. It is activity that positively affirms the other as it affirms itself.

Free conscious activity is activity that is a *"free manifestation of life and an enjoyment* of *life."*[49] It is activity springing from internally felt needs, exclusive of course of such internally felt needs that involve the domination over other people. Free conscious activity is activity that no longer serves merely as a means to ends external to it. Rather, it is activity in which the radical separation of means and ends has been overcome. It is the expression of life activity as an end in itself. It is the expression of human beings as ends in themselves in *concrete practice.* As such, it is activity that involves joy and pleasure as an attendant feature of everyday conscious-activity-in-the-world.

The Categories of Freedom

Up to this point in the development of the first chapter, the concern has been providing a sketch of the broad lines of Marx's conception of man. In later chapters we shall go on to develop a more concrete elaboration of the themes brought into this sketch. But in order to provide orientation for those more concrete elaborations to come, the rest of this chapter distinguishes and explains three categories under which these more concrete elaborations will be undertaken. The categories we distinguish are (a) the category of freedom-as-spontaneity, (b) the category of freedom-as-transcendence, and (c) the category of freedom-as-a-mode-of-being. A characterization of these categories follows.

(a) The category of freedom-as-spontaneity is drawn in relation to all those aspects of the discussion about human freedom that see the meaning of the term "freedom" to be parasitic on the meaning of the term "determined." One need only recall the continual reference to the so-called freedom–determinism debate in order to realize how familiar this category of freedom is. First, one specifies, or more often assumes, the meaning of causal determinism. Then one says that freedom means *not* to be causally determined in some respect or other. The kind of freedom at issue here has come to be understood as involving at least a margin of freedom from causal determinism by antecedent causal factors. A free choice has come to be understood as a spontaneous choice that is not completely determined to be what it is by antecedent events. And in this work we shall take the core meaning of the category of freedom-as-spontaneity as projecting that the human being, in some respects at least, is not subject to causal determination by antecedent factors.

(b) With the meaning of the first category specified, consider now the category of freedom-as-transcendence. This category is drawn in relation to all those aspects of the discussion about human freedom which insist that human beings are more than given circumstances have made them be, since they have the capacity to go beyond or transcend what they have become, and by their activity become something different. Perhaps a reference to one of the existentialist thinkers would be of help here, inasmuch as this category of freedom has received more emphasis from existentialist philosophers than from most other contemporary philosophers. In *Man in the Modern Age*, Karl Jaspers speaks as follows:

> Man is always something more than what he knows of himself. He is not what he is simply once for all, but is a process; he is not merely an extant life, but is, within that life, endowed with possibilities through the freedom he possesses to make of himself what he will by the activities on which he decides. Man is not a finished life which repeats itself from generation to generation. . . . He "breaks through" the passivity of perpetually renewed identical circles, and is dependent upon his own activity, whereby the process of his life is carried on toward an unknown goal.[50]

This passage exemplifies our category in a more or less obvious way. It conveys that man is a process; that he is never fully made, but is always in the process of making himself; that man is always more than he has made himself in the past; and this no matter how he may have made himself in his past, because he can make himself in different ways; that possibility is constitutive of man; that man is free just because he is the actualization of those of his possibilities that he decides upon; that man's freedom is the activity of actualizing those possibilities; that man can always "break through" to new ways of making himself, and so forth.

From this passage and the brief comment made upon it, let us extract and specify what will be regarded as the core meaning of the category under discussion. The core meaning of the category of freedom-as-transcendence is that human beings are always more than antecedent conditions may have made them be. They have the capacity to make what they become by their own activity. They can continue to remake themselves in the same specific ways as they did in the past. Or they can go beyond those past ways, and make themselves in new ways.

(c) Consider next the third category of freedom-as-a-mode-of-being. This category is drawn in relation to all those aspects of the discussion about human freedom that maintain that freedom is the attainment of some desirable mode of being regarded as constitutive of self-fulfillment, some desirable way of comporting oneself toward the world, toward other people, and toward one's own self as well. To specify a particular mode of being, one would have to specify particular structures in terms of which one was related to the world, other people, and one's self. And to specify freedom-as-a-mode-of-being, one would have to give a specification of self-fulfillment—or what might be called positive freedom—in terms of such structures.

With this characterization of the three categories behind us, some remarks on the status of categories are in order. First, the categories proposed here should not be taken as having some kind of *a priori* status, nor should they necessarily be taken as prescriptive. These categories are intended to be reflective of and even, in an abstract way, descriptive of the numerous array of particular positions that have actually been taken throughout the tradition on the issue of human freedom. The three categories have been abstracted from this wide array of different particular positions. They can be used to introduce some kind of order and intelligibility into the often confusing discussion about human freedom. The justification for employing these three categories consists in the extent to which the categories would permit the introduction of order and intelligibility into the discussion of at least the main views. In any case, we introduce them as categories for organizing our own discussion of freedom in Marx, and, we hope, for making it intelligible. This is a practical justification the value of which may be left to the assessment of the reader.

2

The Dialectical Movement
from the Abstract to the Concrete

At various points throughout the sketch of Marx's view of man that was provided in the first chapter, reference was made ahead to more concrete elaborations to be provided in later chapters. Inasmuch as these more concrete elaborations will be structured along the lines of the method of explanation developed by the mature Marx, we present a methodological interlude that will bring out the structures of Marx's method of explanation, as well as provide some philosophical warrant for the viability of this method.[1] We set out from the vantage point of the central core of Marx's own formulation on method that appears in the Introduction to the *Grundrisse*. Marx writes:

> [T]he method of rising from the abstract to the concrete is only the way in which thought appropriates the concrete, reproduces it as the concrete in mind. But this is by no means the process by which the concrete itself comes into being. . . . The concrete is concrete because it is the concentration of many determinations, hence unity of the diverse. It appears in the process of thinking, therefore, as a process of concentration, as a result, not as a point of departure, even though it is the point of departure in reality and hence also the point of departure for observation and conception.[2]

Our central concern in what follows will be the exploration of just what is involved in this movement from the abstract to the concrete. A proper understanding of this method requires a clear comprehension of the following points: (a) A distinction must be made between the concrete-in-thought and the concrete-real. (b) The movement from abstract to concrete does not purport to be generative of the concrete-real. (c) Neither is the movement from the abstract to the concrete a movement in which the concrete-in-thought can be deductively inferred from the abstract. (d) This movement is undertaken within a framework

17

of internal relations. (e) The internal relations at play in Marx's thought must be interpreted in terms of the notion of the concrete universal. (f) The movement from abstract to concrete aims at the construction of the concrete-in-thought, which is constituted as a complex of interconnected factors whose pattern of interconnection represents in thought the structures of the concrete-real. (g) The movement proceeds in stages from more abstract to more concrete levels of analysis. (h) The laws that figure in Marx's explanations have to be interpreted as dialectical tendencies. (i) Marx's model of scientific explanation is a synthesis of the "covering law" model and the genetic model. We proceed now to develop each of these points.

The Concrete-Real, the Concrete-in-Thought, and the General Nature of the Dialectical Movement

The distinction that Marx makes between the "concrete in mind" and the "concrete itself," in the above-quoted passage, must be clearly drawn if Marx's formulations on method are not to be subjected to systematic distortion—and even mystification. Louis Althusser, for one, has clearly underscored this distinction in his essay "On the Materialist Dialectic" in *For Marx*, and we shall adopt his comments here. In relation to Marx's suggestion that "'the correct scientific method' is to start with the abstract to produce the concrete in thought," Althusser explains that care must be taken "if we are not to believe that the *abstract* designates theory itself (science) while the *concrete* designates the real." He points out that there are *"two different concretes:* the *concrete-in-thought* which is a knowledge, and the *concrete-reality* which is its object."[3]

However, the movement from abstract to concrete as understood by Marx, in contradistinction to Hegel, simply does not fall into the position of maintaining that the concrete-real is itself generated out of thought, thinking, or the abstract. It is important to note here that Marx explicitly distinguishes himself from Hegel who, in Marx's view, "fell into the illusion of conceiving the real as the product of thought concentrating itself, probing its own depths, and unfolding itself out of itself."[4] Marx makes this distinction in the very context in which he speaks of his own method as "the method of rising from the abstract to the concrete." Along these same lines Althusser points out that the movement "whereby the 'abstract' becomes the 'concrete,' only involves the process of theoretical practice, that is, it all takes place 'within knowledge.'"[5] The movement from the abstract to the concrete is a theoretical movement through and through. It is a movement from the abstract to the concrete-in-thought, not to the concrete-real, although to be sure the objective is always the comprehension in thought of the concrete-real. We note here, and shall explain more fully later, that "the abstract" connotes a more general theoretical characterization of a given ontological domain in the concrete-real, whereas "the concrete" connotes a more specific theoretical characterization of the same domain.

It is equally important to note that the movement from the abstract to the concrete-in-thought is not a movement in which the concrete-in-thought is deductively derived from the abstract. As Marx points out, the concrete-in-thought is "not in any way a product of the concept which thinks and generates itself outside or above observation and conception; [the concrete-in-thought is] a product, rather, of the working-up of observation and conception into concepts."[6] This means that the conceptual elaborations presented in the movement from abstract to concrete are not established by the movement itself. Rather, the movement from the abstract to the concrete-in-thought is a movement that systematically reconstructs conceptual interconnections which have been drawn in relation to dialectical–empirical inquiry,[7] which has preceded the movement itself. That is to say, the method of moving from the abstract to the concrete is essentially a method for systematic presentation of the results of prior dialectical–empirical research. Such systematic presentation proceeds from more abstract levels of analysis that provide a more general comprehension of the ontological structures of a given domain, to more and more concrete levels of analysis that provide more specific comprehension of the given ontological domain. It is definitely not an attempt to give an *a priori* elaboration of what is the case. It is rather a method of explanation that arranges the material gathered in research into a coherent whole in which diverse phenomena can be explained in their interconnectedness. Through all phases of the movement from the abstract to the concrete-in-thought, the particular content of the particular relations that are introduced into this movement *as* factors is a content that derives from the findings of prior dialectical–empirical research.[8] The research preceding the explanatory movement is of course undertaken and interpreted within a framework that comprehends reality as a developing process of internally related aspects.

Preliminaries on Internal Relations and
the Concrete Universal

As we turn now to the theme of internal relations in Marx, we note first that V. I. Lenin and, before him, Engels have already brought out the central importance of internal relations in Marx's thinking—as well as the intellectual debt that Marx owed to Hegel in this regard.[9] Hegel's own view of internal relations is summarily indicated in this striking formulation that Lenin quotes in his *Philosophical Notebooks*, in the long section dealing with Hegel's *Science of Logic*—a work which had a powerful influence on Marx, even as he was writing *Capital*. (No suggestion, though, that Marx followed Hegel all the way on this theme.) Hegel writes:

> A determinate or finite Being is such as refers itself to another; it is a content which stands in a relation of necessity with other content or with the whole world. In view of the mutually determinant connection of the whole, metaphysics could make the assertion—which is really a tautology—that if the least grain of dust were destroyed the whole universe must collapse.[10]

More recently, Bertell Ollman has addressed the issue of internal relations in Marx in his fine book *Alienation: Marx's Conception of Man in Capitalist Society*. Ollman brings out that all Marx's social factors have to be understood in terms of internal relations. He writes:

> According to the common sense view, a social factor is taken to be logically independent of other social factors to which it is related. The ties between them are contingent, rather than necessary. . . . One can logically conceive, so the argument goes, of any social factor existing without its relations to others. In Marx's view, such relations are internal to each factor (they are ontological relations), so that when an important one alters, the factor itself alters; it becomes something else.[11]

In bringing out the critical importance of internal relations in getting at Marx's dialectical method of inquiry, Ollman writes that "the dialectical method of inquiry is best described as research into the manifold ways in which entities are internally related."[12] However, Ollman's view of Marx's "method of inquiry" has an important lacuna, which ramifies in such a way that his treatment of Marx's "method of explanation" becomes deficient in important ways. We speak here of the notion of the concrete universal. Ollman gives no attention to this. But, as will emerge in the text ahead, the notion of the concrete universal is just as important for understanding Marx's dialectical method of analysis as is the notion of internal relations. Indeed, the two are conceptually interwoven in Marx's thinking so as to go hand in hand.

Along with internal relations this is part of the Hegelian heritage that Marx never abandoned. (In this connection we cite Lenin's excited comment made in relation to one of Hegel's formulations concerning the concrete universal. He writes in his *Philosophical Notebooks:* "A beautiful formula: 'Not merely an abstract universal, but a universal which comprises in itself the wealth of the particular, the individual, the single' (all the wealth of the particular and single!) !!Très Bien!"[13] Moreover, the conceptual interconnection between internal relations and the concrete universal, in both Hegel and Marx, has already been well brought out in the literature—for example, by Carol C. Gould in *Marx's Social Ontology*.[14] However, Gould's treatment of Marx's "logic of explanation" does not address the scientific dimension of Marx's method of explanation.

Internal Relations, Critical Appropriations, and Individuation

Since it is the special concern of this chapter to bring into clear focus the structure of Marx's mature method of scientific explanation, we must provide formulations of a theory of internal relations and of the concrete universal that will be in keeping with this objective. In developing such formulations we will deliberately avoid the thickets of Hegel, and instead take recourse outside Hegelian and even Marxist circles to Brand Blanshard's work *The Nature of Thought*.[15] However, we shall present a critical appropriation of Blanshard's analysis. We do this because of the clarity of his analysis of internal relations and the concrete universal; because he understands the conceptual interconnection between internal relations and the concrete universal;[16] and because Blanshard gives his formulations at a level of abstraction that will be extremely helpful in our task of bringing Marx's method of scientific explanation into clear focus. We deal first with the analysis of internal relations, and then later with the analysis of the concrete universal.

Blanshard's view of the theory of internal relations is indicated by the following three theses:

> (1) That every term, i.e., every possible object of thought, is what it is in virtue of relations to what is other than itself; (2) that its nature is affected thus not by some of its relations only, but in differing degrees by all of them, no matter how external they may seem; (3) that in consequence of (2) and of the further obvious fact that everything is related in *some* way to everything else, no knowledge will reveal completely the nature of any term until it has exhausted that term's relations to everything else.[17]

In developing our critical appropriation of Blanshard's formulation, it is important to indicate first that Blanshard's analysis of internal relations is cast within the framework of a philosophical idealism. Thus we cannot simply adopt his analysis just as it stands, but will instead work toward a critical appropriation that will serve our main objective of bringing Marx's method of scientific explanation into clear focus.

As we proceed to do this, we note next that Blanshard intends to project his view of internal relations as having linguistic and ontological dimensions.[18] We mention this distinction in emphasis, in view of the frequent attempt to discharge the theory of internal relations, on the basis of linguistic conventions that operate within a universe of discourse already committed to an ontology of *external* relations.[19] The formulation of internal relations that we present below is intended to have an ontological emphasis, but the formulation is cast within a universe of discourse in which linguistic conventions suitable to an adequate understanding of an ontology of internal relations are already operative. And it points in the direction of what language and thought must do if they are to comprehend the concrete-real as understood by Marx.

To bring out what is involved in our critical departure from Blanshard, let us focus attention on the third thesis of his formulation. As we bear in mind the reference to terms in the concrete that Blanshard intends to make with his usage of "the nature of any term",[20] we recognize that his third thesis raises the question of the degree to which reality can be regarded as intelligible. Is reality intelligible through and through, or only to a degree? Is it possible in principle for thought to achieve an exhaustive grasp of the internal relations that obtain in the concrete? Is exhaustive knowledge of the concrete theoretically possible?

If we go beyond Blanshard's formulation of the theory of internal relations to the wider conceptual framework within which it functions, it seems clear that Blanshard's view of the relation between thought and reality, together with his view of coherence as the nature of truth, involves a commitment to the view that reality *is* intelligible through and through.[21] Blanshard certainly does not mean to suggest that exhaustive knowledge of the concrete is required in order to have any knowledge at all.[22] Yet the main thrust of his thought seems to rest on the theoretical possibility of a unique coherent system-in-thought, which would articulate without residue all the infinitely complex internal relations that obtain in the concrete.[23] As against Blanshard's position, the formulation of the theory of internal relations that we shall develop explicitly rules out the possibility of exhaustive knowledge of the concrete. Moreover, our formulation indicates a direction in which it is possible to understand how there can be partial knowledge of the concrete-real in a framework of internal relations. The key element in understanding this possibility is the introduction of the notion of structure into the very meaning of the theory of internal relations. This is another critical departure from Blanshard's formulation of internal relations.

One key thinker who has done much to develop an understanding of the kind of structure at play in Marx's conception of "concrete totality" is Louis Althusser.[24] In *For Marx* Althusser speaks about the projection by Marx of "the ever-pre-givenness of a structured complex unity."[25] He says that for Marx "the complex whole has the unity of a structure articulated in dominance."[26] Now Althusser does not himself explicitly associate what he says about structure with a philosophy of internal relations. Yet it seems clear that he all along presupposes a framework of internal relations in his discussions about structure, so that "each essential articulation of the structure" is internally related to the other articulations of the structure.[27] In any case, the formulation of internal relations we shall present is further differentiated from Blanshard's by the explicit introduction of the notion of structure into the theory of internal relations.

In Althusser's treatment of Marx, structure is emphasized, whereas internal relations are left more or less implicit. This contrasts with Ollman's treatment where internal relations are emphasized and structure is more or less implicit—although Ollman himself does not want to use the term "structure." However, although Althusser's analysis of the structures in Marx's conception of "concrete totality" is quite important as far as it goes, there is a significant lacuna in his treatment, inasmuch as Althusser fails to address explicitly the notion of the concrete universal. He does not give an account of the level-by-level development of integrated dialectical structures leading from the abstract to the concrete—a cognitive process that characterizes Marx's mature dialectical method of explanation. Moreover, without taking explicit account of concrete universals, together with an explicit account of internal relations and structure, he cannot do so. The methodological result is that Althusser winds up getting stuck on one level of abstraction that blocks his view of a more concrete "concrete totality" than the one he presents—and which blinds him to the recognition of the central importance of alienation for the mature Marx, and to the possibility of taking account of alienation on the more concrete levels of analysis.[28]

We return now to the theme of internal relations. Remember that our formulation of the theory of internal relations is intended to have an ontological emphasis. Although this formulation very clearly abstracts from specific content, it is projected with an eye on the concrete-real and thus with an eye on the diversity and differentiation that obtain therein. Care must be taken that an emphasis on interconnection and integration within the concrete-real—a proper emphasis considering the current predominance of the theory of external relations—be balanced by due attention to differentiation and diversity within the concrete-real. The theory of internal relations does not view things as interconnected in a way that obliterates differentiation. Rather, the concrete-real is viewed as a field of differentiation-in-integration. And knowledge of the concrete-real is possible to the extent that the internal relations obtaining in the concrete field of differentiation-in-integration establish themselves in articulable structures.

We stress that the structures to which reference is made here cannot be conceived as structures ontologically independent of the internally related concrete field of differentiation-in-integration. The structures referred to are structures embedded right within the concrete field, and thus share the relational quality of the concrete field itself. This means not only that the structures arising within the concrete field are internally related to the concrete field, but also that the various articulations of the structure of the concrete field are articulations that themselves bear internal relations to one another.

With this critical discussion of Blanshard behind us, we formulate the theory of internal relations in Marx by the following six theses:

1. If the very being (i.e., the ontological structures) of two entities in the concrete-real is constituted to be what it is by the interconnections that the entities have with one another, we shall say the entities are internally related.
2. If the very being of two entities in the concrete-real is not constituted to be what it is by the interconnections that the entities might have with one another, we shall say that the entities are externally related.
3. Every concrete-real is constituted to be what it is through the internal relations it has with some other entities.
4. The nature of every concrete-real is constituted to be what it is not by some of its internal relations only, but in differing degrees by all of them.
5. Complete knowledge of any concrete-real would require an exhaustive comprehension of the relation of that concrete-real to everything else with which it is internally related; and since this is not possible, complete knowledge of the concrete-real is not possible.
6. Even so, some knowledge of the structure of the concrete-real is possible to the extent that the infinitely complex internal relations that obtain among concrete-reals establish patterns of concrete differentiation-in-integration whose broader structures can be grasped in thought.

(A comparison of our formulation with Blanshard's will reveal that our third and fourth theses are adopted from the first two theses of Blanshard's, but with minor changes in terminology that serve to underscore the ontological emphasis of our own formulation. However, the fifth thesis of our formulation constitutes a departure from Blanshard, a departure which is further developed in our sixth thesis. The first two theses we give round out the formulation.)

All this, especially the concept of structure that is at play in the framework of internal relations, will become clearer as we go on with our explanation of the remaining points in our treatment of Marx's method of moving from the abstract to the concrete. But prior to further development along these lines, some indication of how individuation is possible within a framework of internal relations is in order. We shall draw from Ollman's explorations of this issue, which were undertaken in *Alienation*.

Linking his own discussion of individuation back to the work of Joseph Dietzgen, Ollman explains:

> According to Dietzgen . . . the whole is revealed in certain standard parts (in which some thinkers have sought to re-establish the relations of the whole), because these *are* the parts in which human beings through conceptualization have actually fragmented the whole. The theoretical problem of individuation is successfully resolved by people in their daily practice. The fact that they do not see what they are doing as individuating parts from an interconnected whole is, of course, another question and one with which Dietzgen does not concern himself.[29]

The central thesis of this passage is that individuation is a function of everyday practical activity lifting into conceptual relief some particular aspect of the concrete field of differentiation-in-integration. Carrying this theme further forward we cite Karel Kosik's great work on *Dialectics of the Concrete*, and we adopt his resolution to the problem.

He writes that reality stands out to man primarily

> as the realm of his sensory-practical activity, which forms the basis for immediate practical intuition of reality. . . . Immediate utilitarian praxis and corresponding routine thinking . . . allow people to find their way about in the world, to feel familiar with things and to manipulate them, but it does not provide them with a *comprehension* of things and of reality. . . . The collection of [individuated] phenomena that crowd the everyday environment and the routine atmosphere of human life, and which penetrate the consciousness of acting individuals with a regularity, immediacy, and self evidence that lend them a semblance of autonomy and naturalness constitutes the world of the *pseudoconcrete*. . . . What lends these [individuated] phenomena a pseudoconcrete character is not their existence as such but the apparent autonomy of their existence. In destroying the pseudoconcrete, dialectical thinking does not deny the existence or the objective character of these phenomena, but rather abolishes their fictitious independence by demonstrating their mediatedness, and counters their claim to autonomy with proving their derivative character.[30]

A particular aspect of the concrete-real is individuated on the basis of practical activity that differentiates it from other aspects. However, dialectical cognition can proceed to make explicit the internal connections that obtain between the given aspect and other aspects which have been individuated in the same way, that is, internal relations that are masked in everyday practical activity. Thus it is through dialectical cognition that individuated phenomena, which have become solidified into the pseudoconcrete on the basis of everyday practical activity, find their adequate comprehension in a structured complex of internal relations.

The Dialectic as Presentation versus the Dialectic as Inquiry

Now let us consider the objective toward which the movement from the abstract to the concrete is oriented. In general terms, perhaps the most significant thing is that the movement from the abstract to the concrete aims at knowledge of the concrete-real, where such knowledge is rendered in terms of a comprehension of the structures of some domain of the concrete-real. (In view of the frequent equation of knowledge with "certain knowledge" in the Western philosophical tradition, care should be taken here to note that "knowledge" as understood in this context carries with it no pretensions as to certainty.)

The concrete-in-thought is essentially a complex hypothesis concerning the structure of some domain of the concrete-real. It constitutes the structure of the concrete-real as grasped in thought. The "grasping in thought and language" of the structure of the concrete-real is rendered through the comprehension of a complex of internally related factors. Their pattern of interconnection in thought constitutes the conceptual model for comprehending the broader structures of the concrete-real. Indeed, the structure of the concrete-in-thought can be regarded as the conceptual reflection of the structure of the concrete-real, but a reflection that is deliberately constructed.[31] All the internally related factors, whose pattern of interconnection constitutes the concrete-in-thought, have been selected with a view toward revealing the structure of some domain of the concrete-real. Thus it is not simply that the concrete-in-thought reflects the structure of the concrete-real, but that it is intentionally constructed with a view toward revealing that structure. The construction of the concrete-in-thought proceeds with continual ontological reference to the concrete-real itself.

Each of the internally related factors—whose pattern of interconnection constitutes the concrete-in-thought for a given domain of the concrete-real—describes and refers to some aspect of the concrete field. A given aspect is projected as an essential articulation of the structure of the given domain of the concrete-real. Each aspect is then lifted into conceptual relief and brought into developed conceptual interconnection with other factors, which have themselves been projected as the conceptual grasping of other essential articulations of the structure of the concrete-real.

Next we consider the problem of the relation between "the abstract" and "the concrete" in Marx's thought. Melvin Rader has a very interesting chapter on "The Abstract and the Concrete" in his outstanding work on *Marx's Interpretation of History*. Therein, Rader explains:

The word "abstract" is derived from the Latin verb *abstrahere*, "to draw away," meaning to withdraw or separate in thought or in objective matter of fact. In thought, abstracting is the focusing of attention on some part or aspect of an object, usually for the purpose of contemplation or understanding. . . . Sometimes the verb "to abstract" means not simply to focus but objectively to separate. Hegel, for example, says that to amputate an arm is to abstract it from the human body. Marx likewise uses "abstract" to designate severance from a larger whole. . . . The term "concrete" is derived from the past participle of the Latin verb *concrescere*, meaning to grow together. As used by Hegel and Marx, the concrete is that which has organically grown together and remains unfragmented. It is the whole in its integrity. If we think of an object *as a whole*, we are thinking of it concretely. "Concrete" means taken all together— "abstract" means taken piecemeal.[32]

Rader goes on to bring out that, whereas Marx uses abstraction as a device to isolate and bring into conceptual relief some aspect of a concrete whole for purposes of investigation, he always "rebinds the parts thus dissected, and he objects to substitution of an abstraction in place of the concrete totality."[33] Rader proceeds to explain the various ways in which Marx inveighs against uses of abstraction which do not thus rebind the isolated aspect with some relevant concrete totality. Such uses of abstraction include the reification of abstract essences; the treatment of some isolated dimension of consciousness, such as reason, passion, volition, and the like as if it were the whole person; and the treatment of economic facts in isolation from the specific organic whole within the context of which they come to be what they are.

Now this kind of concern about "the abstract" and "the concrete" permeates all Marx's thinking. However, there is another kind of relation between "the abstract" and "the concrete" that we must explore if we are to appreciate Marx's distinctive method of scientific explanation. And to do this we must recognize the distinction between the "dialectic as inquiry" and the "dialectic as presentation." Here we cite Marx's own formulation in his Preface to *Capital* where he writes:

> Of course the method of presentation must differ in form from that of inquiry. The latter has to appropriate the material in detail, to analyse its different forms of development, to trace out their inner connection. Only after this work is done, can the actual movement be adequately described. If this is done successfully, if the subject-matter is ideally reflected as in a mirror, then it may *appear* as if we had before us a mere *a priori* construction. (emphasis added)[34]

Ollman picks up on this distinction in his chapter on "Dialectic as Inquiry and Exposition," where he rightly brings out that "the dialectical method of inquiry is best described as research into the manifold ways in which entities are internally related."[35] And Ollman further indicates that in investigating the ways in which entities are interrelated, Marx "began with each part in turn, continuously altering the perspective in which their union was viewed,"[36] all with the objective of trying to get at the "essential connections" of phenomena—the "hidden substratum."

But when we come to Ollman's account of the "dialectic as presentation," the situation is not much different. On this theme Ollman says: "The two outstanding features of Marx's use of the dialectic for presentation are, first, that each subject is dealt with from many different vantage points, and second, that each subject is followed out of and into the particular forms it assumes at different times."[37] The first feature already characterizes Marx's "dialectic as inquiry" on Ollman's own account; the second feature that Ollman mentions also characterizes Marx's own procedure in the "dialectic as inquiry." Thus, if we follow Ollman, the "dialectic as presentation" collapses into the "dialectic as inquiry."

And although Ollman does make passing reference to Paul Sweezy's characterization of Marx's method of explanation as a method of "successive approximations," Ollman gives no mention of Sweezy's position that such successive approximations are rendered in terms of successive "levels of abstraction."[38] We return to Sweezy's formulation in a few paragraphs. But let us first consider some further problems with Ollman's characterization of Marx's method of explanation.

Perhaps the most significant lacuna in Ollman's treatment is the failure to take up the problem of the concrete universal. This problem is one that goes hand in hand with the problem of internal relations not only in Marx, but in Hegel before him. In addition, Ollman shows no appreciation for the crucial importance that Marx attached to finding the proper beginning for the "dialectic as presentation." Indeed, for Ollman the beginning seems to be completely arbitrary. In a revealing footnote he writes: "On my view, in attempting to reconstruct the whole from each major vantage point, Marx is erecting—if we insist on this expression—as many structures of the whole as there are major units in his analysis. . . . The difference in where we begin leads to a difference in perspective, in the size and importance of the other factors, and in the relevance of the various ties between them."[39]

Furthermore, although Ollman gives due attention to the theme of complexity in Marx's thinking, he does not see structure in this complexity. He even chides Althusser on this account, writing that "Althusser has in fact confused structure with complexity. . . . The transition, apparently slight but possessing serious ramifications, from the idea of complexity to that of structure, has no basis in Marx's text."[40] In response we say that although it is true that Marx mostly speaks about an "organic system," an "organic totality," a "feudal system," or a "system of production," Marx is concerned to *analyze* the complexities of these systems and totalities. And what is this, if not to bring out their structures? Perhaps Ollman is reacting against the static connotation that the term "structure" has for many of the French structuralists. However, in Althusser's case we have a dialectical structuralism, albeit a truncated dialectical structuralism—not a static one. Finally, we indicate that, taken all together, the various shortcomings in Ollman's view of Marx's method of explanation ramify in such a way that Ollman sees the meanings of Marx's terms to be much more ambiguous and fluid than they really are.[41]

These criticisms made, we next adopt Paul Sweezy's formulation in *The Theory of Capitalist Development*, where he describes Marx's method of analysis as a "method of 'successive approximations,' which consists in moving from the more abstract to the more concrete in a step-by-step fashion, removing simplifying assumptions at successive stages of the investigation so that theory may take account of and explain an ever wider range of actual phenomena." Referring to *Capital*, Sweezy goes on to explain that:

> Volume I begins and remains on a high level of abstraction. . . . [T]he results achieved in Volume I have a provisional character. In many cases, though not necessarily in all, they undergo a more or less extensive modification on a lower level of abstraction, that is to say, when more aspects of reality are taken into account. . . . [T]he intent of Volumes II and III was to take into account factors which were consciously left out of Volume I, that is to say, to bring the analysis to progressively lower levels of abstraction.[42]

But not only are there successive stages in the movement from abstract to concrete as Sweezy brings out; it is also necessary to recognize that the conceptual elaboration of each more concrete stage is undertaken *within the broader structural framework* of the more abstract stage. This must be clearly grasped if the full explanatory power of Marx's method of analysis is to be understood.

We have seen that the movement from the abstract to the concrete aims at the construction of the concrete-in-thought, which in turn is projected as representing through its structure the structure of some domain of the concrete field. The movement from abstract to concrete can be thought of as the gradual elaboration of a *conceptual field* of differentiation-in-integration, the final result of which is the concrete-in-thought. The elaboration of the conceptual field begins with less complex patterns of differentiation-in-integration, namely, those abstract relations that constitute the first broad strokes in the conceptual field. As the elaboration of the conceptual field continues, more complex patterns of differentiation-in-integration are developed within the dialectical framework of the less complex patterns of differentiation-in-integration, and so on. In the course of this gradual elaboration of the conceptual field, the structure of the concrete-in-thought comes more and more fully, as well as more clearly, into view.

The Concrete Universal versus the Abstract Universal

To further develop an understanding of how the more abstract level of analysis constitutes a dialectical framework for the more concrete levels of analysis, it is necessary now to take up the theme of the concrete universal. This is so because all the universal terms that would describe specific factors introduced at the various levels of analysis have got to be interpreted in terms of the concrete universal, not the abstract universal of traditional Western philosophy. As we explain the concept of the concrete universal, we shall see that the theory of the concrete universal provides a key for understanding Marx's method of moving from the abstract to the concrete. Since the concrete universal can be most clearly understood against the background of the abstract universal, we need to look first at the abstract universal.

Drawing once more on Blanshard's help, we single out these passages from *The Nature of Thought* with a view toward getting clear about the abstract universal. Concerning the general idea as interpreted by traditional formal logic, Blanshard writes:

> Such an idea is the thought of a class, and a class is a set of objects with one or more attributes in common. To think the idea "horse" is to refer at once to the set of attributes in virtue of which we identify an animal as a horse, and to all the Dobbins, Black Beautys, and Man-o'-Wars that possess those attributes. The set of common attributes is called the *intension* of the class name, the individuals in which they occur its *extension*. Of these two sides of the idea's meaning, the intension is more interesting. For it is the intension that gives what is distinctive and characteristic; when we think of anything whatever, we do so through thinking of its character. Now what is the character we think of when we use a general idea? Formal logic answers with its doctrine of the "abstract universal." It answers that what is before us is the logical intension, that when we think of horses in general, we refer, so far as we refer to character at all, merely to the set of attributes which all horses possess in common.[43]

> Suppose that the object of my general idea is an abstract universal in the sense defined; to reach the thought of its species, I shall then keep this as a nucleus and add features from the outside. "From the outside" is important. For the species are not now conceived as forms that the genus must take in order to be at all. The relation is purely casual; you may add to the nucleus any characters whatever, provided only that they are not incompatible, and get a species of a genus.[44]

This view of the universal that interprets the universal as an abstract essence, which inheres unmodified in its species, is quite foreign to the universe of discourse that Marx has adopted for his understanding of reality.[45] In commenting on the theory of the abstract universal Blanshard points out—and Marx would have agreed—that "in spite of its attractive simplicity, this view of the universal is false. . . . Its error lies in misconceiving the relation between the universal and what falls under it, in supposing that genus and species are so externally related that, in thought if not in fact, they may be cut apart without damage to either."[46]

In attempting now to provide an understanding of the concrete universal suitable to Marx's universe of discourse, we again draw from Blanshard's highly valuable discussion of the concrete versus the abstract universal in *The Nature of Thought*.[47] We note in passing, though, that Blanshard's discussion of these issues is cast within the framework of a metaphysical idealism, and therefore could not be taken over as a whole into Marx's universe of discourse without significant modification. Blanshard's discussion would have to be "critically appropriated." One vitally important consideration that would guide such a critical appropriation is the distinction marked above between the concrete-in-thought and the concrete-real—a distinction that for present purposes must be seen as involving a distinction between the "species in thought" and the "species in the concrete real." We shall see that the primary focus for understanding the concrete universal is the relation between the universal and the "species in thought."

With the above caution concerning the critical appropriation of the whole range of Blanshard's discussion of the concrete universal, we cite a particular passage in which Blanshard points to the nerve of the theory of the concrete universal—a passage which as it stands could have been cast within Marx's own universe of discourse. The passage reads:

> [A] genuine grasp of the universal carries a grasp of the species with it. Where such a grasp is really present, the bringing to light of the species is not a random running over of attributes with which the nuclear ones have been associated. . . . It is rather the making explicit and detailed of what was germinally present already, the evolution of the undeveloped; not the enumeration of associates. . . . The universal is not an extract from its species. It is the undeveloped schema of its species, which is neither their lowest common denominator nor their explicitly set out sum, but that which contains them within itself as its alternate possibilities.[48]

It is necessary to examine this passage *as if* it actually had been cast within Marx's universe of discourse; we hope that a clear understanding of the concrete universal as it functions in Marx's universe of discourse will emerge as we go on.

First, concerning the relation between universal and "species in thought," we stress that the relation is an internal one. It is not the case that the universal obtains independently of its concrete elaborations in thought. Instead, the universal is to be understood as a schema projected toward its concrete elaborations in thought. The schema is intentionally oriented toward its concrete elaborations, and implicitly contains them within itself by virtue of the fact that it means them. Thus the concrete universal is itself a movement from abstract to concrete. This will seem less puzzling if the explicit articulation of the schema is viewed as having been developed against the background of a vaguer sense of the more concrete elaborations *so as to be* the schema that in its projection embraces them as its concrete elaborations.

Second, we distinguish a particular type of schema which, although not characteristic of the theory of the concrete universal, can nevertheless be brought compatibly within its framework. This is important because it indicates how the abstract universal can be "converted" into the concrete universal. Consider the set of features that in traditional logic constitutes the class intension which defines a given abstract universal. Drop off from this set of features the interpretation which they receive in the theory of the abstract universal, and reinterpret this set of features as a schema projected toward its concrete elaborations in thought. Under this interpretation the different concrete elaborations could emphasize different features to different degrees and in different ways. Moreover, the concrete elaborations could even fail altogether to represent some feature (or even features) of the schema. This stands in sharp contrast to the theory of the abstract universal according to which the abstract universal supposedly inheres unmodified in the species, thus having all its features fully realized in the species.[49]

However, the type of schema most naturally associated with the theory of the concrete universal is a relational schema that is explicitly cast as a conceptual pattern of differentiation-in-integration. (The "abstract determinations" with which the movement from abstract to concrete begins are of this type, as are all the categories of Marx's analysis.) The different concrete elaborations toward which the schema is projected can emphasize different features of the schema to different degrees, and in such a way that the different concrete elaborations manifest wide differences with respect to the relations that predominate in them and characterize them as concrete elaborations of one particular sort rather than another.

Third, just as the concrete universal is a schema projected toward its concrete elaborations, so too the concrete elaborations in thought can themselves be thought of as potential schemata projected toward still more concrete elaborations in thought. For the "species in thought" does not function like a more concrete *abstract* universal; it functions as a more concrete *concrete* universal—projected, potentially at least, toward its own more concrete elaborations. Thus the "species in thought" is itself a schema which, in principle, can be indefinitely elaborated in more and more concrete ways so as to more and more fully grasp in thought the detail of the "species in the concrete real." However, the "species in thought" is not able to specify that detail in an exhaustive way. It cannot become the "species in the concrete real." But ostensive definition serves in practice to bridge the gap between the "species in thought" and the "species in the concrete real." The "species in thought" at some degree of elaboration or other is projected ostensively toward the "species in the concrete real" as a schema circumscribing in thought the broad features of the concrete-real within whose scope all its finer details would be found to lie.

The Dialectical Nesting of Levels

We have described the movement from abstract to concrete as the gradual elaboration of a conceptual field wherein the more concrete stages of the movement are developed within the dialectical framework of the more abstract stages. Here we are in a position to more fully explain this. Just as the commodity is the economic cell in the analysis of capitalist society,[50] so the concrete universal is the conceptual cell in the movement from abstract to concrete, and is itself to be understood as a movement from abstract to concrete.

The elaboration of the conceptual field is the development of a concatenation of interconnected concrete universals arranged in a dialectical hierarchy. Each of the relations at the various levels in the development of the dialectical hierarchy is a schema projected toward its more concrete elaborations in thought. And the relations at a given level taken as an interconnected whole constitute a complex structured schema projected toward its more concrete elaborations in thought.

The projection of the structured schema from a given level in the dialectical hierarchy circumscribes in the conceptual field the broad structures within which a range of possible more concrete elaborations in thought could be developed, without, however, selecting from among them. The particular concrete elaboration—out of the range of possible concrete elaborations that is actually articulated as the next stage in the movement from the abstract to the concrete—is developed within the more abstract schema in accordance with the findings of the prior dialectic of inquiry.

In turn this more concrete elaboration functions as a still more complexly structured schema projected toward its own more concrete elaborations. And it circumscribes in the conceptual field, but in a closer and more fine-textured way than was the case with the more abstract schema, those broad structures within whose scope the next more concrete stage of elaboration comes to be developed in accordance with the findings of the dialectic of inquiry.[51]

Thus the dialectical hierarchy is such that there is a dialectical nesting of more complexly structured schemata projected from within the projected structures of less complexly structured schemata. However, in this dialectical nesting it should be emphasized that the more concrete elaboration provides the warrant for the more abstract elaboration. The more concrete elaboration does not get its warrant deductively from the more abstract elaboration. Rather, the more abstract elaboration gets its warrant from below, that is, from the success with which the more abstract elaboration functions as a dialectical framework for the more concrete elaboration. Note again that the movement from the abstract to the concrete is essentially an explanatory device for arranging the results of prior inquiry in systematic fashion so as to bring into fuller and fuller view the concrete-in-thought, which is then projected as a hypothesis concerning the structure of some domain of the concrete-real. This hypothesis gets its warrant, as does any other hypothesis, through the success with which it organizes and explains the total available relevant evidence.

Tendencies, Complicating Factors, and the Vertical and Lateral Dialectical Projections

Other features of Marx's method of explanation are crucial for understanding how he extends the explanatory movement from the abstract to the concrete so as to constitute his distinctive method of scientific explanation. First, we explore Marx's conception of a law as a tendency. In doing so we shall focus on the particular example of the "tendency of the falling rate of profit," which Marx presents in the third volume of *Capital* (but only after the preparatory analysis of all the factors involved has been given in the preceding two volumes).

Marx writes:

> This [the capitalist] mode of production produces a progressive relative decrease of the variable capital as compared to the constant capital, and consequently a continuously rising organic composition of the total capital. The immediate result of this is that the rate of surplus-value, at the same, or even a rising, degree of labour exploitation, is represented by a continually falling general rate of profit. . . . The progressive tendency of the general rate of profit to fall, is therefore, just *an expression peculiar to the capitalist mode of production* of the progressive development of the social productivity of labour. This does not mean to say that the rate of profit may not fall temporarily for other reasons. But proceeding from the nature of the capitalist mode of production, it is thereby

proved a logical necessity that in its development the general average rate
of surplus-value must express itself in a falling general rate of profit.[52]

The tendency that Marx singles out here is not a tendency which is
projected independently of initial conditions. It is not a tendency in a
vacuum. Rather, the tendency toward the falling rate of profit is
projected as arising out of the capitalist mode of production. It is the
complex of interconnected social relations of capitalism that constitutes
the "initial conditions" for the tendency. Moreover, development within
the social relations of capitalism constitutes the developing dynamic
basis for the tendency of the rate of profit to fall. To be sure, the passage
quoted does not *show* that this tendency does indeed proceed from the
nature of the capitalist mode of production. But this passage has behind
it the whole previous analysis of *Capital*. And it is this previous analysis
which does show that the capitalist mode of production does indeed
give rise to this tendency; and it is this previous analysis which must
inform the interpretation of the passage quoted.

Now, to comprehend what Marx is doing methodologically with all
the tendencies he distinguishes in *Capital*, we have to see how these
tendencies are situated in the conceptual field as the dialectical movement from the abstract to the concrete proceeds. We have already seen
that the dialectical movement takes place in stages. Any given level in
the elaboration of the conceptual field is constituted by a complex of
internally related factors. This complex of internally related factors
stands as a structured schema projected toward its more concrete
elaboration in thought, and thus as a dialectical framework within
which the more concrete elaboration is undertaken. Thus if we think
of the projection of such a structured schema toward its more concrete
elaborations as a *vertical* dialectical projection, we can go on to distinguish the concept of a *lateral* dialectical projection that will help to
comprehend what is going on methodologically in all Marx's discussion
about tendencies.

The lateral dialectical projection is constituted by the projection of
a complex of internally related factors in their dynamic interplay over
time. Instead of going from one level of analysis to a more concrete
level, as happens with the vertical dialectical projection, the lateral
dialectical projection of a given complex of factors is undertaken at the
same level of analysis. And at any given level of analysis, the lateral
dialectical projection is a projection of the dynamic interplay of the
complex of factors distinguished at that level, as this dynamic interplay
affects these factors themselves over time, or as this dynamic interplay
gives rise to some other related consequence. This means that a given
level of analysis must be understood not only in terms of the complex
of interconnected factors distinguished at that level, but also in terms
of the lateral dialectical projection of this complex of factors.

With the concept of the lateral dialectical projection one has a ready instrument for understanding what is going on methodologically in the dialectical laws that figure so importantly in Marx's thought. For these laws describe tendencies of social development—tendencies which arise out of a complex of interconnected factors. And although such laws are not usually formulated by Marx in terms of universal conditional statements, they can nonetheless be easily rendered in such terms. When these laws are expressly formulated in conditional terms, the antecedent of the conditional points to or specifies some complex of interconnected factors, while the consequent of the conditional statement specifies some contemplated result of the projected dynamic interplay of that complex of factors. So, for example, the broad structure of the tendency of the rate of profit to fall can be indicated by some such universal conditional as the following: "If a complex of capitalist social relations obtains, then as the development of the forces of production takes place within the framework of these social relations there will be a tendency for the general rate of profit to fall." It simply is not the case that Marx projects tendencies in a way that is unconditional. For Marx, tendencies are unquestionably conditional, and the laws that figure in Marx's thought are laws describing such conditional tendencies. (This stands in sharp contrast to the influential but misleading interpretation of Marx on the theme of tendencies, which was advanced by Karl Popper in *The Poverty of Historicism* and elsewhere. Popper's interpretation will be explicitly addressed in Chapter 3.)

The laws that Marx distinguishes are initially presented at a level of analysis which abstracts from other factors that might come into play, on more concrete levels of analysis, in a way that would run counter to the laterally projected dynamic interplay of the complex of factors as viewed on the more abstract level. However, Marx goes on to indicate that the general law "is modified in its working by many circumstances."[53] Elsewhere he notes that there are "counteracting influences at work which cross and annul the effect of the general law, and which give it merely the characteristic of a tendency."[54] Thus, for example, Marx follows the chapter in which he presents the law of the tendency of the rate of profit to fall with a chapter on "Counteracting Influences," which details what he sees as the "most general counterbalancing forces" to this tendency.[55]

To understand what is going on methodologically here, we must explain how the lateral dialectical projection works in connection with the vertical dialectical projection. We saw that the vertical dialectical projection is to be understood as a structured schema of interconnected factors projected from a given level of analysis toward its more concrete elaboration. In explaining the lateral dialectical projection we saw that a complex of interconnected factors distinguished at a given level of analysis was to be understood as being laterally projected in the conceptual field so as to represent the dynamic interplay of the given complex of factors over time.

Now consider that a given dialectical law would articulate some tendency at a level of analysis that abstracts from complicating factors. At this level the dialectical law would bring into thematic focus only the most essential aspects which, in their dynamic interplay over time, delineate the broad structure of the tendency. The complex of interconnected essential factors (from whose matrix the lateral dialectical projection is made) is also to be regarded as a schema vertically projected toward more concrete levels of analysis that could be elaborated within its framework. As the actual elaboration of the more concrete levels proceeds, additional complicating factors would be brought into thematic focus at each successive level. And when the lateral dialectical projection is undertaken at each of the more concrete levels, the result would be more and more concretely elaborated and fine-textured versions of the tendency. Assuming that the original hypothesis concerning the essential broad structure of the tendency was sound, the more concrete elaborations of the tendency would integrate wider and wider ranges of diverse phenomena into a coherent whole.

Thus far in speaking about complicating factors in this context, we have had in mind complicating factors that do not function to counteract the given tendency. However, we must also consider counteracting factors. When complicating factors that counteract a given tendency are introduced into the dialectical movement at a given level of analysis, we would expect the lateral dialectical projection of the whole complex of factors distinguished at that level to be modified thereby. But the degree and kind of modification is methodologically indeterminate. It is all contingent on the specific factors that might be involved—both those additional complicating factors introduced in the more concrete elaborations of the given tendency, and any counteracting factors that might be introduced. A clear implication of these considerations is that there is no methodological warrant for claims concerning the absolute inevitability of the outcome of a given tendency.

Whether counteracting factors in the concrete-real corresponding to those introduced on a given level of analysis will turn out to have sufficient strength to effectively counteract the tendency so as to block its projected outcome is methodologically indeterminate. It all depends on the actual situation. In some situations it might be possible to specify limiting conditions with respect to some counteracting factors. This kind of specification might permit one to maintain that certain particular counteracting factors will not be able to indefinitely block the development of the tendency. Even so it is logically possible for new counteracting factors to come into play, in the course of the ongoing

development of the concrete-real, which would continue to thwart the
development of the tendency and effectively block its projected outcome
in the concrete-real. But this is not to say that it would be practically
possible for such factors to come into play in some actual situation. All
this is meant to bring out the conditional nature of assertions about
projected outcomes. And whenever there is talk about inevitable outcomes, the term "inevitable" should be taken to mean "inevitable *as
long as* certain specified conditions hold and develop, and *unless* certain
other possible conditions obtrude."

The Dialectical-Empirical and the
Deductive-Nomological Models of Explanation

Having given the preceding account of the vertical and lateral dialectical projections, in what sense can we say that these notions constitute
the basis for a scientific method of explanation? In order to bring this
out let us try to imagine some features of the conceptual space within
which the currently dominant model of scientific explanation usually
functions. We refer to the deductive-nomological model of explanation.[56] On this model the explanation of an event consists in the
deduction of a statement describing the event to be explained, from the
conjunction of appropriate existential assertions concerning initial conditions, together with an appropriate scientific law (or laws) formulated
as a universal conditional statement. We note that on this model there
is a sharp separation between the conditional status of the law and the
existential status of the initial conditions. We note also that the factors
designated by the antecedent and the consequent of the universal conditional are externally related.

If we try to imagine the conceptual space of the deductive-
nomological model, we can discern a blocklike laying out of the
universal conditional at some level of abstraction with, of course, an
accompanying blocklike separation of antecedent and consequent. And
then we can discern a blocklike laying out of the existential assertion
of initial conditions, but on a relatively less abstract level of analysis
than the universal conditional statement, which represents some particular instantiation of the universal form indicated in the antecedent
of the conditional. The explanation is consummated by the logical
inference in conceptual space—and according to the rules of formal
logic—from these conceptual blocks to still another conceptual block,
which represents the event to be explained. This conceptual block
represents in conceptual space a particular existential instantiation of
the form denoted by the consequent of the universal conditional. As
with the existential assertion of initial conditions, it is projected in
conceptual space on a more concrete level of abstraction than the

universal conditional statement. Thus we note that even in the deductive-nomological model there is an explanatory movement from abstract to concrete—but of course a nondialectical explanatory movement appropriate to a universe of discourse committed to the notion of the abstract universal and to the doctrine of external relations.

We suggest, however, that the plausibility of the deductive-nomological model really rests on an implicitly assumed network of background conditions and other presuppositions, which are never brought into thematic focus. Nonetheless, they function surreptitiously in the implicitly understood theoretical web within the context of which specific explanations of events in terms of the deductive model are actually given.[57] Of special importance in this theoretical web are certain philosophical commitments to the doctrine of external relations and to the abstract universal. These commitments operate to obscure awareness of the implicitly assumed network at play in the deductive-nomological model.

Against this background we submit that in the dialectical-empirical model of explanation (as we refer to Marx's distinctive method of scientific explanation) an event is explained through the presentation of an intricately elaborated explanatory web, which level by level systematically discloses the concrete structural dynamics of the situation. In doing so it *shows* how the event to be explained issues naturally out of the structural dynamics of a developing complex of internally related factors. Here it is essential to remember how the conceptual space of the dialectical-empirical method of explanation is shaped by the interplay of the lateral and vertical dialectical projections that were analyzed earlier.

The explanatory web projects an appropriate dialectical conditional law as a "covering law" in relation to which a given event is to be explained. This dialectical "covering law" abstracts from some relevant factors and brings into focus those factors that are the most essential for disclosing the broad structural tendency in relation to which the event to be explained is to be articulated. And although the internal relations obtaining among the various factors distinguished in the antecedent of the dialectical conditional may not be apparent initially, and the internal relations obtaining between the antecedent and the consequent of the dialectical conditional may also not be apparent at first, all these internal relations become clear in the level-by-level elaboration of the explanatory web.

In the level-by-level elaboration, additional complicating factors relevant for explaining the event are explicitly brought into focus within the broad structural framework disclosed by the dialectical law. Moreover, this level-by-level elaboration includes the existential assertion of concrete conditions. These represent some particular existential instantiation of the universal form indicated in the antecedent of the dialectical conditional and more concretely elaborated in the dialectical hierarchy of nested structures. This elaboration ideally goes on until the explanatory web is developed concretely enough to represent, in thought, the structural configuration in the concrete-real from out of the matrix of which the event to be explained dynamically arises.

The distinction made by the dialectical–empirical method between the existential and the conditional status of statements in scientific explanations has been obscured, because the intricacy of Marx's analysis in the three volumes of *Capital* is such that most people do not get a clear glimpse of the wood of his position because of the trees of his long-spun-out analysis. Those statements, referring to the factors at play in Marx's explanations, have a conditional status when the factors are understood to function as antecedent conditions of some conditionally projected dialectical law; other such statements have an existential status when the factors are understood to function as existential assertions. And in general, just as in the deductive–nomological method, the existentially asserted initial conditions constitute particular instantiations of the universal form indicated by the antecedent of the "covering law," so do we find it in the dialectical–empirical method. Only here the "covering law" is a dialectical law, conditionally asserting a broad structural tendency of some sort or other, in which a complex of internally related factors is conditionally projected in its dynamic interplay over time.

The explanation is achieved not only by an appropriate deductive inference according to formal rules of a statement describing the event to be explained. Consummation of the explanation also requires an active comprehension of the level-by-level development, which systematically ties specific existential conditions together with a dialectical law. This must be done in a way that brings out the structural enmeshment of events with one another, and makes the concrete event to be explained appear to be all but inevitable when seen in the light of the complicated interplay of factors operating in the actual situation in the concrete-real. All these factors are brought into thematic focus in the nested hierarchy of dialectical structures constituted in the dialectical movement from the abstract to the concrete.

In this movement an explanatory web is presented that shows how the event to be explained emerges out of the concrete structural tendencies disclosed in the elaboration of the dialectical hierarchy of nested structures and conceptually developed within the broad structural framework of the dialectical law. (Just how this "showing" takes place will become clear with the analysis of the next two chapters.) Thus the dialectical–empirical method of explanation is a kind of synthesis of the "covering law" model on the one hand, and the genetic model of explanation on the other—a synthesis in which all the factors at play in the explanation are understood in terms of internal relations and the concrete universal.

The Problem of Beginnings

It is essential to determine the methodological importance that Marx attached to finding the proper beginning for his dialectical explanatory movement. In his discussion of method in the Introduction to the *Grundrisse*, Marx indicates that he arrives at the abstract relations—which will serve as the first broad strokes in the movement from abstract to concrete—through a prior "journey" that sets out from a vaguely apprehended "chaotic conception of the whole," and moves "analytically towards ever more simple concepts," "towards ever thinner abstractions" until the "simplest determinations" have been arrived at.[58]

Here we should note that Marx's characterization of certain abstract relations as the "simplest determinations" is not made in a vacuum, but rather in relation to the domain of the concrete-real that Marx has under investigation, namely, capitalist society as a whole conceived as a transitory stage in the development of man. Thus "simplest determinations" in this context means something like the simplest abstract relations in terms of which one can *begin* to comprehend capitalist society as so conceived.

For Marx the simplest abstract relations, which permit one to begin to comprehend the concrete-real of capitalist society, are relations that obtain for the whole gamut of different types of society, and which thus make abstraction from the particular structures that obtain in capitalist society. In other words, the first broad strokes for comprehending capitalist society conceived as a transitory stage in the development of human history are strokes broad enough to embrace other stages than that of capitalism. Thus Marx explains that in the development of the explanatory movement from abstract to concrete, "the order [of development] obviously has to be (1) the general, abstract determinations which obtain in more or less all forms of society, but in the above-explained sense. (2) The categories which make up the inner structure of society and on which the fundamental classes rest. Capital, wage labour, landed property."[59]

At this point we introduce an important but misleading suggestion made by Martin Nicolaus concerning the movement from abstract to concrete. Nicolaus' suggestion is all the more important because of the context in which it is made, namely, his Foreword to his translation of the *Grundrisse*, the first complete English translation. Nicolaus seems to be suggesting that Marx abandoned the method of moving from the abstract to the concrete soon after the period in which he wrote the

Grundrisse.[60] In partial explanation of the appropriateness for such a supposed shift in Marx's attitude, Nicolaus makes this comment on the passage just quoted from the Introduction to the *Grundrisse*:

> The question of the proper beginning remains unsettled in Marx's Introduction. What he says about it in the summary paragraph . . . is inconclusive: "The order obviously has to be (1) the general, abstract determinants which obtain in more or less all forms of society, but in the above-explained sense." This, however, is a manifest impossibility, since the "above-explained sense" is precisely that *not* the categories obtaining in more or less all societies, but rather those which dominate a particular society in distinction to other societies, ought to form the starting point. This formulation does not solve the problem.[61]

We suggest that the "manifest impossibility" that Nicolaus speaks of here is based on a misunderstanding of what Marx means by the "above-explained sense." Nicolaus assumes that the passage to which Marx makes reference with the "above-explained sense" is one wherein Marx had spoken of the predominant relation of a given society as a "starting point" in the analysis of that society.[62] Follow Nicolaus in this suggestion and the claim about the manifest impossibility that he makes seems well founded. However, there is in Marx's text a much more natural reference for the "above-explained sense," which will help to clarify the crucially important philosophical issues at stake here. Early in his Introduction to the *Grundrisse* Marx writes as follows:

> [A]ll epochs of production have certain common traits, common characteristics. *Production in general* is an abstraction, but a rational abstraction in so far as it really brings out and fixes the common element and thus saves us repetition. Still, this *general* category, this common element sifted out by comparison, is itself segmented many times over and splits into different determinations.[63]

The understanding of this passage is contingent upon a recognition that the universe of discourse within which Marx is operating is a universe of discourse that has adopted the concrete universal rather than the abstract universal as a characteristic instrument of analysis. And in the passage just quoted we have an explicit pointing—undertaken within a universe of discourse that has adopted the concrete universal—toward that very adoption. Marx is here effectively denying that "production in general" can be understood as the abstract universal of traditional logic, which appears as an unmodifiable core in each of its species with the specific differences being externally added to this core. At the same time, Marx is pointing to his own interpretation of "production in general" as a concrete universal "which is itself segmented many times over and splits into different determinations."

Remember the context of Marx's qualifying remark. Marx indicated that in the development of the explanatory movement from abstract to concrete the first stage is constituted by the "general, abstract determinations which obtain in more or less all forms of society, but in the above-explained sense." We suggest that Marx's remark about the "above-explained sense" makes reference to the passage we have singled out. We hold that it is intended as a caution against interpreting the abstract relations, which stand at the head of the movement from abstract to concrete, as the abstract universals of traditional logic, as well as a recommendation that they be interpreted as concrete universals. On this understanding of Marx's remark the "manifest impossibility" that Nicolaus speaks about dissolves quite readily.

This still leaves the problems of what to do with Marx's discussion of the predominant relation of a given society as the starting point in the analysis of that society, as well as with Nicolaus' suggestion to the effect that such a beginning involves an abdication of the method of moving from the abstract to the concrete. To resolve these issues we point out that in a sense there are two beginnings. Or, more properly, the question of where to begin must really be seen in relation to the level of abstraction, that is, the degree of elaboration of the conceptual field that is being considered.

In an explanatory movement from abstract to concrete that was fully developed and explicitly stated, the explanation would begin with abstract relations that obtain for all societies. When such an explanatory movement had reached a stage of development where the analysis of given specific societies was ready to be undertaken, then at that stage the analysis would begin with the predominant relation obtaining in the given specific society.

What then of the fact that Marx's analysis in *Capital* begins with the commodity?[64] Does it mean that Marx has abandoned the method of moving from the abstract to the concrete as Nicolaus suggests? Clearly not. For one thing, there is no getting away from the fact that in the course of the development of the three volumes of *Capital* there clearly is a movement from more abstract to more concrete levels of analysis. In addition, Marx's analysis of the commodity in the first chapter of *Capital* is itself structured in terms of a movement from more abstract to more concrete levels of analysis.[65]

Our present problem concerning beginnings is readily resolved, however, if we keep in mind that Marx's projection of the commodity as the explicit beginning of *Capital* is itself carried out within the framework of the implicitly understood thesis of historical materialism, which hovers here in the conceptual background at a more abstract level of analysis than the analysis of *Capital* itself. And if the full potential of Marx's method of explanation were to be actualized here, this would have to be made explicit. As Marx says in the famous 1859 Preface to the *Critique of Political Economy*, once he had arrived at the thesis of historical materialism it "became the guiding principle of my studies."[66]

We note also that in this Preface Marx writes: "A general introduction, which I had drafted, is omitted, since on further consideration it seems to me confusing to anticipate results which still have to be substantiated."[67] Here Marx is referring to the material that is now known as the Introduction to the *Grundrisse* completed in 1858. The fact that Marx omitted publication of this material in 1859 does not mean that he abandoned the position taken therein on scientific method, but rather that he hadn't yet developed his analysis of the "organic totality" of capitalism to the point where he felt this development would itself substantiate the methodological position taken in the Introduction to the *Grundrisse*.[68]

3

Freedom-as-Transcendence I

In this chapter and the following one we address the category of freedom-as-transcendence. As indicated earlier, the core meaning of this category is that human beings are always more than antecedent conditions may have made them be, by virtue of their capacity to make what they become by their own activity. They have the capacity either to make and remake themselves in the same ways in which they have made themselves in the past, or to go beyond such past ways by adopting qualitatively new ways of actively making themselves.

In Marx's view, the particular way in which human beings actively make themselves at any particular phase of human development is something that develops, and something that is shaped by the cumulative effects of earlier phases as it develops. Thus we will have to consider freedom-as-transcendence on the world-historical level if we are to get at Marx. And this means that we will have to focus on the thesis of historical materialism. It will be our objective in the present chapter and in the next to provide a level-by-level elaboration of this thesis in keeping with the methodological considerations of the previous chapter.

The Thesis of Historical Materialism and Levels of Abstraction

As a point of departure for our consideration of human transcendence on the world–historical level, we cite the famous formulation of the thesis of historical materialism that Marx provides in his 1859 Preface to *A Contribution to the Critique of Political Economy*:

> In the social production of their life, men enter into definite relations that are indispensable and independent of their will, relations of production that correspond to a definite stage of development of their material

productive forces. The sum total of these relations of production constitutes the economic structure of society, the real foundation on which
rises a legal and political superstructure and to which correspond definite
forms of social consciousness. The mode of production of material life
conditions the social, political, and intellectual life process in general. It
is not the consciousness of men that determines their being, but, on the
contrary, their social being that determines their consciousness. At a
certain stage of their development, the material productive forces of
society come into conflict with the existing relations of production,
or—what is but a legal expression for the same thing—with the property
relations within which they have been at work hitherto. From forms of
development of the productive forces these relations turn into their
fetters. Then begins an epoch of social revolution. With the change of
the economic foundation the entire immense superstructure is more or
less rapidly transformed.[1]

This passage is a schema presented in the conceptual field at a level
of analysis which abstracts from the specific differences which obtain
for different social formations. It is an abstract schema for the comprehension of the transition from one social formation to another, and
thus for the comprehension of world-historical transcendence.

On the level of analysis from which the schema described in the
above passage is projected, the correlations among the various factors
mentioned *seem* straightforward. Forces of production operate within
the framework of a given complex of social relations in relation to
which a corresponding complex of social institutions and a corresponding form of social consciousness obtains, and there is social stability.
When the ongoing development of the forces of production is increasingly impeded—as a result of a mounting conflict between the developing forces of production and the established social relations—social
instability ensues. This mounting social instability is resolved through
the establishment of a new complex of social relations that fosters the
ongoing development of the forces of production. And in relation to
the new complex of social relations, a new complex of social institutions comes to obtain.

Although these correlations seem straightforward, it will become
clear that adequate comprehension of this schema requires that it be
comprehended in relation to more concretely elaborated levels of
analysis undertaken within its framework. Adequate comprehension
also requires that it be seen in relation to still more abstract levels that
could be distinguished in the analysis of world-historical transcendence.
We take up these considerations more fully in the following sections.

For now, we point to two aspects of Marx's formulation that have
the effect of obscuring comprehension of the passage. In the passage
just cited, Marx speaks of the social relations into which men enter as
being "independent of their will." And he speaks of the social relations

of production as the "real foundation" on which rises the social super-structure. Taken together in the context of Marx's formulation of the thesis of historical materialism as it appears in the Preface—but in isolation from the wider context of his thought—these two aspects of his formulation tend to suggest an interpretation of historical materialism that reduces human subjects to something like phenomenal playthings of an objective process of social development taking place over their heads. The degree to which this interpretation of the thesis of historical materialism is a fundamental distortion of Marx's position will only become fully apparent as our discussion proceeds. Here we explain how the aspects indicated contribute to the misinterpretation of Marx's thesis. Our explanation presupposes some points made in the methodological discussion given in Chapter 2.

We suggest that Marx's reference to the social relations as the "real foundation" (when this reference is not carefully qualified) tends to blur the distinction between the concrete-in-thought and the concrete-real so that abstract social relations, interpreted as altogether independent of human agency, are viewed as coming into conflict with abstract forces of production in a way which somehow generates concrete social development. But it is not *abstract* social relations that are the real foundation of the social institutions and the form of consciousness, but *concrete* social relations. Concrete social relations are independent of human will in the sense that people are born into a network of already existing, historically developed social relations which they did not choose, but which shape the development of individual consciousness from birth. However, concrete social relations, far from being altogether independent of human agency, are themselves constituted through and by human agency. That is, concrete social relations are constituted in the concrete-real through the whole mass of particular activities, under-taken on particular occasions, by particular concrete individuals inter-acting with one another. This whole mass of particular activities of particular concrete individuals is, in the last recourse, the real founda-tion on which everything else rises—including both the base and the superstructure.

Bearing these comments in mind, we stress that the theory of historical materialism must be clearly distinguished from the histori-cally developing concrete social reality to which the theory refers. The theory of historical materialism is projected within the conceptual field. Within this conceptual field the social relations in play are abstract social relations. But these abstract social relations are not the real foundation of the social institutions and form of consciousness in the concrete-real. Nor are they the real foundation for the social institutions and form of consciousness as grasped in thought.

The relationship between base and superstructure, as this relationship is comprehended in the conceptual field, is misrepresented by the image of the "real foundation" (although the image is quite suitable for understanding the relationship between base and superstructure in the concrete-real itself). Rather, social relations, *as comprehended in thought* at an abstract level of analysis, are broad conceptual structures that circumscribe the conceptual zone within which the elaboration of the superstructure as grasped in thought can then be undertaken.

Thus, the general thesis of historical materialism is a complex structured schema projected toward more concrete elaborations from a rather abstract level in the conceptual field. It serves as a dialectical framework for the comprehension of human transcendence. It circumscribes in the conceptual field the broad structures within the framework of which the more concrete elaboration of human transcendence can then be undertaken. Moreover, the general thesis of historical materialism can itself be viewed as a concrete elaboration of a still more abstractly formulated schema—one which serves in its turn as a dialectical framework for the general thesis of historical materialism. This more abstract schema is the general form of being-in-the-world that was explained in the first chapter. It must be brought into clear focus in the present context.

The general form of being-in-the-world was characterized as "conscious activity which is transformative of the natural world as well as formative and transformative of human existence." Because of previous methodological discussion, it should be clear that the general form of being-in-the-world is not to be interpreted after the fashion of the abstract universal. There is no conscious-activity-as-such. There are only particular forms of conscious activity undertaken by particular human agents. But while the general form of being-in-the-world abstracts from such particular content, even in such abstraction it never loses its underlying intentional orientation toward particular forms of being-in-the-world. The general form serves as a schema projected in thought toward more specific forms of being-in-the-world. And it serves as a dialectical framework within which specific forms of being-in-the-world can be elaborated. It projects a variety of different specific forms of being-in-the-world, but without specifying that variety any further. And it projects a changed practice as the instrument through which a transition is effected from one specific form of being-in-the-world to another specific form.

Thus the general form of being-in-the-world is a structured schema circumscribing the broad structures within the framework of which the general thesis of historical materialism is itself elaborated at a more concrete level of analysis. At that level, forces of production, social relations of production, the social superstructure, and so on, are introduced as social factors at play in the more concrete specification of the particular way in which man makes himself. These social factors are pointed to by the projected schema of the general form of being-in-the-world, but are not further specified thereby. As such, the general form of being-in-the-world stands as the most abstract stage in the conceptual elaboration of world-historical transcendence.

Although this general form stands as the most abstract stage, the general thesis of historical materialism stands in turn as a structured schema that circumscribes the broad structures within which the more concrete elaboration of human transcendence can then be undertaken. Such a more concrete elaboration of the general thesis of historical materialism is implicitly referred to when the universals in its formulation are interpreted as concrete universals. When this more concrete elaboration is explicitly rendered with the introduction of more and more factors, it will become apparent that the correlations among the various factors indicated in the formulation of the general thesis are not so straightforward as they might initially seem. In particular, it will become apparent that the relation between the superstructure and the economic base is such that in certain circumstances the superstructure, or aspects of the superstructure, can have primacy over the base in shaping social development.

In addition, with the more concrete elaboration of the general thesis of historical materialism, it will become apparent that this thesis—far from being a law that stands over concrete individuals in a way which seemingly dictates the course of social development—does not wrest the agency of social development from the hands of concrete individuals.

Against Economic Determinism

The following sections will return to these matters, but here we propose to indicate how economic determinism on the one hand, and an interpretation of historical materialism which has been projected as characteristic of Soviet Marxism on the other hand,[2] each in different ways distorts the meaning of the general thesis of historical materialism. Among other things, each of these interpretations fails to interpret it in terms of the concrete universal and in relation to its more concrete elaborations.

Focusing first on the interpretation referred to as economic determinism, we indicate that this interpretation distorts the relationship between the economic base and the social superstructure. It views the superstructure as a more or less mechanical reflex of the economic base to the extent that the economic base is alone regarded as the determining factor of social development, with everything else being completely determined thereby.

As against the economic determinist interpretation of historical materialism, we cite in passing Engels' rejection of the view that the economic base is the only determining factor in social development. "According to the materialist conception of history the determining element in history is *ultimately* the production and reproduction in real life. More than this neither Marx nor I have ever asserted. If therefore somebody distorts this into the statement that the economic element is the *only* determining one, he transforms it into a meaningless, abstract and absurd phrase."[3]

But it was Lenin who most vigorously rejected economic determinism. In "A Talk with Defenders of Economism,"[4] which first appeared in *Iskra* (the paper founded by Lenin), a document of the "Economists" was provided by Lenin which claimed that: "*Iskra* gives too little consideration to the material elements and the material environment of the movement, whose interaction creates a definite type of labour movement and determines its path, the path from which the ideologists, despite all their efforts, are incapable of diverting it, even if they are inspired by the finest theories and programmes."[5]

Lenin responded: "To say . . . that ideologists (i.e., politically conscious leaders) cannot divert the movement from the path determined by the interaction of environment and elements is to ignore the simple truth that the conscious element *participates* in this interaction and in the determination of the path."[6] A sustained critique of economism was taken up by Lenin in *What Is to Be Done?*[7]

Later we deal more fully with the relationship between the economic base and the social superstructure, but here we explain how the economic determinist distortion of historical materialism arises. If the social factors indicated in the general thesis of historical materialism—the forces of production, social relations of production, and social superstructure—are interpreted in terms of the abstract universal rather than the concrete universal, then the consequence is that the internal connections that obtain among these social factors are completely severed.

To be sure, the internal connections obtaining among these social factors are not explicitly drawn out in the formulation of the general thesis of historical materialism that Marx provides in the Preface to *A Contribution to the Critique of Political Economy*. (For example, in the Preface there is no mention of the fact that the forces of production have a conscious aspect. But the concept of the forces of production includes human needs and labor power as well. And labor power is *conscious* labor power. It is conscious labor power, motivated by need, and having certain skills and knowledge, that employs the means of production within the framework of certain social relations to produce the means of subsistence.) Nonetheless, internal relations still obtain among these social factors. The more concrete elaborations—implicitly referred to when the general thesis of historical materialism is interpreted in terms of the concrete universal—would make more explicit the lines of internal connection among the factors distinguished at the more abstract level. For at the abstract level the lines of interconnection are not so immediately apparent.

However, once interpretation of the general thesis of historical materialism in terms of the abstract universal severs the internal relations among the social factors, this severance of internal relations is then carried through to all those more developed contexts in which the general thesis of historical materialism might be appealed to in the explanation of social development. With the severance of the internal relations among the social factors, and the resultant interpretation of these factors as externally related, it is but a short step to the economic determinist interpretation of historical materialism. This step is mediated by the application of the mechanistic model of laws and of explanation to the factors whose lines of interconnection have been severed.

Against Other Stereotypes

The failure to comprehend the general thesis of historical materialism in relation to its more concrete elaborations contributes to the interpretation of historical materialism that Helmut Fleischer projects as characteristic of Soviet Marxism in *Marxism and History*. The main problem, as Fleischer sees things, is that the emphasis on objective laws of social development (which is characteristic of the Soviet interpretation of history) is such that concrete individuals—the acting human subjects—are seemingly transformed into puppets of objective laws of social development. Fleischer writes:

> In the historical materialism of the Soviet Marxist school . . . subjective activity is regarded as the highly conditioned "product" of material social conditions and as the executive organ of objective laws of social development. The theory of the "productive forces" of history is here developed completely along the lines of "objective logic"; history is the result of the dialectics between productive forces and productive relations.[8]

> Soviet historical materialism . . . puts pseudo-subjects in the place of really acting individuals. Structural concepts are isolated from their concrete link with human subjects and become "subjects" and "factors" of truly marvelous effectiveness, and the human subjects who alone deserve the name of factors are turned into "products" of the abstractions thus raised to the power of factors.[9]

On Fleischer's interpretation of Soviet Marxism, the general thesis of historical materialism would constitute an objective law of social development which, in effect, views the dynamic interplay of objective factors—considered in abstraction from subjective factors—as the generative source of the social development of human subjects. Here the attempt to be objective is construed as falling back on the expedient of filtering all subjective components from the forces of production—as well as the social relations—so as to arrive at purely objective factors to which appeal is made in order to account for the development of human subjects. If this view of Soviet Marxism is really a well-founded view, then Soviet Marxism would imply an implicit return to the economism that it explicitly rejects.

Before responding to the interpretation of historical materialism that Fleischer discusses, we first indicate that the main Soviet text cited by Fleischer in his interpretation of Soviet Marxism is a textbook on *The Foundations of Marxist Philosophy.*[10] As it is, there are relatively few direct citations from this text in the course of Fleischer's characterization of Soviet Marxism. Not only that, there are other citations from Soviet texts that could be given which *prima facie* are in conflict with Fleischer's interpretation of Soviet Marxism as it concerns the relation between laws and conscious human agents.[11]

Moreover, Fleischer is clearly operating with a nondialectical conception of law in his interpretation of the brief extracts cited from this Soviet textbook. And indeed a nondialectical interpretation of law is at play throughout Fleischer's whole discussion in *Marxism and History.* On the face of it, this consideration in itself seems to vitiate Fleischer's whole characterization of Soviet Marxism. And strictly speaking, so it does. On the other hand, there is one conspicuous current in the development of Soviet Marxism that comes close in its implications, although not in its explicit formulation, to the kind of position that Fleischer ascribes to Soviet Marxism as a whole.

The current we speak of derives from Joseph Stalin. In its formulations concerning laws of social development, it derives from two works in which Stalin discusses such laws as objective laws, namely, *Dialectical and Historical Materialism,* and *Economic Problems of Socialism in the U.S.S.R.*[12] (We note that Fleischer does not give any citations from these works in *Marxism and History,* nor does he even refer to them.) Here we do not give a fully developed critique of Stalin's conception of objective laws of social development, but rather an indication of the problematic nature of his conception of objective laws.

We point first to a passage that occurs in the context of Stalin's discussion of laws of social development as "having the validity of objective truths."[13] The passage reads: "If the material world represents objective reality existing independently of the mind of men, while the mind is a reflection of this objective reality, it follows that the material life of society, its being, is also primary, and its spiritual life secondary, derivative, and that the material life of society is an objective reality existing independently of the will of men, while the spiritual life of society is a reflection of this objective reality, a reflection of being."[14]

In this passage the distinction between the economic base and the social superstructure is mistakenly assimilated by Stalin to the quasi-metaphysical distinction between the "material world" on the one hand and the "mind of men" on the other. The implication of this mistaken assimilation is that the objectivity of the laws of social development is construed in abstraction from conscious human subjects. This is a gross distortion of the thesis of historical materialism. For, as we go on to explain shortly, the economic base is *constituted as* the economic base by the activity of conscious human subjects, and it embraces, as part of its meaning, certain dimensions of the human subject.

We point to another place in an addendum to *Economic Problems of Socialism in the U.S.S.R.*, where Stalin attacks the view which holds that "only because of the conscious action of the Soviet citizens engaged in material production do the economic laws of socialism arise."[15] Stalin proclaims: "This opinion is absolutely incorrect. . . . Marxism holds that the laws of the political economy of socialism are a reflection in the minds of men of objective laws existing outside of us."[16]

And in the main body of this work, in a section on the "Character of Economic Laws Under Socialism," Stalin writes:

> One of the distinguishing features of political economy is that its laws, unlike those of natural science are impermanent, that they, or at least the majority of them, operate for a definite historical period, after which they give place to new laws. However, these laws are not abolished, but lose their validity owing to the new economic conditions and depart from the scene in order to give place to new laws, laws which are not created by the will of man, but which arise from the new economic conditions.[17]

We quickly add that it is Stalinist Marxism that holds these positions. These are not the positions of Marx himself. Moreover, these positions are a distortion of Marx's own understanding of historical materialism, as will become evident in the ongoing discussion of this chapter and the next one. Some laws of social development, such as the laws implicit in the general thesis of historical materialism, are invariant for all social formations. But those laws that are specific to a given social formation do "give place to new laws . . . which arise from the new economic conditions." However, it is precisely the activity of conscious human subjects that shapes the new economic conditions. The objective laws of social development are laws in which conscious human subjects concretely figure. And without the "conscious action of the Soviet citizens engaged in material production," the economic conditions on the basis of which the economic laws of the Soviet social reality arise would be nonexistent.

Let us now examine the kind of interpretation of historical materialism that Fleischer characterizes in *Marxism and History*. We have recently seen that the general thesis of historical materialism is projected in the conceptual field within the dialectical framework of the general form of being-in-the-world, that is, the general form of conscious-activity-in-the-world. The forces of production and the social relations of production—both of which are objective factors at play in the general thesis of historical materialism—have to be understood as dynamically interconnected aspects of conscious-activity-in-the-world.

The general thesis of historical materialism projects these two aspects of conscious-activity-in-the-world as constituting the base for still another of its aspects, also distinguished in the general thesis, namely, the social superstructure. The shaping of the superstructure by the base is the shaping of conscious-activity-in-the-world, considered under one aspect, by conscious-activity-in-the-world considered under other of its aspects. When this is considered in relation to its more concrete elaboration, it means that the shaping of the superstructure by the base is the shaping of human subjects considered under one of their aspects, by the conscious activity of these same human subjects considered under other aspects. The shaping of conscious-activity-in-the-world is the self-shaping of human subjects on the basis of their own activity.

The comprehension of the general thesis of historical materialism is contingent upon systematically interpreting the concept of the forces of production, and the concept of the social relations of production, in relation to the more concrete elaboration of these concepts. The *concept* of the forces of production is intentionally oriented toward, and includes as part of its meaning, the concept of a field of conscious human subjects—insofar as the conscious activity of these human subjects is considered in terms of skills, work experience, techniques, and the like, which are consciously brought into play in the course of production. The forces of production in the *concrete-real* are constituted by and are identical with, the conscious activity of concrete human subjects consciously employing skills, techniques, and so on in relation to the nonhuman material factors of production, namely, raw materials, means, and instruments of production. The human subject—the subjective component of production—is the primary force of production, and has this primacy vis-à-vis the means and instruments of production that constitute the nonhuman objective component of production. Here the human subject has ontological primacy, for it is only the conscious activity of human subjects with all their skills and knowledge that *constitutes* the nonhuman material factors of production *as* forces of production.

The *concept* of the social relations of production in turn is intentionally oriented toward, and includes as part of its meaning, the concept of a field of conscious human subjects insofar as the conscious activity of these human subjects is considered in terms of the social relations obtaining among them. Social relations of production in the *concrete-real* are constituted by, and are identical with, the concrete activity of conscious human subjects as they interrelate with each other in the concrete-real so as to constitute the class and property relations that obtain among the human subjects. As with the forces of production, the subjective component of the social relations of production has ontological primacy over the objective component. For it is only the activity of conscious human subjects as they interrelate with each other vis-à-vis the material components of production that *constitutes* the social relations of production *as* relations of production.

The general thesis of historical materialism projects the forces of production and the social relations of production as the base on which the social superstructure rises. This means that the general thesis projects the conscious activity of concrete human subjects—insofar as this activity is considered in terms of the skills and techniques that it consciously brings into play, and insofar as this activity is considered in terms of the class and property relations obtaining among the concrete human subjects as they consciously interact with one another—as the base that shapes still another aspect of the conscious-activity-in-the-world of these human subjects, namely, the aspect referred to as the social superstructure.

With respect to the "dialectic of productive forces and productive relations" when this dialectic is considered as the dynamic center of all social development, the foregoing means that this dialectic can be understood only in terms of the activity of conscious human subjects. In other words, the "dialectic of productive forces and productive relations" is identical with the dynamic interconnected activity of conscious human subjects as that activity is comprehended under the concept of the forces of production, and under the concept of the social relations of production. This in turn means that a mounting conflict between forces of production and social relations of production can be understood only as a mounting conflict among conscious human subjects. The "fettering" of the forces of production, as these forces develop within the framework of given social relations, must be understood primarily in terms of a fettering of the development of conscious human subjects.

It is crucially important not to lose sight of Marx's conception of law. Much of the discussion of historical materialism has centered on the general thesis of historical materialism as constituting a law of social development. In *Marxism and History* Fleischer makes it plain that this is especially true of the Soviet development of Marxist theory.

However, although we are in full agreement with Fleischer's view of the acting human subject as the dynamic center of social development, we cannot adopt Fleischer's own position on the issue of laws of social development as they come into play in Marx's thought. This point of difference with Fleischer is significant, inasmuch as it will bring into focus another primary impediment to the comprehension of historical materialism. We speak of the failure to comprehend that the conception of law at play therein postulates dialectical tendencies, and, moreover, that it does so in a way that is inconsistent with the projection of inevitable outcomes in any hard theoretical sense.

Fleischer attempts to dispel the view that Marx had it seriously in mind to project a law of social development ranging over the whole of human history. About Marx's talk of laws, Fleischer writes: "We may conjecture that he was merely paying a verbal tribute to the predominance in contemporary thought of the idea of scientific law. . . . The talk of law is often merely an affirmation of the nonarbitrary nature of historical phenomena; sometimes it is merely a figure of speech indicating that there is some sort of order behind everything."[18] In any case: "The idea of the whole course of history being governed by a single law is simply inconceivable and the founders of Marxism never attempted to establish any such law."[19]

The attitude that Fleischer takes toward laws of social development in Marx's thought is related on the one hand to his position on the primacy of the human subject as the generative source of social development, but on the other hand to the association of a mechanistic concept of law with what Marx says about laws, when such talk is taken seriously. In this connection Fleischer writes: "Thus it seems that in Marx's view of social development (1) given the initial conditions, and (2) given the ways of behavior of the elements involved, (3) definite laws will necessarily result in a definite sequence of states of the system, *following the pattern familiar to us from Laplace's theory of natural determination.*"[20]

We agree that a mechanistic interpretation would indeed be incompatible with the primacy of conscious human subjects as the generative source of social development. Yet we take the position that a mechanistic interpretation of Marx's talk about laws of social development represents a fundamental distortion of his thought. To develop this, we take recourse to the analysis, given in Chapter 2, of the dialectical conception of law at play in Marx's universe of discourse. This conception of law will be seen to be fully compatible with the primacy of conscious human subjects as the generative source of social development.

Having just said this, we want to acknowledge that Marx himself has precipitated some of the confusion concerning his conception of law through occasional statements clearly suggesting a mechanistic interpretation of laws. For example, we refer to a troublesome formulation wherein Marx speaks of laws "working with iron necessity toward inevitable results."[21] Marx's formulation is especially unfortunate given the prominent place in which it appears, in the Preface to *Capital*. For this formulation, when seen in isolation from the whole fabric of Marx's thought and when seen in isolation from his method of analysis, suggests that Marx is indeed working with some kind of mechanistic conception of law.

We note though that a mechanistic interpretation along Laplacian lines is out of place, simply on the grounds that Laplacian laws apply in principle to discrete individual particles. Thus, the inevitability of results would extend in theory to the finer details of the motion of any particle.[22] In contrast, when relevant formulations of Marx are interpreted momentarily as laws determining inevitable results, even so there is no implication that a purported inevitability of results extends to the details of what individuals do. Marx's laws range over large aggregates of individuals. Claims by Marx about inevitability mainly appear in contexts in which what is projected as inevitable is a transformation in the broad structures of the social order. Such claims never appear in contexts in which the specific concrete activity of given individuals is projected as inevitable.

In this connection we note that on most occasions Marx's talk about inevitability can be interpreted as being rhetorical or elliptical. For example, in the *Communist Manifesto* one reads: "The bourgeoisie produces its own grave-diggers. Its downfall and the victory of the proletariat are equally inevitable."[23] Marx's usage of "inevitable" here seems clearly to be rhetorical, especially when one considers the polemical nature of the *Manifesto* as a whole. On other occasions Marx's usage of "inevitable" seems to be elliptical, as when he maintains in the Preface to *Capital* that throughout Europe "a radical change in the existing relations between capital and labor is as evident and inevitable as in England."[24]

Here Marx's usage of "inevitable" can be interpreted as making implicit reference to empirical conditions that are tacitly presupposed as the basis for a projection of inevitability. Such usage seems elliptical for some tacit argument such as the following: If a socialist revolutionary consciousness develops on a wide scale, then there will be a strong tendency for a radical change in social relations to take place. Make the empirical assumption that a socialist revolutionary consciousness will develop. Then, relative to this assumption, there would be a strong tendency for a radical change in social relations to take place. What is empirically problematic, of course, was Marx's expectation that a socialist revolutionary consciousness actually would develop close to his own lifetime. On the other hand, we suggest that the counteracting factors, which actually prevented the development of a socialist consciousness on a wide scale near to Marx's own lifetime, could be comprehended within the framework of the general thesis of historical materialism—but on more concrete levels of analysis than are undertaken in the present work. This though is a task for the historian of the period.

In any case, Marx's formulation about laws "working with iron necessity toward inevitable results" stands without warrant. It is in fact thoroughly at odds with his own method of explanation. There is really no conceptual room within it for laws of social development that work with "iron necessity" or which have "inevitable results" in any absolute sense. The self-conscious adoption of Marx's method of analysis, together with the requirements of consistency, calls for the revision of all those formulations in which Marx suggests an inevitable transformation in the broad structures of the social order, or an inevitable transition from capitalism to socialism. We bring this out more fully by shifting attention now to some things that Karl Popper has to say on the issue before us. Since Popper is one of the most influential critics of Marx,[25] we present our discussion against the background of what he says and as a critique of what he says.

In the course of an attempt in *The Poverty of Historicism* to dispel the belief that there can be any laws of social development,[26] Popper, who clearly classifies Marx as a "historicist," writes:

> Historicists *overlook the dependence of trends on initial conditions.* They operate with trends as if they were unconditional, like laws. Their confusion of trends with laws makes them believe in trends which are unconditional. . . . This, we may say, is the central mistake of historicism. Its *"laws of development" turn out to be absolute trends*; trends which, like laws, do not depend on initial conditions, and which carry us irresistibly in a certain direction into the future. They are the basis of unconditional *prophecies*, as opposed to conditional scientific *predictions.*[27]

> The existence of trends or tendencies in social change can hardly be questioned. . . . *But trends are not laws.* A statement asserting the existence of a trend is existential, not universal. . . . And a statement asserting the existence of a trend at a certain time and place would be a singular historical statement, not a universal law.[28]

Some of what Popper brings out here is fully acceptable, whereas some of it is misleading, to say the least. For one thing, Popper is quite right when he says that a statement asserting the existence of a trend is an existential statement. But this does not mean that "laws and trends are radically different things,"[29] as Popper declares in the surrounding context from which the first of the above extracts was taken.

Suppose we consider as an example the tendency toward increasing existential meaninglessness in American society in the twentieth century—and in relation to it the existential statement: "There is a tendency toward increasing existential meaninglessness in American society in the twentieth century." (We emphasize the distinction between the tendency as it exists in the concrete-real, and the existential statement that refers to this tendency.) Even though we have an existential statement here, the statement still employs universal concepts. When these concepts are properly interpreted in terms of the concrete universal, it will be seen that the very meaning of the existential statement involves implicit reference to the more concrete elaboration of the universal concepts.

Take, for instance, the concept "tendency" which is at play in the existential statement. Within Marx's point of view this concept must be seen as a relational concept. It involves not only a reference to some direction that the tendency takes, but also an implicit reference to some kind of dynamic basis that gives rise to the tendency. Moreover, beyond implicit reference to some kind of dynamic basis or other, really adequate comprehension of the existential statement would even involve an implicit reference to the particular kind of dynamic basis that gives rise to the tendency toward increasing existential meaninglessness in American society. The succeeding analysis will suggest that the complex of interconnected capitalist social relations, which exists in American society, constitutes the dynamic basis for the tendency toward increasing existential meaninglessness in America. The internal connection between this dynamic basis and the tendency toward existential meaninglessness would be comprehensible within broad structures indicated by some such universal law as the following: "If there exists a complex of capitalist social relations, then as human development within the framework of these social relations is increasingly fettered, there will be a tendency toward increasing existential meaninglessness." Thus the existential statement—when its implicit references are drawn out—calls forth for its own adequate comprehension the universal statement that indicates the broad structures within the framework of which the tendency is comprehended *as* the tendency it is.

Secondly, we would agree with Popper that any position that attempts to project the future direction of social development in a way that would "overlook the dependence of trends on initial conditions"[30] would be vulnerable to the charges which Popper brings against the position that he calls historicism. But we quickly add that any suggestion that Marx is a historicist in Popper's sense of the term is a clear distortion of Marx's position. This is especially true of any suggestion that Marx's interpretation of laws as tendencies is such as to "overlook the dependence of trends on initial conditions."

As we made clear in the analysis of Marx's method of explanation given in Chapter 2, the tendencies that Marx distinguishes in *Capital* are not projected independently of initial conditions. They are tied to a whole complex of interconnected initial conditions that constitute the dynamic basis for the tendencies considered. Assertions about projected outcomes are always conditional in nature. There is no theoretical basis in Marx's method of explanation for the absolute inevitability of any projected outcome. Thus, whenever there is talk about inevitable outcomes, the term "inevitable" should be taken to mean "inevitable *as long as* certain specified conditions hold and develop, and *unless* certain other possible conditions obtrude."

The full force of these remarks will only become apparent in a later section that deals with specific laws of social development. There we shall learn that these laws do not preclude an indefinite prolongation of the social relations of capitalism through the development of a regression to fascism. Nor do they preclude the emergence of highly repressive class societies in a hypothetically projected post-capitalist era. Further, they do not preclude the possible emergence of a genuine socialism. What will happen is contingent on the *kind* of activity undertaken by conscious human subjects—as they face the mounting pressures of the dominion of capital and the dominion of the state over human life—as well as on the *kind* of consciousness that will inform their activity.

The Historical Idealist Background

In previous discussions we have singled out some of the significant factors that have contributed to the misunderstanding of the theory of historical materialism. Still another factor leading to the misunderstanding of this theory has been the failure to keep in perspective the conception of history in reaction to which—and against the background of which—the historical materialist conception of history was developed. Of primary importance in this connection is *The German Ideology*. Therein Marx and Engels undertook a head-on confrontation with the conception of history that had been predominant for centuries. Having explained the real basis of history in terms of the activity of real individuals as they produce and interact with each other in the course of production and exchange, and in terms of the development of this activity, Marx and Engels proceed:

> In the whole conception of history up to the present this real basis of history has either been totally neglected or else considered as a minor matter quite irrelevant to the course of history. . . . The exponents of this conception of history have consequently only been able to see in history the political actions of princes and states, religious and all sorts of theoretical struggles.[31]

But we have to look at a more specific version of the general conception of history just indicated in order to bring into full focus what Marx and Engels were reacting against. Further on in *The German Ideology* they write:

> Once the ruling ideas have been separated from the ruling individuals and, above all, from the relationships which result from a given stage of the mode of production, and in this way the conclusion has been reached that history is always under the sway of ideas, it is very easy to abstract from these various ideas "*the* idea," the notion, etc., as the dominant force in history, and thus to understand all these separate ideas and concepts, as "forms of self determination" on the part of *the* concept developing in history.[32]

It is primarily in relation to the conception of history at play in the passage just cited that the historical–materialist conception of history was developed. The heavy emphasis that historical materialism (as formulated by Marx and Engels) places on economic factors, in understanding historical development, can be understood only in relation to the complete disregard of such factors in the view of history they reacted against. This disregard went to the point of reducing real concrete human history to a phenomenal manifestation of the developing "idea."

Here, however, it is very important to recognize that, although the historical–materialist conception of history rejects the view that political and ideological developments take place in complete independence of economic developments,[33] this does not mean that political and ideological developments are dependent in all respects on economic developments. Nor does it mean that political and ideological developments are without effect on economic developments.

The Dependence of the Superstructure on the Base, and Shifts in Dominance

Concerning the dependence of political and ideological developments on economic developments, we note for one thing that this dependence must be understood as a dependence of the broad structures of these developments on the broad structures of economic development. This dependence does not stretch to the details of political developments in all their particularity, or to the details of ideological developments in all their particularity. The factors that figure in the theory of historical materialism are factors ranging over large aggregates of individuals, and which necessarily abstract from the details that take place within the framework of these broad structures. In passing, we point out as an extension of these comments that the historical–materialist conception of history does not imply that the particular details, of what a particular individual thinks on a particular occasion, is determined in all its particularity by economic conditions. It is the broad lines of an individual's thinking rather than the particular details of thinking on particular occasions into which the economic conditions enter as a determining factor.

Furthermore, while rejecting the view that ideological and political developments take place independently of economic development, the historical–materialist conception of history provides room for an explanation of the "semblance of independence" that characterizes these developments. For example, Engels points out that the specialist who develops an inherited stock of ideas from previous generations has himself been shaped by the material life conditions of the society in which he lives, and that it is through this shaping that the further course of development of the inherited ideas is indirectly shaped by the economic foundation. And similarly, historical materialism explains the "semblance of independence" of political development by tracing the political activity of individuals back to the material life conditions that have shaped the consciousness of those who participate in political activity.[34]

Concerning the effect that developments in the superstructure can have on the base, Engels writes to counter

> the fatuous notion of the ideologists that because we deny an independent historical development to the various ideological spheres which play a part in history we also deny them any *effect upon history*. The basis of this is the common undialectical conception of cause and effect as rigidly opposite poles, the total disregarding of interaction. These gentlemen often almost deliberately forget that once an historic element has been brought into the world by other, ultimately economic causes, it reacts, can react on its environment and even on the causes that have given rise to it.[35]

To be sure, Engels' many comments concerning the effect of developments in the superstructure on developments in the economic foundation go a long way toward clarifying the relationship between superstructure and base. However, we suggest that they do not go far enough in recognizing the place of developments in the superstructure in shaping the course of economic development. This is largely due, perhaps, to the underlying assumption, on the part of both Marx and Engels, that a complex of classless social relations was the most likely alternative to the social relations of capitalism. Neither of them had the historical example of the "statist"[36] complex of social relations which developed in the Soviet Union in the twentieth century as a practical refutation of such an assumption. (We shall see later that Marx did argue against one form of "state socialism" in his critique of Ferdinand Lassalle.)

These remarks, however, should not be taken as suggesting that Marx or Engels failed to recognize that conscious activity on the part of large masses of people was the *sine qua non* for actually bringing about a possible transition to a classless society.[37] It is rather that they assumed that the development of a revolutionary consciousness would move in the direction of a genuine classless society, since only the social relations of a classless socialist society seemed to them to be empirically compatible with socialized production as it had developed in the framework of the social relations of capitalism.[38]

In any case, we agree with Engels that the reaction of the superstructure on the base has the character of a "secondary effect"[39] in periods of relative social stability. However, we suggest that, in periods of social transition from one complex of social relations to another, developments in the superstructure have a relative primacy vis-à-vis economic developments in shaping the whole subsequent course of social development, including the subsequent course of economic development.

To understand this one has to be mindful of the changing weight that given factors have in different phases of dialectical development. Each aspect of the concrete-real is an aspect dynamically interrelated with other aspects therein so as to constitute a dialectical interplay of mutually interacting forces, tensions, and conflicting energies. To emphasize such mutual dynamic interactions, the term "contradiction" is often used within Marx's universe of discourse to refer to *each one* of the various aspects of a complex structured whole of internally related aspects. And the whole itself is often said to be a "unity of contradictions." Such a unity of contradictions has to be understood as a structured field in which each contradiction, and each aspect of a contradiction, finds the conditions of its existence in the existence of the other contradictions and other aspects. And the structured field is one wherein some contradictions and aspects have a relative dominance over other contradictions and aspects.

Moreover, such a structured "unity of contradictions" has to be understood in its organic development over time. One must be mindful of the qualitative and nonqualitative variations in each factor, as it undergoes change in the course of the ongoing dynamic interaction with all the other factors in a moving and changing unity of contradictions. Furthermore, as Mao Tse-Tung brings out in his important essay "On Contradiction,"[40] the changes in the various factors due to such ongoing organic development can be extensive enough to cause pronounced shifts in the patterns of dominance and subordination of the various factors, depending on the phase of development of the moving "unity of contradictions."

Mao is very careful to explain that such shifts-in-dominance in the relation between the economic base and the superstructure can take place in a period of cultural upheaval and transition. And we share his position that it "is the view of mechanistic materialism, and not of dialectical materialism" to maintain that "there is no change in their respective positions" in such periods.[41] However, the notion of the relative primacy of developments in the superstructure over developments in the economic foundation in periods of transition does not mean that the general dependence of the superstructure on the base has been entirely done away with in such periods. Rather, in periods of transition from one complex of social relations to another, there is a shift in what general dependence means.

Thus, in periods of relative social stability, the reactive impact of political and ideological developments in shaping economic developments takes place within the framework of a stable complex of social relations. Within this framework superstructural developments may have a far-reaching causal impact on the details of economic developments. Yet the general dependence of superstructural developments on the framework of existing social relations still holds, and the existing social relationships are even reinforced by superstructural developments.

By contrast, the general dependence of superstructural developments on the existing social relations is *disrupted* in periods of transition from one complex of social relations to another—although it is important to remember that the disruption itself is brought about by mounting conflicts in the economic foundation. In periods of relative social *instability* involving a transition from one complex of social relations to another, developments in the superstructure have a primary role in shaping a new complex of social relations. In transitional periods the general dependence of the superstructure on the base is confined to a general dependence on the degree of development of the forces of production. This circumscribes a range of possibilities for the development of a new complex of social relations, but without settling what the specific new complex of social relations will be.

Social Character and the Existential Viability
of the Form of Social Consciousness

To examine another theme, which will clarify further the relationship between the superstructure and the base, we look at the place of human character in understanding this relationship, and in understanding the notion of the existential viability of the "form of social consciousness." This notion will play a central role in the more concrete elaboration of the general thesis of historical materialism presented later. Of course, Marx himself did not have access to the dynamic theories of character developed by Freud and others after his death. Yet the thesis of historical materialism presupposes the dynamic nature of human character. So on this theme we draw on the work of Erich Fromm, who has done so much to clarify the vital link between the base and superstructure.[42]

Critically developing Freud's dynamic theory of character, Fromm views human character as "the specific form in which human energy is shaped by the dynamic adaptation of human needs to the particular mode of existence of a given society."[43] Drawing a distinction between individual character and social character, Fromm explains that

> the concept of *social character* refers to the matrix of the character structure *common to a group*. It assumes that the fundamental factor in the formation of the "social character" is the *practice of life as it is constituted by the mode of production and the resulting social stratification. The "social character" is that particular structure of psychic energy which is molded by any given society so as to be useful for the functioning of that particular society.* The average person must *want* to do what he *has* to do in order to function in a way that permits society to use his energies for its purposes. Man's energy appears in the social process only partly as simple physical energy (laborers tilling the soil or building roads); and partly in specific forms of *psychic* energy. . . . The social character is the form in which human energy is molded for its use as a productive force in the social process.[44]

In this context we apply one of the methodological tools explained in the second chapter, namely, the notion of broad structures within the framework of which more concrete elaborations could be undertaken. Fromm's concept of "social character" ranges over large aggregates of individuals and refers to the broad structures of human character shared by the members of a given society—broad structures within which the more specific character differences of specific individuals in a given society could be undertaken on more concrete levels of analysis. Fromm indicates a dynamic correlation between the broad structures of human character that typify a given society and the broad structures of the economic foundation of that society. It is the practice of life in the concrete-real on the part of a given aggregate of conscious human subjects that actively shapes their social character in dynamic congruence with the economic conditions which prevail in the society. The individuals do not choose the economic conditions, but nonetheless must adapt to them.

So far we have indicated a dynamic correlation between social character and the economic foundation. Fromm goes on to draw a dynamic correlation between social character and the superstructure—more specifically, the ideological aspects of the superstructure—and explains that character shapes thinking. He writes:

> [W]e all tend to share the conventional belief that thinking is an exclusively intellectual act and independent of the psychological structures of the personality. This is not so, however, and the less so the more

our thinking deals with ethical, philosophical, political, psychological, or social problems rather than with the empirical manipulation of concrete objects. Such thoughts, aside from the purely logical elements that are involved in the act of thinking, are greatly determined by the personality structure of the person who thinks. This holds true for the whole of a doctrine or of a theoretical system, as well as for a single concept, like love, justice, equality, sacrifice. Each such concept and each doctrine has an emotional matrix and this emotional matrix is rooted in the character structure of the individual. . . . Different societies or classes within a society have a specific character, and on its basis different ideas develop and become powerful.[45]

So then a given social character is shaped by "the dynamic adaptation of human needs"[46] to the economic foundation that obtains in the given society. Once formed, the social character "tends to produce and to hold onto ideas and ideologies which fit and are nourished by it."[47] Thus the economic foundation shapes the ideological domain through the mediation of the social character. But Fromm is careful to add that ideas in turn can also react back and "influence the social character and, indirectly, the social economic structure."[48]

With the help of Fromm's concept of the "social character" we are now in a better position to explain the notion of the *existential viability of the form of social consciousness.* This will be crucial in the more concrete elaboration of the general thesis of historical materialism to which we turn shortly.

A word first on the meaning of the "form of social consciousness." We take our cue from the section of *The German Ideology* where Marx and Engels speak of "the ruling ideas" as the "ideal expression of the dominant material relationships."[49] We construe the "form of social consciousness" as the array of interconnected ruling ideas—an array of general categories of social-economic-political interpretation and valuation—in terms of which the members of a class or social group interpret social reality and orient themselves to it. A distinction is intended here between such an array of general categories as more or less vaguely comprehended by nonspecialists, and the articulate expression and conceptual elaboration of such categories undertaken by specialists in the various ideological spheres. Such elaboration by specialists serves, however, to reinforce and stabilize the form of social consciousness as it comes into play in the consciousness of nonspecialists.

Proceeding from Fromm, we indicate that a given "form of social consciousness" must be understood as being dynamically rooted in the emotional matrix of a corresponding social character. The existential viability of a given form of social consciousness is thus dynamically bound up with the existential viability of the corresponding social character. In turn the existential viability of a given social character is basically contingent upon whether or not life in the concrete-real—as lived in terms of that social character, and in terms of the corresponding form of social consciousness—is successful in satisfying human needs in the context of the objective economic conditions. A breakdown in the existential viability of a given social character, and in the corresponding form of social consciousness, can be viewed as the result of an intolerable frustration of human needs experienced by conscious human subjects. This happens to people who have attempted to go on living in terms of a given social character and corresponding form of social consciousness, while the ongoing development of the objective conditions has rendered them nonviable. Upon the breakdown in the existential viability of a given social character, and the corresponding form of social consciousness, brought about by developing economic conditions, developments in the superstructure then take on a relative primacy in shaping and crystallizing a new social character and a new form of social consciousness.

At this point we note a significant respect in which the position we have just taken differs from the position that Fromm takes in his analysis of the transition from feudalism to capitalism in *Escape from Freedom*. Therein Fromm seems to be suggesting that it was changes in the economic conditions which directly generated a change from a feudal social character to a new social character, and that it was this already formed new social character to which the Protestant ideology appealed, and in relation to which the Protestant ideology could then function as a stabilizing factor.[50]

We adopt the following variant hypothesis on this issue. Transformations in economic conditions generated a breakdown in the existential viability of the feudal social character, and the corresponding feudal form of social consciousness. This caused a kind of "existential vacuum."[51] Because there was no viable social character or form of social consciousness, existential needs at a deeper level of the psyche than the social character took on ascendancy. These deeper-level existential needs had to be addressed in the context of the changed economic conditions. The Protestant ideology, by appealing to these deeper level needs in a way that also served to foster the ongoing development of the productive forces, thereby acted as a psychic catalyst in shaping and crystallizing a new social character and a new form of social consciousness.

The very influential work by Max Weber, *The Protestant Ethic and the Spirit of Capitalism*, is often cited as a counter to the kind of explanation that historical materialism would provide for social development.[52] Weber projects his work as "a contribution to the understanding of the manner in which ideas become effective forces in history."[53] In a number of places throughout his work, Weber dissociates his own analysis from what he *takes* to be historical materialism. For example, Weber speaks of "the doctrine of the more naive historical materialism" according to which "ideas originate as a reflection or superstructure of economic situations."[54] And he goes on to say: "We must free ourselves from the idea that it is possible to deduce the Reformation, as a historically necessary result, from certain economic changes. Countless historical circumstances, which cannot be reduced to any economic law, and are not susceptible of economic explanation of any sort, especially purely political processes, had to concur in order that the newly created Churches should survive at all."[55] And assuming that historical materialism is indeed one-sided, Weber indicates that it "is not my aim to substitute for a one-sided materialistic an equally one-sided spiritualistic causal interpretation of culture and of history."[56]

Now we suggest that what Weber is actually dissociating himself from is a *caricature* of Marx's own understanding of historical materialism—namely, what is known as "economic determinism" or "economism." Furthermore, we suggest that the main lines and even most of the detail of Weber's analysis in *The Protestant Ethic* can readily be embraced within the framework of the thesis of historical materialism—provided that it is properly understood. While Weber offers an analysis of "the part which religious forces have played in forming the developing web of our specifically worldly modern culture,"[57] historical materialism would not deny that religious ideas and forces had important impact in shaping the development of the material culture of full-fledged capitalism.

However, a historical–materialist analysis would go on to explain the historical reasons underlying the fact that the Protestant ideology did have such an important causal impact in shaping the development of capitalism. Such an explanation would involve reference to transformations in the economic foundation, *prior to the Reformation itself*, on the basis of which the Protestant ideology evolved. A concretely developed historical–materialist analysis would also involve reference to the impact of these changes on human character and on the existential viability of the feudal form of social consciousness. It would also bring out the way in which the general dependence of ideological developments on the forces of production circumscribed the range of possibilities of ideological development—the Protestant ideology originally constituting only one of those possibilities.

Existential Needs

We must examine the sort of existential needs that have been presupposed in the foregoing discussion. In developing an articulation of these needs, we shall take our point of departure from a famous formulation that Marx gives concerning religion. Marx writes that:

The struggle against religion is . . . mediately the fight against the other world of which religion is the spiritual aroma. Religious distress is at the same time the expression of real distress and the protest against real distress. Religion is the sigh of the oppressed creature, the heart of a heartless world, just as it is the spirit of a spiritless situation. It is the opium of the people. The abolition of religion as the illusory happiness of the people is required for their real happiness. The demand to give up the illusions about its condition is the demand to give up a condition which needs illusions. The criticism of religion is therefore in embryo the criticism of the vale of woe, the halo of which is religion. Criticism has plucked the imaginary flowers from the chain not so that man will wear the chain without any fantasy or consolation but so that he will shake off the chain and cull the living flower.[58]

The general target of Marx's criticism here is religion in the sense of religious beliefs and doctrines that project a dualistic worldview, that is, a dualism of the natural world on the one hand and a supernatural world on the other. And the specific although unnamed target is traditional, establishment Christianity, together with its adherence to such a dualism, its doctrines of a personal god, a substantial soul, and an afterlife, and so on. Marx sees such religious views as illusions serving to perpetuate oppressive and exploitative social, political, and economic conditions, even though they might also provide some solace for believers in the face of those conditions.

But in this strikingly beautiful passage, Marx is also giving full recognition to certain existential needs that, in his view, misguidedly seek fulfillment in illusions. He is calling for a nonillusory fulfillment of these same needs—not in some imagined supernatural world, but in this world. Of course, this would require dramatic transformations of the prevailing social and economic conditions, and in due time we shall examine this issue. Here, though, let us explore whether there is some positive view of the religious dimension of human experience that one might consistently adopt within Marx's own worldview—although Marx himself does not do this. We set out from some brief glimpses of views about this dimension of experience that do not invoke a personal god, or a supernatural realm.

In *Ideas and Opinions*, a collection of Albert Einstein's essays, there are a number of essays in which Einstein gives his views of the relation between religion and science. He rejects the notion of a personal god and even holds that "teachers of religion must have the stature to give up the doctrine of a personal god."[59] Yet we find Einstein taking a positive view of what he calls "cosmic religious feeling." This "religious feeling takes the form of a rapturous amazement at the harmony of natural law."[60] Einstein goes on to say that "the cosmic religious feeling is the strongest and noblest motive for scientific research."[61]

If we turn to someone like Paul Tillich, we find a major theologian who *has* had the stature to give up the notion of a personal, conscious god. In the *Courage to Be* and elsewhere, Tillich speaks of religious sentiment that finds the "ground of Being" in the "god above the god of theism."[62] The "god above god" is a way of speaking and has no connotation for Tillich of a personal or conscious god. Nor does it invoke the supernatural. It is essentially the ongoing world process understood as the ultimate reality. And Tillich is advocating a way of being in which individuals ground their own identity in an experiential recognition of themselves as internally related to the world process—as being one of its temporary manifestations, as participating in its dynamic energy, and as having characteristic energies that seek expression in a process of self-actualization. For Tillich, this requires the "courage to be," that is, the courage for the "self-affirmation of being in spite of the fact of nonbeing."[63] Furthermore, in Tillich's view, this experiential recognition is one in which the radical dichotomy between subject and object has been overcome.

To take an example from a completely different tradition, we turn to the work of D. T. Suzuki,[64] and his account of the experience of *satori*, which is said to constitute spiritual enlightenment in Zen Buddhism and other forms of Eastern religion. We emphasize that in the accounts we draw from, Suzuki is providing a phenomenological description of this experience. He strips away the metaphysical baggage, religious doctrines, and disciplinary rituals so often associated with this experience in Eastern religions, all of which in Suzuki's opinion really stand in the way of understanding what is meant by *satori*.[65]

As Suzuki presents it, the experience of *satori* involves a transformation of consciousness in which the individual has moved away from ordinary ways of thinking and perceiving that are structured in terms of sharp dichotomies, dualistic antitheses, and "rigid rules of intellection."[66] This experience is characterized by "an intuitive looking into the nature of things,"[67] and a mode of cognition and perceiving in which "opposites and contradictions are united and harmonized into a consistent organic whole."[68] In this experience, "the mind is so completely possessed or identified with its object of thought [or of perception] that even the consciousness of identity is lost as when one mirror reflects another."[69] For in this experience, "the subject has struck a new path and is not at all conscious of the duality of his act; in him life is not split into object and subject or into acting and acted."[70] However, Suzuki is not talking about some trancelike state, but rather about a way of experiencing the world, and one's activity in it, in an aesthetic mode. He speaks of a mode of consciousness wherein cognition, feeling, and sensuousness are completely integrated, wherein all the different sense modalities are heightened, and wherein one is so completely immersed in one's activity that there seems to be no separate ego-consciousness. One, so to speak, "becomes the activity." In such experience, the ego-self as a discrete entity is conspicuous for its absence.

Bringing the discussion back to Marx now, we indicate that, although Marx is strongly critical of religious positions that invoke a personal god and a supernatural, interpretations of the religious dimension such as those adopted by Einstein, Tillich, and Suzuki all resonate strongly with various aspects of Marx's conception of unalienated activity. This will become clear when we present an analysis of unalienated activity in Chapter 5. Here, though, our primary concern is with existential needs. To begin to bring them into focus, consider interpretations of the religious dimension that do not invoke a personal god (such as those just briefly mentioned) together with other interpretations that do make such invocations (such as establishment Christianity). Then go on to ask what the common need, or set of needs, might be which underlies religious experience, and which manifests itself in these varying interpretations of the religious dimension. It should not take long reflection to be convinced that the existential need to be interconnected with reality, and the existential need for meaning are two such underlying needs. Furthermore, we indicate that it is these same needs which are implicitly recognized in the passage from Marx cited earlier. More strongly, we indicate that the postulation of these existential needs (together with others, soon to be distinguished) is a necessary presupposition of Marx's understanding of social development.

Focusing first on the existential need to be interconnected with reality, we distinguish two aspects of this need that are crucially important for understanding Marx, namely, the need for community with nature, and the need for community with other people. Here it is necessary to keep in mind that, for Marx, the human being is a part of nature. As Marx puts it in the *Economic Manuscripts*: "That man lives from nature means that nature is his body with which he must maintain a constant interchange so as not to die. That man's physical and intellectual life depends on nature merely means that nature depends on itself, for man is a part of nature."[71]

Over the eons prior to the advent of civilization, human beings lived in tribal and clan communities of one sort or another, such that they were "at one" with nature (relatively speaking) by virtue of the kind of relationship they had to their "natural conditions of existence." As Marx explains in the *Grundrisse*:

> These *natural conditions of existence*, to which he relates as to his own inorganic body, are themselves double: (1) of a subjective and (2) of an objective nature. He finds himself a member of a family, clan, tribe etc., . . . and, as such a member, he relates to a specific nature (say, here, still earth, land, soil) as his own inorganic being, as a condition of his

production and reproduction. As a natural member of the community he participates in the communal property, and has a particular part of it as his possession.[72]

Human life as lived for eons in such modes (together with the even longer period during which our species evolved on the basis of the more rudimentary forms of "labor activity" undertaken in nature on the part of our simian ancestors, who were themselves gregarious)[73] constitutes the formative ground for the existential need for community with nature, and the existential need for community with other people,[74] and in more general terms, the existential need to be interconnected with reality. With the advent of civilization, economic conditions developed that separated human beings from the "natural conditions of their existence" so that the alienation of human beings from nature, and from one another, *appears* as the natural condition of the human being. Marx explains that this separation becomes completely developed only in the context of the capitalist social relations: "It is not the *unity* of living and active humanity with the natural, inorganic conditions of their metabolic exchange with nature, and hence their appropriation of nature, which requires explanation or is the result of a historic process, but rather the *separation* between these inorganic conditions of human existence and this active existence, a separation which is completely posited only in the relation of wage labour and capital."[75]

These comments having been made concerning the need for community with other people and with nature, we turn now to some other existential needs that must also be postulated if the thesis of historical materialism is to make sense. We list the existential need for a believable worldview, the need for meaning, the need for a viable character structure, the need for self-actualization, and the need for wholeness. To bring the first three of these existential needs into focus, we draw from some of Erich Fromm's formulations in his great work, *The Anatomy of Human Destructiveness.*

Concerning the existential need for a believable worldview, Fromm writes:

> Man's capacity for self-awareness, reason, and imagination . . . requires a picture of the world and of his place in it that is structured and that has inner cohesion. Man needs a map of his natural and social world, without which he would be confused and unable to act purposefully and consistently.[76]

Concerning the existential need for meaning, he writes:

> But a map is not enough as a guide for action; man also needs a goal that tells him where to go. . . . [M]an, lacking instinctive determination and having a brain that permits him to think of many directions in which he could go, . . . needs an object of devotion to be the focal point of all

his strivings and the basis for all his effective—and not only pro-claimed—values.[77]

And concerning the existential need for a viable character structure, he writes:

[M]an, being still less determined by instinct than the chimpanzee, would have been a biological failure if he had not developed a substitute for the instincts he lacked. This substitute also had to have the *function* of instincts, enabling man to act *as if* he were motivated by instincts. This substitute is the human *character*.[78]

In bringing out the "existential" nature of these needs, Fromm goes on to explain that human existence is characterized by inherent conflicts, which

have their root in the biological dichotomy between missing instincts and self-awareness. Man's existential conflict produces certain psychic needs common to all men. . . . I have called these needs existential because they are rooted in the very conditions of human existence. They are shared by all men, and their fulfillment is as necessary for man's remaining sane as the fulfillment of organic drives is necessary for his remaining alive. But each of these needs can be satisfied in different ways, which vary according to the differences of his social condition.[79]

We add that a given "form of social consciousness" and a corresponding "social character" constitute specific ways in which these existential needs are addressed in a specific society. Thus the breakdown in the existential viability of a given form of social consciousness, and the corresponding social character, would open the pathway for fulfilling these deeper-level existential needs in qualitatively different ways.

As for the existential need for self-realization, this need is implicit in Marx's notion of the general form of human being as "praxis", that is, as conscious activity that shapes nature as well as the socioeconomic realm, and in so doing shapes itself. Drawing this out a little further, we cite Rader again, who writes: "All organic beings are replete with potentialities. Human beings, as part of their species–nature, strive to fulfill them. Because they are internally related to their environment, they cannot realize them in isolation but only in fellowship with others and in 'metabolic' interaction with nature."[80]

And finally, concerning the existential need for wholeness, we project this need in the sense of an existential need for a psychic integration of needs. Here we emphasize that the various existential needs that have been postulated should not be thought of as discrete, atomic needs, which operate independently of one another. Rather, they should be seen as interrelated aspects of a psyche's relatedness to its environment. Thus the existential need for wholeness demands that the specific way in which the various existential needs are addressed in a given context be constitutive of a general psychic integration as well as an existentially viable relationship to the environment.

A More Concrete Formulation of the Thesis of Historical Materialism

With this discussion of existential needs behind us, we are now in a position to take up the next stage in the analysis of world historical transcendence. Remember that this stage of the analysis is to be undertaken within the framework of the general thesis of historical materialism. This will yield what amounts to a somewhat more concrete formulation of the theory of historical materialism. It will, we hope, clarify the interconnections between those aspects of conscious-activity-in-the-world that Marx refers to as the forces of production, the social relations, and the superstructure. In particular this more concrete formulation of the theory of historical materialism will bring into focus the manner in which consciousness can have primacy in shaping the material base in periods of social transition.

A key factor figuring prominently in this stage of the elaboration of world-historical transcendence is the notion of the existential viability of a given form of social consciousness—a notion that has been explained earlier. First, we shall indicate the theoretical juncture at which Marx implicitly presupposes a breakdown in the existential viability of a prevailing form of social consciousness as an *essential* factor figuring in the transition from one complex of social relations to another. We can do this by considering some relevant passages from *Capital* within the framework of the general thesis of historical materialism.

In the chapter on "The General Law of Capitalist Accumulation" in the first volume of *Capital*, Marx is concerned with the existential impact of the accumulation of capital on the members of the working class. At one point he writes that the "accumulation of wealth at one pole is, therefore, at the same time accumulation of misery, agony of toil, slavery, ignorance, brutality, mental degradation, at the opposite pole."[81] Later on, in the chapter on "The Historical Tendency of Capitalist Accumulation," referring again to the existential impact of the accumulation of capital on the members of the working class, Marx writes that with the growth in "the mass of misery, oppression, slavery, degradation, exploitation . . . grows the revolt of the working class, a class always increasing in numbers, and disciplined, united, organized by the very mechanisms of the process of capitalist production itself."[82] In Marx's view such a revolt will lead to the transcendence of the capitalist social relations and the establishment of socialist ones.

Here we temporarily leave aside the issue of the applicability of Marx's analysis of the "general law of capitalist accumulation" to the contemporary phase of the development of capitalism (later we shall see that it still applies in the monopoly phase). And we have already dealt with the suggestion of inevitability that hovers in the background of some of Marx's assertions concerning the transition from capitalist social relations to socialist ones. Let us go on to consider the connection which Marx draws here between the devastating existential impact of the accumulation of capital on conscious human subjects and the development of a transcending activity on the part of these human subjects that could lead to a new complex of socialist relations of production. Let us consider this connection within the framework of Marx's formulation of the general thesis of historical materialism. In that formulation Marx speaks of social relations as "the real foundation on which rises a legal and political superstructure and to which correspond definite *forms of social consciousness.*"[83]

Now consider that an associated form of social consciousness corresponds to the complex of capitalist social relations. And consider further that this form of social consciousness reacts back on the complex of capitalist social relations so as to sustain them in existence. Consider still further that the vast majority of the workers share the form of social consciousness associated with the complex of capitalist social relations as long as these relations are still predominant. With these considerations in mind, we ask what is it that must be presupposed in order to explain how such conscious human subjects could ever undertake a transcending activity leading beyond capitalism to a new complex of social relations?

We suggest that a breakdown in the existential viability of the form of social consciousness associated with the social relations of capitalism must be presupposed as an essential factor in the development of such a transcending activity. In other words, because the ruling ideas associated with capitalism have to lose their effective force before the consciousness for such a transcending activity could develop, a breakdown in the existential viability of the form of social consciousness associated with capitalism is a necessary condition for a transition to socialism. This does not mean, however, that such a breakdown can be simply equated with the development of a socialist form of social consciousness.

Such a breakdown would indeed prepare the ground for the development of a socialist form of social consciousness and for a complex of socialist social relations, but it would not be identical with such a development. For presumably the emotional rooting of a new form of social consciousness in a new social character would be generated only by a *concrete practice* that actively reshapes character structure—but a practice undertaken in terms of a theoretical acceptance of the new form of social consciousness, that is, with its guidance. Along these lines we recall Marx's formulation in the "Theses on Feuerbach": "The coincidence of the changing of circumstances and of human activity or self-changing can be conceived and rationally understood only as revolutionary practice."[84]

We have indicated the theoretical juncture at which a breakdown in the existential viability of the form of social consciousness associated with the social relations of capitalism must be presupposed. We suggest that the notion of the existential viability of the form of social consciousness has general, as well as essential, significance for the thesis of historical materialism. In keeping with this, we project the following guide for the more concrete elaboration of the thesis of historical materialism.

In situations of relative social stability, the form of social consciousness associated with a given complex of social relations is existentially viable. It reacts back so as to stabilize, and sustain in existence, the given complex of social relations. And so do the prevailing legal and political institutions, and the prevailing ideological positions, also associated with this complex of social relations. However, when the developing forces of production come into increasing conflict with the given complex of social relations to the point of social crisis, a breakdown in the existential viability of the form of social consciousness occurs. And this prepares the ground for the development of a new form of social consciousness. This development—cultivated and sustained by ideological developments which until the period of crisis had been nonpredominant—acts as a social catalyst to crystallize and bring into predominance a new complex of social relations that will foster the ongoing development of the forces of production. With the crystallization of a new complex of social relations, there comes a corresponding change in the legal and political institutions. And new ideological positions become predominant to such an extent that a new period of relative social stability ensues.

To more fully grasp the import of this somewhat more concrete elaboration of the general thesis of historical materialism, we must transcribe its most critical points into the form of universal conditional statements that explicitly express *laws* of social development. In doing so we recall the earlier discussion of the laws that figure in Marx's universe of discourse. We saw that these laws are to be interpreted as describing tendencies—tendencies tied back to an interconnected complex of factors out of whose dynamic interplay the tendencies arise. And remember that tendencies have to be viewed in relation to counteracting factors. We articulate the following three laws:

L1. If the framework of social relations, within which productive forces develop, has a tendency over the long run to inhibit such development with increasing intensity, then there will be a tendency for social pressures to mount for a transition to a new set of social relations more compatible with the developing forces of production.

L2. If the framework of social relations, within which productive forces develop, has a tendency over the long run to inhibit such development with increasing intensity, then there will be a tendency for the form of social consciousness associated with those social relations to undergo a breakdown in existential viability on a mass scale.

L3. If there is a breakdown in the existential viability of a given form of social consciousness—then there will be a tendency for social pressures to mount for a transition to a new form of social consciousness, and therewith a transition to a corresponding new set of social relations. The new form of social consciousness must be capable of responding to existential and other human needs, in the context of the changed conditions. And the new social relations must be more compatible with the developing forces of production.

The first of these laws involves no specific mention of the breakdown in the existential viability of the form of social consciousness. It can be thought of as a transcription into conditional form of the most critical relationship indicated in Marx's own formulation of the general thesis of historical materialism that was quoted above from the Preface. L2 and L3, on the other hand, both involve specific mention of the breakdown in existential viability of the form of social consciousness. Taken together they are a transcription, into conditional form, of the most critical relationships indicated in the more concrete elaboration of the thesis of historical materialism, undertaken here within the dialectically projected structures of Marx's own formulation.

From reflection upon these general laws of social development, a number of significant conclusions can be drawn. First, these laws taken singly or in combination do not permit an inference to the effect that there is a definite sequence of particular stages of historical development.[85] These laws are projected in the conceptual field at a level of analysis that makes abstraction from the specific factors which characterize specific social formations. And although these laws do articulate the broad structures within which transformations from one specific complex of social relations to another must be comprehended, no deduction can be made from these laws concerning some particular sequence of stages of historical development that must be passed through in all cultures.

Second, and as a related consequence of the first, these laws do not allow one to infer that a complex of genuine socialist social relations would come into being in the aftermath of a hypothetical breakdown of the capitalist social order. They allow the inference that there will be a tendency for *some* new complex of social relations to come into being after such an event, but do not allow an inference that some *particular* complex of social relations would do so. Contrary to Marx's own expectation, the twentieth century has borne witness to the emergence of a new complex of post-capitalist social relations that are not socialist in Marx's sense, namely, those that prevail in the Soviet Union and elsewhere. (We note, however, that Marx did argue against one form of "state socialism" in his critique of Lassalle,[86] which suggests that Marx did regard the possibility of the attempt to respond to the fettering of the forces of production along state socialist lines as a real but undesirable possibility. This suggests in turn that Marx's talk about the inevitability of socialism is indeed rhetorical or elliptical.) Svetozar Stojanović carefully distinguishes this complex of social relations from genuine socialist ones in *Between Ideals and Reality*. Therein he refers to the social relations that obtain in the Soviet Union as "statist" social relations.[87] This complex of social relations constitutes another form of class society, in which a class ruling in its own interests stands over an oppressed and exploited working class. As Stojanović puts it:

> Short of irony or cynicism, there is no sense in which the working class in the Stalinist system may be called the ruling class, not even in the most liberal sense of the term. The working class is completely subjugated and severely exploited. Not only is it barred from controlling production and making decisions concerning the distribution of surplus-value (either directly or indirectly); it does not even possess certain rights that it has realized in capitalism—the rights to choose one's employer and to negotiate over working conditions and wage levels.[88]

Third, no inference can be drawn from these laws to the effect that a mass breakdown in the existential viability of the capitalist form of social consciousness will in fact occur, or that an accompanying breakdown of capitalist social relations will in fact occur. That is, these laws do not permit one to say with scientific warrant that a breakdown of the capitalist social order is inevitable. This is so, irrespective of what kind of social order might be claimed to follow such a breakdown. Here we recall the discussion concerning the operation of factors that counteract a given tendency. On methodological grounds we have seen that it is always logically possible for some new factor to come into being which could effectively block the realization of a given tendency. This is not to say that such factors will indeed emerge, but only that it is possible for them to emerge. Thus, even though there may be an objective tendency toward the breakdown of the capitalist social order, new counteracting factors may emerge, in addition to those already in operation, which could effectively block a breakdown in the capitalist social order. One such factor might be the reemergence on a worldwide scale of a fascist version of the capitalist form of social consciousness, together with a fascist political practice undertaken within the framework of the existing capitalist social relations. Such a development might indefinitely block a breakdown of the capitalist social relations by providing a destructive vent[89] for the mounting frustration of existential needs that the ongoing development within the framework of these social relations generates.

Fourth, these laws bring into focus the crucial role that developments in the superstructure play in a transition from one social formation to another. A breakdown in the existential viability of the capitalist form of social consciousness would leave indeterminate the new form of social consciousness that would eventually come into predominance. After such a breakdown, developments in the superstructure would have primacy in determining which of the culturally available ideological positions that had been nonpredominant up until the period of breakdown would become predominant thereafter. This in turn underscores the crucial importance of developments in the superstructure *prior* to such a looming breakdown. In the face of such a prospect, superstructural developments would be predominant factors in shaping whether or not there would be a mass regression to a fascist version of the capitalist form of social consciousness. Such a development would perhaps preserve for a time the capitalist complex of social relations, but at the cost of a universal barbarism and perhaps an eventual universal annihilation. On the other hand, supposing that a fascist regression within the framework of capitalism does not occur, superstructural developments prior to a looming breakdown in the capitalist social order would be pivotal in shaping the kind of social order that would come into being in the aftermath of its actual breakdown—whether "Brave New World," or "statism," or statism-cum-fascism, or genuine socialism.

This does not imply, though, that each of these possible outcomes would be an equally stable, an equally satisfactory, or an equally life-affirming resolution of frustrated existential needs on the one side, or an equally satisfactory resolution of the problems concerning the ongoing development of the forces of production on the other side. Thus the notion of the unfettering of the forces of production—through the establishment of new social relations—is an unfettering that can take place in many different ways, and thus with quite different kinds of impact on modes of consciousness and on the quality of life all around. This brings the issue down to a basic value decision concerning which modes of life *ought* to be cultivated. In Chapter 5, we shall find that practical reason, as understood by Marx, has much to say about this "ought."

4

Freedom-as-Transcendence II

In this chapter we continue the exposition of freedom-as-transcendence. As the discussion proceeds, we shall examine the concrete application of the theory of historical materialism, as presented in the last chapter, to the dynamics of male–female social relations and to the dynamics of the capitalist social order as well. It should follow clearly that freedom-as-transcendence, viewed from Marx's perspective, involves the transcendence of the capitalist social order.

Before proceeding, we stress that the concrete applications of the theory of historical materialism undertaken in this chapter are not to be understood simply as the application of abstract theory to specific social practice. For in the concrete applications we explore, the theory of historical materialism is itself being more concretely elaborated. In this elaboration the projected meaning of the more abstract theoretical formulations given in the last chapter is more fully disclosed.

Historical Materialism and Male–Female
Social Relations

The problem of the social relations between men and women is a crucially important one for Marx's perspective. However, there has been pervasive misunderstanding about it because of a failure to comprehend Marx's method of explanation. This will emerge in what follows. We approach our subject through a critique of a position concerning the dynamics of the oppression of women that is advanced by Shulamith Firestone in *The Dialectic of Sex: The Case for Feminist Revolution*,[1] a work that has had wide influence in feminist circles. At the outset we emphasize that we have no disagreement with Firestone concerning the fact of the oppression and exploitation of women—or concerning its extent. Our disagreement with her has to do with the connection

80

between male–female social relations on the one hand, and economic-social relations on the other. And it has to do with the way in which this connection affects the theoretical comprehension of a possible transcendence of the oppression of women.

Firestone projects the relation between men and women in the "biological family" as having had primacy in shaping human culture throughout the whole course of human history. In her view, this primacy extends to all other factors, including economic "social relations" and the class structure embedded therein. The "biological family" is "the basic reproductive unit of male/female/infant."[2] And Firestone takes the "biological family" as necessarily generating the general social oppression of women by men. For her, such social oppression is necessitated by the biological differences in the reproductive functions of men and women in procreation. She writes: "Unlike economic class, sex class sprang directly from a biological reality: men and women were created different, and not equally privileged. Although, as [Simone] de Beauvoir points out, this difference of itself did not necessitate the development of a class system—the domination of one group by another—the reproductive *functions* of these differences did."[3]

Moreover, Firestone even projects Marx as unwittingly admitting such a connection against himself when she writes: "Marx was onto something more profound than he knew when he observed that the family contained within itself in embryo all the antagonisms that later develop on a wide scale within the society and the state." She adds immediately: "For unless revolution uproots the basic social organization, the biological family, . . . the tapeworm of exploitation will never be annihilated."[4]

We shall see that Firestone misrepresents Marx on this issue. But right now we emphasize that the "biological family" can hardly be considered "the basic social organization" throughout all human history. For one thing, there is the evidence that suggests that "group marriage" was the norm in the earliest primitive societies.[5] The form of the family associated with such societies, suggested by the wide range of people whom one called father or mother, son or daughter, brother or sister, and so on, makes clear that the basic *social* organization in such societies could not have been the "biological family."

Furthermore, Firestone's claim that the biological reproductive functions are such as to necessitate a general social oppression of women by men is in conflict with the wide array of evidence attesting to the historical existence of societies in which women were not subject to general social oppression. Evidence of this sort is cavalierly dismissed by Firestone when she writes:

> For no matter how many tribes in Oceania you can find where the connection of the father to fertility is not known, no matter how many

matrilineages, no matter how many cases of sex-role reversal, male housewifery, or even empathic labor pains, these facts prove only one thing: the amazing *flexibility* of human nature. But human nature is adaptable *to* something; it is, yes, determined by its environmental conditions. And the biological family that we have described has existed everywhere throughout time.[6]

The phenomena mentioned bespeak "the amazing flexibility of human nature." But human nature is "adaptable to something," and for Firestone this "something" is the "biological family." She gives no explanation as to how the particular sort of flexibility mentioned could ever take place, given her assumption that the social oppression of women is necessitated by the differences in the biological reproductive functions of men and women. These are just the sort of phenomena you would not expect to find, given her assumption. They stand, *prima facie* at least, as disconfirming evidence for her thesis.

As one striking example of the sort of evidence that is meant, we refer to Marx's *Ethnological Notebooks*,[7] where among other things one can find very extensive extracts (plus notes and comments) made by Marx from Lewis Morgan's *Ancient Society*.[8] In one of these extracts we find Morgan relaying firsthand testimony from a missionary who lived for many years among the Iroquois Senecas, an American Indian tribe. The passage reads:

> As to their families, when occupying the old longhouses . . . some one clan predominated, the women taking in husbands from the other clans. . . . Usually, the female portion ruled the house. . . . The stores were in common; but woe to the luckless husband or lover who was too shiftless to do his share of the providing. No matter how many children or whatever goods he might have in the house, he might at any time be ordered to pick up and budge, durfte nicht [he dare not] attempt to disobey. The house would be too hot for him, . . . he must retreat to his own clan; or, as was often done, go and start a new matrimonial alliance in some other. The women were the great power among the clans, as everywhere else. They did not hesitate, when occasion required, "to knock off the horns," as it was technically called, from the head of a chief, and send him back to the ranks of the warriors. The original nomination of the chiefs also always rested with them.[9]

How important this, and other such evidence, was to Marx is attested to by Engels. He relates that Marx "often said" that in the American Indians he had "found the key to the understanding of our own primitive age."[10] Although this sort of evidence counts against Firestone's position, it counts as confirming evidence for Marx's thesis of historical materialism. In the *Grundrisse* (written some twenty years before Morgan's work was published), Marx had made certain speculations about primitive human beginnings from the perspective of the thesis of historical materialism.[11] In Morgan's work he found empirical confirmation for much of this speculation.

In this context, we also mention a social practice concerning menstruation that was common among the Iroquois and other similar societies, namely, the practice of segregating women who were menstruating. Such a practice has often been projected as a direct manifestation of the social oppression of women in the societies where it occurs. However, if we consider this practice not in isolation, but in connection with other practices such as women "knocking the horns off the chief," another interpretation of the segregation of menstruating women becomes plausible—an interpretation that does not connote the social oppression of women. Inasmuch as the Iroquois was a tribe that hunted animals for food, and inasmuch as men were the hunters, the social institution of segregating women who were menstruating may have developed at the behest of women. It may have been a way of "protecting" the daily sexual interplay between men and women from the intrusion of deep images and memories of death—associated by men with the sight of blood, as a result of hunting animals, and as a result of earlier cannibalistic practices.

Consider in this connection a major theme that Evelyn Reed advances in her work on *Woman's Evolution: From Matriarchal Clan to Patriarchal Family*. She holds that the social institution of the ancient matriarchy originally developed in order to elevate the evolving hominid line out of an earlier cannibalistic stage. In her view, one of the most important aspects of the ancient matriarchy was an elaborate system of "totemism and taboo," which became institutionalized as a result of the collective efforts of female hominids, or "feminids." Among other things, it was taboo to kill a member of one's clan. It was taboo for males to seek mates from among the females of their own clan. And it was not only taboo to kill women, but women placed themselves in a condition of taboo when they were in childbirth, or were menstruating. And as Reed suggests: "Savage men's horror of menstrual blood was connected with their dread of women and of *infringing women's taboos*, which in the first instance prohibited men from shedding the blood of women"[12] (emphasis added).

In any case, we return now to the suggestion that we heard Firestone make earlier, to the effect that Marx unwittingly acknowledged that the "biological family" was the dynamic basis necessarily leading to general social oppression of women—and of other exploited groups. Although Firestone does not give any documentation for such a claim, presumably she has in mind a passage from Marx's *Ethnological Notebooks*, which is cited by Engels in his work, *The Origin of the Family, Private Property, and the State*, a work that Firestone does mention in passing. Marx's own formulation reads as follows: "The modern family contains in germ not only slavery (*servitus*), but also serfdom, since from the beginning it is related to agricultural services. It contains *in miniature* all the contradictions which later extend throughout society and its state."[13]

Here though, Marx is not speaking about some mythical "biological family," but rather about a particular form of the *social* family, which came into being on the basis of very definite economic developments that supplanted the earlier forms of the family. (Marx's use of the phrase "modern family" in the above formulation carries a meaning which contrasts with earlier forms of the family associated with the stages of "savagery" and "barbarism.")[14] From the context of Marx's formulation as it appears in his *Ethnological Notebooks*—and also from the context in which Engels presents Marx's formulation in *The Origin of the Family*—it is unmistakably clear that Marx has in mind the monogamous family as it developed in its Roman patriarchal form. This family form *was* oppressive of women. It projected monogamy for women only, and involved the absolute subjugation of women in all spheres of social life. It also involved the subjugation of a number of slaves who were originally considered part of the family. In fact, as Engels brings out (following Morgan and Marx), the term "family" originally meant "the total number of slaves belonging to one man."[15] The term was extended "by the Romans to denote a new social organism, whose head ruled over wife and children and a number of slaves, and was invested under Roman paternal power with rights of life and death over them all."[16]

Having already brought out some of the problems with Firestone's concept of the "biological family"—and her contention that it necessitates general social oppression of women—we now examine Firestone's interpretation of historical materialism. Against the contrasting background of a brief formulation of the thesis of historical materialism that Engels gives in *Socialism: Utopian and Scientific*, Firestone gives her own idiosyncratic formulation of historical materialism—one that seems to turn Engels on his side, if not his head, and with him Marx too. She writes:

> Historical materialism is that view of the course of history which seeks the ultimate cause and the great moving power of all historic events in the dialectic of sex: the division of society into two distinct biological classes for procreative reproduction, and the struggles of these classes with one another; in the changes in the modes of marriage, reproduction and childcare created by these struggles; in the connected development of other physically-differentiated classes (castes); and in the first division of labor based on sex which developed into the economic-cultural class system. . . . All past history . . . was the history of class struggle. These warring classes of society are always the product of the modes of organization of the biological family unit for reproduction of the species, as well as of the strictly economic modes of production and

exchange of goods and services. The sexual-reproductive organization of society always furnishes the real basis, starting from which we can alone work out the ultimate explanation of the whole superstructure of economic, juridical and political institutions as well as of the religious, philosophical and other ideas of a given historical period.[17]

There are many problems with this formulation. Not the least of these is the fact that the concept of the "biological family" is itself an inherently confused concept. If we consider that the category "family" is a social category, then the very attempt to project a concept such as the "biological family" suggests strong reductionist currents concerning the relation between sociology and biology. In Chapter 6 we will take up the issue of the relation between the different sciences within the context of a dialectical, nonreductive conception of the unity of science. Anticipating that discussion somewhat, we maintain here that the biological dimension of human sexual reproduction requires that there be *some* form of social relations between men and women, and *some* form of the family. Yet the biological dimension does not, and cannot, determine what the specific form of the relations between men and women, or of the family, will be. Rather, the biological dimension allows for a broad spectrum of very different forms in the social relations between men and women, and very different forms of the family.

In Marx's view, all these specific forms come to be what they are by virtue of the dominating influence of some specific form of the social relations of economic production and reproduction. Marx can account for the specificity in the form of the social relations between men and women on the basis of the specificity of the economic social relations, while at the same time taking account of the role of the biological factors in what occurs. However, the biological–reductionist thesis, which Firestone seems to be pushing, cannot account for the specificity of the wide range of different historical forms in the economic social relations, or for the specificity of the different forms of the family, or for the specificity of the different forms in the social relations between men and women. This is the fatal flaw in Firestone's version of "historical materialism."

Now at times it seems that Firestone is really pushing for a somewhat weaker thesis on these issues, namely, that it is not the biological dimension of sexual reproduction, by itself, that has primacy in shaping cultural developments all around, but rather the social relations between men and women within the context of which biological reproduction is actualized. This may be what Firestone means in the passage recently quoted, when she speaks of the "sexual-reproductive organization of society." But how then account for the specificity in the form of these social relations? If one says that they are necessitated by the biological dimension of sexual reproduction, then the fatal flaw of the strong reductionist thesis confronts us again.

For his part, Marx holds that the form of a society is the result of a complex combination of different dynamically interrelated factors the relative weight of which, in determining the form of the social whole, undergoes shifts over the course of historical time. The crucially important factors here are "the social relations between men and women in the family," second, "the economic social relations," and then the biological dimension. In Chapter 1, we cited a passage from *The German Ideology* wherein Marx wrote: "The family, which to *begin* with is the *only social relationship*, becomes *later*, when increased needs create new social relationships and the increased population new needs, a *subordinate* one . . . and must be treated and analysed according to the existing empirical data"[18] (emphasis added).

As we explained in the earlier context, Marx is here alluding to shifts in the relative weight of the "social relations between men and women in the family" vis-à-vis the "social relations of economic production" in shaping the social whole. In the earliest human societies, the family is the "only social relationship." But the family must here be understood as the extended clan family. And the social relations of economic production, characteristic of these earliest societies, are best understood as being coextensive with the social relationships of the extended clan family. In this situation there was a relative parity between male–female social relations and economic social relations.

However, this relative parity was upset in the course of the development of economic conditions that led to the advent of "private wealth in the means of production." With this development, new social relations of economic production came into being, and they were hierarchical in character—with one class dominating another class. The hierarchical character of the new economic relations was gradually superimposed on male–female social relations in the family. Therewith, an all-around social oppression of women was generated. Moreover, Marx holds that, subsequent to the advent of "private wealth in the means of production," the specific form of male–female social relations in the family has continued to be subject to the dominating influence of the specific form of economic social relations that might obtain.

But none of this should be taken to mean that male–female social relations in the family are an epiphenomenal by-product of economic social relations. Nor should it be taken to mean that all the concrete, specific details of what transpires in male–female social relations, in ongoing daily life, are determined to be what they are by the economic social relations. Nor should any of this be taken to deny that the biological differences between males and females play an important role in shaping social life. But even when such biological differences seem more decisive vis-à-vis other factors in shaping the "division of labor"—as in the earliest clan communities—the relative weight of the biological differences between men and women in this shaping must be understood in relation to the whole complex of contributing factors. This includes the geographical environment—the biotic environment of flora and fauna existing in a geographical area, and thus the kind of food sources that are naturally available—the techniques that are available to utilize such food sources, and such factors as the distance traveled and the time away from home in securing various types of food, and so on. But it also includes social factors, such as the kinds of taboos that were operative in the days of the ancient matriarchy. (For example, the institution of women putting themselves in a condition of taboo while menstruating would presumably have been in conflict with the participation of women in an extended hunt away from home.) Thus, the biological differences between men and women do not in themselves necessitate a general social oppression of women—contrary to Firestone's thesis.

We bring this out by taking recourse to Reed's analysis in *Woman's Evolution*. While acknowledging a division of labor based on sex differences in the matriarchal clan communities, she writes: "Neither sexual nor social inequalities could exist in the matriarchal epoch when society was both communalist and egalitarian."[19] As her analysis proceeds, Reed makes the case that the matriarchal clan community was a cooperating sisterhood–brotherhood of clan members in relation to which the biological father was considered an outsider from another clan, which had formed a mating alliance with the first clan. The biological father had visiting privileges for mating purposes. Thus, the male–female social relations, which had primacy in shaping the clan community, were social relations between men and women for whom sexual mating was proscribed. Thus, instead of the biological father, it was the "mother's brother" who was the key male personage. All this speaks from yet another direction against Firestone's position. And obviously, her projection of "class struggle" in early primitive times has to be rescinded in the light of the vast array of evidence attesting to the actual historical existence of the matriarchal clan community.

There is one further problem concerning the strategy of explanation at play in Firestone's position that should be addressed. It is the explanatory impetus to take things back to some simple unit that is somehow given—some "simplest beginning" from which everything else can then be explained. In Firestone's case this "simplest beginning" is the "biological family." We contend that in the explanation of human phenomena such a strategy is a mistake, inasmuch as what is given is not some simple unit, but, to use Althusser's phrase, "the ever-pre-givenness of a structured complex unity."[20] In any situation, the human being is on the scene as the ontological mixture of the physical, the chemical, the biological, the psychological, and the social. It is the task of science, and the philosophy of science, to sort out these different domains—as well as the interrelations between them—and to determine which factors are the essential ones for understanding any given domain. And the real basis for understanding any individual or any society is not the simple unit, but the complex whole, the given "concrete totality."

To be sure, specific social relations between specific men and women are partially constitutive of a given "concrete totality." But the specific form of such relations—and the specific form of consciousness associated with them—come to be what they are under the influence of other factors at play in the "concrete totality." This is not to say that the concrete details of male–female social relations are determined by economic relations. For it is only the broad structure of these relations that is so shaped. Thus it is not that the relations between men and women are without determining influence on the "concrete totality," but rather that, for the most part, these relations between men and women have already been shaped by the dominating influence of other factors. These other factors (primarily economic in nature) mold the consciousness of both men and women to fit into social roles which, for the most part throughout human history, have involved the objective oppression and exploitation of women by men—although not necessarily the subjective consciousness of that oppression on the part of women, or men. Here, though, it is important to bear in mind that, in periods of increasing social instability, the general thesis of historical materialism allows for shifts-in-dominance in the interplay of the various factors at play in a given "concrete totality." We have already spoken about a relative primacy of superstructural developments over economic ones in periods of transition. Later we return to this theme in connection with the growing consciousness of the oppression of women in our culture, on the part of both women and men.

Before taking up this issue, however, we need first to give a fuller explanation of the way in which Marx's thesis of historical materialism provides conceptual room for understanding the social relations between men and women. This is quite important, inasmuch as many feminists have dismissed Marx's work as failing to contribute to an understanding of male–female relations—or as reducing male–female relations to an epiphenomenal by-product of economic social relations. This is partly a result of Marx's conspicuous emphasis on the analysis of economic social relations, but it is primarily due to the prevalent stereotypic interpretations of Marx, which fail to comprehend his method of explanation and which dismally distort his view of human reality all around—including his view of the development of the social relations between men and women.

We admit that Marx's formulations along these lines are sketchy. But remember that Marx's ultimate objective was to provide a theoretical comprehension of the development of the concrete-real of social life. This concrete totality is one of interacting individuals and social groups—composed of individual men and women—engaged in definite activities, responding to definite needs, establishing definite patterns of relationship among themselves, and having definite forms of social consciousness. Marx is concerned to penetrate the swirling mass of surface phenomena, through which the unanalyzed human world appears to us, in order to get at, and *comprehend*, the essential underlying reality within the context of which the surface phenomena come to be what they are. This swirling mass of surface phenomena includes, of course, the surface phenomena that pertain to the relations between men and women.

That Marx himself was able to carry the analysis of the concrete totality only so far in his own life's work, and that he himself did not give us anything like a definitive analysis of male-female social relations, should not blind us to the scientific achievements that he did leave us. Nor should it blind us to the theoretical potential which his scientific and philosophical perspective harbors for eventually developing an adequate comprehension of the dynamics of male-female relations. Engels did take things a long way in *The Origin of the Family, Private Property, and the State* (and with the help of Marx's *Ethnological Notebooks*). And there is the provocative work by Evelyn Reed in the tradition of evolutionary anthropology, *Woman's Evolution: From Matriarchal Clan to Patriarchal Family*. Nonetheless, a really adequate, all-around comprehension of male-female social relations still stands as a continuing "research problem" for Marx's theoretical perspective.[21] In what follows here, however, the main focus will be on some methodological considerations.

With the problem of male-female social relations, as with so many other problems, it is crucial to become aware of the various levels of abstraction that are, or can be, distinguished in the dialectical movement of cognition from abstract to concrete. Earlier we distinguished the general form of being-in-the-world at the most abstract level. We went on to distinguish the general thesis of historical materialism at a more concrete level. And then we distinguished a somewhat more concrete version of the thesis of historical materialism, which made explicit mention of the notion of the "existential viability of the form of social consciousness." Within Marx's perspective, the social relations between men and women have to be comprehended *at a still more concrete level of analysis*—but within the framework of the dialectically projected structures presented at the more abstract levels.

Such a methodological arrangement of levels is intended to reflect the fact that social relations between men and women, as they obtain in any given concrete totality—and the associated male and female forms of social consciousness—are shaped to be what they are under the dominating influence of the prevailing economic system in the given concrete totality. The form of social consciousness typical of a given concrete totality is constituted by the general categories of interpretation and valuation in terms of which the members of that totality interpret social reality and orient themselves to it. These include categories in terms of which males and females interpret, and orient to, one another—and to their own selves as well. In the same way, the associated social character typical of the given concrete totality has its male and female counterparts, which are distinguished by whatever differences (in disposition and in psychic structuring) characterize males and females in that totality.

Male and female individuals are born into a given concrete totality. They are shaped from birth under the influence of various socializing agents, both male and female, who are themselves bearers of the forms of social consciousness and social character (in their respective male and female modes) typical of the given concrete totality. But the specific nature of male–female social relations typical of a given society—and the specific associated forms of social consciousness and social character in both their male and female modes—all come to be what they are under the dominating influence of the specific economic system in the given society.

Still in this context, we turn attention briefly to the theme of "mothering" and a position that Sandra Harding takes concerning it in her essay, "What is the Real Material Base of Patriarchy and Capital?" Reacting against the reductionist economic determinism of "traditional Marxism," Harding argues that "[t]he material base [as concerns social relations] is not in fact limited to economic relations."[22] For she has her eye on the social relations of "mothering"—the social relations in which women (who "are universally devalued" and who devalue themselves)[23] undertake the infant care of both boys and girls. And it is these social relations that Harding takes to be the "real material base" of both capitalism and patriarchy. Thus, while rejecting "traditional Marxism," Harding seems to be tending toward a reductionism of her own.

This is not meant to deny the importance of the social relations of infant care for understanding the psychodynamics of human development—especially the psychodynamics of the gender-identification process. And we are in agreement with Harding concerning the importance of Nancy Chodorow's work on *The Reproduction of Mothering*.[24] This is one of the key works that Harding herself stands by as she makes her own case for the "real material base."

Chodorow's work is a feminist critical appropriation of psychoanalytic theory. It has a primary focus on the gender-identification process.

Among other things, she gives extended analysis of the asymmetries that characterize the developmental processes of male and female infants as they *both* go through the process of "separating and individuating" in relation to a woman as the primary infant caretaker. And she connects such asymmetries to the gender-based personality differences that emerge between boys and girls. Further, she gives a great deal of explicit attention to the way in which mothering, as it occurs in capitalist society, shapes males and females differentially for life in that form of society. But it is also important to recognize that Chodorow's *general case* concerning "mothering" seems implicitly to presuppose "mothering" as it functions in capitalist society.[25]

In any case, it is Harding, and not Chodorow, who projects "mothering"—and the social relations of mothering—as the "real material base." Perhaps this is an exaggeration on Harding's part, an overemphasis due to the neglect, until very recently, of the social relations of child-rearing in theoretical explorations across the board. Perhaps her stance on the "real material base" is primarily intended to focus practical attention on activity aimed at changing patterns of family life that foster sexism and oppression. One might gather this from her statement that "the family is not in this theory an isolated cause of social ills but, instead, the intergenerational conduit for interests in reproducing them."[26] Be this as it may, we hold it is very misleading to project the social relations of mothering as the "real material base" in contradistinction to economic social relations. This does not mean that these social relations are unimportant, or that they are an epiphenomenon of the economic structures. On the other hand, mothering is always a specific form of mothering, undertaken in a definite kind of family structure, by a socializing agent (or agents) who has a definite form of social consciousness, who projects definite sorts of expectations for male and female children and who employs definite child-rearing techniques and practices, and so on. Thus, mothering must itself be understood historically. And although we agree that the social relations of infant care are an important component of the material base, they are a component already shaped under the dominating influence of that other component of the material base that Marx refers to as the social relations of economic production. And as long as hierarchical economic social relations generally obtain, we can expect them to have an impact on the social relations of mothering so as to adjust the psyches of male and female infants to hierarchical patterns of social life.

If we are to understand the objective oppression and exploitation of women, which has characterized male–female social relations for most of human history, we must understand the structural dynamics whereby hierarchical and exploitative economic systems shape the consciousness and psyche of both men and women, so as to sustain such economic systems and perpetuate oppressive social relations between men and women. In order to bring out more fully that the general social oppression of women throughout most of human history is indeed grounded on exploitative economic systems, we present some considerations drawn from Engels' *The Origin of the Family, Private Property, and the State.* However, before we discuss Engels in this connection, it is important to keep in mind the distinction between isolated instances and broad structures constituted by an aggregate of many individual instances, that is, the distinction between the individual case and the prevailing norm in a given society. In any society there are individuals who deviate from the norm—for a variety of reasons and in a variety of directions. And although the norm, in American society, for example, clearly reflects a general social oppression of women by men, there are individual men who are not objectively oppressive of women, just as there are individual women who happen to be oppressive of men. With that caveat made, let us turn to Engels.

Basing his work largely on Lewis Morgan's *Ancient Society* and Marx's *Ethnological Notebooks,* Engels explores the development of the human family through various stages in human history from the perspective of historical materialism. Of special importance for our purposes is Morgan's analysis of the "primitive matriarchal gens." This was a historical predecessor to the later patriarchal gens (or clan), and to the still later forms of the monogamous family associated with "civilization." Engels highlights its importance in the following way: "This rediscovery [by Morgan] of the primitive matriarchal gens as the earlier stage of the patriarchal gens of civilized peoples has the same importance for anthropology as Darwin's theory of evolution has for biology and Marx's theory of surplus-value for political economy."[27]

Taking the matriarchal gens of the American Iroquois Indians as an exemplar of this societal form, Engels (after Morgan) tells about a kind of society where everyone was "personally free"[28] and where there was full political and social equality between men and women. In shaping the social organization as a whole, the social relations between men and women had at least parity with, if not a relative primacy over, the economic factors as they obtained in this primitive stage. Pairing marriage was predominant, and was dissolvable at will by either party. However, descent was reckoned in the female line. Almost all the women in a given gens were originally from the same gens, whereas the men came from different gens. Marriage within the gens was prohibited, so that men had to leave their own gens and join another in order to marry.

There was no private wealth in the means of production, and thus no economic class divisions. Hunting and fishing grounds were owned communally by the various gens composing a tribe; households were communally owned by the members of the individual gens. The little personal property that individuals possessed remained within the gens at death, and was shared by the closest gentile relatives. Moreover, the practice of "mother right" prevailed, whereby the property of a deceased woman could be inherited "by her children and her sisters, but not by her brothers";[29] and "man and wife could not inherit from one another, nor children from their father."[30]

There was a division of labor oriented around sex differences, but not one that signified general social oppression of women. Men were primarily hunters, and they made and owned the implements for hunting and tending animals. Women were primarily domestic workers and they made and owned their implements. However, domestic work was communal domestic work, not private service, and was regarded by both men and women as important social productive labor. Men who did not fulfill their responsibilities could in effect be pushed out of the gens by the women—by ostracism, for instance. But the sovereign power in the governance system of the gens was "the democratic assembly of all male and female adult gentiles, all with equal votes."[31] The leaders were elected, and could be deposed at will, as we indicated earlier in connection with the Iroquois practice of "knocking the horns off the chief."

Societies of this general type were the precursors of the patriarchal gens that flourished in the Old World among the ancient Greek and Latin tribes, and among other social groups like those reflected in the Old Testament writings. The demise of this social form in the Old World was *due primarily to transformations in economic conditions* that led to the amassing of private wealth in the means of production. Foremost among such economic transformations were the development of large-scale agriculture and the domestication of livestock, especially cattle. The food surpluses, made available by the development of agriculture, made it possible to sustain larger concentrations of people. It also made possible new divisions of social labor and provided a practical basis on which a potential power elite could be formed. The practice of stock-raising, in turn, provided the first really valuable "movable property," and therewith one of the most essential factors that led to the development of private wealth.

In Engels' account in *The Origin of the Family* from which we have been drawing, he also brings into focus an important tradition that was significant in the development of the concentration of wealth in men's hands, rather than in those of women. This was the tradition of men being hunters, and the associated tendency for men to base their very "identity" on the "praxis" that developed in relation to the ritual preparations and purifications associated with hunting, as well as in the actual hunt itself. Often this was a cooperative activity of many men working to trap and kill large game, but also, in some geographical locations, to capture animals which could be domesticated. Because in their work men had physical disposition over most animals—especially larger animals—their work gave them physical control over herds of livestock accumulated beyond what was required for the immediate consumption needs of the clan. This made it very easy for ownership of these herds by males to become institutionalized—at first as collective ownership.

Here we turn again to *Woman's Evolution*, where Reed sustains and develops the analysis of these themes originally given by Engels. Among other things, she explains a tradition not mentioned by Engels himself, namely, the tradition of primitive "gift interchange" between men of hostile clans. This tradition interacted with the tradition of "men as hunters" to generate the accumulation of private wealth in men's, rather than women's, hands. Token gifts, that had high symbolic value in formalizing a mating alliance between the clans, were periodically interchanged among the men of the clans, especially in the "marriage gift exchanges" of food and other things. Later, with the domestication of cattle in those areas of the world where cattle were to be found, it was natural for cattle eventually to be brought into this "marriage gift exchange." Cattle represented the first "real wealth" in movable property.

At first the same cattle would circulate back and forth between two clans, as various members of the two clans formed "pairing marriages" with partners from the other clan. Here the interchange did not affect the disposition of children. Gradually, however, the interchange of cattle between clans on the occasion of a marriage deteriorated into an exchange relationship, in which the men of the different clans essentially bartered cattle for wives. This exchange involved the sort of agreement in which the clan, accepting the cattle, forfeited any claims concerning children that might be born. But that clan had to provide a replacement woman if no children were forthcoming. On the side of the male, the agreement was that "the cattle exchanged for his wife gave him claims to her children as his own." As Reed puts it: "Subtly but inexorably cattle marriage passed over from an interchange relationship to an exchange relationship involving ownership of property. With the advent of the bride price and child price the road was paved for the private ownership of cattle in the hands of the husband and father who, as an individual, could dispose of them as he wished."[32]

With the increase of private wealth in men's hands, the position of men in the family took on an ascendancy. An impetus developed to overthrow "mother right," which blocked inheritance by children of their father's wealth. With the overthrow of "mother right" came "the *world historical defeat of the female sex*."[33] Eventually woman's work in the family deteriorated from communal productive labor to private domestic labor, and her position to that of being "a mere instrument for the production of children."[34] Thus arose monogamous marriage—but important to note, monogamy for women only. It first "comes on the scene as the subjugation of one sex by the other; [and] it announces a struggle between the sexes unknown throughout the whole previous historical record."[35] Thereafter, the hierarchical social relations between men and women in the family (and elsewhere) have been shaped and dominated by various hierarchical economic formations, instituted around the various forms of private wealth in the means of production. Such domination has persisted to this day, in all the various social formations that have been founded on private wealth in the means of production.

Engels advocated "the abolition of the monogamous family *as the economic unit of society*."[36] He did so because traditional forms of the monogamous family involved the economic control over women by men and thus the economic oppression of women, as well as their general social oppression. Notice that Engels does *not* advocate abolition of the family, or abolition of monogamy. He has his eye on a higher form of the family that would not be dominated by the capitalist social relations. And he seems to hold out for a species of marriage in a future society in which "monogamy, instead of collapsing, at last becomes a reality—*also for men*."[37] In passing, we mention here Marx's position in *Capital*, that "modern industry," despite the alienated form in which it does so, "creates a new economical foundation for a higher form of the family and of the relations between the sexes."[38]

To extend Engels' argument concerning the issues under discussion, we draw from an insightful essay by Iris Young, in which she brings out that the capitalist system is essentially patriarchal in character.[39] Young develops her case in critical reaction to the "dual systems theory." The various versions of this theory "start from the premise that patriarchal relations designate a system of relations distinct from and independent of the relations of production described by traditional marxism."[40] Although not herself accepting the position of "traditional marxism," Young rejects the position that there is a separate system of patriarchal relations "distinct from and independent of" the economic relations of capitalism.

It is important to stress here that the dual systems theory arose originally because of the failure of "traditional marxism" to address systematically the specific oppression of women. This failure was connected with the economic determinism of "traditional marxism," which saw male-female social relations as an epiphenomenon of economic social relations. Moreover, "traditional marxism" was preoccupied with the theme of class structure and took "class as its central category of analysis." This preoccupation, combined with a distorted view of Marx's method of explanation, resulted in concern for the specific oppression of women being pushed out of thematic focus. Dual systems theory developed in reaction to this. Since class as the central category of analysis provided "no place for analysis of gender differentiation and gender hierarchy," there seemed "no alternative but to seek another category and another system in which gender relations can appear."[41]

Young, however, does see an alternative. She recognizes that the category of "division of labor" is just as important for Marx as the category of "class." And then she has the crucial methodological insight that, for Marx, these categories function on different levels of abstraction. She writes:

> Each category entails a different level of abstraction. *Class analysis* aims to get a vision of a system of production as a whole, and thus asks about the broadest social divisions of ownership, control, and the appropriation of surplus product. At such a level of abstraction, however, much pertaining to the relations of production and the material bases of domination remains hidden. *Division of labor analysis* proceeds at the more concrete level of particular relations of interaction and interdependence in a society which differentiates it into a complex network. It describes the major structural divisions among the members of a society according to their position in laboring activity, and assesses the effect of these divisions on the functioning of the economy, the relations of domination, political and ideological structure.[42]

Thus a complete analysis of the economic relations of a given society would require an analysis of the division of labor characteristic of that society. And since the division of labor includes an elaborate *gender division of labor*, "a complete analysis of the economic relations of production in a social formation requires specific attention to the gender division of labor."[43]

Concerning the specific case of capitalist society, Young takes the position that the *"marginalization of women"* and their *"functioning as a secondary labor force is an essential and fundamental characteristic of capitalism."*[44] She points to the fact that the capitalist economic system is one that precludes the employment of all potentially productive people, and it "requires a fluctuation in the proportion of the population employed."[45] Thus the existence of the capitalist system requires that "some criteria be found to distinguish the core of primary workers from marginal or secondary workers. The preexistence of patriarchal ideology, coupled with the necessity that women be near small children, operated to make sex the most natural criterion by which to divide the workforce."[46] So, from the very beginning, capitalism was *"founded on* gender hierarchy which defined men as primary and women as secondary. . . . [Thus the] specific forms of the oppression of women which exist under capitalism are essential to its nature."[47] These include the general devaluation of women's work, exclusion from certain job categories, a lower pay scale than men for equivalent work, and so on.

Another aspect of the oppression of women by men manifests itself in the sexual dimension of human experience. It consists in the tendency for men to relate to women as sexual objects and not as whole persons. Whatever disagreement there might be among the various schools of the women's movement in the last few decades, there seems to be unanimous agreement on this. And we agree that this is indeed one of the most pervasive and significant forms of the oppression of women in capitalist society. This is not to say that this phenomenon has not occurred in other social formations. But there are a number of factors characteristic of capitalism that work in conjunction with a traditional sexist ideology—and a traditional devaluation of women—so as to promote this tendency within capitalist society on a scale unprecedented in other social formations.

Consider especially the central place that advertising has in the capitalist economy—and consider the prominent use of women as sexual symbols in capitalist advertising to sell all kinds of products. And consider also the general transformation of the human being into a commodity that occurs in capitalist society. Therein, attitudes and habits concerning personal relationships have been shaped under the dominance of social relations in which people systematically relate to each other—and to their own selves—as objects. All this spreads over into the sexual dimension so as to constitute, and reconstitute, alienated modes of sexuality.

Here we must remember that the mode of being-in-the-world associated with capitalist social reality has its male and female counterparts, with its corresponding male and female modes of social consciousness and social character. The differences in social consciousness and social character between men and women account for, and reflect, the different ways in which men and women treat one another as objects under the dominating influence of the capitalist social relations. While the way in which men relate to women as objects is often obvious, and even blatantly so, there are "compensatory" ways in which women relate to men as objects, although this takes place in more subtle and concealed ways.[48] Moreover, many women feed the phenomenon of men relating to women as sexual objects by cultivating the use of "sex as a weapon" in the battle to secure psychological and economic security in a world perceived to be economically controlled by men.

Certainly the perception of economic control by men in capitalist society is not incorrect. But it does not go far enough, if it does not also recognize that the men involved are men whose psyches have been shaped from infancy under the dominating influence of the capitalist social relations—and that they are men who are committed to the idols of capitalism. And it does not go far enough if it does not also recognize that women in capitalist societies share complicity in sustaining the capitalist social relations in existence. For without the ongoing commitment and approval of women, the capitalist social relations could not be sustained in existence. Of course, such complicity is most developed in the case of upper-class women. As Evelyn Reed brings out in *Problems of Women's Liberation*: "Upper-class women are not simply bedmates of their wealthy husbands. As a rule they have more compelling ties which bind them together. They are economic, social and political bedmates, united in defense of private property, profiteering, militarism, racism—and the exploitation of other women."[49]

None of this is meant to excuse men. It is meant, rather, to bring out that the alienated social relations between men and women that obtain in capitalist social reality are aspects of the alienated mode of being-in-the-world which is structurally generated therein. And although the way in which women become "victims" in the capitalist socialization process is fairly obvious, large masses of men are also, in a sense, victims of the socialization process, although victims in different ways than women are.

As we will see ahead, Marx projects an intensification of alienation with the development of capitalism. It manifests itself, among other ways, as an intensification of the alienation between men and women. That is, the ongoing development of the capitalist system, and its structural tendency to generate an intensification of alienation all around, intensifies the alienation between men and women in all classes. In recent decades, many women have personally experienced a breakdown in the existential viability of the traditional female form of social consciousness, which has been prevalent in the United States and other capitalist cultures. This happened as a result of an intolerable frustration of existential needs stemming from their attempt to live in terms of that form of social consciousness under the existing conditions.

One very influential work of the early sixties that reflected this phenomenon was Betty Friedan's *The Feminine Mystique*.[50] Therein, the plight of middle-class suburban wives (whom Friedan interviewed) was described as a condition in which these women suffered from "the problem which has no name,"[51] that is, the problem of existential meaninglessness. Though Friedan's book went a long way toward helping these, and other women, become subjectively conscious of their oppression and exploitation, it did not go far enough. Men as such tended to come across as "the enemy," whereas the real enemy is an inherently exploitative economic system that systematically warps the psyche of both men and women, and whose perpetuation requires the complicity of women along with that of men. In addition, the book implicitly projected to women the remedy of adopting a life-style under the aegis of the form of social consciousness typical of men in American culture—more particularly, that of men who had made it in the system. This in the long run amounted to a self-defeating recommendation that women attempt to overcome alienation within the form of alienation. After all, one primary reason for the sense of alienation and meaninglessness that these women experienced was their mode of family living, as played out in relation to men who were so molded by their professional lives that they had become the living exemplars of alienation. Moreover, Friedan's remedy was not available for the great mass of women.

For other women, and for some men, there has been a more complete breakdown in the existential viability of the traditional forms of consciousness—one that has extended to the capitalist form of social consciousness as a whole. Such people are in rebellion, although where things will go from here remains to be seen. Later in this chapter, the theme of the alienated relationship between men and women will be examined further in connection with the question of whether a potential revolutionizing agency exists, in the contemporary stage of capitalist development, that could carry the culture beyond the capitalist social relations.

We shall find that there is no theoretical reason that a superstructural focus on male–female relations could not have a relative primacy in carrying out a movement toward a new culture. However, this would be contingent upon understanding the capitalist system as an essentially exploitative system that took advantage of whatever traditional patterns of exploitation and oppression existed when it came on the historical scene, that regenerated and extended those patterns in modified form under the dominance of the capitalist social relations, and that continues to sustain them in existence. Further, it would be contingent upon recognizing the historical and contemporary dominance of economic relations over male–female relations in capitalist society, even while recognizing a potential shift in this dominance in a period of cultural transition. Before taking up this issue, however, it is necessary to develop an understanding of the structural dynamics of the capitalist system, to bring out important tendencies of development that Marx discloses, and to mark the crisis potential that their long-term development holds.

Understanding the Tendential Fall
in the Rate of Profit

Thus far in the course of our treatment of the notion of world-historical transcendence, three major levels of abstraction have been distinguished.

We move now to a significantly more concrete level of abstraction which
will bring into focus Marx's view of the long-term structural dynamics
of the capitalist system. Here we turn attention to some of the major
dialectical laws of the development of capitalism that Marx distinguishes. However, we stress that adequate comprehension of these
dialectical laws requires that they be situated within the framework of
the conceptual structures circumscribed in the conceptual field as a
result of integrating the structures dialectically projected from each of
the three levels of abstraction distinguished in Chapter 3. Moreover,
adequate comprehension of them also requires that they be seen in
relation to their own more concrete elaborations.

We shall consider first the dialectical law of the "progressive tendency of the general rate of profit to fall." There has been a great deal
of confusion in most of the various interpretations, given in the literature on Marx, concerning this crucially important dialectical law. We
must get it straight, inasmuch as it stands at the heart of Marx's
explanation of the dynamics of capitalism. Moreover, it has the same
degree of importance for Marx's scientific explanation of the development of capitalism as Newton's law of universal gravitation has for his
scientific explanation of motion, or as Einstein's $E = mc^2$ has for the
explanation of energy–mass transformations in quantum mechanics. In
the case of the "progressive tendency of the general rate of profit to
fall," much of the confusion in the literature is tied back to the failure
to understand Marx's method of explanation.

What is at stake here becomes clear via a critique of a confused
position that Paul Baran and Paul Sweezy adopt with respect to this
law in their very influential work *Monopoly Capital: An Essay on the
American Economic and Social Order*.[52] We are especially concerned to
clarify this confusion in the case of Baran and Sweezy, since so much
of the rest of their analysis in *Monopoly Capital* constitutes a working
out of what stands as an undeveloped research problem in Marx's own
exposition of the development of capitalism. This will be explored in
due course. First, however, Baran and Sweezy discuss the "law of rising
surplus" replacing the "law of the falling rate of profit" in monopoly
capitalism. They write:

> If we provisionally equate aggregate profits with society's economic
> surplus, we can formulate as a law of monopoly capitalism that the
> surplus tends to rise both absolutely and relatively as the system develops.
> This law immediately invites comparison, as it should, with the clas-
> sical-Marxian law of the falling tendency of the rate of profit. Without
> entering into an analysis of the different versions of the latter, we can
> say they all presuppose a competitive system. By substituting the law of
> rising surplus for the law of falling [rate of] profit, we are therefore not
> rejecting or revising a time-honored principle of political economy; we
> are simply taking account of the undoubted fact that the structure of the

capitalist economy has undergone a fundamental change since that theorem was formulated. What is most essential about the structural change from competitive to monopoly capitalism finds its theoretical expression in this substitution.[53]

What prevented both the classics and Marx from being more concerned with the problem of the adequacy of modes of surplus absorption was perhaps their profound conviction that the central dilemma of capitalism was summed up in what Marx called "the falling tendency of the rate of profit." Looked at from this angle, the barriers to capitalist expansion appeared to lie more in a shortage of surplus to maintain the momentum of accumulation than in any insufficiency in the characteristic modes of surplus utilization.[54]

Whereas Baran and Sweezy maintain that the law of rising surplus replaces the law of the falling rate of profit, we maintain that the tendency toward a rising surplus is a correlative tendency of the tendency toward a falling rate of profit. Also we hold that both tendencies are operative in the pre-monopoly phase as well as in the monopoly phase. First, let us hear Marx as he speaks in the third volume of *Capital:*

The law of the progressive falling of the rate of profit . . . does not rule out in any way that the absolute mass of exploited labour set in motion by the social capital, and consequently the absolute mass of the surplus labour that it appropriates, may grow. . . . [T]he absolute mass of the profit produced by it, *can*, consequently, increase, and increase progressively, in spite of the progressive drop in the rate of profit. And this not only *can* be so. Aside from temporary fluctuations it *must* be so, on the basis of capitalist production. . . . [T]he same development of the social productiveness of labour expresses itself with the progress of capitalist production on the one hand in a tendency of the rate of profit to fall progressively and, on the other, in a progressive growth of the absolute mass of appropriated surplus-value, or profit [and in the absolute mass of commodities produced].[55]

Here we must remember that for Marx all the various forms of profit are grounded in surplus-value as their ultimate source. Surplus-value refers to that value generated in "surplus labor time," or that portion of the working day during which workers produce value for which they get no equivalent,[56] although this is masked by the appearances of the wage form.[57] And the rate of profit is expressed as the ratio between surplus-value and the total capital advanced.[58] This includes capital to cover wages (Marx's "variable capital") and capital to cover instruments and materials of production (Marx's "constant capital").

Since the specific aim of capitalism is the generation of profit, and since profit is grounded in the surplus-value generated in surplus labor time, there is a structural impetus to increase surplus labor time as much as possible, and thus also the surplus-value and profit generated by the workers for the capitalist. This involves an increase in productivity through the ongoing introduction of new machinery, and other factors, into the production process. And here the increase in productivity means an increase in the mass of commodities produced—in the mass of surplus-value that is generated and in the mass of profit that can be realized. (However, there will be a relative decrease in the surplus-value embodied in any given commodity because of the reduction in labor time required for its production, and thus in the surplus-value it represents.)

But the same conditions that generate an increase in the mass of commodities, surplus-value, and potential profits also lead to a decrease in the rate of profit. For the increases in productivity made possible by bringing new machinery on line mean changes in the total composition of capital to such an extent that there are progressive relative increases in the "constant capital" vis-à-vis the "variable capital." In the ongoing development of capitalism this involves "the relative decline of appropriated surplus labour [i.e., surplus-value] compared to the mass of materialized labour [i.e., constant capital] set in motion by living labour."[59] And since profit is determined in relation to the total capital, the rate of profit will tend to decline.

So far we have tried to bring out that Marx sees the tendency toward a falling rate of profit, and the tendency toward a rising surplus, as correlative tendencies. Not only that, but the crisis potential of the falling rate of profit is connected by Marx with the problems that capital increasingly encounters in the actual realization of the surplus-value embodied in the increasing mass of commodities produced. The commodities must be sold at a profit in order for the surplus-value to be realized as profit for the capitalist. When there is production on such a scale, and of such a sort, that the surplus-value cannot be realized through sale, then there is a crisis of overproduction. This is followed by production slowdowns, stoppages, and the underutilization of human resources. As against what Baran and Sweezy suggest, it simply is not the case that Marx understood the crisis potential of the falling rate of profit in the pre-monopoly phase as a problem of "a shortage of surplus to maintain the momentum of accumulation." Nor is it the case that he understood it in isolation from the problems of actually realizing the surplus-value embodied in the increasing mass of commodities produced.

None of what we say here is meant to deny that there are important differences between the monopoly phase of capitalism and the pre-monopoly phase, but the theoretical difference between these phases is not reflected in the substitution of laws that Baran and Sweezy suggest. For in Marx's view, both the laws we have been discussing hold in the pre-monopoly phase—and in our view they hold in the monopoly phase as well. Such considerations should serve to undercut a good bit of the rationale behind Baran and Sweezy's suggestion that Marx's analysis in *Capital* does not apply to the monopoly phase. Obviously, though, the problem is much more complicated in the monopoly phase. Consider, for example, the existence of the international corporation, state intervention in the economy, the vast increase in productivity in all spheres of production, and the development of modes of surplus absorption such as "the sales effort" and "the absorption of surplus through militarism" (analyzed by Baran and Sweezy), which were only in their infancy in Marx's era.[60]

But how are we to take account of the difference between the two phases within the framework of *Capital?* The main clue, as we see it, is Marx's method of explanation. It is fully in keeping with Marx's method of moving from the abstract to the concrete, that he should focus first on the "general nature of capital" and then proceed to take account of more and more complicating factors on more concrete levels of analysis. From various letters of Marx, and various sections of the *Grundrisse*, we know that the three volumes of *Capital* constitute only a partial fulfillment of Marx's projected plans.[61] Not only were separate works planned on "the State," "International Trade," and the "World Market," but, more importantly for present purposes, Marx's 1858 plans for work on "Capital in general," the subject matter of the three volumes of *Capital*, called for this analysis to be supplemented by additional works on credit and competition.[62] Moreover, in the third volume of *Capital* (written some ten years later), we find Marx still speaking the same way in a chapter on "The Effect of Price Fluctuations" where he writes:

> The phenomena analysed in this chapter require for their full development the credit system and competition on the world market, the latter being the basis and the vital element of capitalist production. These more definite forms of capitalist production can only be comprehensively presented, however, after the general nature of capital is understood. Furthermore, they do not come within the scope of this work and belong to its eventual continuation.[63]

Note the contrast here between "the general nature of capital" and "these more definite forms of capitalist production." Note also Marx's concern that these matters "be comprehensively presented"—and, we would add, "comprehensively presented" along the patterns of the dialectical movement from more abstract to more concrete levels of analysis, which would more and more fully disclose the concrete totality. Had Marx lived longer, he would undoubtedly have given much attention to monopolies in his projected works on credit and competition in the world market, especially in view of the many references to monopolies scattered throughout *Capital* and the growing importance of monopolies in the latter part of the nineteenth century. In any case, we hold that the analysis of monopolies *can* be given within the framework of *Capital*. Moreover, the first stage of such an analysis has already been given within the framework of *Capital* by Lenin, in *Imperialism: The Highest Stage of Capitalism*.[64] And much of the analysis that Baran and Sweezy give in *Monopoly Capital* can also be factored into the framework of *Capital* at a more concrete level of development.

Before we leave Baran and Sweezy there are some other issues that we must address. Drawing a contrast between "competitive capitalism" and "monopoly capitalism," they find Marx's analysis in *Capital* inapplicable to the monopoly phase since, in their view, "the Marxian analysis of capitalism still rests in the final analysis on the assumption of a competitive economy."[65] It is clear from their later analysis in *Monopoly Capital* that the chief stumbling block for them has to do with the way prices get determined. Although they see prices as being determined by competition in the pre-monopoly phase, they see them as being determined by noncompetitive corporate decisions in the monopoly phase. As they put it: "[U]nder competitive capitalism the individual enterprise is a 'price taker,' while under monopoly capitalism the big corporation is a 'price maker.'"[66]

We respond that we do not agree that Marx's analysis in *Capital* "rests in the final analysis on the assumption of a competitive economy." In the final analysis it rests on "value" and "surplus-value". Thus in *Capital* III, we find Marx saying:

> What competition does *not* show . . . is the determination of value, which dominates the movement of production; and the values that lie beneath the prices of production and that determine them in the last instance. . . . *Thus everything appears reversed in competition.* The final pattern of economic relations as seen on the surface . . . is very much different from, and indeed quite the reverse of their inner but concealed essential pattern and the conception corresponding to it.[67]

> Whatever the manner in which the prices of various commodities are first mutually fixed or regulated, their movements are always governed by the law of value. If the labour–time required for their production happens to shrink, prices fall; if it increases, prices rise, provided other conditions remain the same.[68]

In this context it is quite important to bring out that in *Monopoly Capital* Baran and Sweezy provide no analysis of the concept of "value," nor do they even mention it. We note also that in their formulation of the law of monopoly capitalism cited earlier, they speak of "surplus" whereas Marx speaks of "surplus-value." This may seem innocuous at first sight but it really is not, when we consider that the notion of surplus-value is at the very center of Marx's explanation of exploitation, and that for Marx "capitalist production is not merely the production of commodities, it is essentially the production of surplus-value."[69]

Soon we return to the theme of surplus-value. But first we address the problem of competition and pricing. We agree with Baran and Sweezy that there are some differences, within pre-monopoly and monopoly capitalism, concerning the role of competition in determining the market prices of commodities, with prices in both phases, however, generally deviating from the actual value of commodities, but oscillating around their value as a center. On the other hand, we would say that monopoly capitalism, taken as a whole, is every bit as competitive as pre-monopoly capitalism, although there are differences in the ways in which competition gets played out in the two phases.

In any case, although the role of competition in determining prices is much more pronounced in the pre-monopoly phase, it is not completely absent in the later phase. But even here Marx recognizes the evolution, *within* the earlier phase, of pricing policies that require consensus among groups of capitalists so as to maximize the profit of the whole class of capitalists. And as Baran and Sweezy put it themselves: "Maximization of the profits of the group constitutes the content of the pricing process under monopoly capitalism."[70] Here we just point to Marx's resolution of this problem, while recognizing that an adequate analysis would require an extensive technical discussion that is beyond the province of this book. Marx writes:

> [C]ompetition levels the rates of profit of the different spheres of production into an average rate of profit and thereby turns the values of the products of these different spheres into prices of production. This occurs through the continual transfer of capital from one sphere to another, in which, for the moment, the profit happens to lie above the average.... This incessant outflow and inflow of capital between the different spheres of production creates trends of rise and fall in the rate of profit, which equalise one another more or less and thus have a tendency to reduce the rate of profit everywhere to the same common and general level.... As soon as capitalist production reaches a certain level of development, the equalisation of the different rates of profit in individual spheres to general rate of profit no longer proceeds solely through the play of attraction and repulsion [i.e. competition], by which marketprices attract or repel capital. After average prices, and their corresponding market prices, become stable for a time it reaches the *consciousness* of the individual capitalists that this equalisation balances *definite differences*, so that they include these in their mutual calculations.[71]

With the cumulative experience of capitalists over many years, the consciousness is reached that it serves the interests of the capitalist class as a whole to eschew competition in determining prices, in favor of mutual consent in determining them. Such mutual consent will allow an individual capitalist to set prices to compensate himself for any special contingencies incurred in his given line of production that would stand in the way of his receiving a proportionate share of the total surplus-value. This is allowed "without always requiring the renewed action of competition to justify the motives or factors for calculating this compensation."[72] Behind this practice is the unwritten recognition that all the capitalists "have an equal claim, *pro rata* to the magnitude of their respective capitals, to the common loot, the total surplus-value."[73] The practice of setting prices in this way, so as to augment the common loot as much as possible, comes to the fore in monopoly capital. But it is anticipated by Marx in *Capital,* and can be accommodated within its framework on more concrete levels of analysis.

To proceed with further exploration of the theme of surplus-value, we draw on the help of Marx W. Wartofsky and his paper "Karl Marx and the Outcome of Classical Marxism."[74] Against persistent attempts to dismiss Marx's notion of surplus-value "as excess metaphysical baggage, as Hegelian vestige, as inherited error from Locke, Smith, Ricardo, as rhetorical redundancy, or worse yet, as standing in direct and systematic contradiction to what in Marx remains scientific," Wartofsky argues that the theory of surplus-value "*is the paradigm case of Marx's own scientific work.*"[75] And in passing he indicates his agreement with Engels' assessment that "Marx's major contribution to science was the theory of surplus-value."[76]

Wartofsky proposes a reconstruction of Marx's theory, "in terms of its historical *Problematik,*" in order to present and assess its scientific character. He asserts that Marx's theory of surplus-value evolved on the basis of wide-ranging empirical studies which he undertook concerning the history of prices and crises—and concerning the overall workings of the production process in capitalist England. And he brings out that it also evolved out of a fine-grained, internal critique of the work of the major classical political economists, from whom Marx inherited much of his terminology and many of his themes (for example, "the tendency of the rate of profit to fall," and "the labor theory of value.")

Wartofsky explains how the unique form of the labor theory of value that Marx developed involved

> the introduction of the concept of abstract labor not simply as a theoretical entity to be construed in the computations and arguments of the theory, but as a *concrete socio-economic fact* which exhibits itself daily in the contexts of market exchange, where one of the commodities exchanged is labor–power itself, bought and sold at a time rate at a monetary price—the wage—which obliterates or masks the concrete and differentiated qualitative characteristics of this labor as human work,

skill, the "expenditure of brain and muscle," as Marx puts it. It is in the difference that Marx sees between the cost of the production of this commodity and the value of what is produced by it that Marx locates the surplus-value, the *Mehrwert*, which then serves as the Archimedean point upon which the lever of his critique of capital as a system of exploitation rests.[77]

Wartofsky indicates the domain of facts, both practical and theoretical, with which Marx had to come to grips in his own theoretical project. For example, Marx had to come to detailed critical grips with positions, predominant among classical economists, to the effect that the condition of the working class was a permanent natural condition of the human situation. Against this position, Marx had to explain and account for the exploitative nature of the capitalist system—the historical generation of the working class and its ongoing subjugation to capital. He had to account for the variations in the rate of profit in different spheres of production, and at different times. And he had to account for the historical tendency of the rate of profit to fall—something that was never explained by the classical economists. Finally, Wartofsky brings out that the theory of surplus-value—with its elaboration to account for the falling rate of profit—does just what Marx intended it to do. It explains the phenomena that Marx set himself to explain. Wartofsky even provides a sketch of the way in which Marx's theoretical project can be put into standard hypothetico-deductive form for scientific explanations.

We add to what Wartofsky brings out, that Marx's presentation of the historical tendency of the rate of profit to fall is not given until well into the third volume of *Capital*, and that there are more than fifteen hundred pages of prior analysis within *Capital* leading up to its presentation. This is an intricate, systematic, and artistic analysis that begins with the commodity and gradually proceeds to disclose the structural dynamics of the capitalist system. In the case of the structural tendency toward a falling rate of profit, Marx succeeds in scientifically explaining it. He develops, in the conceptual movement of *Capital*, the explanatory theory that not only allows the conceptual deduction of the tendency—given the appropriate initial conditions and boundary conditions—but which does so in a way that brings out how the tendency develops out of the dynamic interplay of the interacting factors in the concrete totality.

On the theme of the deducibility of the tendency of the falling rate of profit from the explanatory theory of *Capital*, Wartofsky writes:

> If one is to offer a logical reconstruction of Marx's theoretical project in standard hypothetico-deductive form . . . it would be this: The explanandum is the dynamic variable, changes in the rate of profit; the boundary conditions are then to be constructed in terms of the prices of com-

modities which function as the variables in the economic structure: the costs of labor, of raw materials, of plant, of interest, etc. But the crucial element in the explanation is the theory of how these costs come to be determined in the exchange of commodities that takes place on the market. The hypothesis which serves as the major premise in the *explanans* of the hypothetico-deductive model must therefore be such that from its theory of the relations among value, price, and profit, together with the values of the empirical variables given in the boundary conditions, changes in the rate of profit can be explained, that is, can be deduced. To put this in another way: the phenomena which serve as the paradigmatic *explanandum* of the theory are not just any changes in the rate of profit, but rather those concerning the historical tendency of the rate of profit to fall over the long run.[78]

But to elaborate the "theory of the relations among value, price, and profit"—which could function as the *explanans* in Wartofsky's reconstruction—would be to elaborate Marx's theory of the structural dynamics of capitalism. To see what this involves in a way that is in keeping with Marx's dialectical movement from abstract to concrete, we indicate that Marx begins his dialectical explanatory movement in *Capital* with an analysis of the commodity. Then as Kosik explains: "From the elementary form of capitalist wealth and from an analysis of its elements (the two-fold character of labor as a unity of use-value and value; exchange-value as the phenomenal form of value; the two-fold character of a commodity as an expression of the two-fold character of labor), the investigation proceeds to the *real* movement of commodities, to commodity exchange."[79] And thereafter Marx proceeds to disclose the movement of commodities as it takes place in capitalism, including, of course, the movement of the commodity labor–power. He lays bare the structural dynamics of the capitalist system and shows how the dynamic interplay of the various factors he articulates in the course of his explanatory movement generates the structural tendencies he distinguishes.

The analysis of the first book of *Capital* focuses on the production process of capitalism, as opposed to the circulation process. It brings into play the most essential factors for understanding this side of the capitalist system. Each of the factors articulated by Marx, such as wage labor, necessary labor time, surplus labor time, value, surplus-value, and the like, is given extended analysis, and in the course of the analysis is tied back to the empirical base. Moreover, the factors are systematically interrelated with one another, and with the analysis of the commodity with which the explanatory movement begins, so as to constitute a complex whole of interconnected factors. Of special concern is the dynamic interplay of these factors over time. The analysis brings out the way in which the various factors are affected in the course of the ongoing development of the productive process. It brings out the way in which their dynamic interplay gives rise to important structural tendencies of the capitalist system, such as the inherent structural impetus toward the expansion of the capitalist system and the "accumulation and concentration of wealth at one pole" and "the accumulation of misery, agony of toil, slavery, brutality, mental degradation at the opposite pole."[80]

In the second book of *Capital* the focus shifts to the circulation process. Essential factors for comprehending this dimension of the capitalist system are given extended analysis. These include the conversion of surplus-value into money and the turnover time of fixed capital, of commodity capital, and of money capital. Moreover, structural tendencies arising from this side of the capitalist system are given extended analysis. Of special importance is the analysis of the structural tendency toward reproduction of capital on an extended scale, arising out of the conversion of surplus-value into new capital.

With the third volume of *Capital*, the focus shifts to an analysis of the structural dynamics of the capitalist system as a whole. Extended analysis is given of the conversion of surplus-value into profit, of the changing rates of surplus-value and profit at different times and in different spheres of production, and of the formation of the general rate of profit, as a statistical average across the various rates of profit in different spheres of production. In connection with all this, Marx also gives an extended analysis of the structural impetus toward an equalization of the rate of profit in different spheres to the general rate of profit through the action of competition. Only after all this preceding analysis is the structural tendency toward a historical decline of the general rate of profit articulated. And then we hear Marx speaking as follows:

> The progressive tendency of the general rate of profit to fall is therefore, just *an expression peculiar to the capitalist mode of production* of the progressive development of the social productivity of labour.... [P]roceeding from the nature of the capitalist mode of production, it is thereby proved a logical necessity that in its development the general average rate of surplus-value must express itself in a falling general rate of profit. Since the mass of employed living labour is continually on the decline as compared to the mass of materialized labour set in motion by it, i.e., to the productively consumed means of production, it follows that the portion of living labour, unpaid and congealed in surplus-value, must also be continually on the decrease compared to the amount of value represented by the invested total capital. Since the ratio of the mass of surplus-value to the value of the invested total capital forms the rate of profit, this rate must constantly fall.[81]

From Marx's elaboration of the explanatory movement of *Capital*, it becomes intuitively clear that the historical tendency of the rate of profit to fall is logically deducible from the explanatory theory of *Capital*. It also becomes intuitively clear that such a tendency would develop as a structural outgrowth of the projected dynamic interplay of the specific interacting factors distinguished in *Capital*, as these factors undergo systematic modification in the development of the organic totality of capitalism. We say "intuitively clear" here because the explanatory web of *Capital* is spun out fully enough so that one can follow the internally related links among the factors differentiated therein in a way that permits the factors in their interconnection to be seen as a structural matrix out of which the tendency toward a falling rate of profit is structurally generated. Thus, just as Einstein's $E = mc^2$ cannot be adequately comprehended in isolation, but only when it is seen in relation to the whole network of interrelated concepts that constitute its theoretical milieu, so is it with Marx's formulation of the tendency toward a falling rate of profit. To adequately comprehend this formulation it must be seen in conceptual interconnection with the whole network of interrelated concepts that are elaborated in the previous fifteen hundred pages of *Capital*.

Internal Contradictions of the Law

With this discussion behind us, we turn now to a consideration of what Marx projects as the internal contradiction of the law of the progressive tendency of the rate of profit to fall. This is quite important because it brings out the major structural conflict in capitalism between the forces of production and the social relations of production. Earlier we indicated that adequate comprehension of the dialectical laws, which Marx articulates in *Capital*, requires that they be situated within the projected conceptual structures elaborated on the more abstract levels previously explained in this chapter. The rationale for this will emerge more clearly as we explore the internal contradiction that Marx brings to light. First, we cite Marx from his chapter on the "Exposition of the Internal Contradictions of the Law."

> The contradiction, to put it in a very general way, consists in that the capitalist mode of production involves a tendency towards absolute development of the productive forces, ... while, on the other hand, its aim is to preserve the value of the existing capital and promote its self-expansion to the highest limit. ... [However] the limits within which the preservation and self-expansion of the value of capital resting on the expropriation and pauperisation of the great mass of producers can alone move—these limits come continually into conflict with the methods of production employed by capital for its purposes, which drive towards unlimited extension of production, towards production as an end in itself, towards unconditional development of the social productivity of labour. The means—unconditional development of the produc-

tive forces of society—comes continually into conflict with the limited purpose, the self-expansion of the existing capital. The capitalist mode of production is, for this reason, a historical means of developing the material forces of production and creating an appropriate world-market, and is, at the same time, a continual conflict between this its historical task and its own corresponding relations of social production.[82]

In order to grasp the contradiction that Marx projects as an internal contradiction of the tendency toward a falling rate of profit, it is necessary to keep in mind the connections (which we noted earlier in our discussion of Baran and Sweezy) between this tendency and the correlative tendency of an increasing mass of commodities produced and of surplus-value generated. And one must remember that all these tendencies are structurally generated by the capitalist system as productivity develops. In addition it is necessary to keep in mind that the crisis potential of the tendential fall in the rate of profit is due to the ever-present problems of selling an increasing mass of commodities at a profit, and thereby realizing the surplus-value embodied in them.

On the one hand, there is a structural impetus toward unlimited extension of production, including the ongoing development of up-to-date and more costly machinery and other instruments of production, the greater and greater diversification in the types of commodities produced, and an ever-increasing mass of commodities. On the other hand, the social relations of production within which capitalist production takes place require that the commodities produced be sold in a way that will contribute to the self-expansion of capital. Furthermore, the dynamics of the capitalist system are such that the ever-increasing capacity of the system to produce commodities, together with its inherent tendency toward an overproduction of commodities, outstrips its capacity to actually realize the surplus-value embodied in the commodities on behalf of the owners of capital. Thus rhythms of crisis and relaxation of crisis are inherent to the system. The overproduction referred to is, however, not absolute overproduction, but overproduction relative to the functioning of the system. As Marx puts it:

> Too many commodities are produced to permit of a realisation and conversion into new capital of the value and surplus-value contained in them under the conditions of distribution and consumption peculiar to capitalist production, i.e., too many to permit of the consummation of this process without constantly recurring explosions. . . . Not too much wealth is produced. But at times too much wealth is produced in its capitalistic, self-contradictory form.[83]

Economic crisis is attended by production slowdowns and stoppages, worker layoffs, and depreciation of existing capital (in the forms of both circulating capital and fixed capital in the means of production). All this means a structural inhibition of the development of the forces of production, due to the particular nature of the capitalist social relations of production. Here it is especially important to stress that one of the most problematic dimensions of such inhibition is the structural inhibition of the development of the concrete individuals who are the ontological center of the forces of production.

In the pre-monopoly phase of capitalism, where the market is the regulator of what gets sold, economic crises, when they do occur, do so with full fury. However, in the monopoly phase—where the state intervenes in the process of the realization of surplus-value by its adoption of market-replacing functions (among other things)—economic crises have thus far been more readily controlled. But problems concerning the absorption of surplus still threaten potential crisis. For, as Jürgen Habermas explains in *Legitimation Crisis*, "the activity of the state cannot compensate for the tendency of the falling rate of profit. It can at best mediate it, that is, itself consummate it by political means."[84] Only now, because of the deep enmeshment of the state in the economic process, the range of the sources of potential crisis has greatly widened.

An extremely important, unintended side effect of such enmeshment, which Habermas brings out, is the erosion of the justification potential of cultural traditions and belief systems that have functioned in the past to support the activity of the capitalist states. The expansion of state activity into new areas at home—and in more and more controversial ways on the international level—pulls these traditions into public focus, subjects them to intense critical scrutiny, and pushes them before the court of discursive justification, wherein "universalistic value systems"[85] are dominant. As Habermas explains in *Legitimation Crisis*: "At every level, administrative planning [on the part of the state] produces unintended unsettling and publicizing effects. These effects weaken the justification potential of traditions that have been flushed out of their nature-like course of development. Once their unquestionable character has been destroyed, the stabilization of validity claims can succeed only through discourse."[86] When these traditions fail to survive the critical gauntlet of universalistic discursive justification, the tendency toward a general "legitimation crisis" increases. (We return to this theme later in the chapter.)

One especially ominous source of growing world crisis is the activity of the capitalist states—especially the United States—in the support of the economic interests of capitalist investment in Third World countries. Marx explained (in a chapter on "Counteracting Influences" to the tendential fall in the rate of profit) that one of the key means of offsetting the fall in the rate of profit was investment in undeveloped countries. Such investment promises a higher rate of profit because of the especially good chances of exploiting very cheap labor. Marx writes: "As concerns capitals invested in colonies, etc., . . . they may yield higher rates of profit for the simple reason that the rate of profit is higher there due to backward development, and likewise the exploitation of labour, because of the use of slaves, coolies, etc."[87] When this statement is adjusted for the contemporary reality of Third World countries, the same principle holds.

Investment in Third World countries, at a level of exploitation very much greater than that which obtains in the capitalist powers themselves, is one of the key ways in which the crisis potential of the fall in the rate of profit is alleviated within the capitalist countries. Thus the capitalist states have a vested interest in maintaining the political power of those who will continue to ensure that native populations in the Third World will be especially ripe sources of exploitation. And although practical and political action in this direction, on the part of the capitalist states, alleviates the short-run economic problems in the capitalist countries, it adds to the long-run world crisis. For the means of maintaining such political and economic power in Third World countries is generative of an increasing world militarism.[88] Among other things, this involves the intensification of the threat of catastrophic nuclear confrontation between the Western bloc and Soviet bloc countries as both sides vie for influence among the political factions confronting each other in the class struggles taking place in Third World countries.

In the monopoly phase of capitalism, investment in undeveloped countries becomes a prominent counteracting factor to the tendential fall in the rate of profit. Along with other counteracting factors (such as expansion of foreign trade, increasing intensity of exploitation, depression of wages below the value of labor power, etc.), it serves to temporarily offset overt economic crisis within the capitalist countries. But this does not mean that the structural inhibition of the development of the forces of production by the social relations of production is thereby overcome *within* the capitalist countries in the monopoly phase. It is simply managed better—at least so far.

As Baran and Sweezy have brought out very clearly, the monopoly phase of capitalism is characterized by "chronic underutilization of available human and material resources."[89] For monopoly capitalism "tends to generate ever more surplus, yet it fails to provide the consumption and investment outlets required for the absorption of a rising surplus and hence for the smooth working of the system. Since surplus which cannot be absorbed will not be produced, it follows that the *normal* state of the monopoly capitalist economy is stagnation."[90] Here, of course, stagnation is not to be thought of in absolute terms, but in relation to the productive potential of the system. Moreover, with the ongoing development of the capitalist system, the structural inhibition and oppression of the human beings—who form the ontological center of the forces of production—intensifies. This will come out more fully as we now examine dialectical tendencies concerning the existential impact of the ongoing development of capitalism on workers—and on social life in general.

The Existential Impact of the Development of Capitalism

As with the other dialectical tendencies Marx discloses, those we examine here are projected as structural outgrowths of the dynamic interplay of the complex of internally related factors that Marx articulates as the most essential factors for comprehending the capitalist system. Taken together, the tendencies we examine connote an increasing dominion of capital and commodities over human life as the capitalist system develops.

The first tendency we consider is that the ongoing accumulation of capital involves a reproduction on an expanding scale of wage-laborers who are indentured to capital for life. Here we must stress that surplus-value (which is generated by wage-laborers in surplus labor time) is the "formative element of accumulation" of capital.[91] Thus, all methods for augmenting the surplus-value that can be generated are methods for the accelerated accumulation of capital. Such accelerated accumulation serves in turn as the basis for production on an extended scale, and thus for an accelerated production of surplus-value. Marx explains that:

> [Capitalist] reproduction on a progressive scale, i.e., accumulation, reproduces the capital relation on a progressive scale, more capitalists or larger capitalists at this pole, more wage-workers at that. The reproduction of a mass of labour-power, which must incessantly re-incorporate itself with capital for that capital's self expansion; which cannot get free from capital, and whose enslavement to capital is only concealed by the variety of individual capitalists to whom it sells itself, this re-production of labour-power forms, in fact, an essential of the reproduction of capital itself. Accumulation of capital is, therefore, increase of the proletariat.[92]

This reproduction on an expanding scale of wage-laborers who are indentured to capital for life carries with it no structural implication of a *general* increase—within the capitalist countries themselves—of misery rooted in material impoverishment. Rather, such reproduction is fully compatible with a rise in the price of labor that would give most workers access to commodities and services well above the level of material impoverishment. But this does not eliminate the reality of exploitation. For as Marx explains:

> Just as little as better clothing, food, and treatment, and a larger peculium, do away with the exploitation of the slave, so little do they set aside that of the wage-worker. A rise in the price of labour, as a

consequence of accumulation of capital, only means, in fact, that the
length and weight of the golden chain the wage-worker has already
forged for himself, allow of a relaxation of the tension of it. . . . [T]he
very nature of accumulation excludes every diminution in the degree of
exploitation of labour, and every rise in the price of labour, which would
seriously imperil the continual reproduction, on an ever enlarging scale,
of the capitalist relation.[93]

On the other hand, Marx does disclose a tendency correlative to the
one we have been considering, which does imply an increase in the
misery of the "surplus population" generated in the capitalist countries,
as the system develops. For together with a tendency toward an absolute
increase in the number of wage-laborers indentured to capital, Marx
projects a structural tendency toward an absolute and a relative (to the
working population) increase in "surplus population," which Marx
sometimes refers to as the "lazarus-layers of the working class."[94] As
Marx explains:

[Capitalistic accumulation] constantly produces, and produces in the
direct ratio of its own energy and extent, a relatively redundant population of laborers, i.e., a population of greater extent than suffices for the
average needs of the self-expansion of capital, and therefore a surplus
population. . . . It forms a disposable industrial reserve army, that
belongs to capital quite as absolutely as if the latter had bred it at its
own cost.[95]

This "disposable industrial reserve army" tastes the dregs of degradation, despair, impoverishment, and misery. The perception of its existence by employed workers pressures them to accept their own conditions of alienated work, out of fear for their own livelihood, and because
there is no perceived alternative. For as Marx indicates: "The advance
of capitalist production develops a working class, which by education,
tradition, habit, looks upon the conditions of that mode of production
as self-evident laws of nature."[96]

We also note that Marx's analysis makes it quite clear that the
structural generation of such a "surplus population" is dynamically tied
to changes in the composition of capital that attend its ongoing accumulation. Thus Marx can say that "accumulation of wealth at one
pole is, therefore, at the same time accumulation of misery, agony of
toil, slavery, ignorance, brutality, mental degradation, at the opposite
pole, i.e., on the side of the class that produces its own product in the
form of capital."[97] That is, in the form of "an alien power that
dominates and exploits"[98] wage-laborers, and that arises out of the
surplus-value generated by wage-laborers themselves.

Marx anticipated that the correlative tendencies of an extensive and
intensive increase in the exploitation of workers, and in the growth of
the "surplus population" and its attendant misery, *could* issue in the

development of a revolutionizing agency out of the industrial proletariat, that is, a revolutionizing agency which would have the motivation and the power to initiate a movement to transcend capitalism. Furthermore, Marx anticipated that this *would* happen, provided that the necessary transformation of consciousness among workers had taken place, and that they were ready to jettison the form of social consciousness that sustains capitalism.

Historical developments in the twentieth century have been such as to belie Marx's anticipation. The industrial working class in capitalist countries has for the most part become less revolutionary rather than more so. This is largely a result of the provision of enough goods and services to the workers in the capitalist countries to offset, at least so far, the kind of general misery in those countries that Marx projected as a stimulus of revolutionary change, and thus to secure, at least so far, the consciousness of workers to the tether of capital.

Concerning the projected tendency toward an increase in the size of the "surplus population," however, Harry Braverman has made it clear in *Labor and Monopoly Capital* that actual historical developments in the United States in the twentieth century are in concert with this projected tendency.[99] But even from this quarter no transcending agency has been forthcoming. There are a number of reasons for this, including the isolation and lack of unity of such unemployed workers; the general absence of the consciousness of the possibility of an alternate complex of social relations; the perception that employed workers are generally loyal to the system; and partial mitigation of the effects of unemployment by welfare and the like.

Now the fact that in the contemporary stage of capitalist development there has not been a general increase in physical misery within the capitalist countries themselves (as measured, say, by the level of consumption of goods and services on the part of workers), and that therefore the working class has not become more revolutionary, has often been advanced as one of the arguments against the applicability of the analysis of *Capital* to the monopoly phase. The main problem with such an argument is that Marx's analysis in *Capital* does not in the first place project a structural tendency (arising out of the dynamic interplay of the factors he distinguishes) toward an ongoing increase in the misery of material impoverishment among the *employed* workers of the capitalist countries, *once capitalist development is well underway.*[100] To be sure, though, Marx's assessment of the likelihood of a revolutionary transformation of capitalism—at a historical juncture near to his own time—assumed the *de facto* continuance in capitalist countries of very low standards of living, close to those that obtained in his own era.

In this context, we should also indicate that a projection of an increasing misery of material impoverishment among employed workers, within the capitalist countries, would not even be methodologically appropriate to the level of analysis on which Marx was working in the first volume of *Capital*. The factors distinguished in this volume (wage-labor, capital, surplus-value, rate of exploitation, composition of capital, degree of productivity of labor, etc.) are factors that abstract from many of the specific conditions of capitalist social reality that obtained in Marx's own time. Yes, Marx initially exemplifies many of these factors in relation to those specific conditions. Be that as it may, Marx's factors have to be understood in terms of the concrete universal, and thus as allowing for a range of varying specific conditions. That is, we have to see Marx's factors in their historical variation, as they change, and are modified, in their ongoing dynamic interaction with other factors. The laterally projected dynamic interplay of the factors Marx distinguishes in *Capital* does indeed provide a warrant for the projection of a tendency toward an increasing dominion of capital and commodities over human life, and with this, an increasing psychological alienation. But it does not provide a warrant for the projection, within the capitalist countries themselves, of the more specific kind of dominion which was characteristic of the capitalist social reality that obtained in Marx's own time. As for Marx's projection of an inherent structural tendency toward an increasing dominion of capital over workers, we cite the following:

> Within the capitalist system all methods for raising the social productiveness of labour are brought about at the cost of the individual labourer; all means for the development of production transform themselves into means of domination over, and exploitation of, the producers; they mutilate the labourer into a fragment of a man, degrade him to the level of an appendage of a machine, destroy every remnant of charm in his work and turn it into a hated toil; they estrange him from the intellectual potentialities of the labour-process in the same proportion as science is incorporated in it as an independent power; they distort the conditions under which he works, subject him during the labour-process to a despotism the more hateful for its meanness; they transform his life-time into working-time, and drag his wife and child beneath the wheels of the Juggernaut of capital. But all methods for the production of surplus-value are at the same time methods of accumulation; and every extension of accumulation becomes again a new means for the development of those methods. It follows therefore that in proportion as capital accumulates, the lot of the labourer, *be his payment high or low*, must grow worse.[101] (emphasis added)

Although this passage speaks directly of the dominion of capital over industrial workers, some minor adjustments would have to be made to extend it to workers in the various job categories throughout the service sector of the economy, where the alienation is no less real than it is for industrial workers. In any case, Marx's focus here on "the lot of the laborer" must be understood as a focus on the *existential lot* of the laborer. For Marx's qualifying phrase, "be his payment high or low," clearly indicates that it is not something as simple as a low standard of living that he is projecting here. Marx is projecting a structural tendency toward an intensification of alienation—or a worsening in the existential lot of the laborer—as capital accumulates in the ongoing development of the system. We return to the theme of the increasing dominion of capital over human life, in connection with the question of a potential transformative agency that could go beyond capitalism. But before doing so, we point to another dimension of the misery of alienation and of material impoverishment which is structurally generated by the capitalist system.

So far, in our discussion of these matters, we have confined our attention to the existential impact of the development of capital on workers within the capitalist countries. But capitalism is a vast international system that has extended its tentacles into every accessible place throughout the world. We indicated in earlier discussion that one of the chief counteracting factors to the crisis potential of the tendential fall in the rate of profit is capitalist investment in Third World countries. The especially high rate of profit from such investment is due to the especially high degree of exploitation of native workers in such countries. And capitalist investment has not only taken advantage of an original material impoverishment in such countries. It has regenerated and sustained such impoverishment by holding wages below subsistence level, and by giving active support to governments in Third World countries that promise to ensure the continuance of ripe conditions for the exploitation of native workers. Furthermore, this support is reinforced by the activity of the capitalist states in sustaining such governments in existence.

Thus if we consider the existential impact of the ongoing development of capitalism on the world level, taking account of all wage-laborers indentured to capital throughout the international system, we have to conclude that the development of capitalism structurally generates a perpetuation of, and an increase in, the misery of material impoverishment throughout the world. And we have to conclude that it structurally generates an intensification of alienation everywhere. Thus, the continuing viability of the capitalist system *within* the capitalist countries themselves rests on an exploitative practice that perpetuates and generates misery of one sort or another throughout the world.

A Potential Transcending Agency

Now Marx projected the development of a revolutionizing agency out of the working class as a result of the combined effect of the crisis potential of the dialectical tendencies we have been considering. Up to the present the crisis potential of these tendencies has been contained by the capitalist social relations. Moreover, we have gone beyond the historical juncture at which a revolutionizing agency could be expected to emerge out of the industrial workers of the capitalist countries as Marx envisioned. For one thing, the large increase in service-related jobs since Marx's time means that industrial workers no longer constitute the largest job category.[102] In addition, the contemporary pay scale of industrial workers within the capitalist countries assures employed workers of access to commodities and services well above the level of material impoverishment. And it is clear that there is still strong commitment to the capitalist form of social consciousness among such workers. Thus we have gone beyond the historical juncture at which the background conditions presupposed by Marx as underlying empirical conditions for actualizing the revolutionizing potential of industrial workers could be empirically fulfilled.

But have we then reached a new historical juncture in the contemporary stage of capitalist development? Have we reached a juncture at which the ongoing development of capitalism could culminate in the emergence of a transformative revolutionizing agency from some other quarter than the industrial proletariat? If so, where can a potential transformative agency be discerned, within the capitalist countries themselves, that could lead to a development beyond capitalism?

In order to adequately resolve this research problem, we will eventually have to take the analysis down to a still more concrete level of abstraction where we can present an extended analysis of an alienated mode of being-in-the-world. This analysis will be presented in Chapter 5. It will be developed within the framework of the nested levels of abstraction distinguished thus far. Moreover, it will be interwoven with an analysis of an *unalienated* mode of being-in-the-world elaborated against its contrasting background. With such a contrast we can bring into clear focus the way in which the continuing development of capitalism structurally generates an intensification of alienation, issuing in a *crisis of the human person*.

We present the developed analysis of alienated and unalienated modes of being-in-the-world in the next chapter. However, we indicate in the present context that a pervasive existential meaninglessness is one of the chief ways in which the crisis of the human person manifests itself, as the increasing dominion of capital over human life continues to develop. Here we do not refer to existential meaninglessness in general, but rather existential meaninglessness and its growth in the context of monopoly capitalism. The underlying presupposition is that the growth of existential meaninglessness, in any given society, must be explained in terms of the particular concrete conditions that obtain in that society. And the suggestion here is that the primary cause of

existential meaninglessness in the contemporary phase of the development of capitalist social reality is the concrete activity of life as lived in
terms of the capitalist form of social consciousness and its corresponding social character. This concrete activity is increasingly dominated by
capital, and, in turn, it increasingly subjugates all the dimensions of
the human being to the commodity form.

The further presupposition here is that in most cases such activity
generates an increasing frustration of a whole complex of interrelated
existential needs. Such frustration eventually culminates in a crisis of
alienation and the attendant phenomenon of existential meaninglessness. We recall the various existential needs distinguished earlier,
namely, the need for meaning, the need for community with other
people and with nature, the need for self-actualization, the need for a
believable worldview, the need for a viable character structure, and the
need for wholeness. The crisis of alienation generated by the ongoing
development of capitalism involves not just the frustration of one or
the other existential need. It involves the systematic frustration of this
whole complex of existential needs. And this phenomenon is a prelude
to the breakdown in the existential viability of the capitalist form of
social consciousness.

We explain that in speaking of existential meaninglessness here, we
are referring to the same phenomenon to which Friedrich Nietzsche
referred when he wrote:

> What I relate is the history of the next two centuries. I describe what is
> coming, what can no longer come differently: *the advent of nihilism.*
> This history can be related even now: for necessity itself is at work here.
> This future speaks even now in a hundred signs, this destiny announces
> itself everywhere.... For some time now our whole European culture
> has been moving as toward a catastrophe, with a tortured tension that is
> growing from decade to decade: restlessly, violently, headlong, like a river
> that wants to reach the end, that no longer reflects, that is afraid to
> reflect.[103]

We are referring to the same phenomenon that the existentialists and
phenomenologists have been so concerned to comprehend—the same
phenomenon reflected in different ways in Fyodor Dostoevski's "Under-
ground Man," Hermann Hesse's *Steppenwolf*, the plays of Bertolt
Brecht, and the poetry of Pablo Neruda; the same phenomenon that is
reflected much more closely in the contemporary output of the culture
industry, across the whole spectrum of television, movies, magazines,
papers, and books; the same phenomenon to which Betty Friedan
referred as "the problem which has no name."

At this juncture we refer to a contrast, concerning the crisis of the
person, which Rader makes in *Marx's Interpretation of History*, between
existentialist perspectives and "traditional Marxism". First, Rader ex-

plains: "The [outer] dialectical conflict between the forces and relations of production is matched by an inner dialectic—the disparity between thought and being, ideal and fact, hope and accomplishment, 'ought' and 'is.'"[104] And then he continues: "Traditional 'Marxism' has largely ignored the inward dialectic and has emphasized only the outer. Consequently it has been quick to recognize the crisis of institutions and slow to recognize the crisis of the human person. It has presented a one-sided interpretation of Marx. The existentialists have countered with an equally one-sided emphasis on personal crisis and inner life. Both the 'Marxists' and the existentialists fail to realize that Marx himself had supplied the corrective."[105]

We add that "traditional Marxism" developed in isolation from Marx's theory of alienation, and long before key works by Marx dealing with alienation were even published.[106] And when these works finally were published, "traditional Marxism" largely wrote them off as early philosophical meanderings by Marx, from which he later radically dissociated himself. This attitude toward Marx's writings on alienation, in combination with a distorted understanding of Marx's method of analysis and explanation, deflected the attention of "traditional Marxism" away from the crisis of the person. The attention was focused, instead, on the structural conflict between the forces of production and the social relations, but in a way that reified this conflict so that concrete individuals tended to become something like puppets of history. (In earlier discussion we have already explored the way in which this interpretation of Marx thoroughly distorts his position.)

Although "traditional Marxism" neglected the crisis of the person, the existentialists put so much emphasis on it that they largely lost sight of the underlying dynamics of the capitalist socioeconomic reality whose ongoing development is concretely generative of alienation in Western cultures. For example, Nietzsche's projection of the advent of nihilism—or the era of existential meaninglessness—is made in detachment from any consideration of the capitalist form of concrete praxis that systematically alienates people from one another. Instead, Nietzsche ties it back to cultural factors such as the "death of god."[107] If, however, we take the "death of god" as a symbol for the decline and fall of traditional Christian values, then from Marx's perspective we could say that the phenomenon Nietzsche referred to as the "death of god" had its historical roots in the concrete development of capitalism. This had already become so pervasive by Nietzsche's time that the believability of the traditional Christian values *as values for action* in the economic world of capitalism had already widely eroded. And their believability *as values for religious thinking and feeling* was often rendered hypocritical by an adherence to a concrete practice that actively negated those values. (In this connection we note Søren Kierkegaard's *Attack on*

Christendom[108] in which Kierkegaard inveighs against "inauthentic" modes of Christianity, and the psychic split that obtains when one pays only lip service to one's stated values, while concretely acting in a way that contradicts them.)

In addition, the tendency of existentialists to interpret the crisis of the person in abstraction from the dynamics of capitalist social reality—together with the existentialists' insistence on the primacy of the "concrete individual"—led many existentialists to absolutize the particular form in which the concrete individual *appears* in capitalist society into the form of the "individual as such." And this in turn shaped the kind of "resolution" to the crisis of alienation, which various existentialists viewed as possible and as choiceworthy in the circumstances.

In any case, the vast existentialist literature that has come out in the last fifty years attests to the pervasiveness of the phenomenon of existential meaninglessness in Western cultures. And when this pervasive phenomenon is considered in connection with Marx's analysis in *Capital*, it can be situated within a theoretical framework that enables us to understand it, and explain it, as a structural outgrowth of the development of capitalism. Moreover, it can be understood as a precursor of the potential transcendence of the capitalist system. For our hypothesis is that the great mass of the people in capitalist society who experience the meaninglessness of life as lived in terms of the capitalist form of social consciousness—and the corresponding social character—constitute a potential transcending agency that could lead beyond capitalism to a genuine socialism. This mass of people is not confined to the industrial workers. It includes people from the service sector of the economy as well as most other job categories. It includes the unemployed and the unemployable, as well as those who have not yet entered the job market. It includes women and men. And it includes people from socioeconomic classes other than the working class.

We stress immediately that the realization of such a potential transcending agency is contingent upon organized, many-sided, creative activity aimed at cultivating a movement of this potential in the direction of a socialist consciousness, and a socialist practice. We also note that the growing sense of existential meaninglessness is not itself equivalent to the breakdown in the existential viability of the capitalist form of social consciousness and corresponding social character. The basic reason for saying this is that one could experience existential meaninglessness, even while in practice there was still a retention of the capitalist form of social consciousness and corresponding social character—as well as a retention in subconscious and unconscious levels of the psyche. Nonetheless, the growing sense of meaninglessness is a precursor of a breakdown in the existential viability of the capitalist form of social consciousness. And it is a precursor that would actually tend in that direction with growing awareness in the United States and elsewhere of the real causes of the growing existential meaninglessness.

We can think of the transformation of a form of social consciousness as a process that begins with a phase of existential meaninglessness arising in relation to a given belief system and form of social consciousness. We can go on to distinguish a phase in which various aspects of an individual's belief system come progressively into critical thematic focus, in a way that amounts to a kind of personal legitimation crisis[109] for each of the separately considered beliefs and ideas constituting the belief system. To understand the breakdown in the existential viability of the given belief system and form of social consciousness, however, we have to distinguish still another phase in which the legitimation crisis is experienced as extending to the individual's belief system as a whole, and not just separately considered beliefs. The catalyst for such a systemic legitimation crisis for the old belief system is the exposure to, and tentative acceptance of, a new belief system that the individual perceives as addressing basic existential needs in a believable way. Such exposure serves as a contrasting background against which the old belief system can be seen as a whole (perhaps for the first time) and can be critically judged as a whole.

Although the capitalist system structurally generates a vast pool of individuals from all classes and all job categories who are lost in existential meaninglessness, it is also clear that increasingly large numbers of individuals within the capitalist societies have gone through, or are going through, a personal legitimation crisis concerning traditional values, traditional views of human nature, and traditional views of male-female relations, and so on. It is also clear that for many, this process has culminated in a partial or complete breakdown in traditional worldviews and in the capitalist form of social consciousness. So far, however, there has been no broad consensus on new directions, no consensus on how to deal with what seems recognized on every front as a mounting world crisis in our era. Moreover, a broad consensus around Marx's position has been inhibited because of the systematic distortions of Marx that continue to be promulgated, largely because of the failure to comprehend his method of analysis and explanation.

Now Marx anticipated that a revolutionizing consciousness would develop because of the tendencies toward an increasing misery of alienation and material impoverishment, but *only* on the presupposition that a transformation of consciousness would take place in which the capitalist form of social consciousness would be jettisoned on a wide scale. Such a result would itself be contingent on a wide recognition of what Marx projected as objective, scientific laws of social development. Such recognition would allow individuals to understand how they might act together to end systematic oppression. Even though such a transformation has not yet taken place on a broad scale in the capitalist countries, such a projected transformation still stands as a necessary condition for the development of a revolutionizing agency that could go beyond capitalism to a genuine socialism. For as Rader, among others, has pointed out: "Considered in isolation Marx's economic theory does not entail breakdown and resolution. It entails no more than economic crises that function as necessary restorative forces through which the whole economic system is recharged. . . . Without the active intervention of human beings *conscious* of their suffering and *determined* to end it [i.e., active intervention guided by knowledge of the dialectical laws of social development], the crises will recur without forseeable limit."[110]

Marx's anticipation that such "active intervention" would eventually be forthcoming rested on his tacit conviction that the revolutionizing scientific theory of social development which he had elaborated was so sound and compelling *as a scientific theory* that it held within it the theoretical power to serve as a believable base for the crystallization of a new form of social consciousness—and with it a new common sense. This implied in turn that it could pass through the critical gauntlet of "universalistic discursive justification" (to use contemporary philo-sophical parlance) through which all scientific claims must be able to pass, if they are to win consensus on their scientific merits.

Thus far, the various versions of Marx's theory that have been presented or dragged before the critical gauntlet have mostly been systematic, as well as gross distortions of his theory. Obviously the critical factor here is the development of an adequate understanding of Marx's revolutionizing scientific theory—and for this an understanding of Marx's dialectical method of scientific explanation is essential. Whether a broad recognition of Marx's theory *as* a revolutionizing scientific theory will be forthcoming in the capitalist countries remains to be seen. Clearly such recognition cannot be taken as a foregone conclusion in the face of vested capitalist interests, which can be expected to do everything possible to distort Marx. But if such recognition were to be forthcoming, then it would serve as a catalyst for the crystallization of a new form of social consciousness on a broad scale. And the potential revolutionizing agency to which we pointed earlier would begin to be activated.

We return to an earlier theme: We saw that no theoretical reason stands in the way of a superstructural focus on male–female relations taking on a relative primacy in a period of cultural transition from the capitalist system to a new social order. Indeed, at this historical juncture at the end of the twentieth century, such a focus may represent the best hope within the capitalist countries for eventually transcending the growing world crisis in which we find ourselves enmeshed. However, there is still much confusion about male–female dynamics, and its relation to the economic structures.

On the one hand, large numbers of women have already experienced a breakdown in the existential viability of the traditional female mode of the capitalist form of social consciousness. This has come about as a result of an intolerable frustration of existential needs stemming from the attempt to live in terms of that form of social consciousness. On the other hand, many of these women have adopted a modified capitalist form of social consciousness. Some of them believe that sexism can be overcome without transcending the capitalist social formation. Others believe that sexism is an uneliminable aspect of the male psyche—and that sexism is the historical root of oppressive class structures.

For our part, we hold that it is crucially important to recognize the historical and contemporary dominance of economic relations over male–female relations, even as one recognizes the possibility of a shift in this dominance in the course of a future cultural transition leading beyond capitalism. Among other things, this would help in understanding the growing alienation between men and women in our time as an aspect of the growing alienation that is structurally generated *among people all around,* as development continues within the framework of the capitalist social relations. If a consensus develops concerning "positive freedom"—and if a consensus develops in the women's movement concerning the dominance of economic social relations *over* male–female social relations in capitalist society—a pathway would open up toward a reconciliation of the sexes. A powerful impetus would develop to jettison the capitalist form of social consciousness altogether. And the women's liberation movement would evolve, and merge with other movements, to become a movement for general human emancipation.

At this point, we refer to a striking formulation that Marx gives in the *Economic Manuscripts* concerning the relation between men and women:

> The immediate, natural, and necessary relationship of human being to human being is the relationship of man to woman. In this natural relationship of the sexes man's relationship to nature is immediately his relationship to man, and his relationship to man is immediately his relationship to nature, his own natural function. Thus, in this relationship is sensuously revealed and reduced to an observable fact how far for man his essence has become nature or nature has become man's human essence. Thus, from this relationship the whole cultural level of man can be judged. From the character of this relationship we can conclude how far man has become a species-being, a human being, and conceives of himself as such; the relationship of man to woman is the most natural

relationship of human being to human being. Thus it shows how far the natural behavior of man has become human or how far the human essence has become his natural essence, how far his human nature has become nature for him.[111]

Letting go of the capitalist form of social consciousness altogether, *in both its male and female modes*—and cultivating a new form of social consciousness with Marx's guidance—would infuse into the social relations between men and women a revolutionizing practice that would reshape these relations. It would be a revolutionizing practice that had overcome the polarization of thinking and feeling in the psyche. It would be a revolutionizing practice in which "reason had become sensuous, and sensuousness had become reasonable" (Marcuse). It would be a revolutionizing practice that had transcended the psychic polarization into traditionally "male" and traditionally "female" dimensions through a merging of these dimensions into the whole person. And it would be a revolutionizing practice constitutive of nonoppressive, nonviolent, nonsexist, nonracist ways of being in the immediate relations between men and women. (As will become clear in the following chapter, all the foregoing characteristics are injunctions of *practical reason* as presupposed by Marx.) Moreover, such a revolutionizing practice on a wide enough scale would, in turn, ramify beyond immediate male–female social relations so as to eventually reshape the social relations of economic production and reproduction.

5

Freedom-as-a-Mode-of-Being

We are now in a position to proceed with the concrete elaboration of the category of freedom-as-a-mode-of-being. We recall from the first chapter that the core meaning of this category is that freedom means the attainment of some desirable mode of being regarded as constituting self-fulfillment—some desirable way of comporting oneself toward the world, toward other people, and toward one's own self as well. Here we shall try to unfold the particular way in which this category is applied in Marx's view.

The analysis of this chapter will be presented within the framework of the dialectically projected structures analyzed in the last two chapters, but at a still more concrete level of elaboration. Moreover, the analysis of freedom-as-a-mode-of-being will be developed against the contrasting background of the alienated mode of being that Marx sees as being structurally generated within the framework of the capitalist social relations.

We take our cues from Marx's analysis of estranged labor—that is, his analysis of objectification within the framework of alienation—as it appears in the *Paris Manuscripts*.[1] In that analysis Marx singles out four aspects of estranged labor all of which are deeply interconnected with one another. In estranged labor, human beings are alienated with respect to the product of their labor, the activity of labor, the "species essence," and other people. It is important to stress that these different aspects of alienation are dynamically interrelated with one another. Marx is providing an analysis of a mode of conscious-activity-in-the-world, within which the different aspects of alienation can be differentiated. But what is differentiated in analysis is dynamically interconnected in practice. So deeply interconnected are these four aspects of alienation in Marx's thought that, in order to overcome alienation with

127

respect to any one aspect, it is necessary to overcome alienation with respect to the remaining aspects.

Against this contrasting background we can get a preliminary sighting on an unalienated mode of objectification. For in such a mode, all the various aspects of alienation that Marx distinguishes would have been overcome. In the following discussion we shall bring out the structures of such an unalienated mode of being-in-the-world. The guide for this discussion is as follows: People in an unalienated mode of objectification are consciously active in such a way that they continuously bridge the separation between themselves, and other people, the products of their activity, the "species essence," and their own activity.

Alienated versus Unalienated Social Relations: Kant and the Categorical Imperative

The social relationship among human subjects is not only a convenient, but also a natural, point for beginning the sketch of an unalienated mode of objectification. This is suggested by the consideration that "man's relation to himself only becomes for him *objective* and *actual* through his relation to the other man,"[2] and also the consideration that "[t]he estrangement of man . . . is first realized and expressed in the relationship in which a man stands to other men."[3] Since the self relation of a person is first realized in the relation in which a person stands to other people, we have every reason to expect that the transcendence of alienation would also first be expressed through the relationship of human beings with one another.

Here we must remember that the individual is for Marx a social individual. Individuals are constituted, or rather constitute themselves, as individuals of a particular sort through the social relationships in which they stand to other people. If individuals are social individuals, then the specific nature of their social relationships will be constitutive of the specific nature of the individuals. And indeed if individuals are social individuals, then the most positive development of individuals is intimately bound up with the most positive development of their social relationships. Thus, insofar as the social relationships obtaining among specific groups of individuals are of an antagonistic nature—insofar as the individuals are pitted against one another in their social relationships—then so far are the individuals pitted against their own positive unfolding, so far are the individuals pitted against themselves.

It is not that the individuals of capitalist society are not social individuals. It is rather that these individuals are interconnected with one another in antagonistic social relationships. Although such individuals may seem to themselves to be individuals who are such independently of society,[4] they are in reality *antagonistic* social individuals—but social individuals nonetheless. Although these "individuals appear to be independent . . . they appear so, however, only to someone who abstracts from the conditions of existence in which these individuals come into contact."[5] They are "atoms only in imagination."[6]

Since all individuals, even the seemingly independent individuals of capitalist society, are social individuals, then both the kind as well as the degree of individual development will be contingent on the specific kind of social relationships that obtain. To the extent that the social relationships obtaining among individuals are antagonistic in nature, then the development of these individuals will be the development of antagonistic individuals. To the extent that individuals develop within the framework of social relationships in which people are pitted against one another—and in which each treats the other only as a means to further his own ends—to that extent individual development will be development within the form of antagonism. It will be development *as against* other individuals, and therefore development that negates other individuals.

It would be illuminating here to make a short digression. There is a very common view about the nature of human freedom that interprets freedom as the ability to do whatever one chooses to do.[7] What is usually lost sight of by those who would adhere to this view in a simpleminded way is the particular view of human nature often associated with it. To hold that freedom is the ability to do as one chooses, and to hold this in abstraction from a particular view of human nature, is to offer not much more than a platitude. However, to offer such a view of freedom in either explicit or implicit connection with a view of human nature which holds that the individual is by nature an egoistic individual who is engaged in a war of all against all, is virtually to offer tyranny as freedom. For consider, *if* the individual is by nature such an egoistic individual, and *if* the freedom of such an individual rests on his capacity to do as he chooses, then freedom *in concrete practice* comes down to so many socially acceptable—or at least socially accepted—forms of tyranny (more or less attenuated) over other people.

In very clear contrast to the general character of the social relationships prevailing in capitalism—where antagonistic individuals systematically treat each other only as a means, and where individual development is development *as against* other individuals—the general form of unalienated social relationships can be understood as one in which individuals relate to other individuals as ends in themselves in concrete practice. We will develop the meaning of this against the contrasting background of Kant's discussion of the "categorical imperative" in the *Foundations of the Metaphysics of Morals*.[8]

In perhaps its most well known formulation, Kant's categorical imperative reads: "Act so that you treat humanity, whether in your own person or in that of another, always as an end and never as a means only."[9] On the face of it, this principle might seem to be pointing toward the unalienated social relationships, which we have just initially characterized as ones in which people relate to one another as ends in themselves in concrete practice. That this is not the case will become clear as we go on to consider the abstract notion of the person that is at play in Kant's formulation, as well as the abstract notion of treating a person as an end.

Kant projects three different formulations of the categorical imperative, as "fundamentally only so many formulas of the very same law, and each of them unites the others in itself."[10] This means that we can take recourse to the other formulations of the categorical imperative in order to help clarify what Kant means in the formulation already given by "persons," and by treating a person "always as an end, and never as a means only." Thus a second formulation reads: "Act only according to that maxim by which you can at the same time will that it should become a universal law."[11] Another formulation reads: "[Act in accordance with] the idea of the will of every rational being as making universal law."[12] The net effect is that, relating to a person as an end, is assimilated to relating to that person in a way that can consistently be projected as a universal law—by one's self, that person, and all others. But this is a highly ambiguous and highly questionable assimilation, in view of the *a priori* nature of Kant's approach.

Kant abstracts from all empirical considerations in the derivation of the categorical imperative (holding it to be "derived from the universal concept of a rational being generally").[13] He abstracts from all those historically conditioned factors that enter into the shaping of individuals as individuals of one sort rather than another. He abstracts from all those conditions that shape the mode of consciousness of individuals. And he abstracts from the fundamental ontological structure of human reality, which has been explained in the first chapter as being-in-the-world. This means of course that Kant abstracts from those conditions that have historically conditioned the form of reason, in relation to which he attempts an *a priori* derivation of the categorical imperative.

The projection of universal law, which stands at the center of the categorical imperative, is modeled on the projection of the *a priori* structuring principles of "theoretical reason" (which enter into the constitution of universal laws of nature as explored in the *Critique of Pure Reason*). Running parallel to the position of the *Critique of Pure Reason*—that there is a common realm of nature by virtue of objective *a priori* structuring principles which are common for all people—Kant assumes that there is an *a priori* "objective principle of the will."[14] It is on this basis that Kant projects a common "realm of ends," in which there is a "systematic union of different rational beings through common laws."[15]

But the great danger of Kant's position is that it tends to blur the distinction between existing political law and moral law.[16] For it allows not just the projection of one unambiguous "realm of ends," but rather the projection of a whole array of different possible realms, according to the different social and political conditions obtaining in different societies. Once the empirical factors that shape human reality are taken into account, it would become clear that modes of consciousness are historically conditioned. And thus it would become clear that a historically conditioned mode of consciousness would, in turn, condition the formulation of the particular maxims that might be advanced on particular occasions to describe particular acts whose justification in terms of the categorical imperative is sought. And it would also condition the general social acceptance in particular contexts of such maxims *as* universal laws.

In this connection we note that none of the examples that Kant cites to illustrate the categorical imperative brings into thematic focus ways of acting and interacting with other people that are drawn along class lines, and which are not universalizable on that account.[17] However, there might be a general consent to such ways of acting and interacting, due to the predominance of the ideas of the ruling class. Thus the "realm of ends," which Kant projects in connection with the categorical imperative, is an abstract realm of ends. It can be projected in relation to a concrete social practice in which people relate to one another along class lines to such an extent that one class holds practical power over another class, oppresses and exploits the other class in its own interests, and therefore treats it as a means in concrete practice. Against the background of all these considerations, and as a critical appropriation of Kant, we suggest the following formulation of a fundamental ethical principle:

> So act that the particular mode of being-in-the-world in terms of which you act can become universal.

As with Kant's categorical imperative, this principle makes explicit reference to the principle of universality that has become one of the canons of Western culture. Only in contrast to Kant, the principle of universality is interpreted here in terms of the concrete universal, rather than the abstract universal. It projects a practice in which persons concretely relate to other persons as ends in themselves. And instead of focusing moral attention on isolated maxims of action (as in the case of Kant's categorical imperative), our fundamental ethical principle focuses attention on a whole complex array of interconnected maxims, which are implicit in the notion of the universalization of a mode of being-in-the-world. This principle directs the moral attention away from Kant's abstract "realm of ends" toward concrete practice in the world—concrete practice that involves the social distribution of power, privilege, property, and wealth. And we note that only a nonoppressive, nonracist, nonsexist, classless mode of being-in-the-world is concretely universalizable, that is, universally realizable in the concrete–real for all people.

Taking the principle of acting, so that the particular mode of being-in-the-world in terms of which one acts can become universal, as pointing toward unalienated social relationships in which people concretely relate to one another as persons, we consider now another closely associated aspect of unalienated social relationships. It concerns the contrast between private interest and general interest.

Private Interest, General Interest, and the Human Interest

Departing from the bounds of Kant's own position on these issues, we bring this aspect into view in another way. Consider a group of individuals, who in concrete practice relate to one another so that each regards his own private interest as uppermost, and so that each becomes only a means for the other. Suppose further that each of these individuals subscribes to the abstract formula that "each of the other individuals should be considered as an end in himself." These individuals would have an abstract community with one another, by virtue of their common intellectual adherence to the same abstract principle. But in concrete practice, they would not have any positive community with one another, since each in his concrete practice pursues his own private interest as against the rest. The effective meaning that the abstract formula would have for these individuals is the practical recognition that all the other individuals have their own private interest—which they have a right to pursue, provided that they also recognize the right of others to pursue their private interest.

Here, regarding others as ends in themselves means regarding others as having a right to pursue their private interest in competition with one another. It means that each regards the other as a means—and recognizes that the other regards him as a means—in the competitive pursuit of private interest. As Marx explains in the *Grundrisse*: The relations between one individual and another in capitalism are such that "the other is also recognized and acknowledged as one who likewise realizes his self-seeking interest, so that both know that the common interest exists only in the duality, many-sidedness, and autonomous development of the exchanges between self-seeking interests. *The general interest is precisely the generality of self-seeking interests.*"[18]

In the framework of capitalist social relations, the affirmation of private interest, as against other people, means the concrete negation of other people as ends in themselves in the pursuit of private interest. For when the concrete practice of all individuals takes the form of an affirmation of private interest, as against the interest of other people, then there can be no affirmation of the general interest in concrete practice. Here there is a cleavage between individual private interest and the general interest.

For Marx, the general interest that might emerge out of the widespread pursuit of private interest, as against the interest of others, would be *an alienated form of the general interest.* It would be an alienated form of the interest of society as a whole, but, importantly enough, a form grounded in the political state, projected as the active representative of the common interest. Thus the cleavage between private interest and general interest takes on the form of a cleavage between man as a private individual who pursues his own private interest as against others and man as the member of the political state united together with others.[19] In this connection Marx explains:

> By its nature the perfected political state is man's *species–life* in *opposition* to his material life. . . . Where the political state has achieved its full development, man leads a double life, a heavenly and an earthly life, not only in thought or consciousness but in *actuality.* In the *political community* he regards himself as a *communal being*; but in *civil society* he is active as a *private individual*, treats other men as means, reduces himself to a means, and becomes the plaything of alien powers.[20]

The situation described is one in which people associate with one another in antagonistic ways, so that they do not have any positive concrete community with one another. The forms of association of antagonistic individuals result in a real concrete negation of community. Such antagonistic individuals have only an abstract political community with one another, by way of a common adherence to a common set of principles. But practical activity along the lines of these principles results in the concrete negation of community. Each individual regards himself as having community with the others, because they all subscribe to the same principles. But at the same time each individual views "the *essential bond* connecting him with other men as something unessential so that the separation from other men appears as his true existence."[21] Such community is as little genuine community as there would be if two people upon seeing the same pot of gold fought each other for its acquisition. The abstract community of antagonistic individuals serves the practical function of preventing real community from developing.

Marx's position on this issue opposes the view of Hegel, whose thinking along these lines founders on the same problem that we have seen beneath Kant's attempt to establish his categorical imperative. We speak of an abstract interpretation of the principle of universality, which leads in turn to an understanding of community simply in terms of a general recognition of political laws held in common—in spite of the nature of the concrete social practice that might be associated with such recognized laws in a given social context.

Thus in the *Philosophy of Right*, Hegel had projected the political state as "the actuality of concrete freedom." Here a "substantive unity" is established among individuals, when the self-seeking individuals regulate the ongoing development of their self-seeking interests, in terms of political laws—which they can will to be universal, and which therefore they can take as prescriptive for the general interest.[22] The short response to Hegel is that he construes "substantive unity" (or community) in terms of an abstract principle of universality, which allows the reification of bourgeois community into the final form of human community. Now we proceed, against the background of the foregoing considerations, to a further clarification of unalienated social relationships.

In order to overcome the double life of the abstract citizen, who regards himself as a member of the political community, and the private individual who in his practice negates community with other people, and thus in order to overcome the dichotomy between the general interest and the private interest, it is necessary for people to affirm their social nature in their concrete practical activity.

Only when the actual, individual man has taken back into himself the abstract citizen, and in his everyday life, his individual work, and his individual relationships has become a *species-being*, only when he has recognized and organized his own powers as *social* powers so that social force is no longer separated from him as *political* power, only then is human emancipation complete.[23]

In unalienated social relationships, the *social* nature of the individual is recognized and fully affirmed, not merely in abstract formula, but in concrete practice. If the concrete practical activity of individuals is such that each affirms the other as he affirms himself, and each treats the other as an end in himself, then in such concrete activity the gap between the private interest and the general interest would be overcome, through the emergence of the *human interest*. Moreover, through concrete practical activity in which people positively affirm each other, even as they affirm themselves, the illusory abstract community of supposedly independent individuals would be superseded by a real concrete community of human individuals.

In unalienated social relationships, society is no longer regarded as an external framework that hinders the development of supposedly independent individuals. Rather, individuals recognize that they are internally related with other people through the concrete practical affirmation of their own social nature and therefore through the concrete practical affirmation of other people as ends in themselves. Community with other people is no longer recognized as, and no longer operates as, a limitation of individual fulfillment, but rather as a pathway toward human fulfillment. And this because community no longer means the common pursuit of private interest, as against the interest of others. It means instead the common affirmation of the unfolding of all people, within frameworks that give full, positive, practical recognition to the social nature of human being.

These considerations have a crucial bearing on individual development, for, insofar as individual development takes place within the framework of antagonistic social relationships, it is trammeled in fetters that block its development as an end in itself. Therein, all individual development is distorted into active alienation from other people and from one's own self. However, within the framework of unalienated social relationships, individual development would no longer be fettered by the repressive need to develop in a way that negates other people. Individual development would no longer subserve the overriding compulsion to dominate and tyranize others.

It will be seen how in place of the *wealth* and *poverty* of political economy comes the *rich human being* and rich *human* need. The *rich* human being is simultaneously the human being *in need of* a totality of human manifestations of life—the man in whom his own realization exists as an inner necessity, as *need*. Not only *wealth*, but likewise the *poverty* of man—under the assumption of socialism—receives in equal measure a *human* and therefore a social significance. Poverty is the passive bond which causes the human being to experience the need of the greatest wealth—the *other* human being.[24]

Individual development that has thrown off its fetters, and which has taken on a specifically human face, is development in which individuals simultaneously have a need for the realization of a "totality of human manifestations of life," and a need for the other person as a person. It is individual development in which people—both men and women—concretely regard their own development and the development of other people as an end in itself.

In a framework of unalienated social relationships, individual development would be shaped by a new form of practical reason. And the moral imperative of the form of practical reason implicit in Marx calls for a transformation toward a *new common sense*. It calls for a common sense that is sensitive to the dynamic interplay of the social factors that constitute and reconstitute the form of social reality; a common sense that recognizes that the growing dominion of things over human life is grounded in an oppressive and dehumanizing social practice; a common sense that requires the concrete extension of democracy to the workings of the economic process; a common sense that gives full positive recognition to the social nature of human being; a common sense that comprehends that community with other people need not operate as a limitation on individual fulfillment, but rather as a pathway toward individual fulfillment; a common sense that affirms the need for a manifold of human expressions of life, and which affirms as well the need to be related to the other person as a person; a common sense that rejects the oppression and exploitation of women, blacks, and others, and which rejects their degradation to second-class semi-persons.

Freedom as the Recognition of Necessity

In working toward an understanding of an unalienated mode of production, we consider first the view that "freedom consists in the recognition of necessity." This is an often misunderstood aspect of Marx's view of human freedom. Much of the misunderstanding resides in a failure to comprehend clearly what is meant by "necessity" in this context. To dissolve the misunderstanding we must give a clear indication of what "necessity" means when it is said that "freedom consists in the recognition of necessity." And we will also attempt to situate this particular aspect of Marx's view of human freedom within the overall view encompassing it.

The precondition for a transition from society characterized by alienated modes of being to society characterized by unalienated modes of being is the development of effective control over the productive apparatus. The suggestion, of course, is that the predominance of alienated modes of being is intimately bound up with the domination of human life by the productive apparatus. To overcome their own alienation human beings must overcome the domination that the productive apparatus has over them. "Freedom in this field can only consist in socialized man, the associated producers, rationally regulating their interchange with Nature, bringing it under their common control, instead of being ruled by it as by the blind forces of Nature."[25]

In order to regulate human interchange with nature rationally—to control this interchange rather than being controlled by it—it is necessary that people have genuine knowledge of the way in which social development takes place. And it is also necessary that they have genuine knowledge of the real possibilities to be actualized in ongoing social development. In addition, it is necessary that people take practical action, in the light of this knowledge, with a view toward bringing these real possibilities to fruition. People must have knowledge, and they must act in the light of that knowledge. Conscious-activity-in-the-world must be intentionally guided by genuine knowledge of the principles of social development, if people are to regain control over the productive apparatus, and thereby regain control over their own lives. The classic formulation of these considerations is in the words of Engels, rather than of Marx, so we cite them here.

> Hegel was the first to state correctly the relation between freedom and necessity. To him, freedom is the appreciation of necessity. "Necessity is *blind* only *insofar as it is not understood.*" Freedom does not consist in the dream of independence of natural laws, but in the knowledge of these laws, and in the possibility this gives of systematically making them work toward definite ends. . . . Freedom of the will means nothing but the capacity to make decisions with real knowledge of a subject. . . . Freedom therefore consists in the control over ourselves and over external nature which is founded on knowledge of natural necessity.[26]

The understanding of this frequently quoted passage turns on an understanding of the conception of necessity which is at play in it, and thus also on the conception of law that is implicitly bound up with this conception of necessity. This passage, although often quoted, is often misunderstood, even by thinkers who are sympathetic to the philosophical orientation of Marxism and to the humanistic thrust of Marx's thought. To develop our own understanding of this passage, we must consider it against the background of an often encountered misinterpretation of it. A particular example that applies comes from a work of one of the contemporary East European thinkers, Gajo Petrovic.

In his critique of the theory of freedom that construes the essence of freedom to be knowledge of necessity (together with action in the light of such knowledge), Petrovic makes the somewhat surprising suggestion that this whole theory has at its core a fundamental contradiction. Obviously, if this is so, the whole theory must collapse. Let us hear Petrovic:

> The idea that freedom is the knowledge of necessity is based tacitly on two mutually irreconcilable assumptions: (1) that everything is necessary, and (2) that man can (but does not have to) know that necessity. But if everything is necessary, then man's knowledge (or failure to know) necessity must also be necessary. Therefore, to consider the knowledge of necessity as freedom and lack of knowledge as unfreedom is senseless.[27]

In discussing this passage it is not our intent to take issue with Petrovic concerning his own positive stance on human freedom and human agency. Indeed it is precisely because of his positive stance on these issues that Petrovic finds it important to reject the view that freedom is knowledge of necessity. This is clearly manifested when he says that "[i]f everything occurs of necessity, it is natural to accept what is and not attempt to change it."[28] And again, when he says, "in order to be able to adjust freely, we would have to be, at least to a certain extent, excepted from necessity."[29]

Furthermore, it may be that Petrovic is himself reacting against a widespread misinterpretation of the view that freedom is knowledge of necessity, in which case his criticism is well taken. Be that as it may, we suggest that an interpretation of freedom as the knowledge of necessity can be given which would not be touched by the kind of criticism that Petrovic offers against it. In order to bring this out, let us specify the particular way in which the term "necessity" is interpreted by Petrovic, as he gives his criticism of the view that freedom is the recognition of necessity.

We suggest that the concept of necessity at play in Petrovic's criticism is one in which "the necessary" can provide no room for "the contingent." The phrase that "man can (but does not have to) know that necessity" leaves open contingencies that the phrase "everything is necessary" would close off. Here we have a rigid, nondialectical concept of necessity from which all elements of contingency have been entirely excluded. It is a concept of necessity in which everything that happens is preordained to happen, precisely in the exact way that it happens and in no other way. It is a concept of necessity in terms of which what happens could not possibly fail to happen.

And now we come to the crux. The concept of necessity at play in Engels' formulation of freedom as the recognition of necessity is a completely different concept of necessity. Whereas the position under criticism by Petrovic presupposes a nondialectical concept of necessity, Engels' formulation is committed to a dialectical concept of necessity. And from it no such contradiction, as envisaged in the position under criticism by Petrovic, arises. This means, of course, that the criticism advanced by Petrovic leaves untouched the theory that freedom is the recognition of necessity—so long as it is understood in terms of a dialectical conception of necessity.

So then, we must attempt to clarify the dialectical conception of necessity which is operative within the view that freedom is the recognition of necessity—and without which it does not even make sense. Inasmuch as Engels' classic formulation of the view under discussion was introduced above, it would be well to refer to some of Engels' remarks concerning necessity in his notes to *Dialectics of Nature*.[30]

At one point therein, Engels writes of the nondialectical conception of necessity associated with mechanistic determinism. As characterized by him, this view sees all events as "produced by an irrevocable concatenation of cause and effect, by an unshatterable necessity of such a nature indeed that the gaseous sphere, from which the solar system was derived, was already so constituted that *these events had to happen thus and not otherwise.*"[31] To this characterization Engels adds, as if to emphasize his disagreement, that "[w]ith this kind of necessity we . . . do not get away from the theological conception of nature."[32]

This conception of necessity is an iron-rigid one that obliterates contingency entirely. (It is the same concept of necessity that is at play in the view of freedom as knowledge of necessity with which Petrovic takes issue.) Not only does Engels dissociate himself from this view of necessity, but in the course of doing so he points to an alternate conception of necessity. We speak of the view derived from Hegel according to which, "necessity determines itself as chance," while "on the other hand, this chance is rather absolute necessity."[33] In explicitly adopting such a conception of necessity, Engels writes:

> In historical development, *chance* plays its part, which in dialectical thinking . . . *is comprised in necessity.*[34]

> [And further:] Chance overthrows necessity, as conceived hitherto (the material of chance occurences which had accumulated in the meantime smothered and shattered the old idea of necessity). The previous idea of necessity breaks down. To retain it means dictatorially to impose on nature as a law a human arbitrary determination that is in contradiction to itself and to reality, it means to deny thereby all inner necessity in living nature, it means generally to proclaim the chaotic kingdom of chance to be the sole law of living nature.[35]

The "previous idea of necessity" from which Engels dissociates himself is, of course, the one at the theoretical center of "mechanistic determinism." And although Engels' formulations do not fully clarify the issue, they point toward a dialectical conception of necessity that somehow involves a dialectical unity of "the necessary" and "the contingent."[36] It is a conception in relation to which a range of as yet unrealized possibilities can be projected as real possibilities, although not predetermined ones. It is a conception of necessity drawn along such lines to which Engels' formulation of freedom as "founded in knowledge of natural necessity" makes implicit appeal, and in relation to which it must be understood.

To resolve the problem of "the dialectical unity of necessity and contingency" fully, Marx's mature method of scientific explanation would have to be brought into explicit play, as will appear when we pick this problem up again in Chapter 6, where we explore a theory of dialectical determination. Engels himself did not take explicit account of Marx's mature method of scientific explanation, perhaps because he was still too closely tied to Hegel in certain respects to realize fully the way in which Marx had developed dialectical thinking beyond Hegel.

In any case, we comment here in preparation for the later analysis, in order to dispel the view that any talk of a "unity of necessity and contingency" is inherently contradictory.

"The necessary" and "the contingent" are projected as having reference to different complementary aspects of the concrete process of becoming. We interpret "the necessary" as having reference to those broad ontological structures in the concrete-real that can be comprehended in terms of articulated laws projected at a given level of abstraction. We interpret "the contingent" as having reference to those events that take place in the substructures of these broad ontological structures. The articulated law abstracts from such contingent events, but nonetheless, contingent events, in their mass effect, enter into the constitution and reconstitution of the broad ontological structures, but without being completely determined in all their concrete detail by the reactions of the broad ontological structures upon them. Concrete reality is the unity of "the necessary" and "the contingent" as so understood. Furthermore, specific articulated laws projected in terms of given factors (at whatever level of abstraction, and in whatever scientific domain) can be said to be "necessary" only in relation to the assumption that the background contingencies left out of account in the articulation of the laws can be legitimately neglected in the domain of application of the given laws. Such "necessity" is not absolute necessity, but conditional necessity.

This relativization of necessity and contingency, made possible in connection with a dialectical conception of determination, allows us to understand that the "knowledge of natural necessity," which constitutes the basis for holding that freedom is the recognition of necessity, means knowledge concerning the broad ontological structures that arise on the basis of contingent events. Thus, even in nonhuman contexts, "knowledge of natural necessity" involves the recognition of the place of contingent events in shaping the ontological structures that are comprehended in terms of articulate laws.

Moreover, as one moves from less to more complexly structured ontological domains, say from nonhuman to human contexts, we go on to explain that "knowledge of natural necessity" involves the recognition of the increasing possibilities for contingent events in the present to make a significant difference in shaping and reshaping the ongoing development of the concrete-real. This is due to a broadening of the zone of ontological indeterminacy, between antecedent events and present events, as one moves from less to more complexly structured ontological domains. And in the domain of human events "knowledge of natural necessity" involves the recognition of the increasing possibilities for conscious activity, undertaken in the present, to make a significant difference in reshaping the ongoing development of the concrete-real, on both the individual level and the social level.

As applied to the view that freedom is the recognition of necessity, these considerations have the following meaning. Freedom as the recognition of necessity is at the same time the recognition of contingency—that is, of the place of contingent events in the generation of the ontological structures that obtain in the concrete-real. Freedom as the recognition of necessity is the recognition of the dialectical interconnection between concrete necessity and concrete contingency, and of the real possibilities for future development that can legitimately be projected on the basis of this recognition. It is the theoretical and practical recognition of the general principles and laws in terms of which development in the human and nonhuman environment occurs. But it is also the theoretical and practical recognition of the way in which contingency figures in the constitution of the ontological structures that are comprehended in terms of articulate laws. And thus, it is also the theoretical and practical recognition of the real possibilities for the development of *human* mastery over the productive apparatus. Freedom in this sense is an aspect of freedom-as-mode-of-being, the meaning of which goes beyond freedom as the recognition of necessity while nonetheless embracing it.

Social Control over Production and the
Creation of "Real Wealth"

With this explanation of the kind of necessity implicit in the notion of freedom as the recognition of necessity, we can proceed to consider the general form that control over the productive apparatus would have in unalienated production. In alienated modes of objectification the products produced, and indeed the whole productive apparatus, dominate the people who have produced them. This relationship is reversed in an unalienated mode of objectification, and it is the producers who dominate and control the productive apparatus instead of being dominated by it. Let us look more closely at the first kind of situation, in order to understand more fully the second situation by contrast with it.

If in the alienated mode of objectification the product stands over against the producer as an alien and hostile force, this is not because the product possesses within itself any mystical force whereby it is able to maintain such domination over human beings. Rather, it is because the production and distribution of products, within the framework of the antagonistic social relations of capitalism, is such that "the mutual relations of the producers . . . take the form of a social relation between the products."[37] The social character of human productive activity—when this activity is undertaken within the framework of antagonistic social relationships in which each takes the other as a means—is opposed to the individuals, and takes on in their eyes "the fantastic form of a relation between things."[38] The human being appears as a commodity among other commodities. And human beings appear to be dominated by things, and the relations between things.

In sharp contrast to this situation, the social character of human productive activity—when this activity is undertaken within the context of unalienated social relationships in which people relate to each other as ends in themselves—is not opposed to the individual and does not appear as a relationship between things. In addition to social control over the productive apparatus, however, there are other important factors that would enter into the constitution of an unalienated mode of production. These other factors are embedded within the notion of the positive practical affirmation of the social nature of human being. And we must explicitly draw them out, in order to provide a clear notion of what an unalienated mode of objectification might look like.

To help draw them out let us single out one key dialectical interconnection within capitalism that is important for understanding the unalienated mode of objectification which we are presently investigating. The dialectical interconnection in mind is the interrelation between the tendency within capitalism toward universal development of the productive capacities on the one side and the framework of antagonistic social relationships within which this tendency is operative on the other side. This dialectical interrelation is one of the major contradictions within capitalism.

> Capital is itself contradiction in action, since it makes an effort to reduce labour time to the minimum, while at the same time establishing labour time as the sole measurement and source of wealth. Thus it diminishes labour time in its *necessary* form, in order to increase its *superfluous* form; therefore it increasingly establishes superfluous labour time as a condition (a question of life and death) for necessary labour time. On the one hand it calls into life all the forces of science and nature, as well as those of social co-operation and commerce, in order to create wealth which is relatively independent of the labour time utilized. On the other hand it attempts to measure, in terms of labour time, the vast social forces thus created and imprisons them within the narrow limits that are required in order to retain the value already created *as* value.[39]

In order to gather the import of this passage, the dual meaning of necessary labor time as understood within the framework of capitalism must be kept in focus. In one sense, socially necessary labor time means the working time required in given social conditions for the production of any given object.[40] But in a different sense, necessary labor time is contrasted with surplus labor time.[41] In this sense necessary labor time means the working time required in given conditions for the reproduction of labor power as a commodity. It refers to that segment of the working day during which this reproduction takes place, whereas surplus labor means the working time during which surplus-value is created.[42] It refers to that segment of the working day during which the worker creates value for which the worker is unpaid.[43]

Pari passu with increases in efficiency and effectiveness as the productive apparatus develops within the capitalist framework, there are decreases in the amount of necessary labor time required for the production of any given object and decreases in the time required for the reproduction of labor power. *But* there are increases in the amount of surplus labor time. This surplus labor time is not time spent outside specifically economic conscious activity. It is time still confined within the form of economic conscious activity. Inasmuch as the accumulation of wealth within capitalism is grounded upon the exploitative appropriation of the value created in surplus labor time, increased wealth means an increase in surplus labor time.[44]

Since value is determined within capitalism by labor time, any increase in surplus-value, and also any increase in wealth, is contingent upon an increase in surplus time, but also upon a decrease in necessary time (both in the sense of time necessary for the reproduction of labor power and in the sense of time socially necessary for the production of any given commodity). As the productive apparatus develops, the vast increase in efficiency, made possible by the growing sophistication of machinery, involves an increasing reduction in the labor time required for the production of goods. Thus, as the development of machinery becomes more sophisticated, the less does direct labor figure in what is produced. But the less that direct labor figures in the actual production of what is produced, the more does direct labor cease to be the real source of wealth. As capitalism develops,

> the creation of real wealth depends less on labour time and on the quantity of labour utilized than on the power of mechanical agents which are set in motion during labour time. The powerful effectiveness of these agents, in its turn, bears no relation to the immediate labour time that their production costs. It depends rather on the general state of science and on technological progress, or the application of this science to production.[45]

But to the extent that direct labor ceases to be the real source of wealth, the less can labor time continue to effectively operate as the measure of wealth.[46] In other words, the more direct labor ceases to be the real source of wealth, the more artificial and the more contradictory the retention of the value form (which construes labor time as the measure of wealth) becomes.[47] This increasingly artificial and contradictory character of the retention of the value form is not merely, or even primarily, an abstract consideration. For the retention of the value form, in concrete practice, is the retention of the social relations of production constitutive of capitalism as a social form. It is the retention of capitalism. This, of course, means that the contradiction between the growing reduction of direct labor as the real source of wealth on the one hand, and the retention of the value form on the other hand is identical with the contradiction between the developing forces of production and the framework of capitalist social relations of production. This is a contradiction that steadily increases, and in the long run makes practically possible a transformation of the capitalist framework.[48]

At this point we diverge to consider a problem raised by the foregoing remarks in relation to the position that Marx takes concerning machinery and the generation of exchange value. In *Capital*, Marx holds that machinery "creates no new value." Rather, machinery stores value that has been appropriated as surplus-value from past labor, and then "yields up its own value to the product that it serves to beget."[49] At first glance this position seems to conflict with the suggestion just indicated that, as capitalism develops, "the creation of real wealth depends less on labor time" than on the productive power of machinery. How resolve this issue?

In the first place, when Marx says that machinery "creates no new value," the reference is clearly to exchange value. In capitalism it is labor that creates value, not machinery. The use value of machinery in capitalism is subsumed under the requirement of extending surplus labor time as much as possible. This is necessary to realize increasing profits through the exchange of commodities whose value is measured in terms of labor time, and thus with reference to the wage levels that capitalists pay out for the *timed* use of labor power. However, in socialism the hegemony of exchange value is broken.[50] Labor time no longer serves as a measure of value in determining the proportion in which goods are exchanged for one another. Rather, a transformed conception of value comes into play, so that one can no longer properly speak of the exchange of commodities in genuine socialism. Remember that, in Marx's usage, commodities are "material depositories of exchange value."[51]

Instead, one can speak of the exchange of use values, where the proportion in which use values of various kinds are exchanged for one another would be determined in accordance with the estimate of social needs. The estimate would be undertaken in the light of the concrete recognition of people as ends in themselves. That is, exchange in socialism would be mediated by the recognition that the people facing each other in exchange are social individuals who are to be treated concretely as ends in themselves. Whereas in capitalism there is a one-sided measure of the value of all commodities in terms of labor time, in genuine socialism there would be a many-sided estimate of the value of products. This would all vary from occasion to occasion, from product to product, and from side to side, in accordance with the needs of fully developed social individuals.

Thus, in a given exchange of use values, the social individuals on one side might exchange on the basis of an estimate of the degree to which disposable time would be promoted by the product received. On the other side the social individuals might exchange on the basis of an estimate of the degree to which the products received might contribute directly to aesthetic satisfaction, say, in the form of materials for creative activity in free time. But on both sides the estimate of use value would be mediated by the explicit recognition and affirmation of the social individuals on the other side, and thus by the concern to promote universal disposable time for all people. And although some degree of labor time would indeed be embodied in the use values exchanged, it would not serve as a measure of their value in exchange.

We return now to the consideration that "the creation of real wealth depends less on labour time . . . than on the power of mechanical agents which are set in motion during labour time."[52] We stress that "real wealth," as used in this context, cannot be equated with exchange value. Thus there is no conflict with Marx's position in *Capital* on the theme that machinery does not create exchange value. This becomes clearer when Marx explains: "[R]eal wealth is the developed productive force of all individuals. It is no longer the labour time but the disposable time which is the measure of wealth."[53] Thus "real wealth" must be understood primarily in terms of the wealth of human development and not primarily in terms of the command over things and people.

The wealth of human development is contingent on available free time in which such development can be undertaken outside the pressures of economic constraint. Thus the development of machinery is essentially connected with the development of "real wealth," for it is the technological basis on which it can come to realization for all people. Here we recall a passage in the *Communist Manifesto*: "In bourgeois society living labor is but a means for increasing the amount of stored labor. In communist society, stored labor is but a means for enlarging, enriching, furthering the existence of the worker."[54]

Necessary Labor Time

Next we focus on the connection between the reduction of necessary labor time within capitalism and the supersession of the predominance of economic activity and the emergence of conscious activity as an end in itself within socialism. This is all with a view toward further clarification of an unalienated mode of production. As we will see, the increasing reduction in necessary labor time (which is a constituent feature of capitalism) is taken over in socialism as an increasing reduction in time spent within the sphere of material production. The reduction in time spent in the "realm of necessity" develops to the point where "it is no longer the labour time but the disposable time which is the measure of wealth."[55]

In order to develop the explanation of these connections, it will be helpful to make two important distinctions at this stage. The first concerns the meaning of necessary labor time. We point out that the meaning of "necessary labor time" that Marx associates with capitalism is somewhat different from the meaning of "necessary labor time" that he associates with socialism. The second distinction concerns the meaning of the predominance of economic conscious activity. We distinguish between the quantitative predominance of economic conscious activity and its qualitative predominance.

Concerning the first distinction, let us recall that within capitalism, "necessary labor time" (in one of its meanings) is "the time necessary for the production [i.e., reproduction] of the particular commodity labour-power." Recall further that, as far as the laborer is concerned, Marx contrasts necessary labor time not with nonworking time but with surplus labor time. This is a contrast made within working time. To this we add here that, though Marx does make a contrast within capitalism between working time as a whole and nonworking time, it is drawn as a contrast between capital and labor. Witness the following: "Capital creates a great deal of disposable time. . . . This creation of non-working time is, from the capitalist standpoint, and from that of all earlier stages of development, non-working time or free time for the few." And again: "Labour time as the measurement of wealth . . . implies that all an individual's [i.e., the laborer's] time is working time."[56]

Given the above understanding of necessary labor time within the framework of capitalism, how then is necessary labor time within socialism to be understood? It should be clear, for one thing, that the definition of necessary labor time associated with capitalism cannot simply be adopted verbatim as a definition of necessary labor time within socialism. In the definition of necessary labor time associated with capitalism, there is a reference to labor power as a commodity. Strictly speaking, as long as labor is taken as a commodity, we are still within the sphere of exchange value, still within the sphere in which labor time is taken as the measure of wealth, still within capitalism. In socialism a situation obtains in which "[p]roduction based on exchange value . . . falls apart"[57] and disposable time, that is, nonworking time, is the measure of wealth rather than is labor time.[58]

To see the transformation in the meaning of "necessary labor time" in socialism, consider, first, that in socialism Marx contrasts necessary labor time with nonworking time—instead of with surplus time, as in capitalism.[59] Also consider that the contrast between working time and nonworking time in socialism is not drawn in an antagonistic way. It is not drawn along class lines, causing working time to be concentrated in the many, while nonworking time is concentrated in the few. It is drawn so that working time is at a minimum for everyone whereas nonworking time is increased for everyone.[60]

We can proceed nearer to a formulation of the meaning of necessary labor time in socialism by becoming clear on just what is involved in the reproduction of labor power within capitalism. This comes out in the following:

> But there are some peculiar features which distinguish the *value of the labouring power*... from the values of all other commodities. The value of the labouring power is formed by two elements—the one merely physical, the other historical or social. Its *ultimate limit* is determined by the *physical* element, that is to say, to maintain and reproduce itself, to perpetuate its physical existence, the working class must receive the necessaries absolutely indispensable for living and multiplying.... Besides this mere physical element, the value of labour [power] is in every country determined by a *traditional standard of life*. It is not mere physical life, but it is the satisfaction of certain wants springing from the social conditions in which people are placed and reared up.[61]

Given the above statement on the value of labor power, and given that labor time is the measure of value within capitalism, then necessary labor time in capitalism amounts to the time necessary to provide for the satisfaction of subsistence needs, *plus* the "satisfaction of certain wants springing from the social conditions" of the particular phase of capitalism that might be considered.

This gives us just what is needed to understand the meaning of necessary labor time in socialism. Just as the satisfaction of subsistence needs, plus the "satisfaction of certain wants springing from the social conditions," figures into the determination of necessary labor time in capitalism, so do they figure into the determination of necessary labor time in socialism. But what is significantly different in socialism is the particular social conditions that obtain—and the kind of "wants" that are dialectically related to those different social conditions. The differences in social conditions, and in the "wants springing from the social conditions," can be summed up for present purposes in the change in focus that necessary labor time has in socialism. The focus of necessary labor time in capitalism is the reproduction of the wage laborer—who will be able to come back, and who will have to continue to come back, to sell his labor power as a commodity. The focus of necessary labor time in socialism is not this at all, but rather the reproduction of the social individual. And necessary labor time in genuine socialism can be construed as the working time necessary for the reproduction of the social individual *as* a social individual.[62] The implications of this will unfold as we continue. (Of course, the meaning of "necessary labor time" in the sense of the time necessary for the production of a given object under given social conditions is preserved in the socialist context.)

Quantitative and Qualitative Predominance of Economic Activity

Now we shall investigate the other distinction mentioned, namely the one between the quantitative and qualitative predominance of economic conscious activity. In making this distinction we must examine whatever conceptual relationships might obtain between them, and particularly whether the quantitative predominance of economic conscious activity implies the qualitative predominance of economic conscious activity.

The meaning of the quantitative predominance of economic conscious activity has to do with the amount of time during which conscious activity is focused on earning a living—that is, the amount of time taken up by working time. (Here the stress should be laid on working time as opposed to necessary labor time. For in capitalism the duration of working time extends far beyond the duration of necessary labor time.) However, the determination of whether economic conscious activity is the predominant form of activity cannot be made merely by adding up the total number of hours spent in working time, subtracting this total from the twenty-four hours of the day, and then comparing this total with the remainder. For clearly it is not possible for people to be consciously active throughout the whole twenty-four hours of the day on a continuing basis. For "[w]ithin the 24 hours of the natural day a man can expand only a definite quantity of his vital force. . . . During part of the day this force must rest, sleep; during another part the man has to satisfy other physical needs, to feed, wash, and clothe himself."[63]

Nor can the ratio between leisure time and working time be taken as a reliable index of the degree to which economic conscious activity might be the predominant form of activity. For most leisure time in capitalist society is anything but active time in which people creatively develop themselves. As Ernest Mandel points out, most nonworking time is

> time spent in getting rid of physical and nervous fatigue. . . . The com-
> mercialization of leisure is adapted to this condition of things. It starts
> from the recognition that after an ordinary working day the average
> contemporary proletarian is incapable of an intellectual or physical
> effort. But on the pretext of providing him with "relaxation" or "diver-
> sion," commercialized leisure causes either an atrophy of critical capacity
> or a morbid and lasting excitement which ends by degrading and disin-
> tegrating his personality to some degree.[64]

Along the same lines, Fromm proceeds: "If a man works without genuine relatedness to what he is doing, if he buys and consumes commodities in an abstract and alienated way, how can he make use of leisure time in an active and meaningful way? He always remains the passive and alienated consumer."[65]

But if neither the natural day nor commercialized leisure time will properly serve as a point of reference to assess the degree of predominance of economic conscious activity, we can readily find a proper reference in that span of time in which people are actively and creatively engaged in objectifying their own powers. And if the amount of working time in some social context exceeds the amount of nonworking time during which people are creatively active in objectifying their powers (say, in a context in which working time is not creatively active time), we can legitimately speak of the quantitative predominance of economic conscious activity.

On the other side, if in some social context the amount of nonworking time during which people are creatively active exceeds the amount of working time (say, in the case where working time is not creatively active), we will say that economic conscious activity does not quantitatively predominate in that context. But, if in some social context the amount of creatively active time (viewing together now free time, and that portion of working time which might be creatively active time in that context) exceeds the amount of working time that is not creatively active, we will say that economic conscious activity does not qualitatively predominate in the context.

What we need to distinguish, so as to specify more fully the meaning of the qualitative predominance of economic conscious activity, is whether in a given context conscious activity as a whole is experienced merely, and only, as a means, or whether it may not also be experienced as an end in itself that is intrinsically satisfying. Speaking of alienated conscious activity in the *Economic Manuscripts*, Marx says "that *life-activity, productive life* itself, appears in the first place merely as a *means* of satisfying a need—the need to maintain physical existence."[66] If in some social context the quality of life is such that conscious activity is primarily experienced sheerly as a means for earning a living—or sheerly as a means for the acquisition of wealth—we shall refer to such a situation as one in which the qualitative predominance of economic conscious activity obtains. But if in some other social context the situation is such that conscious activity is experienced on the whole as intrinsically satisfying, creatively active, and as an end in itself (even if it is also a means for earning a living), we will say that the qualitative predominance of economic conscious activity does not obtain in that context.

At this point the question of the relationship between the quantitative and the qualitative predominance of economic conscious activity arises. This relationship cannot be abstractly set forth in isolation from specific social contexts. For example, among the craftsmen of feudal society the quantitative predominance of economic conscious activity was apparently not accompanied by its qualitative predominance. However, in the case of the wage-laborer of capitalism, both the quantitative and qualitative predominance go hand in hand. Thus it seems that the predominance of economic conscious activity (under both aspects) in any given social context is really shaped by the interplay between the social relations of production and the level of development of the forces of production, in that particular context. And in view of the nature of dialectical development, we would expect the relative weight of the social relations, versus the forces of production, in determining the degree of predominance of economic conscious activity (under both aspects) to be different in different contexts. As we pursue the explanation of this in what follows, we shall draw from previous discussion concerning the increasing reduction of necessary labor time in capitalism and in socialism.

If we focus attention on the qualitative predominance of economic conscious activity in capitalism, it will be readily seen that this qualitative predominance is grounded on the capitalist social relations. For present purposes they can be concretely summed up by reference to the predominant aim of capitalist production, for which "production is the aim of man and wealth the aim of production."[67] The "production of surplus–value, or the extraction of surplus-labour, is the specific end and aim, the sum and substance, of capitalist production."[68] Here, there is a constant and implacable pressure from all directions that reduces conscious activity to a means for the fulfillment of this overriding end. This, of course, involves the sacrifice of conscious activity as intrinsically satisfying activity, as an end in itself.

The process through which this overriding end is realized is such that the worker finds himself in a situation where he is "obliged to offer for sale as a commodity that very labour-power which exists only in his living self."[69] Indeed, the worker "is compelled by social conditions, to sell the whole of his active life, his very capacity for work, for the price of the necessaries of life."[70] And it is the capitalist "process itself that incessantly hurls back the labourer on to the market as a vendor of his labour-power, and that incessantly converts his own product into a means by which another man can purchase him."[71] For the capitalist himself, conscious activity becomes transformed into a means for the unlimited acquisition of wealth—that is, the unlimited "extraction of surplus labour."

Clearly then, the qualitative predominance of economic conscious activity in capitalism is grounded on the social relations of capitalism.

These relations actively subsume conscious activity to ends that are in dynamic conflict with the realization of conscious activity as an end in itself. We can in turn regard the qualitative predominance of economic conscious activity as the immediate ground for its quantitative predominance in capitalism. We have seen that the development of capitalism is characterized by an increasing reduction in necessary time (both in the sense of the working time necessary for the reproduction of labor power, and in the sense of the time necessary for the production of any given item). Capitalism "necessarily tends toward an increase in the productivity of labour and as great a diminution as possible in necessary labour."[72] Thereby it provides the technical ground for overcoming the quantitative predominance of economic conscious activity. Yet such an outcome is blocked by the effective power of social relations that militate against the realization of conscious activity as an end in itself. In the case of the capitalist, they shape conscious activity into a means for the unlimited acquisition of wealth, and in the case of the worker, they shape "the whole of his active life" into a means for acquiring "the price of the necessaries of life."

The continuing quantitative predominance of economic conscious activity in capitalism finds its immediate ground in the qualitative predominance of economic conscious activity that prevails therein.[73] The quantitative predominance of economic conscious activity is sustained by its qualitative predominance. The import of this, for the unalienated mode of production under investigation in this chapter, consists in the fact that the positive practical affirmation of the social nature of human being involves the supersession of the predominance of economic conscious activity altogether—in both its quantitative and its qualitative aspects. But before proceeding in this direction, we consider briefly a social context in which the quantitative predominance of economic conscious activity is not grounded on its qualitative predominance.

In *Capital*, Marx points out that "it is . . . clear that in any given economic formation of society, where not the exchange-value but the use-value of the product predominates, surplus-labour will be limited by a given set of wants which may be greater or less, and that here no boundless thirst for surplus-labour arises from the nature of the production itself."[74] Feudal society is a convenient example of a society in which use-value predominates over exchange-value. Presumably the quantitative predominance of economic conscious activity was the norm within the framework of feudal society. What is significant for present purposes is that there was no implacable pressure emanating from the very structure of the feudal economic formation—as one of its essential features—that would undermine the possibility of the expression of conscious activity as an end in itself. There was "no boundless thirst for surplus-labour" which would operate to reduce conscious activity into a means, and only a means, to quench itself. Instead of being sustained by the qualitative predominance of economic conscious activity as in capitalism, the quantitative predominance of economic conscious activity in feudalism was primarily grounded on the level of development of the productive apparatus.[75] This does not mean, of course, that conscious activity was always experienced as an end in itself in feudalism. But it does mean that the negation of conscious activity as an end in itself was not a necessary function of the feudal economic formation. And it does mean that, other factors being favorable, the feudal economic formation did permit the emergence of conscious activity as an end in itself in certain circumstances. Conscious activity of the craftsman in medieval society is a case in point.[76]

Transcending the Predominance of Economic Activity

After this discussion, we are in a position to appreciate the connection between the reduction of necessary labor time in capitalism, and the supersession of the predominance of economic conscious activity in socialism, and the emergence of conscious activity as an end in itself. Through those forces in capitalism that operate to reduce necessary labor time to a minimum, capitalism "is instrumental in creating the means of social disposable time, and so in reducing working time for the whole of society to a minimum and thus making everyone's time free for their own development."[77] To be sure, the actual realization of this potential reduction of working time to a minimum is blocked within capitalism. As Marx says, "although its tendency is always to create disposable time, it [capital] also converts it into surplus labour."[78] The increasing reduction of necessary labor time toward a minimum is not attended by an increasing reduction of working time toward a minimum. It is attended by an expansion of surplus labor time, and surplus-value—and also by an expansion of the social power that actively negates the expression of conscious activity as an end in itself and compels the worker to expend his active life on earning "the price of the necessaries of life." The reduction of necessary labor time toward a minimum is accompanied by the quantitative and qualitative predominance of economic conscious activity.

And now we come to the crux. In production within an unalienated mode of objectification—of a sort that involves the positive practical affirmation of the social nature of human beings—the reduction of necessary labor time toward a minimum is realized in a way that involves the supersession of the predominance of economic conscious activity in both its quantitative and qualitative aspects. This makes possible the free development of the individual.

Individuals are then in a position to develop freely. It is no longer a question of reducing the necessary labour time in order to create surplus labour, but of reducing the necessary labour of society to a minimum. The counterpart of this reduction is that all members of society can develop their education in the arts, sciences, etc., thanks to the free time and means available to all.[79]

Let us consider first the supersession of the qualitative predominance of economic conscious activity. In capitalism the qualitative predominance of economic conscious activity is grounded on social relations whose very structure actively negates the expression of conscious activity as an end in itself. We have mentioned that these social relations can be concretely summed up in the phrase "production is the aim of man and wealth the aim of production." In contrast, the social relations of full-fledged socialism actively promote the expression of conscious activity as an end in itself. For present purposes such social relations can be concretely summed up in the phrase "the social individual is the aim of production." This aim is especially manifest in the mode of appropriation associated with an unalienated mode of objectification.

One of the chief characteristics of an unalienated mode of objectification is a mode of appropriation, of the products in which labor power has been objectified, that is in harmony with the social nature of production. This would be a social mode of appropriation, a mode of appropriation which recognized and affirmed the social nature of the individual and the social nature of production. Each person sees that the products of human productive activity are the objectification of social individuals, and each person recognizes this in practice. Here it will be "seen how on the assumption of positively annulled private property man produces man—himself and the other man; how the object, being the direct embodiment of his individuality, is simultaneously his own existence for the other man, the existence of the other man, and that existence for him."[80]

Individuals in their practical activity within the productive apparatus relate to the others as ends in themselves. They recognize that the products of social production are an objectification of social beings, which are to be appropriated in ways that affirm the existence of people as ends in themselves. To the extent that individuals in social production recognize others as ends in themselves—through a mode of appropriation that bears within itself the affirmation of others as ends in themselves—to that extent the products cease to loom over against people as alien hostile forces. And to that extent people cease to be related to one another in antagonistic ways that spell the negation of people by one another. A corollary of the union of a social mode of production and a social mode of appropriation is social control over the productive apparatus. Social control means control by individuals united together in ways that give positive practical affirmation to the social nature of human being.

So then, the qualitative predominance of economic conscious activity that obtained in capitalism is overcome in full-fledged socialism by the institution of social relations promoting the expression of conscious activity as an end in itself—by actively affirming in their very structure human beings as ends in themselves. Moreover, the quantitative predominance of economic conscious activity that had obtained in capitalism is overcome in socialism through the institution of these social relations as well. It will be recalled that in capitalism, the quantitative predominance of economic conscious activity is grounded not on the level of development of the productive apparatus but rather on the qualitative predominance of economic conscious activity. However, with the institution of the social relations of socialism this qualitative predominance is overcome. Thereby the ground that sustained the quantitative predominance of economic conscious activity is removed. Through the removal of this ground, the reduction of working time to a minimum is made possible, and thereby the quantitative predominance of economic conscious activity is overcome. Thus we see that the positive practical affirmation of the social nature of human being conceptually entails the supersession of the predominance of conscious activity that is specifically economic in character. This means a consequent liberation of human conscious activity from economic constraint, and its expression as an end in itself.

From the above considerations it should be clear that the positive practical affirmation of the social nature of human beings can only be a product of history. It can emerge only out of the historical development of the productive apparatus, and thus out of a prior alienated development of the productive apparatus—and a prior alienated expression of the social nature of human being.[81] In order for there to be "universally developed individuals," the practical presupposition of "the universal development of productive forces" must have been fulfilled.[82] This practical presupposition is prepared by the capitalist mode of production, which "forces the development of the productive powers of society, and creates those material conditions, which alone can form the real basis of a higher form of society, a society in which the full and free development of every individual forms the ruling principle."[83] Through the reduction of necessary labor time to a minimum—and the corresponding development of the productive apparatus to the point where it is practically possible to fulfill the material needs of individuals without those individuals consuming themselves in economic activity—the practical presupposition for the transition toward an unalienated mode of objectification is fulfilled.

Unalienated Activity in the "Realm of
Necessity"

There are a few remaining issues having to do with an unalienated mode of production that require some attention. The first of these bears on the possibility of unalienated activity within the "realm of necessity." The second concerns the place of surplus labor within socialism. As a point of departure for considering whether or not conscious activity within the "realm of necessity" is unalienated activity, let us examine this passage from *Capital*. (We assume a situation in which the predominance of specifically economic activity has been overcome.)

> [T]he realm of freedom actually begins only where labour which is determined by necessity and mundane considerations ceases; thus in the very nature of things it lies beyond the sphere of actual material production. . . . [The sphere of material production] remains a realm of necessity. Beyond it begins that development of human energy which is an end in itself, the true realm of freedom, which, however, can blossom forth only with this realm of necessity as its basis.[84]

There seems to be a sharp bifurcation in this passage between the realm of necessity and the realm of freedom. Inasmuch as unalienated activity has been characterized as free activity, this passage would seem to imply that any activity within the realm of necessity would perforce be alienated activity. And indeed so prominent a figure as Marcuse has spoken of the obsolescence of the Marxian conception of socialism in connection with this bifurcation of the two realms.

In relation to the specific problem before us now, he says that "[t]his division implies that the realm of necessity remains so in the sense of a realm of alienated labor."[85] Having made this suggestion, Marcuse goes on to suggest that "the development of the productive forces beyond their capitalist organization suggests the possibility of freedom *within* the realm of necessity."[86] In this suggestion Marcuse takes himself to be at variance with Marx's own thinking about activity within the realm of necessity. As against Marcuse's suggestion, it is our suggestion that, in his own vision of full-fledged socialism, Marx envisioned activity within the sphere of material production proper, and thus within the realm of necessity, as unalienated activity.

On this point we can do no better than to refer to some of Marx's own formulations that appear significantly enough in the *Grundrisse*. Let us listen to Marx:

> Really free labour . . . is at the same time damned serious and demands the greatest effort. The labour concerned with material production can only have this character if (1) it is of a social nature, (2) it has a scientific character and at the same time is general work, i.e., if it ceases to be human effort as a definite, trained natural force, gives up its purely

natural, primitive aspects and becomes the activity of a subject controlling all the forces of nature in the production process.[87]

It is also self-evident that immediate labour time [within socialism] cannot remain in its abstract contradiction to free time—as in the bourgeois
economy. . . . Free time—which includes leisure time as well as time for
higher activities—naturally transforms anyone who enjoys it into a different person, and it is this different person who then enters the direct
process of production. The man who is being formed finds discipline in
this process, while for the man who is already formed it is practice, experimental science, materially creative and self-objectifying knowledge,
and he contains within his own head the accumulated wisdom of society.[88]

A close examination of these passages in their surrounding context
clearly suggests that Marx is providing therein a picture of unalienated
activity within the sphere of material production itself—that is, right
within the realm of necessity. But what shall we do then with the
passage quoted from *Capital* in which Marx speaks of the two realms?
Did Marx recant his earlier view? To this suggestion, we remark that
the three volumes of *Capital* cover only part of the ground for which
the *Grundrisse* served as an extended plan.[89] Had Marx lived to complete
his plans beyond *Capital*, we may have seen him taking up an even
more extended analysis of unalienated activity within the production
process. The passage quoted from *Capital* seems to provide the only
significant textual evidence, which might be interpreted as a change of
mind sometime after the period in which the *Grundrisse* was written.
There is no other clear evidence suggesting such a change of mind. And
the passage from *Capital* can be interpreted in a way that does not imply
that activity within the sphere of material production is necessarily
alienated activity. Thus, it is not unwarranted to contend that Marx did
not change his mind about this issue and that under certain conditions
he did envision the possibility of unalienated activity within the sphere
of material production proper.

Before providing an interpretation of the passage from *Capital* along
such lines, it would be well to point out the antidialectical nature of
the interpretation which suggests a sharp bifurcation between alienated
activity within production and unalienated activity outside production.
This is especially important in view of other significant antidialectical
interpretations of other metaphors used by Marx. We speak in particular
of the antidialectical interpretation of the metaphor of the "economic
base" and the "social superstructure." This has led to many interpretations of Marx's thought later recognized to be mistaken. Consider, for
example, the theory of economic determinism. It is true that Marx did
use the metaphor, and his use of such a metaphor was perhaps unfortunate. But in any case, the metaphor of the "economic base" and the

"social superstructure" has already found its proper dialectical interpretation in the wider context of Marx's thought. We suggest further that the metaphor of the "two realms" would find its proper dialectical interpretation if it were seen in the wider context of Marx's work as a whole. For to see it in isolation from this wider context is surely, in most cases, to see it with a nondialectical set of structuring principles. This said, how shall we interpret the passage from *Capital?*

We suggest something like the following. The presupposition of genuine, fully developed freedom is the supersession of economic conscious activity as the predominant mode of activity. Only under this condition can conscious activity first develop in a way that is multidirectional, open-ended, and free from economic constraint. Conscious activity that is free cannot first begin within material production, and this is especially so as long as economic conscious activity is the predominant mode of activity. But this does not mean that the unalienated character of such activity cannot extend back to material production, once having developed (or having begun to develop) outside material production proper.

With the supersession of the predominance of economic conscious activity, and the significant quantitative decrease in time spent in economic conscious activity, a qualitative transformation of the time spent in activity that is specifically economic becomes possible. The development of conscious activity in free time "naturally transforms anyone who enjoys it into a different person." And it is this qualitatively different person who undertakes conscious activity within the sphere of material production. And such activity, for this transformed person, could be activity of an unalienated sort. The development of genuine freedom, and of unalienated activity, begins beyond the sphere of material production. It is sustained through a continued capacity of the developing productive apparatus to meet material needs without the predominance of economic activity. But once taking deep root outside the sphere of economic activity, and once cultivating a transformation of the emotional structures, this development can also radiate through conscious activity undertaken within the realm of necessity. For it is this changed person, with changed emotional structures, who enters into the realm of necessity, and for whom activity within that realm could be unalienated activity. To be sure, the activity of this changed person within the realm of necessity would be activity that served as a means for the provision of the necessaries of life. But it would *also* be activity in which this changed person experienced himself as an agent having control over the productive apparatus. It would be activity affirming other human beings as ends in themselves, and activity experienced as a satisfying self-objectification of human powers.

Surplus Labor and the Reproduction
of the Social Individual

We turn now to another problem deserving some attention in this context. This problem concerns the understanding of surplus labor within the framework of the unalienated mode of production of full-fledged socialism. That there is such a problem should be clear upon investigation of the following passages:

> The essential difference between the various economic forms of society, between, for instance, a society based on slave labour, and one based on wage labour [and presumably one based on the labor of the social individual], lies only in the mode in which this surplus-labour is in each case extracted from the actual producer, the labourer.[90]

> Surplus-labour in general, as labour performed over and above the given requirements, must always remain. In the capitalist as well as in the slave system, etc., it merely assumes an antagonistic form and is supplemented by complete idleness of a stratum of society. A definite quantity of surplus-labour is required as insurance against accidents, and by the necessary and progressive expansion of the process of reproduction. . . . [Capitalism] creates the material means and embryonic conditions, making it possible in a higher form of society to combine this surplus-labour with a greater reduction of time devoted to material labour in general.[91]

Our discussion of this problem is two-pronged. It aims at showing, first, that necessary labor time in socialism (in the sense in which it is contrasted with nonworking time) embraces within itself an element of surplus labor. And it establishes that this element of surplus labor does not serve to negate the supersession of the quantitative predominance of economic conscious activity, which is a feature of the unalienated mode of objectification under analysis in this chapter. Our discussion here serves to clarify the particular manner in which the reduction of necessary labor time toward a minimum in capitalism (understood in its dual meaning) is taken over in socialism as a reduction of working time toward a minimum.

We note again that the working day in capitalism is not coextensive with necessary labor time. It is divided into necessary labor time in which the worker creates value in which he has a share, and surplus labor time in which he creates value in which he has no share. This division of the working day reflects the antagonism between wage-labor and capital. It might be put like this. For part of the working day, the worker is for himself; for another part of the day, the worker is against himself. Moreover, the worker is increasingly against himself as surplus labor time expands with the development of capitalism and as the power of capital over the worker grows out of the worker's own activity.

Since social conditions compel workers to consume most of their active life in economic activity, it will not be stretching things unduly to formulate a sense in which surplus labor time, as well as working time as a whole, is necessary. Thus, just as necessary labor time in capitalism is the working time socially necessary for the reproduction of the worker as worker (i.e., labor power as a commodity), so surplus labor time in capitalism can be considered as the working time socially necessary for the reproduction of the capitalist as capitalist. Thus, working time as a whole in capitalism can be considered as the working time socially necessary for the reproduction of the capitalist relationship on an expanding scale. It is quite clear that the working day as a whole reflects the antagonism between wage-labor and capital. Thus, the length of the working day cannot be understood in abstraction from this antagonism, but is rather concretely based upon it.

Standing in sharp contrast to the situation as it obtains in capitalism is the corresponding situation as it would obtain in socialism. Necessary labor time in socialism—the working time required for the reproduction of the social individual—is coextensive with the length of the working day. It embraces in a nonantagonistic way two complementary aspects, which can be understood as the dialectical transformation of the antagonistic division between necessary and surplus labor time in capitalism. Thus the working time necessary for the reproduction of the social individual embraces (a) the working time necessary for the immediate reproduction of the social individual and (b) surplus labor time (beyond what is required for the immediate reproduction of the social individual) required for the maintenance and development of the productive apparatus, so as to provide for the continuing reproduction of the social individual over the long run, in accordance with a standard of life that is dynamically shaped by the need for an all-around creative development and manifestation of life.

The chief factors that would affect the temporal duration of necessary labor time in socialism would be the continuing development of productivity, the nonantagonistic social relations of socialism, and a standard of life that is dynamically shaped by the need for all-around development. Taken in dynamic conjunction with one another, these factors would operate to reduce *working time* within production to a minimum.

Thus, the duration of working time in socialism would tend to decrease as a result of the continuing development of productivity. This would continue to reduce the time socially necessary for the production of given objects of consumption. The duration of working time would tend to decrease even more significantly because of the shift toward new social relations. The new social relations would block the private appropriation of the surplus product. They would spread the requirement of necessary labor evenly throughout the society as a whole. They would reorient the economy away from the overriding concern with profit, and thus away from the impetus to augment as much as possible the sheer mass of products in which surplus-value is embodied. And the new social relations would counter the tendencies toward production of undurable goods, planned obsolescence, and massive waste.

The standard of life, which would become the traditional standard of life for socialism, would be one shaped by the need for all-around development. It would be a standard that called for the cultivation of an all-around creative manifestation of life—maximization of creative life. As such, it would be a standard of life that would dynamically operate to "economize on labor time" within direct production.[92] It would function so as to reduce to a minimum working time within production in order to extend creatively active time to a maximum for all people. And although the needs of the social individual would undoubtedly develop, this does not mean that such development would be primarily concerned with the acquisition of more and more things. Furthermore, the need for such things as are socially reasonable would itself be mediated by the demand for durable quality products for all people, so that the ongoing replacement of nondurable, low-quality goods does not cost workers their lives.

The "Species Essence" and Free Conscious Activity

Up to this point in our elaboration of an unalienated mode of being, we have dealt with unalienated social relationships and with an unalienated mode of production. We have also had to deal with some aspects of unalienated activity. Now we complete our analysis of an unalienated mode of being by focusing on the "species essence." Then, we draw together the different aspects of unalienated activity already discussed and consider other aspects of unalienated activity not yet explored.

In approaching the concept of the "species essence," it might be well to mention the controversy in the literature concerning the relation between the "early Marx" and the "mature Marx" on the whole matter of alienation. Now, the view that the later Marx dropped the notion of alienation entirely, or that it became unimportant for him, has been refuted elsewhere.[93] But there still seem to be some lingering problems with the concept of the "species essence," especially with respect to the role that this concept might or might not play in the later work of Marx. Perhaps the major issue in this connection is whether or not Marx dropped the concept of the "species essence" in his later work. Whatever the outcome, we must first be clear about the meaning that Marx attaches to the phrase "species essence" in his early works (as well as associated phrases like "species being" and "species life").

As an instrument for providing focus to our discussion, let us point to the view of Ernest Mandel who maintains that, although Marx did not abandon the theory of alienation in his later work, he nonetheless did abandon the concept of the species essence.[94] In his discussion of the *Economic Manuscripts*, Mandel claims that Marx has presented therein two contradictory theories of alienation. On the one hand, "Marx gives a remarkable explanation of alienated labor as the product of a *particular form of society*."[95] But then "[t]he thought diverges and gives us a passage in which the origin of alienated labor is no longer sought in a *specific* form of human society but in *human nature* itself, or more precisely in *nature in general*. . . . There is thus indeed a *contradiction* within the *Economic and Philosophical Manuscripts*."[96] Marx supposedly goes on to resolve this contradiction by "[r]esolutely abandoning the concept of generic man, the 'species being.' . . . [Moreover,] a year later, in *The German Ideology*, he was to blame [Max] Stirner for holding onto it."[97] So far, the view of Mandel.

We go to relevant passages in *The German Ideology* in order to form a clear idea of the view of man which Marx does indeed reject. Having done this, we can return to the *Economic Manuscripts*, and other early texts, to examine passages in which the phrases "species essence" or "species being" occur. Thereupon we shall see that the view of the human being that Marx rejects in *The German Ideology* is quite different from the concept of the "species essence" as it figures in Marx's thought. Further, it will be clear that the contradiction that Mandel has in mind simply does not obtain (or better, that Mandel's contradiction is really based upon a misunderstanding of the "species essence"). Then we shall be in a position to see that the concept of the "species essence" is an essential component of Marx's theory of alienation—for the late as well as the early Marx. Consider then the following passages from *The German Ideology*:

> There is no need for a true socialist, absorbed in his intimacy with "human essence," to know anything about what "may arise from the economic position and the political constellation" of a country.[98]

> The conceptions and ideas of people, separated from actual things, are bound, of course, to have as their basis not actual individuals, but the individual of the philosophical conception, the individual separated from his actuality and existing only in thought, "Man" as such, the notion of man.[99]

> By setting aside this factor [i.e., the need for liberation as actually experienced by real people], "Man" appeared instead of actual individuals, and the striving for a fantastic idea, for freedom as such, for the "freedom of Man" appeared instead of the satisfaction of actual needs.[100]

> [Stirner] constantly foists "Man" on history as the sole *dramatis persona* and believes that "Man" has made history.[101]

The individuals, who are no longer subject to the division of labour, have been conceived by the philosophers as an ideal, under the name "Man." They have conceived the whole process which we have outlined as the evolutionary process of "Man," so that at every historical stage "Man" was substituted for the individuals and shown as the motive force of history. The whole process was thus conceived as a process of the self estrangement of "Man."[102]

Passages such as these can be found throughout the work, and the whole work can be interpreted as an extended rejection of the view of man outlined in the extracts above. In any case, these passages clearly reveal Marx's impatience with any attempt to understand man in abstraction from the world. Marx is here rejecting the notion of "abstract man" or "man in general" who has been separated from the concrete world, or who has been separated from interconnection with the whole of society, or who has been separated from the material conditions that enter into the constitution of actual individuals as individuals of a particular sort. He is also rejecting the projection of modes of consciousness, associated with particular concrete historical material conditions, as the "consciousness of man as such." To be sure, if the view rejected in *The German Ideology* is what Marx meant when he spoke earlier of the "species being" and the "species essence," then Mandel's claim that Marx later rejected the concept of the "species essence" would obviously be correct. But it seems clear that this is not what Marx means by the "species essence" at all. (Before turning to passages that will provide a textual basis for understanding what Marx does mean by the term, we note that, even before the *Economic Manuscripts* were written, Marx was no champion of abstract man—to wit, "man is not an abstract being, squatting outside the world."[103])

In order to form a picture of what Marx does mean by "species essence" and "species being," consider these passages:

Man is a species being.[104]

Man's individual and species life are not *different*.[105]

[W]e must avoid postulating "Society" again as an abstraction *vis-à-vis* the individual. The individual *is the social being*. . . . Man, much as he may therefore be a *particular* individual (and it is precisely his particularity which makes him an individual, and a real *individual* social being), is just as much the *totality*.[106]

[The man, which political democracy regards as man, is] man in his uncivilized and unsocial aspect, in his fortuitous existence and just as he is, corrupted by the entire organization of our society, lost and alienated from himself, oppressed by inhuman relations and elements—in a word, man who is not yet an *actual* species-being.[107]

Only when the actual, individual man has taken back into himself the abstract citizen and in his everyday life, his individual work, and his individual relationships has become a *species-being* . . . only then is human emancipation complete.[108]

The *real*, active orientation of man to himself as a species-being (i.e. as a human being) . . . is only possible by the utilization of all the *powers* he has in himself and which are his as belonging to the *species*—something which in turn is only possible through the cooperative action of all mankind, as the result of history.[109]

The whole character of a species—its species character—is contained in the character of its life activity; and free, conscious activity is man's species character [i.e., species essence].[110]

If we momentarily leave out of account the last section, in which Marx speaks of free conscious activity, there is nothing in the remaining passages requiring, or even suggesting, an interpretation that is anything like the abstract human being whom Marx rejects in *The German Ideology*. The species being that Marx speaks of is rooted in the world and is interconnected with other people. Marx's species being is a concrete species being, not an abstract one. Thus, these passages do not permit the identification of Marx's concrete species being with the "abstract man" of *The German Ideology*. Yet they do point to a distinction in meaning between two different aspects of the concept of species being. One of these aspects is drawn in relation to some concrete context or other, with the particular sort of context left unspecified. The other aspect is drawn in relation to the concrete context of full-fledged socialism. To say that the human being is a species being from the first aspect (at play in the first three of the above passages) is to say that the human being is a social individual who is constituted as a social individual of a given sort, through the particular concrete context within which that individual develops. Whereas to say that the human being is a species being from the second aspect (at play in the next three passages) is to say that the human being can become the fully human social individual who is dynamically associated with the concrete context of socialism. And to say that an individual was a "real" or "actual" species being would be to say that in concrete practice he or she had actually become this fully human social individual. To be sure, the fully realized species being is not rooted in the real material conditions and social relations that obtain when people are lost in alienation. But nonetheless, the fully realized species being is not conceived of by Marx in abstraction from material conditions altogether.

We can work toward a more developed formulation of the concept of the species being if we now bring back into account the passage in which Marx speaks of "free conscious activity" as the "species essence." Having seen that the species being is not the "abstract man in general" of *The German Ideology*, there will be nothing amiss if we take some clues from this work concerning the meaning of "free conscious activity." Therein, "free activity" is referred to as "the creative manifestation of life arising from the free development of all abilities, of the 'whole fellow'."[111] At another point in *The German Ideology* the idealist attempt to construe "free activity" in abstraction from concrete material conditions is rejected out of hand.[112] Taking both clues together it seems clear that what constitutes the "creative manifestation of life" arising from the development of the "whole fellow" must be understood in dynamic interconnection with concrete material conditions, and moreover with the concrete material conditions which are constitutive of socialism. In other words, the very nature of "free conscious activity" is internally related to the projected concrete conditions of socialism—and thus gets its shape from these conditions. For Marx then, the species essence, that is, free conscious activity, is the character which life activity would have in a concrete context within which the human being had become an "actual" species being, that is, the fully human social individual of socialism.

Putting all this together with what has already been said about an unalienated mode of production and unalienated social relationships, we arrive at the following formulation of the concept of the species being. To say that the human being is a species being is to say, first, that the human being is a social individual who is constituted as a social individual of a particular sort, through a totality of particular dialectical relationships with other people and the world at large. It is also to say that human beings *can become* the kind of social individuals who have a totality of dialectical relationships such that (a) they have real community with other people in their everyday life and in their individual relations; (b) their life activity is constituted as a creative manifestation of the whole self, and is experienced as an end in itself; (c) they have dominion over the products into which they have objectified themselves, and have this dominion vis-à-vis a developed productive apparatus that permits the supersession of the predominance of economic conscious activity. And the species essence refers to the particular character that life activity would have for such a concretely established social individual. The activity of this fully realized species being would be activity of an unalienated sort. In other words, the concept of the species essence and the concept of unalienated activity—as these concepts are understood by Marx—are really the same concept.

On the basis of this understanding of the species being and the species essence, it should now be clear that Mandel's claim, to the effect that Marx abandoned the concept of the species being, is simply mistaken. Mandel identifies the species being of the *Economic Manuscripts* with the "abstract man" of *The German Ideology*. But this identification is not made by Marx himself. Marx does indeed drop the terms "species being" and "species essence" from the time of the writing of *The German Ideology* onward.[113] But he never abandons these concepts.

Indeed, these concepts are ingredient to Marx's theory of alienation, which was never abandoned. The fully developed species being is identical with the unalienated fully developed social individual of socialism. And the mode of activity of this unalienated social individual is identical with what Marx meant by the species essence in the *Economic Manuscripts*.

Unalienated versus Alienated Modes of Appropriation

This will all become clearer as we elaborate the meaning of unalienated activity more fully. We can sum up the results of the previous sections as they bear on the meaning of unalienated activity in the following way. Unalienated activity is activity undertaken and experienced as an end in itself. It is activity undertaken in a context within which the supersession of the predominance of economic conscious activity in both its quantitative and qualitative aspects has been established. It is activity concretely affirmative of the social nature of the individual. It is activity which, in concrete practice, recognizes the internal ontological bond between human beings in a positive way. Thus, it is activity that objectifies itself in a way that concretely affirms the unobstructed objectification of the other person, insofar as the activity of the other person is also a concrete affirmation of the social nature of human being. Bearing in mind these cardinal features of unalienated activity, we turn to other aspects of unalienated activity that have not yet been explicitly addressed, or which require more developed treatment.

The next aspect we address is the notion of an unalienated mode of appropriation. The meaning of this can be more clearly understood if it is contrasted to the alienated mode of appropriation, which is associated with the antagonistic social relations of capitalism. Within the framework of capitalism, forces are operative in such a way that the specific activities, capacities, powers, and needs through which individuals objectify themselves are all expressed within the confines of a single mode of appropriation—the mode of appropriation of "having." Referring to "seeing, hearing, smelling, tasting, feeling, thinking, observing, experiencing, wanting, acting, loving," Marx maintains that within capitalism "*[a]ll* these physical and mental senses have therefore—the sheer estrangement of *all* these senses—the sense of *having*."[114] And he indicates that within capitalism, appropriation is understood "merely in the sense of *immediate*, one-sided *gratification*—merely in the sense of *possessing, of having*."[115]

At this juncture, we should note in passing the deep internal connection that obtains between "having" as the single mode of appropriation, and activity as a means. We saw earlier that conscious activity within the framework of capitalism is not experienced as an end in itself. Here, activity is distorted into a means for the realization of some external end (that is, some end that stands in consciousness as external to the activity directed toward the realization of the end). Within capitalism, particular activities, and particular relationships to the world, are undertaken and expressed within the overarching mode of appropriation of "having." And the underlying meaning of all particular activities and relationships is that of "having." Thus, it seems clear that the appropriative activity of "having," in its capitalist form, must also reflect the dichotomy between means and ends. In other words, "having" in its capitalist form appears as a means to an external end. Put in still another way, we might say that "having," in its capitalist form, *appears* as an external relation between a possessing agent and that which is possessed. For in its capitalist form, the appropriative activity of "having" interposes the appearance of an external relation between the human being and the world. In so doing it distorts the awareness of the internal relation which actually obtains between the human being and the world, and more especially the internal relation which obtains between human being and human being.

In capitalism particular activities are undertaken, and particular capacities are expressed, within the overarching appropriative activity of "having." This means that all individual development is the development of "having." But, too, individual development within capitalism is restricted concerning the range of activities that can be undertaken by any given individual within the overarching mode of "having." As Marx makes clear: "If the circumstances in which the individual lives allow him only the one-sided development of a single quality at the expense of all the rest, if they give him the material and time to develop only that one quality, then this individual achieves only a one-sided, crippled development."[116] Forces within capitalism operate so that "each man has a particular, exclusive sphere of activity, which is forced upon him and from which he cannot escape."[117] Thus individual development within capitalism is a confined development in two respects. It is development confined to a narrow range of activities; and it is development confined within the overarching mode of "having."[118] Moreover, a dynamic internal connection exists between these two aspects. Confinement in one respect is reinforced by confinement in the other respect; and confinement in both respects is rooted in the social relations of capitalism. We shall see that unalienated development within the framework of socialism involves the emergence of individual development, both from "having" and from a "narrow range of activities."

Against the background of the alienated mode of appropriation of capitalism, we can now begin to sketch the unalienated mode of appropriation which is constitutive of unalienated activity. We point out, first, that in an unalienated mode of appropriation, "having" is no longer the dominant, let alone the single, mode of appropriation. Some idea of the range of unalienated appropriation can be brought out by the following example (which is modeled very loosely upon a brief description of human production provided by Marx in his early work[119]). Suppose someone makes something for a friend, let us say, a desk. Suppose that the person making the desk enjoys the actual process of making the desk. This very enjoyment would be a mode of appropriation of the desk. After the desk is made, suppose that this person, in looking at the desk, experiences the gratification of recognizing the sensuous objectification of him or herself in the desk that he or she had made. This gratification would also be a mode of appropriation of the desk. But the moment of appropriation of the desk need not stop here. For insofar as this person finds satisfaction in the recognition that the desk has fulfilled the need of the friend who will actually use the desk, so far does the appropriation of the desk continue in this satisfaction, although in a different mode. So here we have three different modes of appropriation of the desk on the part of the person who made the desk, no one of which is a mode of "having." Within the context of unalienated activity, "having" is just one mode of appropriation among others—and is conspicuously *not* the predominant mode of appropriation. An unalienated mode of appropriation is constituted by a manifold of different types of appropriation. In unalienated activity, "[m]an appropriates his total essence in a total manner, that is to say, as a whole man. Each of his *human* relations to the world . . . are in their *objective* orientation or in their *orientation to the object*, the appropriation of that object."[120]

Within the framework of the antagonistic social structures of capitalism, individual development is such that human beings appropriate only part of their essence, and in segmental ways, and as fragmented individuals. In contrast, the unconfined, unfettered development of human beings within the framework of socialism is such that human beings appropriate their total (that is, manifold and many-sided) essence in a total and many-sided way. The manifold, many-sided character of appropriation is conspicuous in a succession of different activities and varied relationships with the world, as they are undertaken over an extended span of time. But even in a given activity undertaken in the present, the manifold and many-sided character of appropriation is apparent.

Within capitalism particular activities are undertaken and expressed within the overarching mode of "having"—that is, within the need-to-have as the overarching need. This renders the development of particular activities into the development of "having"—and it prevents the open-ended development of anything else but "having." In socialism, on the other hand, particular activities are undertaken and expressed within the overarching *need of* a totality of human manifestations of life."[121] This fosters the open-ended development of a number of different particular activities. Appropriation by the whole person in socialism is appropriation in which human beings actively constitute themselves as whole persons, through a manifold and many-sided objectification of themselves in their relationship with the world and other people. Rich appropriation—and through this the "rich human being"—is founded on the rich, many-sided objectification of human powers, through the rich, many-sided appropriation of human reality.[122]

At this point we should dwell briefly upon the specifically human character of appropriation, when appropriation is undertaken in an unalienated mode—for clearly not every manifestation of life is a human manifestation of life. In doing so, we should point out initially that the model of activity that is *human* must be drawn in relation to the fully developed condition of the social nature of human beings. Since the human individual is a social individual, then clearly the determination of the meaning of activity that is *human* must take into account the social nature of the individual. Moreover, it must take into account its fully developed condition. Earlier in this chapter, an exposition of unalienated social relations was presented. It is these unalienated social relations which must figure in the determination of just what constitutes *human* activity. For it is these social relations that reflect the full development of the social nature of the individual. In unalienated appropriation the human being actively constitutes himself as a "totality of human manifestations of life" by way of a multitude of particular modes of objectification undertaken within the framework of nonantagonistic social relations, such that the "*other* person as a person has become for him a need."[123]

Not only must the very meaning of *human* activity be understood in reference to the fully developed social nature of humankind; the human character of unalienated appropriation must also be understood in dynamic interconnection with the many-sided character of unalienated development. For the human factor, and the many-sided factor, of unalienated appropriation are dynamically interconnected with each other. The development of each factor affects, shapes, and is shaped by the development of the other factor. Moreover, these factors are dynamically interconnected, so that the dynamic tendency of one factor is in harmony with the dynamic tendency of the other. The full practical development of many-sided activity requires, and is based on, the full practical development of human activity, and vice versa.

Just consider: Within the antagonistic social structures of capitalism, "having" is the overarching mode of appropriation. This means, among other things, that "having" is the only activity affirmed in an open-ended way. It means that particular activities are affirmed only insofar as they are affirmations of "having." It is in the nature of "having" as the overarching mode of appropriation to project itself as the general form of all activity, and thus to exclude the open-ended development of anything else. If "having" is the only kind of appropriation that is affirmed in an open-ended way, then a many-sided appropriation is dynamically impossible. The whole person simply cannot be affirmed in an open-ended way, in a context within which only one mode of appropriation is affirmed so. In order for the whole person to be affirmed in an open-ended way, it is necessary that many-sidedness be affirmed in an open-ended way.

"Having" precludes the development of the whole person, by precluding the open-ended affirmation of any other kind of appropriation than itself. It also constitutes individuals in their relations with one another as antagonistic centers of one-sided appropriative activity, in which each engages in a one-sided affirmation of himself or herself against the others—that is, one-sided appropriation in which each appropriates for himself or herself only, in competitive antagonism with other people. "Having" as the overarching mode of appropriation generates one-sidedness in all directions. It transforms the activity of the self into one-sided activity, both within the self and between selves.

In this context, also, we indicate that the one-sided development of activity within the antagonistic social structures of capitalism provides the *necessary basis* for the many-sided and human development of activity, within the nonantagonistic structures of socialism. The universal development of the productive forces in capitalism is obviously attended by the development of new needs, capacities, and abilities. It is also attended by a growing variety in the types of activity that are undertaken in the society at large (although this growing variety is not characteristic of most individuals in capitalist society because of division of labor and overspecialization). Moreover, the universal development of the productive forces in capitalism brings people, more and more, into general interconnection with one another through the instrument of exchange value. Only on the basis of the universal development of the productive forces in capitalism can the "universally developed individual" of socialism become a reality.

> Universally developed individuals . . . are the product not of nature but
> of history. The extent and universality of the development of capacities
> which make possible this sort of individuality, presupposes precisely
> production on the basis of exchange value. The universal nature of this

production creates an alienation of the individual from himself and others, but also for the first time the general and universal nature of his relationships and capacities.[124]

To be sure, the concrete realization of individuals who are "universally developed individuals"—that is, the concrete realization of free conscious activity—means a supersession of exploitative private property, and the other social relations of capitalism. But more than this, the social relation of exploitative private property can only be superseded through an activity of individuals, which is concretely developing toward the full realization of free conscious activity. Thus, the degree to which the social relation of exploitative private property is superseded is identical with the degree to which free conscious activity has been concretely realized. "Private property can be abolished only on condition of an all-round development of individuals, because the existing character of intercourse and productive forces is an all-round one, and only individuals that are developing in an all-round fashion can appropriate them, i.e., can turn them into free manifestations of their lives."[125]

There is one further aspect of the concept of a many-sided mode of appropriation which can be suitably addressed in the present context. István Mészáros points out that it would be a mistake to hold that the realization of unalienated activity was simply a matter of "job-diversification." He maintains that what Marx

> was after was not a more extensive collection of hierarchically arranged functions in place of their presently more limited number. For it is simply inconceivable that the individuals could master even a small proportion of activities that characterize contemporary society, let alone all of them. And it is by no means self-evident why the exercise of half a dozen or so functions should be *in itself* inherently more rewarding than that of a smaller number of them.[126]

How are we to respond to this passage? To begin with, we are quite in agreement with Mészáros when he says that Marx did not advocate the development of a more "extensive collection of hierarchically arranged functions." In this context this phrase suggests a principle of ordering in terms of which particular activities are ordered as means to some external end, rather than affirmed in an open-ended way as ends in themselves. An extension of "hierarchically arranged functions," as so understood, can in no way be identified with the concept of a many-sided mode of appropriation at play in Marx's thought. If "job-diversification" means varied activity within the form of "having," such varied activity cannot be construed as a many-sided activity in which a manifold of different modes of objectification are affirmed as ends in themselves. Such varied activity is only a complex manifestation of "having," and not yet a complex manifestation of the whole person. Job-diversification undertaken within the framework of "having," and hierarchically ordered within this framework, is still alienated activity.

But whether, as Mészáros says, it is "inconceivable that the individuals could master even a small proportion of the activities that characterize contemporary society," this would really seem to depend on the complexity and difficulty of the particular activities that might be considered. Perhaps Mészáros has in mind some of the more especially complex activities characteristic of contemporary society, such as the activity of a versatile experimental biochemist or neurophysiologist. Surely, however, there are other much less complex activities. And one might even say that the activity of most people, within the antagonistic social structures of capitalism, is not only uncomplex relative to the activity of a versatile experimental biochemist, but even uncomplex to the point of monotonous routine. Moreover, a mastery of a number of different activities, which taken separately might be relatively uncomplex, might in combination be complex enough to provide ample scope for a many-sided objectification of human powers. (It should be clear, however, that an attempted combination of such activities within the framework of "having" would not be constitutive of unalienated activity.)

This brings us to the last part of the passage from Mészáros upon which we have been commenting. We agree with Mészáros that it is not "self-evident why the exercise of half a dozen or so functions should be in itself inherently more rewarding than that of a smaller number of them." It is also not self-evident that the exercise of one function is in itself inherently more rewarding than that of a larger number of them. In any case, the issue at hand is not really an issue of the diversity of function. The issue is the entirely different one of a diversity of modes of appropriation. Depending on the nature of the particular functions considered, such diversity can be realized within a given function or through a number of different functions.

As we have seen, the structure of unalienated activity is characterized by a manifold of different modes of objectification affirmed in an open-ended way as ends in themselves. In the present context it is important to emphasize that this structure of unalienated activity can be concretely realized in different ways. What is crucial is not whether a given life is job-diversified, but whether it is characterized by a manifold of different modes of objectification affirmed in an open-ended way. A manifold of different modes of objectification can be realized within a given activity undertaken over an extended temporal span, provided the activity as concretely practiced is rich-textured and diverse enough to provide the practical ground for such a manifold of different modes of objectification. But such a manifold can also be concretely realized through a number of diverse activities undertaken over an extended period of time. In either case, it is clear that Marx does regard activity that manifests a manifold of diverse modes of objectification as inherently more rewarding than activity which does not, because only such activity can give rise to the full expression of human powers.

Reason, Sensuousness, and Unalienated Activity

We turn now to another aspect of unalienated activity that concerns the mode of integration of the different mental functions in such activity. With respect to this aspect, Marx himself has not provided anything like a clearly formulated and explicit position, let alone an extended analysis. In spite of this, it seems clear that a presupposition of much of Marx's thinking, as it bears on the issue of unalienated activity, is that the dichotomy between cognition and conation is overcome in unalienated activity. The background against which this presupposition is here singled out is the sharp separation, which is so deeply rooted in our tradition, between the rational faculties on the one side and all the so-called lower faculties on the other—including feeling, desire, emotion, will, and so on. We are suggesting that in Marx's understanding of unalienated activity, the separation of these different faculties that obtains in alienated activity is overcome. Unalienated activity requires a structural transformation of consciousness in which an interpenetration and harmonious integration of these different faculties takes place. In slightly different terms, we might say that unalienated activity is activity in which the dichotomy between reason and sensuousness has been overcome, so that "reason is sensuous and sensuousness rational" (Marcuse).[127]

To substantiate adequately that this presupposition is implicit in what Marx says in connection with unalienated activity would require an extended textual analysis beyond the scope of this work. There are, however, some general points that may provide, we hope, some clear indication that such a suggestion is not without warrant. In the course of these considerations, it will also be seen that an understanding of the mode of integration of the different mental functions in unalienated activity will help to further clarify what it means to speak about appropriation by the whole person.

As indicated earlier, the general form of being-in-the-world is conscious activity that is transformative of the world, as well as formative and transformative of the self. Because such activity is intentional in character, it is obvious that such activity must be activity guided by concepts, for without concepts there can be no intentions. So even alienated activity is concept-laden activity. But by definition, alienated activity as it obtains within the antagonistic social relations of capitalism is not spontaneous, it is not pleasurable, and it does not provide satisfaction of the sensuous aspects of human nature.[128] For example, Marx points out that in alienated work the worker "does not affirm himself but denies himself, does not feel content but unhappy . . . and therefore only feels himself outside his work, and in his work feels outside himself." So "his labor is therefore not voluntary, but coerced," and "so is the worker's activity not his spontaneous activity."[129]

In alienated activity within capitalism, the operative cognitive faculties are not in harmonic integration with the noncognitive, sensuous faculties. Not only are the cognitive faculties alienated from the noncognitive sensuous faculties, and vice versa, but the cognitive faculties that are operative in alienated activity within capitalism are *antisensuous* in character. This will come out more clearly if we look at some aspects of the concept of reason that is embedded within alienated activity in the framework of capitalism—and reflective of it. The aspects in mind have been captured very clearly in Marcuse's formulation of the "logic of domination," or "rationality of domination," which he gives in *Eros and Civilization*.[130]

Whatever the implications of the original Greek conception of Logos as the essence of being, since the canonization of the Aristotelian logic, the term merges with the idea of ordering, classifying, mastering reason. And this idea of reason becomes increasingly antagonistic to those faculties and attitudes which are receptive rather than productive, which tend toward gratification rather than transcendence—which remain strongly committed to the pleasure principle. They appear as the unreasonable and irrational that must be conquered and contained in order to serve the progress of reason.[131]

As the scientific rationality of Western civilization began to bear its full fruit, it became increasingly conscious of its psychical implications. The ego which undertook the rational transformation of the human and natural environment revealed itself as an essentially aggressive, offensive subject, whose thoughts and actions were designed for mastering objects. . . . The struggle begins with the perpetual internal conquest of the "lower" faculties of the individual: his sensuous and appetitive faculties. Their subjugation is, at least since Plato, regarded as a constitutive element of human reason, which is thus in its very function repressive.[132]

The "rationality of domination" is antisensuous as well as nonsensuous. Alienated activity within capitalism is characterized by the "rationality of domination," and by the antagonistic bifurcation of reason and the feeling-sensing-striving dimension of human being. Thus, it seems clear that the supersession of alienation must also involve the supersession of this mode of rationality—and the supersession of the antagonistic bifurcation of the "higher" and "lower" faculties.

A second general consideration, which will provide some warrant for the suggestion that unalienated activity presupposes a structural transformation of the cognitive and conative faculties as they obtain in capitalism, is the theory of historical materialism. This theory provides a framework within which the supersession of this bifurcation can be understood. The theory of historical materialism was worked out by Marx against the background of (and as an alternative to) the view that cognition and abstract reason have primacy in the understanding of human activity. This view has deep roots in our intellectual tradition and can be traced back at least as far as Plato. Moreover, the belief in the primacy of cognition and abstract reason in understanding human activity also has had a long partnership with a dualistic conception of the relation between mind and body.

Diametrically opposed to the primacy of abstract reason and the dualistic conception of the relation between mind and body, the theory of historical materialism bases its understanding of human activity on the primacy of "praxis," that is, on the primacy of conscious-activity-in-the-world. It contends that the conceptual life of man emerges and develops out of his practical activity in the world.[133] If practical activity in the world is taken as primary, and if our conceptual life (our cognitive nature) develops on the basis of our practical activity, then there are grounds for saying that our cognitive nature undergoes change through history. This means that reason must be understood histori-cally. And thus it means that the content of reason is different at different stages in human history.[134]

The suggestion that the concept of reason undergoes development is quite at odds with the traditional view, which sees reason as basically ahistorical and unchanging. But the conflict is resolved, if we consider that any concept of reason when fully unfolded—even the traditional concept of reason—embraces much more than the abstract principles of logic. The extralogical content of any concept of reason embraces, among other things, (a) specific presuppositions in terms of which the world is understood and explained, (b) specific presuppositions about the nature of reality, both human and nonhuman, and (c) specific value presuppositions.

To be sure, such presuppositions are not always made explicitly, let alone given extended analysis and defense. One conspicuous exception, of course, is the case of Kant, who actually did provide extended analysis of most of the presuppositions which, taken together, constitute his concept of reason as a whole. (On the side of theoretical reason these presuppositions include the "Categories of the Understanding" and the "Ideas of Reason"; on the side of practical reason they include the

"Postulates of Practical Reason" and the "Categorical Imperative.") However, one significant presupposition of Kant's concept of reason that is not made explicit by him, but which nonetheless is operative throughout his thought, is his presupposition concerning the ahistorical and unchanging character of reason. Kant projects his view of reason as the view for all humanity and for all time.[135]

Moreover, the presupposition of the ahistorical and unchanging character of reason is not in any way unique to Kant. It runs through the mainstream of Western thinking about reason from as far back as Plato and Aristotle, and even earlier.[136] To be sure, there is much variety among individual Western philosophers with respect to the particular constellation of presuppositions that, taken together, constitute a given philosopher's view of reason. However, despite such variety in the particular constellation of presuppositions adopted by given philosophers in their view of reason, there is much less variety with respect to the subset of presuppositions that make up theoretical reason as opposed to practical reason. In fact, theoretical reason, in some of its chief features, has been fairly constant throughout the mainstream of the Western tradition. This is not surprising considering the predominance of the view throughout the tradition that being is ahistorical—the view that "ultimate reality" does not change. The predominant view of theoretical reason is drawn in relation to the predominant view of being. More than that, the predominant view of being has been lifted right up into the predominant way of understanding reason. Inasmuch as any full-fledged view of reason embraces within itself specific presuppositions about the nature of reality, it is clear that "reason" is metaphysical through and through. A view of reason that regards reason as unchanging reflects within itself metaphysical commitments which see "ultimate reality" as unchanging. The long shadow of Parmenides lies over the mainstream of the tradition in its thinking about being, but *also* in its thinking about reason.

In any case, the theory of historical materialism provides a framework for understanding the supersession of the rationality of domination, and the emergence of a new mode of rationality. For within the framework of the theory of historical materialism, our cognitive life, including the concept of reason operative therein at any phase of human development, develops on the basis of practical activity in the world. And the conceptual array constitutive of alienated reason (whose central core has been summed up above as the rationality of domination) is one which has emerged out of practical activity which is itself alienated. The predominance of the alienated concept of reason, and the alienated mode of rationality, is grounded upon the predominance of an alienated material and social practice. Once it is seen that abstract reason does not have primacy in the understanding of human activity, and that reason is historical and grounded in the primacy of man's material practice, then it becomes possible to envision a changed mode of rationality arising on the basis of a changed material and social practice.

Suppose that the changed material practice was an unalienated material practice, in which people related to one another so as to give sensuous, practical recognition to each other as ends in themselves. Suppose that conscious activity was unforced and spontaneously creative and provided full opportunity for the simultaneous expression of all the different faculties of the mind. Out of such practical activity, what would be the mode of rationality to arise? Although we will attempt nothing like a full analysis, there seems every reason to contend that (on the assumption of the soundness of the theory of historical materialism) a mode of rationality could emerge that would not be repressive of our sensuous nature and would even overcome the split between the cognitive and the noncognitive faculties. Overcoming this split would mean a modification of the structures of both reason and sensuousness, as they generally obtain in the framework of the antagonistic social relations of capitalism. It would mean their harmonious integration into a unitary mode of rational-sensuousness or sensuous-rationality. The dimension of human experience in which the paradigm for such a mode of rationality can be found is the aesthetic dimension. At this point we turn again to Marcuse's work for help.

Although acknowledging the secondary role to which the aesthetic dimension has been consigned within the social structures of capitalism, Marcuse is quick to point out in *Eros and Civilization* that this situation must be understood in dynamic interconnection with the predominance of a mode of rationality that is repressive of the sensuous nature of man. Developing his discussion largely from the aesthetic philosophy of Kant and Johann Christoph Schiller,[137] Marcuse goes on to explore the aesthetic dimension as "a realm which preserves the truth of the senses and reconciles, in the reality of freedom, the 'lower' and the 'higher' faculties of man, sensuousness and intellect, pleasure and reason."[138]

In another work, *An Essay on Liberation*, Marcuse focuses on the central place which the aesthetic sensibility could have in the creation of a new social reality—in which the aesthetic dimension of human experience would no longer be of marginal, secondary importance, but would come into the foreground as a pervasive concern of everyday life and activity in all its various aspects.[139] In a new social reality in which the aesthetic dimension figured pervasively in all aspects of everyday life and activity, the antagonism between reason and sensuousness would have been overcome. (We note here that, while the theoretical roots of this antagonism go back to the Greeks, the concrete practical consequences of this antagonism begin to unfold fully only with the advent of capitalism and the growing intensity of alienation.)

Given the relation between reason and sensuousness within the rationality of domination, it is clear that both reason and sensuousness would have to be transformed if they are to be brought together in mutual harmony in a new mode of rationality. Theoretical reason would have to undergo a transformation from the nondialectical structuring principles at play in the rationality of domination to dialectical structuring principles capable of comprehending reality as process—and capable of comprehending the dynamic interconnections that shape human reality. Sensuousness would undergo a transformation from the repressive and antagonistic domination of the sensuous aspects of the human being to a central concern for the cultivation of their "gratification in an order of freedom" (Marcuse's phrase).

To arrive at a fuller appreciation of the transformation of human sensuousness, which would go hand in hand with the transformation of theoretical and practical reason in a new mode of rationality, we will explore some considerations suggested by the following passage from the *Economic Manuscripts*:

> The *sense* caught up in crude practical need has only a restricted sense.... [T]he senses of the social man are *other* senses than those of the non-social man.... For not only the five senses but also the so called mental senses—the practical senses (will, love, etc.)—in a word, *human sense*—the human nature of the senses—comes to be by virtue of its object, by virtue of *humanized* nature. The *forming* of the five senses is a labor of the entire history of the world down to the present.... Only through the objectively unfolded richness of man's essential being is the richness of subjective *human* sensibility (a musical ear, an eye for beauty of form—in short, *senses* capable of human gratification, senses affirming themselves as essential powers of *man*) either cultivated or brought into being.... The transcendence of private property is therefore the complete *emancipation* of all human senses and qualities, but it is this emancipation precisely because these senses and attributes have become, subjectively and objectively, *human*. The eye has become a *human* eye, just as its *object* has become a social, *human* object—an object made by man for man. The *senses* have therefore become directly in their practice *theoreticians*.... Need or enjoyment have consequently lost their *egotistical* nature, and nature has lost its mere *utility* by use becoming *human* use.[140]

We have already indicated that reason must be understood historically. And we have indicated that the mode of rationality predominant within the antagonistic social structures of capitalism arises from a historically conditioned practice. Running parallel to this notion, the above passage suggests that human sensuousness must also be understood historically. It suggests that the mode of sensuousness that obtains at any given time also arises on the basis of a historically conditioned practice.[141] Human sensuousness gets the particular form it has through the mode of appropriative activity, which characterizes the practice out of which the mode of sensuousness arises. The mode of sensuousness, which arises from the historically conditioned practice associated with the antagonistic social structures of capitalism, is "caught up in crude practical need." It is a mode of sensuousness shaped within the framework of "having" as the overarching mode of appropriation. It is a nonaesthetic mode of sensuousness that is concerned with "mere utility."

At this point, an important distinction between two different aspects of human sensuousness must be drawn, a distinction at which Marx hints when he refers to "not only the five senses but also the so-called mental senses—the practical senses (will, love, etc.)." The two different aspects of human sensuousness can be distinguished, as the sense-perceptive aspect on the one hand, and the conative–libidinal aspect on the other hand.[142] Human sensuousness under both aspects is shaped in a given context by the mode of appropriative activity which obtains in that context. Within the context of the social structures of capitalism, the form that both aspects of human sensuousness take on is shaped by the appropriative activity of "having."

If we focus on the sense-perceptive aspect of sensuousness, we can say that the mode of sense perceptiveness, which is shaped by the kind of appropriative activity predominant in capitalism, is a passive, receptive, nonaesthetic mode of sensuousness. It is a mode of sense perceptiveness whose distinguishing feature is the recognition and discrimination of objects, as objects to be manipulated and used (in the sense of "mere utility"). In such a mode of sense perceptiveness the "cognitive presence" is at a minimum. But even here the cognitive element is not completely absent, because the recognition of something as something requires a cognitive element. Be this as it may, this mode of sense perceptiveness appears in consciousness as passive and receptive. The sensory content appears as simply given without any admixture of cognitive activity. The given is "had."

Shifting attention now to the conative–libidinal aspect of sensuousness, we point out that the conative–libidinal forces as shaped by the appropriative activity of "having" are possessive and tyrannical in their expression vis-à-vis other people. They tend to be "manifested turbulently and forcibly."[143] They are "caught up in crude practical need" and give rise to an enjoyment characterized by its "egotistical nature." And they are confined in their expression to a narrow range of physical and mental zones.

Against the background of this sketch of both aspects of human sensuousness, as they are shaped by "having," we can more clearly understand the transformation of human sensuousness, which would occur on the basis of a manifold of different modes of appropriation affirmed in an open-ended way within the context of full-fledged socialism. Following the suggestion in the above passage, it seems clear that human sensuousness in socialism could be characterized as *aesthetic* and *human* under both aspects.

Consider first the transformed condition of the sense-perceptive aspect of human sensuousness in the context of full-fledged socialism. The following points deserve attention. Here there would be a mode of sense perceptiveness in which the aesthetic dimension of "subjective human sensibility" came fully into prominence, as a pervasive feature of everyday experience. It would be an active, aesthetic mode of sense perceptiveness, in which the cognitive presence was extremely significant—and was felt as such in conscious experience. The senses would have "become directly in their practice theoreticians." It would be a mode of sense perceptiveness that involved the recognition and discrimination of the external world as an objective field, in relation to which "the richness of subjective human sensibility" can be brought into being—and thus as an objective field, in relation to which the social nature of man is concretely mediated through a many-sided human appropriation, which concretely affirms persons as ends in themselves.

Consider next the transformed condition of the conative-libidinal aspect of human sensuousness in socialism. As with sense perceptiveness, the mode in which the conative-libidinal forces are expressed in socialism would be shaped by a human, many-sided mode of appropriation. Here too, the conative-libidinal forces would have "become directly in their practice theoreticians." Thus, they would become human in their practical expression. The concrete practical expression of the conative-libidinal forces would no longer be possessive and tyrannical. Instead, they would be sensuously affirmative of other persons as ends in themselves. Moreover, such conative-libidinal forces would no longer be confined in a one-sided way to a narrow range of physical and mental zones, but would radiate through *all* bodily and mental zones.[144] Corresponding to a many-sided mode of appropriation, there would be a many-sided sensuousness. In their transformed condition, the conative-libidinal forces would no longer be "manifested turbulently and forcibly," but spontaneously, lightly, and naturally. They would give rise to a human many-sided sensuous enjoyment, which would not involve the negation of other people, and which would even find sensuous enjoyment in the human affirmation of other people.

From the foregoing considerations on the transformed condition of human sensuousness in the context of socialism, it should be clear that this transformed condition presupposes the structuring principles of a dialectical reason. The sense-perceptive aspect and the conative-libidinal aspect of human sensuousness would have been informed by dialectical structuring principles so that an order of freedom would obtain. The dichotomy between sensuousness and reason would have been overcome. There would be order, but this order would be a sensuous human order. Reason would have become sensuous—and sensuousness would have become reasonable.

Activity in which whole persons expressed themselves would be *human* activity. It would be activity in which the dichotomy between reason and sensuousness had been overcome by a structural transformation of consciousness. In such activity, individuals would concretely express themselves in the wholeness of their cognitive and noncognitive dimensions. Since such activity is characteristic of artistic activity, all this means that artistic activity is *practically necessary* in dynamically shaping the dialectical interplay between cognition and conation, which is such an important feature of unalienated activity.

6

Freedom-as-Spontaneity

As we turn to the concrete elaboration of the category of freedom-as-spontaneity in this chapter, we recall that human reality, in some respects at least, is not subject to causal determinism—so that a free, or spontaneous, choice is one that is not predetermined to be what it is by antecedent conditions. (We note that our treatment of this category in what follows will be much more schematic than was the case with the other categories of freedom. Full treatment would require a book-length analysis, and that will be a project for a future publication.)

Marx does not explicitly state that the human being has a margin of freedom from causal determinism. Not only that, but it might appear, from Marx's frequent mention of the way in which human activity is conditioned,[1] that his position involves the implicit rejection of the suggestion that there could be any margin of freedom from antecedent causal determinism in human activity. Despite initial appearances, however, it will be our task in this chapter to explain how it is possible within Marx's universe of discourse for human activity to have a margin of freedom from antecedent causal determinism. Since this issue is basically a metaphysical one, a brief word on metaphysics is in order at this point.

We can think of a metaphysical position as constituted by a set of very general but very basic principles in terms of which one interprets, understands, experiences, and explains reality—whether in whole or in part. In one sense, everyone who thinks about reality has some metaphysical position or other, even if the person thinking is not explicitly aware of the particular principles in terms of which that person's understanding and experience of reality are structured. One thinks from a point of view, and a point of view involves a commitment to metaphysical principles—whether this commitment is conscious or unconscious, whether it is acknowledged or unacknowledged. Metaphysics as a special discipline is concerned to bring into full, articulate, conscious awareness the very basic principles in terms of which a given thinker, or a given group of people, structures its understanding of reality.

Marx's thought about human reality—including his thought that bears on the issue of human freedom—is undertaken from a point of view that is quite different from the point of view which has been predominant in Western society. This point of view is constituted, among other things, by a set of basic principles in terms of which Marx himself structures his own understanding and explanation of human social reality. Marx himself does not explicitly deal with these principles in any systematic fashion. But nonetheless they run through his thinking.

A Margin of Freedom from Antecedent
Causal Conditioning

We suggest here that one of the basic general principles running through Marx's thought about human reality is the principle that, even though this reality is indeed subject to antecedent causal conditioning in very definite ways, yet human activity is the activity of natural beings who have some margin of freedom from antecedent causal conditioning. Indeed, this principle is implicit in the category of freedom-as-transcendence—and in the concrete elaboration of this category that was the subject of discussion in Chapters 3 and 4. If it is possible for human beings to transcend or go beyond the ways in which they have made themselves in the past, then perforce there must be some margin of freedom from the ways in which they have made themselves in the past, and therefore some margin of freedom from antecedent causal conditioning.

But we have more direct testimony from Marx concerning the theme of freedom-as-spontaneity in his doctoral dissertation, *The Difference Between the Democritean and Epicurean Philosophy of Nature.* In this work Marx brings out the striking contrast between Democritus and Epicurus concerning their respective philosophies of nature—including the contrast between the inert, solid atoms of Democritus and the dynamic atoms of Epicurus. The pivotal theme is Epicurus' notion of the "declination of the atom"—the famous "swerve" in which Epicurus held the spontaneity of nature to be expressed. Moreover, Marx's open admiration for Epicurus in this work clearly reveals his identification with the metaphysical position that Epicurus adopts concerning the dynamic nature of matter and a dimension of spontaneity immanent in it. And Marx agreed as well with some of the broad implications that Epicurus' metaphysics had for the domain of human action.

Concerning the "declination" and the dimension of spontaneity, we cite Marx's dissertation, wherein he writes: "The declination of the atom from a straight line is in fact not a particular determination appearing accidentally in the Epicurean physics. The law which it expresses runs through the whole Epicurean philosophy." Then, after praising Lucretius as "the only one of all the ancients who understood the Epicurean physics," he goes on to speak of Lucretius' commentary on Epicurus in *De Rerum Natura* in the following way: "Lucretius . . . maintains correctly that the declination breaks through the *fati foedera* [the decrees of fate], and, as he applies this directly to consciousness, it can be said of the atom that declination is that in its breast which can fight back and resist."[2]

This striking formulation points to a dimension of spontaneity in matter that is not subject to antecedent causal conditioning—and that can therefore "break through the decrees of fate." But it also suggests, through the very metaphor Marx uses, that he took the notion of the spontaneity of matter in Epicurus as a model for thinking about spontaneity in the domain of human action—a spontaneity that holds the potential to "break through the decrees of fate" in that domain too. Although Marx never again took up this issue explicitly, there is no indication that he ever abandoned the Epicurean presupposition of a dimension of spontaneity in nature—or in the domain of human events.[3]

So then, having focused on Marx's presupposition of a dimension of spontaneity in *all* domains of nature, and on the special importance that this presupposition has in Marx's understanding of human social development, we set out now to provide a tentative formulation of a metascientific theory of dialectical determination. For it is only in relation to such a theory that Marx's presupposition of a dimension of spontaneity in nature can be adequately understood. The theory of dialectical determination we are to give is partially constituted by an associated dialectical interpretation of the unity of science, which brings out how the spontaneity of nature can be construed in the various scientific domains. Therefore we adopt the strategy of looking first at the classic view of the unity of science. Against its contrasting background we can go on later to explain the dialectical theory.

The Classic View of the Unity of Science

To bring into focus the classic view of the unity of science, we turn to the formulation presented by Paul Oppenheim and Hilary Putnam in their essay, "Unity of Science as a Working Hypothesis."[4] In characterizing the Oppenheim–Putnam view of the unity of science, we shall not deal with the more specific details of their treatment, but look at a number of interconnected aspects of their view that will help to provide a clear sense of the broader conceptual framework of their theory of the unity of science, that is, the framework within which the more specific details of their analysis have been developed.

The Oppenheim–Putnam view of the unity of science construes the unity of science in terms of the reduction of the laws of the different scientific disciplines to the laws of some one of those disciplines. They state that the "Unity of Science . . . is attained to the extent to which the laws of science become reduced to the laws of some one discipline."[5] Moreover, their commitment to a reductive interpretation of the unity of science is followed by their adoption of the principle of causal determinism as a metaphysical principle. They write:

> Let us, as is customary in science, assume causal determinism as a guiding principle; i.e., let us assume that things that appear later in time can be accounted for in terms of things and processes at earlier times. Then, if we find that there was a time when a certain whole did not exist, and that things on a lower level came together to form that whole, it is very natural to suppose that the characteristics of the whole can be causally explained by reference to these earlier events and parts.[6]

From the context, it seems clear that in their classic formulation Oppenheim and Putnam have not only adopted the principle of causal determinism just as a principle of scientific explanation but that they have also extended it to become a metaphysical or metascientific postulate about the fundamental mode of determination that obtains in the nature of things. In other words, the principle of causal determinism—understood in terms of the determination of later events by earlier ones—is implicitly extended by them to have universal validity. All later events, down to their minutest details, are viewed as being completely determined by antecedent events, with no zone of ontological indeterminacy between antecedent events and later ones.

Before turning attention to other features of the Oppenheim–Putnam view of the unity of science, we stress here that there is a deep conceptual interconnection between the adoption of causal determinism as the fundamental mode of determination that obtains in the nature of things and the reductive approach to a theory of the unity of science. Although a reductive approach naturally follows from the adoption of causal determinism as the fundamental mode of determination in the nature of things, we shall see later that a nonreductive approach to the unity of science naturally follows from the adoption of the dialectical conception of determination, which it is our objective to explain in this chapter.

To provide the contrasting background against which we shall develop the dialectical view, we focus now on some other aspects that figure in the broad conceptual framework of the Oppenheim–Putnam view of the unity of science. They order the main branches of science in terms of a number of reductive levels, which, in effect, reflect the differing degrees of organization and integration in the physical objects classified as belonging to the respective levels. They list six reductive levels, namely, elementary particles, atoms, molecules, cells, multicellular living things, and social groups. And they speak of the objects that would be classified as properly belonging to a given level as "wholes which possess a decomposition into proper parts"[7] belonging to the next lower level. In their view nothing seems to be lost in such a decomposition, the whole being merely the sum of its parts.

A corollary of this reductive conception of decomposition is the Oppenheim–Putnam position that there are no emergent phenomena that would be irreducible to laws already in operation prior to the occurrence of so-called emergent phenomena. They write:

> [T]he various successes at synthesizing things of each level out of things on the next lower level . . . constitute an argument against the view that, as objects of a given level combine to form wholes belonging to a higher level, there appear certain new phenomena which are "emergent" in the sense of being forever irreducible to the laws governing the phenomena on the level of the parts.[8]

To complete our brief sketch of the Oppenheim–Putnam view of the unity of science, we indicate their adoption of still another methodological principle characteristic of the nondialectical approach to empirical research that has so far been predominant in the development of the Western scientific tradition. They claim that the reductive theory of the unity of science that they postulate "corresponds methodologically to what might be called the 'Democritean tendency' in science; that is, the pervasive methodological tendency to try, insofar as possible, to explain apparently dissimilar phenomena in terms of qualitatively identical parts and their spatiotemporal relations."[9] We add that the position that Oppenheim and Putnam take on the process of synthesis—and on "wholes which possess a decomposition into proper parts"[10]—really amounts to a transformation of this methodological principle into a metaphysical principle as well.

So far we have distinguished a number of interconnected aspects of the Oppenheim–Putnam formulation of the classic view of the unity of science. We list them as follows: (a) the unity of science understood in terms of the reduction of laws; (b) the adoption of causal determinism as a metaphysical principle; (c) levels of reduction where the wholes of a given level are regarded as reducible to the parts belonging to a lower level; (d) the rejection of irreducible emergent phenomena; and (e) the methodological commitment to the "Democritean tendency" in science.

Now taken together, these aspects constitute an interconnected conceptual whole within the framework of which the details of the Oppenheim–Putnam conception of the reductive unity of science have been worked out. This is not to say that Oppenheim and Putnam explicitly present their view in this way. Indeed they do not. Rather, the interconnected aspects just singled out represent a reconstruction of the logic of the situation as it is presented in their article. Against the contrasting background of the Oppenheim–Putnam formulation of the classic view of the unity of science, we shall posit the dialectical conception of the unity of science.

The Dialectical Conception of the Unity of Science

We abstractly indicate the interconnected aspects of the dialectical conception as follows: (a) the unity of science as understood in terms of nonreductive but lawful connections between relatively autonomous scientific domains; (b) the adoption of a principle of dialectical determination that involves a zone of epistemological *and* ontological indeterminacy; (c) the distinction of a number of irreducible scientific domains; (d) the contention that there are irreducible emergent phenomena; and (e) the adoption of a non-Democritean methodological principle for scientific research of proceeding as if nature were qualitatively infinite.

The first step in the development of a nonreductive theory of the unity of science involves a critical appropriation of the six reductive levels that Oppenheim and Putnam distinguish, that is, elementary particles, atoms, molecules, cells, multicellular living things, and social groups. We can tentatively accept the Oppenheim–Putnam classification of scientific domains without accepting their contention that they constitute reductive levels, such that the characteristics of the wholes on any given level can be fully explained in causal terms by the characteristics of component parts on lower levels.

Thus in our critical appropriation of the six groupings that Oppenheim and Putnam list, we interpret these six groupings as six different ontological domains that can be distinguished in the concrete field of differentiation-in-integration. These ontological domains are characterized by varying degrees of complexity, in the organization and integration of the things in the concrete-real that go toward the constitution of each domain. Moreover, we can readily accept that each more complexly structured ontological domain is dependent upon the existents belonging to less complexly structured ontological domains for the composition of the existents that belong to it. But we quickly add that such dependence does not mean reducibility.

In particular, the existential dependence of one ontological domain upon another does not mean that the laws of the first ontological domain can be reduced to the laws of the other. Nor does it mean that the characteristics of the existents in one ontological domain can be reduced to the characteristics of those existents belonging to a less complexly structured ontological domain that enter into the composition of the existents belonging to the first ontological domain. To be sure, when the notion of the existential dependence of one ontological domain upon another is connected with a commitment to the ontological thesis of causal determinism, then reducibility naturally follows, as it does in the Oppenheim–Putnam view of the unity of science; that is, a reducibility of both laws and characteristics. But it is essential to realize that it is the commitment to causal determinism and not the notion of the existential dependence of one ontological domain upon another that leads in this direction.

This can be more readily seen if we shift focus to the issue of the synthesis of wholes, belonging to a more complexly structured ontological domain, out of existents belonging to a less complexly structured domain. In describing the interconnected conceptual whole within which Oppenheim and Putnam develop their view of the unity of science, we saw that one of its aspects was the rejection of emergent phenomena as irreducible phenomena. Also we saw that the fact of synthesis was construed by them as an argument in support of this position. Here we cite another relevant passage: "Synthesis strongly increases the evidence that the characteristics of the whole in question are causally determined by the characteristics, including spatiotemporal arrangement, of its parts by showing that the object is produced, under controlled laboratory conditions, whenever parts with those characteristics are arranged in that way."[11]

We respond that, only if the process of synthesis is already interpreted in terms of the ontological thesis of causal determinism does it increase the evidence in the direction indicated—and then it is clearly a case of begging the question. The fact that an experimenter first arranges "parts" in the proper way, and that this procedure is followed by the production of a synthetic whole, does not in itself mean that the process of synthesis takes place in accordance with the thesis of causal determinism. Whether this is so or not is contingent upon what takes place among the "parts" themselves. This is not to deny that a legitimate causal law could be formulated in relation to such an experimental situation, that is, at a level of analysis that abstracts from what takes place among the parts themselves, once they have been brought together by the experimenter. To accept the thesis of causal determinism, however, is to go way beyond this. It is to make a theoretical commitment concerning the manner in which the parts combine to form the synthetic whole.

Do the "parts" combine to form a synthetic whole in a way resulting in the generation of characteristics that qualify the synthetic whole, but which cannot themselves be causally explained in terms of the characteristics of the "parts"? Causal determinism clearly rejects this possibility. Instead, it maintains that the mode of combination of the "parts" precludes the generation of such irreducible characteristics in the synthetic whole. With this interpretation of synthesis, as viewed in the context of a commitment to causal determinism, as a contrasting background, how may we interpret synthesis in terms of an ontological commitment to a dialectical mode of determination?

Where the thesis of causal determinism implicitly ruled out dynamic interactions taking place between the substances brought together in the formation of a synthetic whole, a dialectical conception of determination would hold the position that dynamic interactions take place among the substances brought together. It would also hold that these dynamic interactions lead to the formation of a new synthetic whole that has characteristics which cannot be causally explained in terms of the separate substances themselves, and that satisfies laws not reducible to the laws governing the separate substances.

In keeping with the theory of internal relations which was developed in Chapter 2, we postulate that the various substances, which might be brought together with one another to form a synthetic whole, are constituted to be the particular substances they are by internally related energetic interactions occurring below the threshold of determinate human knowledge. Such energetic interactions give rise to broad ontological structures in the concrete field, in terms of which the various substances can be comprehended *as* the particular substances they are. The broad ontological structure of a given substance can be thought of as a dynamic structure in which such a field of internally related energetic forces finds a dynamic balance that accounts for the relatively stable character of the particular substance. Different substances would represent different balanced structures of such internally related energetic forces.

On the basis of such a postulate, we can go on to explain the process of synthesis along the following lines. Suppose a number of different substances, from a given ontological domain, are brought together in a way that forms a synthetic whole belonging to an ontological domain with a more complexly structured mode of integration. We postulate that, as the various substances are brought together, dynamic interactions take place among the substances at a level that is below the threshold of determinate human knowledge. These dynamic interactions modify the balance of interacting forces which had obtained in each of the separate substances—and to that extent modify the ontological structure of each of the separate substances. The disruption of the dynamic balance of each of the separate substances—and the attendant modification in ontological structure brought about by dynamic interactions among the substances when they are brought together in the right way—is then followed by the establishment of the new synthetic whole. The broad ontological structure of the new synthetic whole constitutes a new dynamic balance of internally related energetic interactions occurring below the threshold of determinate human knowledge, but associated with the dialectically integrated substances.

In concluding this brief sketch of a dialectical conception of synthesis, we stress that the postulate of internally related energetic interactions taking place below the threshold of determinate human knowledge carries with it the implication of a zone of epistemological indeterminacy in the knowledge of the concrete–real. Determinate knowledge of the concrete–real requires identification and articulation of the various interconnected factors in terms of which determinate knowledge claims could be rendered. Thus, it should be stressed that our postulate concerning dialectical determination and the associated postulate of a zone of epistemological indeterminacy mean that articulable, determinate factors requisite for determinate knowledge cannot be unambiguously differentiated at the level of the internally related energetic interactions. On the other hand, such a zone of epistemological indeterminacy does not necessarily mean that events occurring below the threshold of determinate human knowledge are unconditioned events. Soon we will take up this issue again. But now we proceed with some considerations concerning the way in which such a dialectical view of synthesis would shape the conception of the relationship between the laws of the different ontological domains.

In view of the foregoing understanding of synthesis rendered in terms of an ontological commitment to dialectical determination as the fundamental mode of determination in the nature of things, it would no longer be conceptually necessary, or even conceptually allowable, to regard the laws of one ontological domain as being reducible to the laws of another. This is so despite the fact that the existents belonging to the first ontological domain were existentially dependent upon the existents belonging to the other.

The emergence of synthetic wholes representing higher levels of integration involves a dialectical synthesis of substances, on lower levels of integration, in which the ontological structures of these substances are modified. Thus, the laws that were drawn in relation to the ontological structures of the separate substances would no longer suffice to explain events in which the new synthetic wholes figured. Rather, new laws, drawn in relation to the new ontological structures of the synthetic wholes, would be required in order to explain events in which they figured. These new laws would be the dominant laws for explaining events in the corresponding ontological domain—and these laws would be irreducible. On the other hand, because of the existential dependence of the existents in one ontological domain on existents in a less complexly structured ontological domain, lawful interconnections *between* the different ontological domains would obtain, even though the laws of one domain were not reducible to the laws of the other. The most conspicuous such laws would be laws of emergence that bridged the various ontological domains.

At this point we suggest a tentative ideal for the unity of science that would be fully consistent with a dialectical interpretation of determination. Focusing first on the issue of unity *within* a given science, we shall say that a unity of laws would obtain in a given science when the laws of that science can be arranged in a dialectical hierarchy, with the more abstract laws of that science constituting a dialectically projected framework within which the more concrete laws of that science are elaborated. In other words, the unity of a given science would be constituted by a dialectical movement undertaken in the conceptual field from more abstract laws to more concrete laws. The dialectical movement would reflect, at different levels of analysis, the ontological structures of the concrete–real corresponding to that science.

With this conception of a unity of laws as construed *within* a given science in mind, how construe the relationship *between* the different sciences from the perspective of a dialectical theory of the unity of science? Corresponding to each of the six ontological domains indicated earlier, we could distinguish six conceptual domains, each of which would represent the province of one of the main branches of science. With the laws in each conceptual domain organized in a dialectical hierarchy through the instrument of a dialectical movement from more abstract to more concrete laws, we could think of the six conceptual domains as parallel dialectical movements undertaken in the conceptual field. These parallel dialectical movements would be relatively autonomous. But each parallel dialectical movement would be interconnected with the next parallel dialectical movement by laws of emergence. Such laws would themselves be arranged in a dialectical hierarchy that reflected, at different levels of analysis, the existential dependence of one ontological domain upon a less complexly integrated ontological domain.

We proceed from the ontological postulate concerning the concrete field of dynamically interacting forces taking place below the threshold of determinate human knowledge, but giving rise to broad ontological structures that do provide a basis for determinate human knowledge. We supplement this hypothesis to bring the dialectical conception of determination more fully into view.

As we have already indicated, this dialectical conception of determination involves the postulate that there is a zone of ontological indeterminacy between antecedent events and present events, such that the present is not completely determined by antecedent events. However, the zone of ontological indeterminacy about which we speak must be clearly differentiated from the indeterminacy principle of Werner Karl Heisenberg if the dialectical conception of determination under development is to be understood. We will approach our objective through a brief consideration of the Heisenberg indeterminacy principle and the position that David Bohm adopts in relation to it in his work, *Causality and Chance in Modern Physics*.[12]

In its most well-known form, the Heisenberg indeterminacy principle maintains that there is a reciprocal relationship between the precision with which the velocity of any microphysical particle can be measured, on the one hand, and the precision with which its position can be measured, on the other.[13] Furthermore, it assigns a definite lower limit to the precision of such reciprocally related measurements.[14] Bohm points out that, on the usual interpretation of the quantum theory, the Heisenberg "principle represents an absolute and final limitation on our ability to define the state of things by means of measurements of any kinds that are now possible or that ever will be possible."[15]

Bohm explains that this has been interpreted as involving a breakdown in causality on the microphysical level. He writes:

[T]he renunciation of causality in the usual interpretation of the quantum theory is not to be regarded as merely the result of our inability to *measure* the precise values of the variables that would enter into the expression of causal laws at the atomic level, but, rather, it should be regarded as a reflection of the fact that no such laws exist.[16]

This means that the precise details of microphysical events are regarded to be uncaused. So that, for example, the precise time of emission of an alpha particle from an individual atomic nucleus in radioactive decay[17] is *completely arbitrary* in the sense that it has no relationship whatever to anything else that exists in the world, or that ever has existed."[18]

In critical reaction to the usual interpretation of the Heisenberg indeterminacy principle, Bohm rejects on methodological grounds (which will be explored later) the projection of the limits to the precision of measurement, which are set by the Heisenberg indeterminacy principle, as absolute limits. And he sets out to develop an alternative interpretation of the quantum theory. His alternative interpretation is based on the hypothesis of a sub-quantum level that contains "hidden variables" which cannot be defined on the quantum level but which could figure in causal laws appropriate to the sub-quantum level.[19] But causal laws on the sub-quantum level could, in turn, lead to the causal laws of the quantum level as approximations.[20]

The detection of "hidden variables" on the sub-quantum level, and the formulation of causal laws in terms of such variables, would "diminish the indeterminacy below the limits set by Heisenberg's principle."[21] We hasten to add, however, that although the thrust of Bohm's analysis is directed toward making a case that it is possible to reduce the epistemological indeterminacy below the level set by Heisenberg's principle, Bohm nowhere suggests that it is possible to eliminate epistemological indeterminacy completely. Bohm is very careful to qualify his alternative interpretation of the quantum theory in the following way: "[I]n our model we have not insisted on a purely causal theory, for we have also utilized the assumption of random fluctuations originating at a deeper level."[22]

Moreover, although Bohm does not explicitly maintain that there is a zone of ontological indeterminacy, his analysis is thoroughly compatible with the postulation of a zone of ontological indeterminacy, as long as it did not imply some specific limit to determinate knowledge of the concrete-real. Of central importance in this connection is the position that Bohm takes on the relationship between causal laws and chance contingencies. His position projects "chance and necessary causal interconnections as two sides of every real natural process."[23] Amidst the endless changes and transformations occurring in nature, scientists discover "relationships that remain effectively constant." And they "interpret this constancy as signifying that such relationships are *necessary*, in the sense that they could not be otherwise, because they are inherent and essential aspects of what things are. The necessary relationships between objects, events, conditions, or other things at a given time and those at later times are then termed *causal laws*. . . . [However,] *the necessity of a causal law is never absolute*"[24] (emphasis added).

Bohm argues that one can properly conceive of a given

> law of nature as necessary only if one abstracts from *contingencies*, representing essentially independent factors which may exist outside the scope of things that can be treated by the laws under consideration, and which do not follow necessarily from anything that may be specified under the context of these laws. Such contingencies lead to *chance*. Hence, we conceive of the necessity of a law of nature as *conditional*, since it applies only to the extent that these contingencies may be neglected.[25]

Thus, in Bohm's view,

> no system of purely determinate law can ever attain a perfect validity. For every such system works only with a finite number of kinds of things,

and thus necessarily leaves out of account an infinity of factors, both in the substructure of the basic entities entering into the system of law in question and in the general environment in which these entities exist. . . . Hence, the determinations of any purely causal theory are always subject to random disturbances, arising from chance fluctuations in entities, existing outside the context treated by the theory in question [e.g., in substructures or in the general environment]. It thus becomes clear why chance is an essential aspect of any real process and why any particular set of causal laws will provide only a partial and one-sided treatment of this process, which has to be corrected by taking chance into account.[26]

We adopt Bohm's position on the relation between causal laws and chance contingencies. (Among other things, Bohm's important work on *Causality and Chance in Modern Physics* clarifies the paradox of the "dialectical unity of necessity and contingency," which hovers in the background of the assertion by Engels that "freedom is the recognition of necessity." See Chapter 5 on this.) Then we take a further step from Bohm's position toward the development of our own formulation concerning a zone of ontological indeterminacy. In taking this step, we recall earlier discussion concerning the concrete universal as the characteristic instrument of analysis in Marx's universe of discourse. The step we take here calls for an interpretation of causal laws in terms of the concrete universal, rather than the abstract universal.

Consider the most concrete causal laws that might be formulated in relation to microphysical reality at any particular time—most concrete in the sense of being cast in terms of the finest specifiable variables in the concrete-real. These most concrete causal laws, when interpreted in terms of the concrete universal, can be seen as abstract structures within the framework of which to understand the internally related energetic interactions taking place in the concrete-real below the threshold of determinate human knowledge. The gap between the most concrete causal laws that might be formulated for microphysical reality at any particular time, and the concrete-real itself, may be narrowed with the actual articulation of still more concrete causal laws (as construed along the lines of Bohm's model for an alternative interpretation of quantum theory). But this gap can never be completely overcome.

Relative to the most concrete causal laws to be formulated for microphysical reality, the internally related energetic interactions taking place in the concrete-real below the threshold of determinate human knowledge would appear as chance fluctuations. But *in themselves* these interactions would be mutually conditioned interactions. The concrete field of microphysical reality can thus be seen as a structured dynamic field that can be known, as it is in itself, insofar as its broad structures are concerned, but which cannot be known, as it is in itself, insofar as all the internally related energetic interactions taking place within the framework of these broad structures are concerned.

The whole mass of internally related energetic interactions taking place below the threshold of determinate human knowledge constitutes and reconstitutes the ontological structures that can be comprehended above the threshold of determinate human knowledge. But these structures must be understood to be dynamically active structures that energetically react back upon the internally related field of energetic interactions taking place below the threshold of determinate human knowledge, so as to circumscribe their broad movements but without completely determining the specific details of their movement. And in addition to dynamic interactions between ontological structures just above the threshold of determinate human knowledge and dynamic activity below this threshold, we also postulate dynamic interactions among the various determinate substances that give rise to still broader ontological structures which, in turn, energetically react back upon the narrower ontological structures on the basis of which they arise, and so on, and so on.[27]

In keeping with this conception of dialectical determination, the state of reality in the present is construed as a function of the accumulated effects of past dynamic interactions—as summed up in the broad ontological structures obtaining at all levels in the concrete-real—*plus* dynamic interactions taking place in the present (below the threshold of determinate human knowledge), whose mutually conditioned activity is not completely determined by the energetic reactions of the broad ontological structures. This would mean a zone of ontological indeterminacy between present events and later events—a degree of freedom from determination by antecedent events. Moreover, on the basis of this conception of dialectical determination, we would expect the degree of freedom from determination by antecedent events to increase, with an increasing complexity in the organization and integration of the existents considered from the various ontological domains, with human reality manifesting the most pronounced degree of freedom.

As we conclude this brief sketch toward a dialectical theory of the unity of science, we single out one last aspect of the conceptual whole within the framework of which this theory could be more concretely elaborated. This aspect is drawn in contrast to the methodological principle, which Oppenheim and Putnam refer to as the "Democritean tendency," in their presentation of a theory for the unity of science. We rely again on Bohm's analysis.

In developing a point of view that goes beyond a mechanistic philosophy[28] (and the methodological principle that Oppenheim and Putnam refer to as the "Democritean tendency" has been ingredient to a mechanistic philosophy), Bohm writes:

Any given set of qualities and properties of matter and categories of laws
that are expressed in terms of these qualities and properties is in general
applicable only within limited contexts, over limited ranges of conditions
and to limited degrees of approximation. . . . [B]eyond the above limita-
tions on the validity of any given theory, the possibility is always open
that there may exist an unlimited variety of additional properties,
qualities, entities, systems, levels, etc., to which apply correspondingly
new kinds of laws of nature.[29]

Thus, while recognizing that "any given domain of phenomena . . . can
be treated in terms of some finite set of qualities and laws,"[30] Bohm
goes on to explain that "any limited number of qualities, properties,
and laws will prove to be inadequate . . . with regard to predictions in
new domains, in new contexts, and to new degrees of approximation."[31]
And therefore, Bohm adopts the methodological principle of proceeding
as if the variety in nature were qualitatively infinite.[32] We shall adopt
the same methodological principle for the dialectical conception of the
unity of science, whose broad lines we set out to delineate.

The Question of a Dialectics of Nature

A major controversy in the current literature bears on the themes under
exploration in this chapter. At the heart of this controversy is the
question of the very possibility of a "dialectics of nature," that is,
whether nonhuman nature can properly be said to be dialectical in its
structure. We define the controversy by citing a position that Alfred
Schmidt takes concerning Engels' attempt, in his famous *Dialectics of
Nature*, to argue the case that nonhuman nature is dialectically structured. Schmidt, a representative of the Frankfurt School, writes in *The
Concept of Nature in Marx*:

> [It] is only the process of knowing nature which can be dialectical, not
> nature itself. Nature for itself is devoid of any negativity. Negativity only
> emerges in nature with the working Subject. A dialectical relation is only
> possible *between* man and nature.[33]

> Engels' attempt to interpret the area of pre- and extra-human nature
> in the sense of a *purely objective* dialectic must in fact lead to that
> incompatibility between the dialectic and materialism which has been
> repeatedly emphasized by a number of critics. If matter is presented as
> being, within itself, dialectically structured, it ceases to be matter in the
> sense required by the exact natural sciences.[34]

In the course of his discussion, Schmidt gives a penetrating analysis
of Marx's conception of nature as it concerns the dialectical relation
between human society and nature, and we agree with the main lines
of that part of his analysis. However, we are thoroughly at odds with

the view Schmidt takes concerning Engels' position and the general theme of dialectics and nonhuman nature. In developing a critique of Schmidt's view, we point first to an important contrast between Marx's *immanent* dialectical critique of the science of "political economy," on the one hand, and Engels' *external* dialectical interpretation of various discoveries made by the natural sciences in his *Dialectics of Nature*, on the other hand. In relation to this contrast Schmidt writes:

> [Engels] interpreted the results of modern natural science, which already lay to hand in a finished form, with the help of dialectical categories. Whereas Marx, in very Hegelian fashion, allowed the dialectically presented science to emerge first from the criticism of its present state, and therefore at no point detached the materialist dialectic from the content of political economy, *Engels' dialectic of nature necessarily remained external to its subject-matter.*[35] (emphasis added)

Now we agree that Engels gave dialectical interpretations of scientific findings "which already lay to hand in finished form." Yet there is a fundamental ambiguity in Schmidt's formulation when he says that "Engels' dialectic of nature necessarily remained external to its subject-matter." Here we must make a distinction between the assertion that Engels' dialectic is external to the theoretical activity of natural scientists (at a given stage in the history of science) and the assertion that Engels' dialectic is external to nature itself. Not only does Schmidt slide over this distinction; but the apparent strength of his ongoing argument against the possibility of a dialectics of nature owes much to this fundamental ambiguity.

If we turn to Robert S. Cohen's superb essay on "Friedrich Engels" in the *Dictionary of Scientific Biography*, we find a much more careful contrast between Marx and Engels on this issue. He writes:

> Marx's dialectic within social nature arose fully from within his critical examination of the social science of his time: economics, political theory, and related social thought; by contrast, while Engels' dialectic accepted that, his writings carried it further, to interpret the theories and empirical findings of the natural sciences. This interpretive process was from without, external to the scientific activities. *Whether* Engels' dialectic was *external* to the object of such scientific investigations—*to nature*—is an *open question* for philosophers and scientists; but it was not posed, nor was it implicitly answered, by Marx. At any rate, nature is dialectical by bringing men into existence, since for Marx human beings were at once forces of nature and social subjects.[36] (emphasis added)

Thus, although Marx did not pose, or implicitly answer, the question whether nature was dialectically structured along the lines of *Engels'* "cosmic dialectic of development," yet Marx's position does presuppose that nature is dialectical in some respects at least. And although Marx's method of explanation does not strictly imply some particular scientific theory about nonhuman nature, we hold that Marx's method of explanation is highly suggestive of possible ways in which a dialectical reconstruction of the sciences of nonhuman nature might be developed. Some of these possibilities were suggested earlier in this chapter, and we will return later to the theme of the heuristic potential that Marx's method of explanation has for science.

But first we examine a methodological confusion on Schmidt's part concerning Engels' use of abstraction. It haunts the entire course of his discussion on Engels in *The Concept of Nature in Marx*. Just as in the case of Marx, so, too, in the case of Engels, there has been a widespread failure to interpret his theoretical formulations in terms of the concrete universal. The result is that many of Engels' interpreters have mistakenly reified many of his abstract formulations concerning nature—especially his abstract formulations concerning matter, as, for example, Engels' statement: "The real unity of the world consists in its materiality."[37] As an example of the methodological confusion we mean, consider the following passage from Schmidt's essay "On the Relation Between History and Nature in Dialectical Materialism." He writes:

> Precisely because he fundamentally accepted the materialist standpoint, Engels had to draw a critical line between himself and vulgarizers of materialism such as Büchner, Vogt, and Moleschott, and he made this distinction by introducing the dialectic into the materialist conception of nature. This raises the question . . . of whether dialectical determinations such as "totality," "contradiction," "productivity," "immanent negation," can in any sense be ascribed to nature when the latter is reduced to abstract matter.[38]

The question of the ascription of "dialectical determinations" to "abstract matter" aside, the clear implication here is the presupposition that Engels did indeed "reduce" matter to "abstract matter." This, however, is a radical distortion of Engels' own position. For whereas it is true that Engels often speaks about matter at a high level of abstraction, he is operating with the concrete universal in such contexts, not the abstract universal. Therefore all his abstract formulations have to be understood in conceptual interconnection with their more concrete elaboration on lower levels of abstraction.[39] However, when Engels' abstract formulations about matter are interpreted in terms of the abstract universal rather than the concrete universal, these detached abstractions become reified, and the result is "abstract matter."

It is also important to stress in this context that Engels' dialectic of nature can be understood only if the concrete universal is taken as a canon of interpretation. For Engels ascribes "dialectical determinations" not to "abstract matter" but to the concrete, ongoing world process of becoming, in all its qualitative diversity, and with all its different levels of structural complexity. This is brought out in R. S. Cohen's essay when he writes:

> Deeply influenced by his grasp of Hegel's logic, Engels saw the essential criterion for understanding nature in a cosmic dialectic of development, from a stellar and galactic universe of physical and chemical evolutionary processes, through the biochemical processes that are the genesis of living matter, to the biological evolution of all life forms, and to the specific historical evolution of the human species, with its particular bodily and mental changes and its social development due to its primary character in labor.[40]

Furthermore, Engels projects the concrete ongoing process of becoming as continuing eternally. And he projects it as manifesting the eternal recurrence[41] of certain broad patterns of development, dissolution, regeneration, and new development—on the various levels of organization of matter (physical, chemical, biological, etc.). Thus Engels cannot be fairly accused of ascribing "dialectical determinations" to "abstract matter."

The Three "Laws" of Dialectics

It is appropriate to examine the way in which Engels approachs the three "laws of dialectics" in the *Dialectics of Nature*, for his approach has inadvertently led to much misunderstanding of his project. Engels lists the "laws" as follows: "The law of the transformation of quantity into quality and *vice versa*. The law of the interpenetration of opposites. The law of the negation of the negation."[42] (A fourth law dealt with by Engels in another context is the "law of spiral development.")

The terminology has itself led to problems. Engels makes no distinction here concerning the term "law" understood as a regulative principle of theoretical reason—"law" understood as a structural pattern in some domain of scientific inquiry—and "law" understood as some specific scientific law (such as the dialectical "law of the tendential fall of the rate of profit" in capitalism). This lack of differentiation has contributed to an interpretation of the three "laws of dialectics," which misconstrues them as having predictive power. On this issue we agree with Bertell Ollman when he says, in *Alienation*, that the "laws which Engels lists as the most important laws of the dialectic are some of the broad patterns in which he and Marx, following upon Hegel, saw change as occurring in the world."[43] In declaring that these "laws" were not projected by Engels as having a predictive purpose, Ollman goes on to say:

To make them applicable to all spheres of reality, the laws of the dialectic were purposely tailored to fit very loosely. They were not meant to offer any details, information true for only certain entities, since this would limit their application to a single realm. These laws are best viewed as a synthesis and reformulation of what Marx and Engels took to be everyone's experience with reality, though people were forever distorting this reality by separating the inseparable.[44]

We agree here, too, but with a difference. While these "laws" may be "best viewed" in this way *to begin with*, there is a significance that these "laws" have for Marx and his conception of theoretical reason that gets lost when these "laws" are not seen in their interconnection. The problem is that, in order to comprehend the way Marx understands these interconnections, one must comprehend his dialectical explanatory movement. We indicated earlier that there has been a general lacuna concerning Marx's mature dialectical method of scientific explanation. (Some of our differences with Ollman concerning Marx's method of "dialectic as presentation" were discussed in Chapter 2.) We go on here to stress that Engels' approach in *Dialectics of Nature* has itself contributed to this gap, by directing attention away from the interconnections that the regulative principles might have with one another. This has inadvertently directed attention away from Marx's method of explanation. At a crucial point in the beginning of his analysis Engels writes:

> We are not concerned here with writing a handbook of dialectics, but only with showing that the dialectical laws are really laws of development of nature, and therefore valid also for theoretical natural science. Hence *we cannot go into the inner interconnection of these laws with one another*.[45] (emphasis added)

Marx, however, *does* go into their interconnection. For in his explanatory movement of dialectical cognition, as it is played out over the course of the three volumes of *Capital*, these "laws," or regulative principles of dialectical reason, are not considered in abstract detachment from the concrete, specific, detailed analysis that Marx provides for each of the various factors he considers, and for their dynamic interconnection. And although there is only very rare explicit mention of these "laws" in *Capital*[46], they permeate the specific analysis over its whole course. Just how they permeate the specific analysis in any given situation is always controlled by the interplay, between the specific detail of the factors under development in a given place, and Marx's instrument of "theoretical reason" (as it obtains in its mature form in the logic of *Capital*).

In Marx's analysis in *Capital*, the three dialectical regulative principles under discussion can be thought of as recurrent "dialectical nodes" of the movement of theoretical reason as it traverses the dialectical explanatory movement from abstract to concrete. To understand the "dialectical nodes" that are brought into focus in any given context of specific interrelated factors, one must always see these factors in interconnection with one another, and in relation to more concrete levels of analysis, on which the increasingly rich interconnection of factors is brought out. In this connection we mention Lenin's caution in his *Philosophical Notebooks*: "The transition of quantity into quality in the abstract-theoretical exposition is so obscure that nothing can be understood."[47] Although directed at Hegel, Lenin's remark applies here too—and also for the other dialectical principles under discussion. Engels' strategy of not explicitly considering these principles in their interconnection in his *Dialectics of Nature* has had the unfortunate result of reinforcing an interpretation of dialectical modes of reasoning that has not cast off the abstract universal as a canon of interpretation. This has led to a reification of many abstract formulations made by both Engels and Marx—as well as to a pervasive and systematic distortion of their dialectical mode of reasoning.

Dialectics of Nature and a World-Mind

Returning to Schmidt now, we look at some further formulations that reveal another fundamental but mistaken presupposition of his argument against Engels. His presupposition is that a dialectical interpretation of nonhuman nature would necessarily imply an ontological commitment to some kind of Hegelian "World-Spirit," or "nature-Subject," or "divine Logos." Schmidt writes:

> [T]he idea of a dialectic of nature working itself out independently of human mental activity and production must necessarily lead to the pantheistic-hylozoic conception of a "nature-Subject" and hence of course to the abandonment of the materialist position.[48]

> [T]here is this essential difference between Engels and Hegel, that the former [*sic*] could not bring these discoveries [i.e., "the empirically reached discoveries of the natural sciences"] to the level of their dialectical "Concept" if he wished to remain strictly scientific, because this would ultimately involve their reduction to the emanations of a divine Logos.[49]

A large part of the problem here is the implicit assumption of a conception of matter from which the dimension of spontaneity has been entirely obliterated[50]—a conception that precludes the emergence of genuine novelty in the development of matter (including the emergence of qualitatively new levels of organization of matter). Although such a conception of matter has often been adopted in the history of philosophy by various adherents of a "divine Logos," immanent or transcendent, nonetheless it is entirely at odds with Engels' dynamic conception of matter.

And just what it might mean to bring "empirically reached discoveries" to the "level of their dialectical 'Concept'" is quite unclear. What is clear, though, is that Schmidt sees Engels' attempt at a dialectical interpretation of various "empirically reached discoveries," in *Dialectics of Nature*, as a fundamentally incoherent project. Such an attempt, on Schmidt's view, is necessarily caught in the predicament of trying to interconnect empirically reached scientific discoveries with a "divine Logos," or "nature–Subject"—a position that cannot be accepted on scientific grounds, since it is insulated against the possibility of scientific refutation. Thus, Schmidt is operating with a notion of dialectics that requires the presence of a mind—cosmic or human, immanent or transcendent—in order for any situation to be a dialectical situation. But this is a distortion of Engels, who, while adopting Hegel's "way of thinking," jettisoned (along with Marx) Hegel's ontological commitment to a "world mind."

It is true that Engels' *Dialectics of Nature* is an external dialectical interpretation of certain "empirically reached discoveries"—that were "givens" for Engels. As such, it is hardly more than fragments and a plan for a dialectics of nature. It is also true that Engels did not successfully integrate these discoveries with his projected metaphysical heuristic of a "cosmic dialectic of development." That is, he did not do this in a way that could scientifically legitimate accepting such a dialectic of development as more than a heuristic instrument. But, granting that it is still an open question whether Engels' "cosmic dialectic of development" is immanent in nature, something that clearly stood in Engels' way was the stage of development of the various natural sciences in his day. After all, Engels did not have the theories of quantum mechanics to draw from, nor Einstein, nor the "synthetic theory of evolution," nor any of the rest. Among other things, we hold that a successful dialectical presentation of any science presupposes that dialectical inquiry has already arrived at a proper understanding of the essential factors for comprehending events in the domain of that science. This condition was not fulfilled for any nonhuman natural science in Engels' day.

Standing against Engels' project, of course, are the currently predominant scientific theories concerning an eventual heat-death of the universe. These theories are in conflict with Engels' projection of an eternally recurrent cosmic dialectic of development. To be sure, such theories may eventually be overthrown in the ongoing development of science. However, even if such theories were to be strongly legitimated as the "praxis" of science evolves, a dialectics of nature developed by using Marx's dialectical method of scientific explanation as a primary heuristic would not on that account be impossible. Here we emphasize the contrast between Marx's method of scientific explanation and Engels' "cosmic dialectic of development." To adopt the first does not commit one to the second.

Yet we see no compelling reason, in the current stage of the evolution of science, for giving up entirely Engels' dialectic as a third-order heuristic for the ongoing dialectic of inquiry in the nonhuman natural sciences. We say "third-order heuristic" here, inasmuch as we project the dialectical, nonreductive theory of the unity of science developed earlier as a second-order heuristic. We stress that, although this second-order heuristic is not strictly implied by Marx's mature scientific method, yet we take it to be a fruitful dialectical extension suggested by it. However, we take Marx's distinctive method of scientific explanation as a first-order heuristic for the ongoing development of science.

The Heuristic Potential of Marx's Method for Science

To bring out the heuristic potential that Marx's thought holds for the evolution of science, let us focus on the theme of scientific revolution in connection with Marx's mature thought. It is our view that Marx has provided the theoretical basis for a "Copernican" revolution in social science. That is, just as the Copernican revolution theoretically displaced the earth as the center around which the sun and planets orbit, so do we hold that Marx has theoretically displaced capitalism as the eternal center around which all human life must necessarily orbit—from now into perpetuity.

To understand Marx's scientific revolution, it is necessary to get at his "disciplinary matrix"—if we may borrow a notion from Thomas Kuhn. In his 1969 Postscript to *The Structure of Scientific Revolutions*, Kuhn explains his concept of a "disciplinary matrix," and he projects it as a clarification of the concept of "paradigm" at play in his main text. This notion is pivotal for Kuhn's analysis, inasmuch as his account of scientific revolution projects a radical shift to a new, or substantially modified "disciplinary matrix" in the course of a scientific revolution.[51]

As major components of the notion of a "disciplinary matrix," Kuhn distinguishes (a) "symbolic generalizations," such as the abstract formulation of Newton's laws; (b) "concrete problem solutions" that serve as "exemplars" of the way in which the symbolic generalizations are to be applied and interpreted in the explanation of given phenomena; (c) "particular models" of explanation and analysis, together with various philosophical presuppositions at play in the theoretical milieu of given scientific theories; and (d) various values that come into play in choosing between competing scientific theories (values such as scope, fruitfulness, consistency, accuracy, and the like).

Now we have many differences with Kuhn concerning the relative importance of economic and social factors in shaping science and its evolution—and differences also with his position on the "incommensurability" of successive scientific theories, and on other important themes. Yet we want to adopt the main lines of his discussion concerning the notion of a "disciplinary matrix" and the central place it has in understanding scientific revolutions. Kuhn himself does not draw from Marx's work to exemplify his analysis of scientific revolution. Nonetheless, for those familiar with it, Kuhn's exposition of the components of a disciplinary matrix can serve as a kind of abstract guide of what to look for in Marx's scientific work in order to appreciate his scientific revolution.

Throughout this work (and especially in Chapters 2, 3, and 4) we have made a concerted effort to bring Marx's "disciplinary matrix" into clear focus. Concerning key "symbolic generalizations" in Marx's disciplinary matrix, we mention especially the general thesis of historical materialism and the abstract formulation of the tendential fall in the rate of profit in capitalism. Throughout the course of Chapters 3 and 4, various "concrete problem solutions" were presented for bringing out the way in which these symbolic generalizations are to be interpreted and applied. As for "particular models" and associated philosophical presuppositions, which stand as constituent features of Marx's disciplinary matrix, we mention Marx's "logic of explanation" (that is, his distinctive dialectical method of scientific explanation, with its dialectically nested explanatory levels), his adoption of the concrete-universal as a canon of interpretation, and the associated commitment to a doctrine of internal relations.

Though all the aspects of Marx's disciplinary matrix mentioned thus far has been given extensive analysis earlier in the text, we have not given very broad attention to the nature of the "values" implicit therein. However, in Chapter 4, we indicated a presupposition of Marx's disciplinary matrix, to the effect that its associated theory of social development must be theoretically strong enough to win consensus as a scientific theory through a process of universalistic discursive justification. And values for judging competing scientific theories such as scope, fruitfulness, and so on are vitally important for Marx's disciplinary matrix.

To accentuate the heuristic potential that Marx's disciplinary matrix has for science in general, we cite Harold Brown's important contribution to the understanding of scientific revolutions, *Perception, Theory, and Commitment: The New Philosophy of Science*, where he writes:

"The most interesting events in the history of science are revolutions: episodes, sometimes lasting decades, which result in the restructuring of the modes of thought of one or more disciplines and in some cases in the relationships between disciplines."[52] Such a process of restructuring in a given discipline is attended, among other things, by an increasingly successful extension of the new theory within the given discipline as more and more "research problems" posed by the theory (whether explicitly or implicitly) are resolved within its framework. This includes, of course, pertinent research problems that defied resolution within the framework of an older theory under challenge (for example, Marx's successful explanation of the tendential fall in the rate of profit—a phenomenon never explained in the theories of the classical economists). But, just how such restructuring within a given discipline might affect relationships between different disciplines depends, of course, on the specific disciplines and theories involved.

In the case of Marx, we have as a constituent feature of his disciplinary matrix a powerful "logic of explanation" which, when made explicit, suggests a fruitful path for a dialectical reconstruction of other scientific disciplines as well as a dialectical reconstruction of the conceptual relationships among the various sciences. Some of the heuristic potential that Marx's disciplinary matrix has for the ongoing evolution of science has been suggested in this chapter. The dialectical theory of the unity of science presented earlier represents a tentative extension of Marx's conception of theoretical reason to new domains of scientific research—and therewith an extension, to those domains, of the explanatory structures constitutive of Marx's mature method of scientific explanation. So far the analysis has been at a metascientific level. Successful future attempts to achieve a dialectical reconstruction of some other scientific discipline, or disciplines, using Marx's mature method of scientific explanation as the instrument for making the reconstruction, would be dramatic actualization of this heuristic potential.[53]

Dialectical Determinism and
Freedom-as-Transcendence

Having discussed a dialectics of nature and the heuristic potential of Marx's method of explanation, we return to the dialectical conception of determination that was presented. The explanation of this conception has been the primary objective in this chapter. Our strategy was to explain it in relation to a dialectical, nonreductive theory of the unity of science, whose interconnected aspects served to bring it into focus.

The dialectical conception of determination we developed postulates a margin of freedom from antecedent causal conditioning. The margin of such freedom increases from less complexly to more complexly structured ontological domains. And the domain of human events (of all the presently known domains) has the widest margin of freedom from antecedent causal conditioning. When seen in relation to the dialectical theory of the unity of science developed earlier, this conception of determination provides a metascientific perspective for comprehending a possible transition from a given mode of being-in-the-world to a qualitatively different mode.

The ontological structures constitutive of a given mode of being-in-the-world, or of different but complementary modes of being-in-the-world that dynamically shape each other, arise on the basis of a whole mass of particular activities, undertaken on particular occasions, by particular individuals. These structures circumscribe the broad lines of the individuals' activity in the present, as well as the broad lines of their consciousness, but without completely determining the concrete details of their ongoing activity in the present, or the concrete details of their conscious experience. This is all due to the margin of freedom from antecedent causal conditioning which such events have.

Whether the ongoing development of the concrete-real will be such that the contingent aspect of activity undertaken in the present will continue, in its mass effect, to reinforce the given mode of being-in-the-world is not predetermined by antecedent causal factors. Similarly, whether the contingent aspect of such activity will lead, in its mass effect, to the development of qualitatively different modes of being-in-the-world is also not predetermined by antecedent causal factors. But there are some critical conditions whose fulfillment would dramatically increase the probability of the contingent aspect of activity undertaken in the present leading, in its mass effect, to a qualitatively different mode of being.

One of them is the condition that concrete life, as lived in the present in terms of a given mode of being-in-the-world, fails to satisfy basic existential needs. Another condition is that this experience be accompanied by the awareness of the possibility of an alternate mode of being-in-the-world that would be more viable in addressing existential (and other human) needs. Moreover, to the extent that the contingent aspect of activity undertaken in the present would be self-consciously guided by knowledge of Marx's conception of "positive freedom," as well as by knowledge of the laws of social development he disclosed, the probability of the development of a genuine socialist mode of being-in-the-world would also dramatically increase. Thus, taking a retrospective glance back to earlier discussion, we can agree with Engels that the realization of "positive freedom" is indeed founded on genuine "knowledge of necessity."[54] But, of course, necessity must here be interpreted dialectically—and thus in a way that makes room for contingency.

7

Postscript to the Second Edition

In developing the exposition and argument laid out in the foregoing chapters, I was concerned at every point with methodological issues. For it was my intent to present a philosophical reconstruction of Marx that was fully in keeping with Marx's dialectical method of explanation—a method that employs an explanatory process moving from more abstract levels to more and more concrete levels. My long years of study and reflection on and about Marx's thought have convinced me that a clear comprehension of Marx's dialectical method of explanation is of immense importance not only for understanding Marx himself, but also for the ongoing development of the social and natural sciences. After all it is a method of explanation that is oriented toward comprehension of the structural dynamics of changing historical and natural processes.

Moreover, in developing the postscript that follows I am also concerned with methodological issues at every point; for once again I make my presentation in a way that is fully in keeping with Marx's method of dialectical explanation. In fact I indicate that this postscript is itself a sort of dialectical explanatory movement from abstract levels to more concrete ones. As in everything that has come before, so here too my primary concern is the philosophical problem of freedom as comprehended from a humanistic Marxist perspective. But in the present context I take up an issue that the exigencies of time did not allow me to address as fully as I had wished in the first edition of this book. I have in mind the issue of a potential revolutionizing agency in the contemporary era. It seems to me, and others as well, that the threats to human freedom in all its various meanings are more ominous now than when the first edition of this book came out. Thus it is all the more fitting to carry through with the philosophical case for a potential revolutionizing agency that could cultivate a more humane stage of cultural evolution at this juncture in world history.

In carrying through with such an enterprise I have found it necessary to focus on the spiritual dimension, and to explain how this dimension can be comprehended from within a humanistic Marxist perspective. This in turn requires a careful integration of the spiritual dimension as presented below into Marx's theory of historical materialism—that is, his theory of human cultural evolution. In the main chapters of this work I believe I have made the philosophical case that Marx's theory of historical materialism can only be properly comprehended when it is seen in relation to a level-by-level explanatory process moving from the more abstract to the more concrete. In this postscript I go on to show how an understanding of the spiritual dimension can be fully integrated into Marx's theory of historical materialism; and once again this exposition and argument centrally involves the notion of a level-by-level explanatory process moving from abstract to concrete.

In part 1 I begin my case via a series of encounters with some published critical reviews of the first edition. These encounters will help to clarify the method of dialectical explanation at play throughout my main text and the new introduction, and throughout this postscript as well. Then in part 2 I proceed, using this dialectical explanatory method, to an exposition of the spiritual dimension that is fully consistent with Marx's philosophical/social-scientific paradigm; and that also serves to establish the philosophical case for a potential revolutionizing agency.

Part 1: Response to Critics

All of the particular published reviews that I focus on below contain many positive and encouraging remarks about the interpretation of Marx that I presented; moreover, all of them project developed and deeply probing critical comments as well. I am very grateful to the various reviewers for the careful attention they gave to my work, and for the seriousness with which they grappled with it. While I very much appreciate their positive comments, I believe it will be much more fruitful for my new readers if I confine myself to addressing their critical comments. For it seems to me that many of my new readers are quite likely to be concerned with many of the very same issues and problems as were brought up by these reviewers. Hopefully the responses I give to their comments in what follows will clarify a number of issues. In the course of carrying things out I will give excerpts from each of the reviews—excerpts that I believe bring out their most significant and challenging critical comments. Then I will respond in a brief but focused way to each set of comments.

1) The first critical remarks I want to address come from Chris Sciabarra, who writes:

> Brien's interpretation of Marx's project suggests inadvertently that communism is fundamentally dependent upon a grandiose epistemological achievement. Marx posits an historically emergent cognitive efficacy which boggles the human mind. On the one level Marx's speculations about man's future imply that he has a synoptic grasp of the movement of history. It is not entirely clear how Marx has access to the inevitable triumph of human efficacy which is central to the achievement of communism.
>
> F. A. Hayek and Michael Polanyi have suggested that a synoptic grasp of the whole is epistemologically impossible. Indeed the idealist belief in the possibility of an exhaustive comprehension of the whole and its internal relations is the hallmark of utopian thinking. . . . Hayek correctly views utopian blueprints for social change as resting on what he describes as a "synoptic delusion." A "synoptic delusion" represents a false belief that one can consciously design a new society as if one had possession of holistic knowledge. . . . Marx does not accept the Hayekian-Polanyian thesis which places strictures on man's cognitive capacity. For Marx these strictures are themselves historically specific to pre-communist social formations.
>
> While Brien's book emphasizes the important links between reason and freedom, it does not adequately question the actualizable potential of Marx's epistemological transcendence. If, indeed, the strictures on human knowledge are *ontological*, rather than historical, then Marx's project may be leading many genuine radicals toward an inherently unreachable, utopian goal.[1]

In responding to these remarks let me first pose the following question. Why can one not consistently accept that there may be *some* significant ontological strictures on human cognitive capacities, while also holding that *other* strictures on cognitive capacities are historically conditioned? Marx certainly does not hold that human knowledge is infallible, or ever could be infallible. Rather human knowledge of the natural world, and of the various social worlds, is *always* conditional knowledge of the conditioned for Marx. Also, such knowledge is always limited; and exhaustive human knowledge of the natural and social worlds would be impossible in any situation. However, just because it is impossible to explain *everything* exhaustively about various natural or social wholes, does not preclude the possibilities of explaining some significant structural features of those natural or social wholes. I ask my readers to recall my efforts throughout this book to elucidate Marx's understanding of the dynamic tendencies of the capitalist social formation that he projects in *Capital*, and the dynamic tendencies of social evolution that he projects in the theory of historical materialism. The projection of such tendencies is the projection of empirically grounded theories that attempt to capture the *broad structural dynamics* of the capitalist social formation, and of social evolution. They aim at a *kind* of holistic or synoptic understanding of these domains. But they are not "holistic" or "synoptic" in the way Hayek interprets these terms. There is no pretense on Marx's part to have exhaustive knowledge of any social formation, or of the dynamics of social evolution—but only partial, limited, fallible, and empirically grounded knowledge of some of the broad structural features of social wholes, and of the dynamic transition from one kind of social whole to another.

Nor does Marx hold that human knowledge could ever be without some sort of contextual limits. However, he would not agree that the contextual limits on human knowledge that might generally hold in *one* kind of social domain (e.g., a capitalist social world) must hold in *all* possible social domains. Nor would he agree that the contextual limits on human knowledge that might obtain in one social domain are equally viable epistemologically as those that might obtain in another social domain (e.g., a humanistic-socialist world). To be sure, a fully developed historical materialist epistemology, that could unequivocally justify a claim that Marx's philosophical/scientific paradigm is epistemologically more worthy than other currently dominant social scientific paradigms, has yet to be worked out. The main point here, though, is that Marx himself does not pretend to have carried out the kind of "grandiose epistemological achievement" my reviewer is concerned about. Quite unfortunately though, there have been many deluded, dogmatic, and totalitarian followers of Marx who, having been caught up in the kind of "synoptic delusion" Hayek warns us about, believed they knew the absolute, complete, and certain truth about social wholes. But not Marx!

2) I turn now to some critical comments from Marilyn Nissim-Sabat. She remarks:

> Another problem is Brien's struggle to do justice to Marx's conception of the relation between subjectivity and nature while at the same time repudiating metaphysical materialism and subjective idealism. But if Marxist ontology is neither of these, nor an ahistorical Kantianism, nor an Hegelian objective idealism, nor a Heideggerian-phenomenological one, what kind of ontology is it? Unless this question is answered, Marx cannot be shown to have been the "philosopher-scientist" to whom Brien dedicated his book.[2]

In engaging my reviewer's concern here, let me first stress that the ontology at play in Marx's thought is one that recognizes that the natural world exists prior to human beings and independently of them for the most part. It is an ontology that construes human beings as biological organisms existing in a natural world before they come to be anything else at all— natural beings interacting within and upon a natural environment, which is constantly undergoing change of various sorts. Thus it is a *naturalist* ontology. It is simultaneously an ontology that recognizes that human beings have the capacity for self awareness, and also that they come to have a subjectivity which is not only historically conditioned, but which changes in accordance with changes in the specific modes of interaction between human beings and their changing social and natural environment. So also it is an ontology that fully recognizes the *historicity of human subjectivity*. Moreover, it is a *dialectical* ontology—and this by virtue of the specific character of the complex dynamic interplay between human beings and their environment as they simultaneously shape their environment and themselves over the course of history; and by virtue of the emergence of new social formations and new modes of consciousness out of the developing tensions and contradictions in earlier ones; and for many other reasons. Furthermore, it is a dialectical *materialist* ontology—and therefore *not* the kind of mechanistic and reductionist materialism that had been characteristic of the main-stream philosophical tradition and of Newtonian science.

Recall the argument that I gave in Chapter 6 in support of a "dialectics of nature" that would be compatible with Marx's own dialectical method of explanation; and recall, too, that working this out involved a critical appropriation of Engels' views. But a Marxist humanist living on the threshold of the twenty-first century can legitimately subscribe to an even more dialectical view of matter than was feasible in the time of Marx and Engels. Among other things the contemporary scientific view of matter is shaped by the development of relativity theory, quantum mechanics, theories concerning the evolution of stars, the synthetic theory of evolution, etc. Thus on the threshold of the twenty-first century a Marxist humanist can legitimately construe matter as being dynamic through and through at every level, from subatomic to galactic; and as being even *more* dialectical in character than the earlier view of matter. A Marxist humanist can well speak of the dialectical interplay between matter and energy in the super-hot interiors of burning stars, say, and in nature at large; of the dialectical emergence of new natural forms out of the recon-figuration of the dynamic energies of less complex forms; of the dialectical emer-gence of life out of prelife forms; of the dialectical emergence of consciousness itself, as well; and of the intricate dialectical interplay between the mental and phys-ical dimensions of those amazing biological organisms we human beings are. All of this, and more, is what I understand a dialectical *materialist* ontology to be.

3) The next set of critical comments comes from Daniel Little, who writes:

> Brien tries too hard for theoretical unity within Marx's corpus. As a result, he is led to treat all of Marx's important writings as deriving from a single well-worked-out philosophical theory or world view, and he eventually constructs a philosophical reading of Marx's later writings that slights their empirical scientific achievements. . . . [T]he Hegelian dialectical reasoner that we find in Brien's reading of Marx is some distance from the flexible, theoretically innovative and empirically sensitive investigator we find in *Capital*. . . . He places a version of dialectical method at the center of Marx's science. And he maintains . . . that Marx's social ontology depends essentially on the concept of internal relations. Neither thesis is convincing however.

> Brien reconstructs Marx's conception of scientific explanation as "dialectical"; but he summarizes it as a combination of covering-law and genetic explanations. This is a plausible view of Marx's explanatory practice but it is difficult to see why this should be described as a "dialectical" model of explanation. . . . My chief objection to the argument as a whole is its tendency to reconstruct Marx as a philosopher rather than an empirical social scientist. This is a reconstruction that will appeal to many readers; but it is one that detracts from the substance of Marx's contribution

to our understanding of the workings of the capitalist system—not as a philosophical construct—but as a contingent system of historically specific structures that can only be known through detailed empirical investigation.[3]

When I first saw a prepublication draft of these comments, I would have been quite puzzled by them were it not for the fact that I had already become familiar with Daniel Little's important work, *The Scientific Marx*.[4] In developing his case for Marx being a traditional sort of empirical social scientist, he attempts in this work to completely dissociate Marx from dialectical method and dialectical thinking. In Little's view dialectical method is explicitly and exclusively identified with Hegel's *a priori* speculative form of it.[5] Thus any recognition of Marx's method as being dialectical *in any way* must inevitably contaminate him as an empirical social scientist. While I fully agree that Marx is an empirical social scientist, I hold that he is *not* a traditional social scientist but rather a *dialectical empirical* social scientist.

Marx's kind of social science does not float on some kind of positivist raft. Rather it is deeply embedded in a nontraditional background of philosophical commitments and presuppositions, canons of interpretation, and methodological tools—a background that must inform all the foreground concepts and empirical findings of his scientific thought. I believe we cannot fully understand Marx the social scientist, unless we become aware of the nontraditional background of his thought. In fact I hold we are bound to distort it in radical ways if we do not understand how his scientific thought is interconnected with his philosophical thought. While Little's book has done very much to bring out various dimensions of Marx's social scientific thought, I believe that, by sloughing off his dialectical method the way Little has, it has obscured and even undermined full recognition of the explanatory power of Marx's scientific thought. Moreover, I believe it has deepened the wedge that separates the philosophical and scientific dimensions of Marx's thought. Even so, with a little adjustment, much of what Little presents can be conceptually integrated within the dialectical empirical method of explanation I have presented.

In his book, Little dialogues with various figures in the tradition of analytical Marxism as he develops his own interpretation of Marx's method of explanation in *Capital*. He presents a convincing critique of various views of macro-explanation such as "functional" and "collective interest" models of explanation—both of which have been hot subjects of debate within that tradition. Drawing from others in the analytical Marxist tradition, he argues that both forms of macro-explanation are inadequate. Against any claim for the sufficiency of functional explanation, he argues that "it is necessary to provide a detailed account of the micropathways by which the needs of the economy, or the interests of a powerful class, are imposed on other social phenomena so as to elicit beneficial consequences."[6] In relation to collective-interest macro-explanations, he argues it is "necessary to provide a microanalysis of the motives, interests, and incentives that cause individuals of the group to act, as well as an account of the various ways in which collective interests both shape and are frustrated by individual interests."[7]

Little then proceeds to advance his own "logic of institutions" model of explanation. He explains:

> Here . . . is the model of explanation that appears to be at work in *Capital*. The capitalist economy is defined by a set of social relations of production (property relations). These relations determine relatively clear circumstances of choice for the various representative actors (the capitalist, the worker, the financier). These circumstances are both motivational and conditioning. They establish each party's interests, they determine the means available to each, and the constraints on action that limit choice. The problem confronting Marx is this: to demonstrate, for a given characteristic of the capitalist mode of production (e.g., the falling rate of profit), that this characteristic follows from Marx's account of the defining institutions of capitalism through reasoning about rational behavior within the circumstances of choice they define. . . . We can describe explanations of this sort as being based on a "logic of institutions" that is created by rational individuals pursuing independent ends under structured conditions of choice.[8]

I am in full agreement with Little's nice critique of the inadequacy of functional and collective-interest macro-explanations. Also his projection of a "logic of institutions" model of explanation is promising. However, I go on to suggest that all three of these types of explanation, when applied to Marx's analysis in *Capital*, can be integrated into the dialectical method of explanation I have presented. Little's "logic of institutions" model, in particular, can be readily encompassed within the dialectical empirical model of explanation. (Soon I return to this issue.) But to recognize this, one first has to see that Marx's method of explanation in *Capital* really is a dialectical method; and this in turn requires a recognition that Marx is indeed working with a notion of internal relations as a basic canon of interpretation.

Concerning my projection of internal relations and dialectical method as being central to Marx's scientific thought, though, my reviewer holds that "[n]either thesis is convincing." To me this really means that, along with others in the analytical Marxist tradition, Little has implicitly adopted a notion of *external relations* as a canon of interpretation for his analysis—a notion that is not conceptually compatible with *any* form of dialectical method. There are serious implications of all this, in my view. Among them are (a) the radical severance of the philosophical and scientific dimensions of Marx's thought, and a consequent distortion of both dimensions; (b) the abandonment of historical materialism as a theory of cultural evolution—at least in the case of Little[9]; and (c) an interpretation of Marx's explanations in *Capital* that sees them as a bundle of disparate, *externally related* explanations that are projected at various levels but without being theoretically unified.

Before returning to the "logic of institutions" model of explanation, let me first try to bring out why I take dialectical method and internal relations to be central to Marx's scientific thought. First, why is Marx's method of explanation specifically a *dialectical* method? Well, primarily because its aim is to bring out the structural dynamics of a complicated developing process that goes through a series of phases.

In such a process any given phase: (a) comes to be what it is out of the dynamic tensions, conflicts, contradictions, and oppositions of an earlier phase; then (b) goes on to attain a kind of dynamic equilibrium; and (c) eventually gives rise to the emergence of later phases out of its own developing oppositions and contradictions. As Marx puts it in a preface to *Capital*:

> [I adopt the "rational form" of dialectical method, because it] includes in its comprehension and affirmative recognition of the existing state of things, at the same time also, the recognition of the negation of that state, of its inevitable breaking up; because it regards every historically developed social form as in fluid movement, and therefore takes into account its transient nature not less than its momentary existence.[10]

Second, why are internal relations central to Marx's scientific thought? The short answer is that all of the main explanatory factors that Marx brings into his scientific analysis of the capitalist system are *social relations* of one sort or another— whether it be those social relations that are necessary for bringing out the structural dynamics of the capitalist production process, or of its circulation process, or of the dynamics of the capitalist system as a whole. Each of the social relations that Marx considers is understood by him to be that sort of social relation whose very nature is constituted to be what it is by virtue of the dynamic interconnections it has with other social relations. Such social relations do not simply stand side by side with one another in an externally related way, like two people shaking hands; rather, they are internally related to one another. The specific nature of each social relation is what it is by virtue of its interrelations with other social relations.

So, then, we have dialectical method and internal relations at the center of Marx's scientific thought. The configurations of internally related social relations whose structural dynamics Marx is trying to help us comprehend are very complicated, many faceted, and in continual flux. To help us understand them he employs a sophisticated explanatory strategy of providing a series of successive approximations, with partial views, followed by more and more complete views projected at various levels of analysis, all of which are theoretically integrated with a view toward gradually bringing out the big picture. Thus as the explanatory movement continues, more and more complicating factors are introduced into the analysis at successive levels on the basis of previous empirical research. Each successive level is elaborated within the projected conceptual matrix of the more abstract level. A given phenomenon is explained by elaborating the explanatory web fully enough so as to show how that phenomenon dynamically emerges out of the concrete dynamic processes that have been disclosed via the conceptual elaboration of the dialectically nested levels of analysis.

At this juncture, let me return to Little's "logic of institutions" model of explanation to indicate how it can be critically encompassed within the dialectical empirical method of explanation I have presented. Focus on part of the passage from *The Scientific Marx* that I cited above: "The capitalist economy is defined by a set of social relations of production. . . . The problem confronting Marx is this: to demonstrate, for a given characteristic of the capitalist mode of production . . . that this characteristic follows from Marx's account of the defining institutions of capitalism through reasoning about rational behavior within the circumstances of choice they define." Remember that Little does not see Marx's method of explanation as a dialectical method, nor does he see Marx's social relations as internally related to one another, and by implication he does not accept the notion of the concrete universal.[11] However, in order to appreciate how the "logic of institutions" model can be encompassed by Marx's method as I present it, all three of these *nontraditional canons of interpretation* have to be brought into play with one another.

Marx begins the explanatory movement of *Capital* at a very high level of abstraction with a focus on the commodity, and then continues to develop his explanatory movement in a level-by-level mode. As he does so he systematically brings into play all the essential social relations for comprehending the production process of capitalism: factors such as wage labor, value, necessary labor time, surplus value, and the like. The explanatory factors distinguished at each level are conceptually interwoven with each other at that level, and each level as a projected whole comes to be interwoven with the succeeding levels as Marx's explanation of the process of production proceeds. *Embedded* in this interweave, and *required for* its development, are the nontraditional canons of interpretation I indicated. At each level the explanatory factors are internally related to one another; and each level in turn is intentionally oriented by Marx as a structured matrix toward more concrete levels in the explanatory movement as additional complicating factors are introduced. In effect each level implicitly calls out for its more concrete elaboration. For this is a large part of what thinking in terms of the concrete universal involves.

Quite importantly, each level is intentionally oriented toward that *most concrete* level whereon the micro-processes of capitalist production are disclosed. This is the level that reflects the activity of the characteristic individuals belonging to the various groups involved in the capitalist production process. But these groups are quite different with respect to their access to resources, their possibilities of action, their scope of effective choice, their needs, their interests, what they get from the system, etc. Nonetheless the individuals of each group interrelate among themselves and with individuals in other groups in accordance with these differences. As the explanatory movement approaches this most concrete level, it becomes more and more apparent that the complex activities of all the various individuals in the various groups who interrelate among themselves in varying ways actually *constitute the concrete microprocesses* of capitalist production. These microprocesses in their totality give rise to the dynamic structures of the capitalist production process. Thus each macro-explanation concerning the structural dynamics of the capitalist production process, and each macrostructure of it, is intentionally oriented by Marx toward the level of those complex configurations of interacting groups of individuals that in their totality actually give rise to the dynamic structures of the capitalist production process which might be delineated in any given macro-explanation. This all means that a *dialectical* "logic of institutions" mode of explanation is actually embedded in Marx's dialectical empirical method of explanation. Now I go on to another issue brought up by my reviewer.

In this book I have brought out how Marx's dialectical explanatory movement can in principle be extended beyond his own application of it in *Capital* to other fruitful applications. One significant merit of extending Marx's explanatory paradigm the way I have, is that it becomes possible to understand the deep conceptual interconnections between Marx the philosopher on the one hand, and Marx the social scientist on the other. This, though, is not to diminish Marx's status as a social scientist, but to enhance it. To be sure Marx himself did not explicitly extend it the way I have; but this is not a good reason to hold back from extending such a promising philosophical/scientific paradigm as far as possible—especially one that has such significant explanatory power.

In the course of the dialectical movement from abstract to concrete that I presented in this book, I projected the notion of being-in-the-world at the most abstract level of the explanatory movement. Then at successively more concrete levels of analysis, I first brought the general thesis of historical materialism into the explanatory movement, and then later a more concrete formulation of it that specified tendential laws of social evolution. At an even more concrete level I went on to bring into the explanatory movement some of the most critically important factors for understanding the dynamics of the capitalist system, as well as some of the most central tendential laws of the capitalist system that Marx projected. As my analysis proceeded I went on to elaborate still more concrete levels in the explanatory movement on which the focus of concern was on male-female social relations, and later on the phenomena of alienation. This is all fully in keeping with the dialectical method Marx is working with in *Capital*; for it is always intentionally oriented at every level toward the most concrete microprocesses of human economic and social life as they are carried out within the capitalist social formation. Each level implicitly calls out for its more concrete elaboration!

Let me emphasize that I am in complete agreement with my reviewer that capitalism is "a contingent system of historically specific structures that can only be known through detailed empirical investigation." But none of what I have said in this book means, as my reviewer maintains, that I "treat all of Marx's important writings as deriving from a single well-worked-out philosophical theory or world view." While I did project the notion of being-in-the-world at the most abstract level of the explanatory movement, I do not derive any other level from it. In fact Marx's dialectical method, as opposed to Hegel's, actually precludes the derivation of *any* lower level in the explanatory movement from some more abstract level. Although the initial appearances may suggest otherwise, more careful examination would dissipate any such appearances. Here, I point to a comment Marx makes in a preface to *Capital* when he refers to what he takes to be a successful dialectical-empirical explanation. He writes: "If this is done successfully . . . then it may *appear* as if we had before us a mere *a priori* construction."[12] (Emphasis added.) That my own exposition of Marx's paradigm appears at first glance to be an *a priori* construction without actually being so, I take to be an indication of it being a successful explanation.

But if the notion of being-in-the-world is not a notion from which Marx or myself purports to derive the general thesis of historical materialism, say, or the dynamics of the capitalist system, what then is its status? And how does it relate to Marx the social scientist? Well, the notion of being-in-the-world is one that definitely involves a set of integrated philosophical presuppositions and commitments, along with some empirical dimensions as well. As I see things, once fully adopting this notion at least by the time of the *1844 Manuscripts*, Marx never abandoned the philosophical presuppositions at play in it—whether in his later articulation of the general thesis of historical materialism, or his analysis of the capitalist system in *Capital*.

And while this notion did not dictate or imply any of these later developments, it did suggest certain sets of possibilities of development, while ruling out others. For example, the philosophical commitments Marx made in this notion ruled out any explanations of human social life and its development that would have invoked a soul substance, and all that might be implied by such a belief—including, say, any projection of human suffering as a punishment inflicted by some god or gods for alleged human transgression of divine dictates. But the particular theory of human social evolution that Marx eventually did articulate was tied to specific empirical factors that Marx brought into thematic focus as he developed his explanatory movement. The theory of historical materialism was not just simply spun out of the abstract notion of being-in-the-world. On the other hand, Marx's theory of social evolution had to be congruent with this notion, just because it served as a kind of conceptual lens through which Marx singled out the particular empirical factors he brought together in this theory.

Once formulated, however, the theory of historical materialism would henceforth carry with it, at least implicitly, the set of philosophical presuppositions at play in the notion of being-in-the-world. When Marx later went on to develop his analysis of the capitalist system, the theory of historical materialism served in turn as a guiding theoretical matrix for carrying out this analysis. But although it guided this analysis in the sense of suggesting certain sets of possibilities while ruling out others, the theory of historical materialism did not dictate or imply the analysis of the capitalist system itself. For this analysis is intricately tied to a vast array of specific empirical factors that Marx brought into thematic focus from various directions as he developed his explanatory movement—factors that are not deducible from the theory of historical materialism itself. Yet the analysis of *Capital* is fully congruent with the theory of historical materialism.

And why would it not be so? For after all, the various empirical and philosophical parameters which taken together form it as a theory, served in turn as a conceptual lens for carrying out the analysis of *Capital*. Marx's analysis of capitalism presupposes the theory of historical materialism. More than this, though, the analysis of the capitalist system Marx gives, when understood in relation to Marx's own method of dialectical explanation, really amounts to a very much more concrete elaboration of the theory of historical materialism itself, but with a specific focus on the capitalist system. This, in turn, means that the theoretical success and empirical plausibility of Marx's social scientific theory in *Capital* lends significant plausibility and theoretical success to his theory of social evolution, as well as to the array of philosophical and methodological commitments that, taken together with the empirical findings of his thought, constitute his philosophical-scientific paradigm.

4) The next set of excerpts come from the critical review by Sean Sayers:

> According to Brien, we have the possibility of transcending our situation: "human beings are always more than antecedent conditions may have made them be, by virtue of their capacity to make what they become by their own activity." This rules out any purely determinist and economistic account of Marxism, and obliges us to acknowledge that there is a measure of indeterminacy in social and economic life. . . . In rejecting determinism in this way, Brien portrays capitalism as a purely oppressive and divisive social system, heading for "breakdown." Such "breakdown" he argues will create an "existential vacuum," out of which can emerge revolutionary new forms of social consciousness, not determined by capitalism.
>
> Like so many other Marxist humanists, in abandoning 'determinism' in this way, Brien is effectively abandoning the whole of Marx's social theory of classes and theory of history. With all this gone, the analysis of social change and the criticism of capitalism rest on the moral notions of 'existential needs' and 'alienation.'
>
> There is a more philosophical issue as well. Brien sees the human impact of capitalism as purely alienating, and its ultimate destiny as mere 'breakdown.' It is questionable, however, whether Marx's theory of history can be understood in these terms. The new order does not emerge out of a 'vacuum,' but from forces, which are created and developed in the old society. The new society, as Marx puts it, develops in the womb of the old. . . . Revolution is not simply a 'breakdown' of the old order; it is also the process which brings forth the new. It is impossible to understand all this in terms of a theory which sees capitalism as a *purely* negative social form; and one which has no determining influence whatever on the new society which emerges out of it.[13]

As I go on to engage these remarks let me first indicate that I am in full agreement with my reviewer's position that "the new order does not emerge out of a 'vacuum,' but out of forces which are created and developed in the old society." Also I fully agree that any theory "which sees capitalism as a *purely* negative social form," or which views capitalism as having "no determining influence whatever" on a newly emerging society would be in conflict with Marx's understanding of the dynamics of social evolution—even radical conflict. Now, it might be the case that some Marxist humanists have inadvertently strayed into such a misinterpretation of Marx. The question here is whether the case can be made that the interpretation of Marx I have given in the foregoing chapters strays in such a way. I suggest that such a case cannot be sustained.

To be sure I have argued for an interpretation of Marx that rejects economistic determinism, or anything like mechanistic determinism. But to reject these positions, and admit some degree of indeterminacy in social and economic life, is not in itself to abandon all kinds of determinism. In fact, I hold it would be a false dilemma to maintain: either economistic determinism on the one hand, or a complete absence of determining influences from the economy on the other hand. Instead the interpretation of dialectical determinism I have presented in this book lies within the wide middle ground that obtains between these two extreme positions.

Nor do I maintain, or even imply, that capitalism is necessarily "heading for 'breakdown.'" In fact, this is really the view of economistic determinism. My own view is quite the opposite. For in various places throughout my text I explicitly argue against any interpretation of the theory of historical materialism, or of the "laws of capitalism," which would imply a *necessary* or theoretically inevitable breakdown of the capitalist order. In doing so I bring out, among other things, that the dialectical method of explanation that Marx is working with is methodologically incompatible with such suggestions. For his methodology of explanation allows for, and even anticipates, the emergence of counteracting factors that can mitigate, or even completely offset a given structural tendency—depending on circumstances.

Furthermore, contrary to what my reviewer suggests, I nowhere claim that capitalism would have "no determining influence whatever" on a newly emerging society. It seems to me that on this issue my reviewer was misled, perhaps, by the metaphor of an "existential vacuum" that I used in trying to explain what happens when an older form of social consciousness loses its existential validity, and a newer form begins to become crystallized. In using the phrase "existential vacuum," I mean to refer to a kind of transitional psychic phase in which old ways of thinking and valuing have lost their viability, but new ways have not yet begun to take hold. I mean a kind of elongated *psychic bifurcation phase* that is analogous to those bifurcation points in natural systems at which an older natural form is on the threshold of breaking up, while a new natural form is on the verge of coming into being via a kind of realignment of the energies at play in the older form. Just as the new natural form "develops in the womb of the old" natural form, so too does the new form of consciousness and the new social form develop out of the older forms. That is, they *develop out* of them, pass through the birth canal of the psychic bifurcation phase I try to capture in the metaphor of the "existential vacuum," and then *go beyond* them.

Unavoidably, any viable postcapitalist society, including a potential socialist-humanist society, would presumably evolve dialectically out of the capitalist social formation and its developing tensions and contradictions. Thus any viable new society would be deeply influenced and shaped by it in a myriad of ways, even as a new society went beyond it. For a socialist-humanist society to actually become established, it would have to preserve many of the positive features of the capitalist system (although in a transformed way)—including the universal development of the productive forces made possible in capitalism; and the general expansion of free time made possible by such a development of the productive forces. Also it would have to embrace many of the projected ideals of capitalism (although in a transformed way), and *then extend* their spheres of application. For example, it would have to fully embrace the ideal of democracy, but then go on to actually extend it beyond the political arena into other arenas, including the economic one. So, too, it would have to fully embrace the ideal of freedom, but also extend it beyond the basic economic meaning it has in capitalism (namely, being free to make a profit, being free to sell one's labor power, and being free to consume) to a concern for the freely unfolding, many-sided, creative development of all social individuals.

Here I should also remind my readers of Marx's concern to help us understand how changes in ways of thinking, and in other dimensions of the social superstructure, are to be construed in relation to the dynamic tensions and contradictions that intensify as a given economic system works itself out. Consider that various tensions that develop within capitalism, and that intensify therein as time passes, are eventually generative of new ways of thinking, new practices, and new experiments in living—all of which become manifest right within the framework of capitalism itself. These then are among the very many ways in which various determining influences of capitalism would work themselves out in a transition to a new society.

Now, concerning the phenomena of alienation, Marx does hold that there are structural tendencies in capitalism that do have oppressive and alienating dimensions. In fact, I have explained that one of the structural tendencies of the capitalist social formation that Marx projects in *Capital* is the tendency toward an increasing alienation all around as the system develops. But I do not believe that those structural tendencies in capitalism that do have oppressive and alienating dimensions can be fairly characterized as being "purely oppressive" and "purely alienating." Rather, in most capitalist contexts there can be not only different degrees, but also different modes of oppression at different times and places. Also, different people in the system can experience different degrees and different modes of alienation (e.g., those characteristic of capitalists versus those characteristic of workers)—perhaps softened here and there by palliatives for members of all classes. Importantly, too, those broad structural tendencies that do have oppressive and alienating dimensions can still harbor within themselves some relatively nonoppressive elements, as well as some elements that can attenuate alienation to some extent—at least temporarily. For here again Marx's methodology of explanation allows for the emergence of counteracting factors that can mitigate, or even offset, a given tendency to some extent.

Nor does Marx himself see alienation simply as a "moral notion" that has nothing to do with his social theory of classes and his theory of history. Rather, Marx construes the complex phenomena of alienation in capitalist social formations as the structural consequences of the capitalist system, and the impact it has on people of all classes. Thus, alienation in its various dimensions is directly connected with the class struggle that occurs in capitalism. It registers on the pained human faces of the concrete, particular individuals that are caught up in the class struggle! As Marx brings out in many places in his *Grundrisse*,[14] and in other texts, one of the main contradictions of the capitalist social formation is the structural tendency toward universal development of the productive forces on the one hand, and on the other hand a structural tendency toward an increasing fettering of the forces of production. But the fettering of the productive forces in capitalism is primarily a fettering of the development of human beings. For in Marx's view, human beings are the *primary* force of production. The index of their increasing fettering is their increasing alienation. I add that it is a cardinal principle of Marx's theory of historical materialism that the increasing fettering of the forces of production in any social formation becomes in time the main catalyst of dramatic social change.

5) Once again I turn to comments from Marilyn Nissim-Sabat:

> Brien offers as a fundamental ethical principle a Marxist-humanist critical appropriation of Kant's categorical imperative: "So act that the particular mode of being-in-the-world in terms of which you act can become universal." Once attained, being-in-the-world as concrete[-ly ?] universal, as actual socialist society, makes possible the fulfillment of human potential as aesthetic self-realization. Will there no longer be ethical dilemmas facing individuals and the species? It seems to me that a full exposition of Marxist humanism requires a richer discussion of the relation between the aesthetic and the ethical dimensions of human existence.[15]

I respond that the critical appropriation of Kant's moral imperative that I projected toward the beginning of Chapter 5 was intended to be seen as a kind of "conceptual haiku" that is oriented toward the field of meanings that I subsequently laid out in the rest of that chapter. It should not simply be seen in isolation at an abstract level, but rather it should be seen as pointing toward the specific mode of being whose broad structures are brought out as my discussion proceeds. To see it in isolation is to distort what I had in mind. Moreover, in part 2 of this postscript I more fully amplify the field of meanings in relation to which my modified formulation of the "categorical imperative" should be understood. (See, especially, the section, "Unalienated Expression of Existential Needs.")

When my adaptation of Kant's imperative is seen in this way, it should become clear that referring to "the fulfillment of human potential as aesthetic self-realization," as my reviewer does, is really misleading. Rather, the unalienated mode of being that I project as constituting full freedom for Marx has deeply interrelated aesthetic and ethical dimensions. But it is not aesthetic self-realization as such; nor is it ethical self-realization as such. Instead it is *human* self-realization involving interrelated aesthetic and ethical dimensions—and other dimensions as well. It is self-realization that affirms the full *human* creative self-realization of the *other* human being, as it creatively affirms its *own* human self-realization in full concrete practical recognition of the interrelation between "self" and "other" as social individuals. Such *human* self-realization, when cultivated generally, would amount to a *pan-eudaemonism* where the well-being of all would be a living concern at play in the being well of each person.

In passing I mention that none of this means that there would be no ethical dilemmas facing individuals and society at large in such a situation. Presumably there will always be ethical dilemmas of one sort or another in any society. For example, ethical dilemmas in personal relationships when given relationships undergo change such that feelings are modified and priorities shift; or ethical dilemmas that arise on the societal level that concern decisions about, say, the allocation of resources in the aftermath of a catastrophic natural disaster.

Consider once more the analogy of those bifurcation points in natural systems at which an older natural form is on the threshold of breaking up, while some new natural form is just on the verge of coming into being via a kind of realignment of the energies at play in the older form. In those circumstances that obtain at a bifurcation point, something so unlikely as the effects of a stray elementary particle, or of the fluttering wings of a butterfly, can be so greatly augmented by successive iterations that the system dramatically changes, and shoots off in quite a new direction. Against the background of this analogy let me conclude my comments with a metaphor.

It seems to me that there is a *species of butterfly* that has been developing for many decades within a chrysalis in capitalism (or more properly within a myriad of chrysalises therein), and right in the midst of the various tensions, conflicts, and contradictions that continue to intensify within the capitalist systems, and indeed throughout our planet. That is, a kind of butterfly that through very many successive iterations has the potential to shift things toward a new phase of human development, a new plateau of human cultural evolution. That butterfly is the sort of spiritual outlook and practice that I associate with the unalienated mode of being I articulate in part 2 below. I take what I say there, by and large, to be a philosophical codification of the very many developments in such directions to which thousands upon thousands, and even millions of people have already contributed so much. As the developing world systems seem to approach an ever-more threatening bifurcation phase, this is the sort of butterfly whose fluttering wings have the potential to shift cultural evolution in the direction of a genuine human pan-eudaemonism—a stage of cultural evolution that *concretely* promotes the genuine well-being of all peoples, and all that this implies concerning nonracist, nonsexist, nonviolent, and nonoppressive modes of being in the world. So then I move now to a treatment of the spiritual dimension.

Part 2: The Spiritual Dimension in Marx[16]

Spiritual Forces vs. Religious Form

The account of both alienated and unalienated modes of being that I gave in the main text of this book was open-ended in the sense that additional complicating factors left out of account there could be woven into the explanatory web at some later time so as to make the account more complete. Among the more significant factors that I previously left out of account were a number that are related to the spiritual dimension of human beings. In this part I want to address some of these spiritual factors. However, I here intend nothing like a full-fledged analysis of the spiritual dimension as it could be understood within the framework of Marx's philosophy. Rather, here I intend to provide a *preliminary and provisional* sketch of the kind of resolution that I propose for an important research problem that calls for resolution within the framework of Marx's philosophical/scientific perspective. In the course of doing so I will focus both on some things that Marx himself explicitly projected about the spiritual dimension, as well as on some things that I take to be implicit in what he explicitly said.

But first some distinctions in terminology are in order. What meanings do "religion" (and its cognates) and "the spiritual" (and its cognates) have for Marx? Do they have basically the same meaning? Or is there a fundamental difference for him between his notion of religion and his notion of the spiritual? It is well known that Marx was quite critical of what he understood religion to be, and that he even rejected religion as illusory. But does this mean that he rejected the spiritual and the spiritual dimension as illusory too? Or can Marx consistently be critical of religion and yet accept some notion of the spiritual?

In order to shed some light on this issue let me refer to a section of *Capital* where Marx is talking about the historical necessity of material production developing through an alienated and antagonistic transitional phase in which the human subject is transformed into an object. He writes:

> It is necessary [for material production] to go through this antagonistic form, just as it is necessary at first to give man's spiritual forces a religious form by erecting them into autonomous power over against him.[17]

It seems quite clear that Marx is here making a distinction between the "spiritual forces" of human beings on the one hand, and what he takes to be the alienated "religious form" that these forces can have when they involve the projection of an "independent realm in the clouds" from which they seem to stand over human beings as an alien and autonomous power. In using the phrase "religious form" in this way Marx seems to be suggesting that religion (in the sense in which he means it) itself involves the alienation of the spiritual dimension. And indeed in other contexts where Marx speaks about religion, it seems clear that his usage of the term "religion" carries with it the connotation of an associated alienation of the spiritual forces of the human being and of the spiritual dimension itself.

This means that Marx's criticism of religion is not a rejection of the spiritual dimension of human being, but rather a call for what he believes to be the unalienated expression of this very dimension. Thus, for example, in a place where Marx advocates the criticism of religion we find him saying:

> Man, who has [previously] found only the reflection of himself in the fantastic

reality of heaven where he sought a supernatural being, will no longer be inclined to find the semblance of himself, only the non-human being, where [in an unalienated future] he seeks and must seek his true reality.[18]

Existential Needs and the Spiritual Dimension

So then if we are to understand Marx's philosophical perspective, a clear distinction must be made between "spiritual forces" and the "religious form" they can take on in specific historical conditions—a clear distinction between the spiritual on the one hand, and religion on the other. However, there seems something paradoxical in maintaining that there is a spiritual dimension of some sort while at the same time being critical of religion in a way that sees the projections of religion as illusory—especially the projection of a supernatural world and the sort of creator god associated with Christianity and other Western religions, and of course the projection of a substantial and immortal soul. The paradox here, though, is due to the long supremacy of various forms of metaphysical dualism in the mainstream Western philosophical tradition and in the various religions that have been shaped within this dualistic framework. A kind of cultural equation has become embedded in the Western psyche that sees the spiritual as necessarily implying the reality of the supernatural, a substantial soul, and the traditional creator god. But this is simply a cultural bias; for there are a number of non-Western philosophies and religions that give full-fledged recognition to a spiritual dimension without advocating metaphysical dualism.

In any case, Marx clearly does not accept the claims of metaphysical dualism. How then can he accept any conception of a spiritual dimension? Simply on the basis of the ontological primacy of the kind of biological organisms we human beings are, and of the kind of organic and inorganic world of nature with which we interact all the time. But to take the natural world as ontologically primary vis-à-vis spirituality and the spiritual dimension, to take the natural world as the necessary basis in order for there to be any spirituality at all, does not mean that you can reductively understand spirituality in terms of matter. Rather, matter itself has to be understood in such a way as to allow for the emergence of complex forms of organization that have qualitatively new features that are irreducible to the material components themselves, that can not be deduced from such components, and that can not be understood in terms of them—even though the actual existence of these qualitatively new features requires the existence of the organized components.[19]

Well then, if Marx can indeed embrace some notion of the spiritual while simultaneously being critical of religion, and while seeing its claims as illusory, just how is the spiritual dimension to be construed within Marx's philosophical framework? To help make this clear I want to cite a famous passage where Marx writes:

Man makes religion, religion does not make man. . . . But man is not an abstract being squatting outside the world. Man is the world of men, the state, society. This state and this society produce religion which is an inverted consciousness of the world because they are an inverted world. Religion is the generalized theory of this world. . . . It is the fantastic realization of the human essence inasmuch as the human essence possesses no true reality. The struggle against religion is therefore indirectly the struggle against that world whose spiritual aroma is religion. Religious suffering is the expression of real suffering and at the same time the protest against real suffering. Religion is the sigh of the oppressed creature, the heart of a heartless world, as it is the spirit of spiritless conditions. It is the opium of the people. The abolition of religion as people's illusory happiness is the demand for their real happiness. The demand to abandon illusions about their condition is a demand to abandon a condition which requires illusions. . . . Criticism has plucked the imaginary flowers from the chain, not so that man will wear the chain that is without fantasy or consolation but so that he will throw it off and pluck the living flower.[20]

There is at play in these striking formulations (and in others like them) an implicit recognition by Marx of an array of existential needs that call for fulfillment from the very depths of the human being. These fundamental existential needs include the need for meaning, the need for interconnection with reality, the need for community, the need for creative expression of potentials, the need for a viable worldview, the need for a viable value system, and the need for wholeness.[21] It is these needs that are at play in the "spiritual forces" that assume a "religious form" in historical conditions of a sort that prevent the full, many-sided, unalienated expression of human powers. Marx is not critical of religion because he is without compassion for human suffering and would take away the little solace that people might have. Indeed this passage manifests Marx's great compassion for suffering humanity—a compassion that seems to flow beneath all his work. And he is not critical of religion because he is unsympathetic with the fundamental existential needs that seek illusory fulfillment in religion.

Rather he is critical of religion because in his view what usually counts as religion constitutes merely a compensatory "fantastic realization" of these existential needs that, while giving people some kind of solace in the context of oppressive social conditions, also functions like blinders that prevent people from recognizing the real possibility of the unalienated fulfillment of these existential needs in concrete social life—a possibility whose realization would require a transformation of many of the existing social conditions which religion tends to see as unchangeable givens. For example, various religions project the notion that what in fact amounts to an exploitative class or caste hierarchy (sexual and otherwise) has been ordained by god.

At this point I want to enter an important caveat for my readers. While I accept that Marx's projection of religion as "the opium of the people" is appropriate with respect to the particular conception of God he was reacting against, the case would presumably be quite different with respect to other possible conceptions of God. In this connection it should be helpful to bring into focus a passage from *A Marxist Looks at Jesus*—a pioneering work by Milan Machovec, who writes in the 1972 original German edition of this work:

Marx developed his "atheism" as a critique of the conventional nineteenth-century representations of God, and should these change, then the genuine Marxist would have to revise his critique. Twentieth-century theologians have worked out new and more dynamic models for thinking about God, so that often we Marxists no longer know whether we are still atheists or not in their regard.[22]

This caveat made, I can proceed now with my provisional exposition of the spiritual dimension as it might be seen from within Marx's philosophic/scientific paradigm, but with the recognition that a full elaboration of what I project in this part would have to take account of *other* conceptions of God than the one which Marx himself had in mind.

So, then, against the background of the foregoing remarks I project the following as a first approximation to the notion of the spiritual dimension that is at play in Marx's philosophical perspective. At one level the spiritual dimension is that dimension of the human psyche within which the fundamental existential needs mentioned above resonate and make themselves felt in lived experience. Moreover, it is a dimension that comes to address these needs in different ways in different concrete circumstances. Since there is a very broad spectrum of possible ways in which human beings can attempt to address these existential needs as historically given conditions vary, this means that the spiritual dimension is itself historically variable in some important ways.

Drawing from the analysis given above in Chapters 3 and 4, I will soon briefly sketch how the theory of historical materialism can help account for the different historical forms that come to obtain at this level of the spiritual dimension. In the course of making this sketch I want to pay special attention to those dramatic transitional periods in human social life when one sort of social formation is replaced by another. What happens within the spiritual dimension during these periods of dramatic transition is crucially important. For it is within this dimension that the awareness of a relative satisfaction, or a relative dissatisfaction, of the fundamental existential needs is experienced, as the case may be in given circumstances; and it is within this dimension that older modes of spirituality break down and new modes arise.

Furthermore, the breakdown in the existential viability of a given mode of addressing the complex of existential needs within the context of a given social formation is the attendant precursor of such dramatic social transitions. Moreover, when such a dramatic transition does in fact occur, a new mode of addressing the fundamental existential needs first becomes crystallized because of an interaction between various ideas that have become culturally available, and dynamic energies flowing at still deeper levels of the spiritual dimension that are below the threshold of consciousness—levels that contain the wellsprings of human creativity—and once crystallized the new mode begins to take hold in the community at large. Thus we have to postulate that the spiritual dimension has both conscious and unconscious levels. Importantly, too, and contrary to the dominant ways of interpreting the theory of historical materialism, I have argued in my main text that in periods of dramatic social transformation elements of the social superstructure have a relative primacy over the economic base—and that this is implicit in Marx's own understanding of the theory of historical materialism.

Historical Materialism and the Spiritual Dimension

As I go on now to a brief sketch of this theory here, I want to stress that what I say here is extremely schematic. My intention at this juncture is to provide just enough of a sketch as will serve to situate the spiritual dimension in the explanatory web of the theory of historical materialism. This theory represents Marx's understanding of the development of human nature through the course of history. It is an understanding that has at its core the notion that human nature has to be understood as a self-evolving process in which human beings make themselves. At the most abstract level the theory projects: (a) that what generates the whole self-evolving process is human conscious activity that is "transformative of the natural [and social world], as well as formative and transformative of human existence itself,"[23] (b) and it projects further that this development gives rise to a succession of particular modes of conscious activity. This abstract schema is to be understood as being projected toward more concrete levels of analysis that bring into play more and more complicating factors.

At a lower level of analysis in the explanatory web that Marx spins out, he introduces some of the most significant factors that help to bring into focus the most conspicuous broad structures of this development—factors that he sums up as the social relations of production, and the forces of production that operate within them. And he projects a succession of specific patterns of such social relations in the course of history; as well as an ongoing development of the forces of production that generates mounting social tensions pressing for a transition from one pattern of social relations to another when a given pattern impedes their development. But all through this explanatory elaboration it is Marx's understanding that both the forces of production and the social relations of production are interrelated aspects of human conscious activity in the world. The shaping of a given mode of conscious activity by given social relations and a given phase in the development of the forces of production is not a shaping of human beings from the outside. It is the self-shaping of human beings inasmuch as both social relations and forces of production are themselves constituted to be what they are in and through the conscious activity in the world of human individuals. They are the overt social manifestations of that conscious activity.

Everything that has just been said about social relations and forces of production must then be understood as a complex schema that is itself projected toward more fully developed levels of the explanatory web that bring into play additional complicating factors. At a more developed level the social and ideological superstructure is then introduced into the explanatory web. At this level Marx projects that dynamically associated with any given complex of social relations and forces of production there will be some set of corresponding dominant ideas and values, plus an elaboration of these in various ideologies (political, religious, moral, etc.) and their corresponding forms of consciousness, some specific form of the family, governance system, and other social institutions, as well as some specific form of social consciousness. He also projects at this level that the succession of specific patterns of social relations that emerge in the course of history as the forces of production develop and evolve—and in their development generate mounting social tensions—will be dynamically accompanied by a succession of changes in dominant ideas and values, forms of consciousness, forms of the family, etc.

Here it is crucially important to recognize—as against most of the interpretations of Marx that have been prevalent—that Marx is not maintaining that the economic base mechanically determines the social and ideological superstructure at any stage in the process; although he does hold that in periods of relative social stability the economic base has a *relative* dominance in shaping its general features. But this simply means that the concrete conscious activity of people as they interrelate with one another in generating and regenerating a specific pattern of social relations has a relative dominance in shaping their form of consciousness, etc. Their conscious practice shapes their form of consciousness and their social institutions. But even here Marx does not mean that what happens in human consciousness (etc.) is determined in its specific detail by the shaping of the economic activity of human beings, but only its broad structure.

Furthermore, it is crucially important to recognize that in periods of mounting social disruption, and especially in periods of social transition from one pattern of social relations of production to another, there is a shift in dominance such that elements of the *superstructure* have, at these junctures, a *relative dominance* over the economic base in shaping ongoing developments all around. But to understand how this is possible it is necessary to orient oneself toward still more fully developed levels in the explanatory web.

Thus everything that has been said so far—about a historical succession of specific patterns of social relations, along with a corresponding succession of dynamically associated forms of consciousness, dominant ideas and values, forms of the family, political institutions, etc.—must all be understood as a complex structured schema that is projected toward still more fully developed levels in the explanatory web. Much of this further story has been given very extensive treatment by Marx himself—especially the part of it that is concerned with the analysis of the dynamics of the capitalist system—although unfortunately and even tragically this analysis has not been properly situated in the explanatory web by most interpreters of Marx. But some of it has been given only scant attention by him, or is even just there by implication in what he wrote; nonetheless some of it has been, or is being resolved by various scholars, while some of it still remains as a research problem for his philosophical-scientific perspective.

Marx's analysis of the dynamics of the capitalist system as presented in *Capital* thus must be seen as his elaboration of the level-by-level explanatory web that is constitutive of the theory of historical materialism; and it must be seen as being elaborated by Marx within the framework of the complex projected schema outlined above and implicitly presupposed by him all through his analysis of *Capital*, as well as his preparatory analysis for it in the *Grundrisse*. And when it is seen in this way we can see the analysis of *Capital* as itself intentionally projected toward still more concrete levels of analysis that would eventually have to bring explicitly into play many additional complicating factors that would be relevant to a fully adequate theoretical understanding of the evolving situation. Among these factors would be many concerning the spiritual dimension of human being and the way it would figure in any possible transition to a different pattern of social relations, as well as many factors concerning the dynamics of the human psyche, and many other factors, too. In any case, Marx himself does give some explicit attention to the spiritual dimension in *Capital* (although he may not use the phrase as such), and even more so in the *Grundrisse* where he projects an extremely ambitious ground plan that *Capital* only partially fulfills.

In the course of Marx's intricate analysis of the complex of internally related factors in terms of which he understands the dynamics of the capitalist system in *Capital*, he brings into focus various structural tendencies that are generated by the ongoing dynamic interplay of these internally related factors over time as the forces of production develop within the framework of the capitalist social relations. Among these structural tendencies are a number that involve the increasing dominion of capital and of commodities over human life as the capitalist system develops. I speak of such tendencies as those which issue in the reproduction on an expanding scale of workers who are indentured to the capitalist system for life; the tendencies toward a relative and an absolute increase in the numbers of the "surplus population" that tastes the dregs of degradation, despair, impoverishment, and misery; the general tendency in the populace at large toward an intensification of alienation and spiritual impoverishment, etc. It is to the existential impact of these tendencies on human beings that we have to look in order to see how Marx situates the spiritual dimension in his analysis.

Recall that I projected the spiritual dimension as that dimension in which fundamental existential needs resonate and make themselves felt in lived experience; and recall also that it is within this dimension that an awareness of a relative satisfaction, or a relative dissatisfaction, of the fundamental existential needs is experienced. These needs include the need for meaning, the need for interconnection with reality, the need for community, the need for creative expression of potentials, the need for a viable worldview, the need for a viable value system, and the need for wholeness. The structural tendencies I just referred to above have a deep and threatening impact upon the traditional ways in which these existential needs have been addressed within the context of the capitalist social reality.

For it is Marx's understanding that the increasing dominion of capital and of commodities over human life as the capitalist system develops leads to the structural generation of an intensifying crisis in the spiritual dimension of human beings all around. As capitalism develops so does the spiritual crisis of the human beings who live under it. Such a crisis increasingly erodes the existential viability of the ways of attempting to address fundamental existential needs that have heretofore been in place, and thus it generates an increasing frustration of these needs. Moreover, such frustration is not the frustration of one or the other of these needs, but rather the systematic frustration of the whole complex of fundamental existential needs. The increasing erosion in the existential viability of those ways of addressing existential needs that had traditionally been operative, and the sort of existential frustration and spiritual crisis that accompany it, is of crucial importance in Marx's understanding of the dynamics of any possible transition beyond the capitalist social relations.

Now, Marx himself believed that a transition from the capitalist social reality to a genuine socialism was a real possibility some time close to his own lifetime; for he believed that the intensity of the combined material and spiritual impoverishment of large numbers of people in his era *could* lead to the emergence of a revolutionizing agency that could bring about such a change. To be sure, historical events belied Marx's expectation, although I myself believe that all of the developments that intervened can be explained within the framework of Marx's perspective. In any case, it is very important for a comprehension of the theory of historical materialism to recognize that Marx's projection of a possible transition to genuine socialism close to his own lifetime was tied to some very important contingencies. Among the most important were the practical necessity of a widespread transformation of consciousness, as well as a widespread commitment to what amounts to a new spirituality—that is, to a new way of addressing the fundamental existential needs. But not just *any* transformation of consciousness, or *any* new spirituality!

In Marx's mind one of the practically necessary prerequisites for any transition to a genuine socialism was *collective effort* that is guided by the moral commitment to a new ethos, a new spirituality, a new mode of addressing frustrated existential needs—an ethos and a spirituality of the sort that would be at the living, pulsating heart of those unalienated modes of being that Marx associates with what he means by genuine socialism. (More about this later on.)

Moreover, such collective effort must be shaped by a *collective understanding* of the following sort. It must understand the real social causes of human suffering—i.e., the external social and institutional causes of such suffering, including oppressive and exploitative social relations; it must involve a recognition of the historicity of the various forms that human nature assumes in the course of history, as well as an understanding of the possibility of new forms of human being that would be more fulfilling and less alienated than those ways in which human beings have made themselves so far; it must involve a comprehension of the broad structures of the theory of historical materialism; and it must also involve a recognition that only collective human effort and commitment can actualize such potentialities.

So in Marx's mind the hoped-for transition from the capitalist social relations to the qualitatively new social relations that he associated with genuine socialism would require the kind of collective effort and collective understanding indicated here. In rough summary outline, the dynamics of the transition Marx envisaged presumably involved the following stages. A mounting conflict would arise between the developing capitalist forces of production and the network of capitalist social relations within which such forces operated. Attending the mounting crisis of the conflicting powers in the economic base there would be mounting tensions in the various institutions of the social superstructure, and there would be a growing proliferation of contradictory ideas in the ideological superstructure that reflected the crisis in the base and in the social superstructure. All this would generate an intensifying spiritual crisis in people at large, accompanied by a deepening erosion in the existential viability of the traditional capitalist modes of addressing existential needs—an intensifying crisis in what might be called the psychic infrastructure.

The exaggeration of all these crises would lead to an extended phase of social upheaval in which there would be a shift in relative dominance such that elements of the ideological superstructure and of the psychic infrastructure would become salient vis-à-vis the economic base in addressing the crisis and in reorienting the direction of spiritual, social, and economic development. Assuming the success of efforts to cultivate and disseminate the sort of socialist ideas with which Marx identified, there would be a social gravitation of more and more people to a genuine socialist ethos and a genuine socialist spirituality that was existentially effective in addressing the frustrated existential needs of people. This would be followed by or accompanied by a growing acceptance among such people of the modes of right understanding described above. There would be a cascading breakdown in the existential viability of the capitalist form of social consciousness and of the traditional ways of attempting to address existential needs within capitalism.

The transition to genuine socialism would be actualized by the widespread commitment of more and more people guided by right understanding and willing to undertake right effort to actualize a socialist reality. Out of these developments a new socialist form of social consciousness would become crystallized. These developments in turn would generate a qualitatively new pattern of socialist social relations of production. As the new social relations were being established there would be an accompanying reorganization of the institutions of the social superstructure. Once the new social relations and the new superstructure were established there would be another shift in dominance such that the socialist economic base would now have a relative dominance in the ongoing regeneration of the genuinely socialist social reality, and of the socialist spirituality. But such relative dominance must be understood as the relative dominance of one dimension of human conscious activity in the world over other of its dimensions. Moreover, the ongoing regeneration of the new socialist spirituality on the basis of the new socialist economic base would be a regeneration on a basis within which the new spirituality had already been concretely embodied.

Up to this point in my discussion I have tried to give a first approximation of the notion of the spiritual dimension that is at play in Marx's philosophical perspective; and I have tried to clarify the way in which it is to be properly situated in the explanatory web of Marx's theory of historical materialism, as well as the way it figures in those dramatic transitions from one mode of social reality to another. I have already indicated that in Marx's philosophy the spiritual dimension has to be understood as being historically variable in important ways inasmuch as particular ways of addressing fundamental existential needs vary from one historical context to another. A proper understanding of the historicity of the spiritual dimension requires that the changing forms in which this dimension becomes manifest in the various historical circumstances be understood in dynamic relation to developments in, and changing forms of, the concrete social reality—including developments and changes in the forces of production, social relations of production, the family, the governance system, etc. But, of course, only empirical research carried out under the guiding parameters of the theory of historical materialism could make clear in any given historical situation the dynamic correlation that obtained between some particular religion or form of spirituality on the one hand, and some particular form of concrete social reality on the other.

Recognizing the historicity of human social practice, as well as the historicity of the spiritual dimension and its dynamic interconnection with changing modes of social practice, involves recognizing that human beings can transcend, or go beyond, the ways in which they have made themselves in the past, and that they can also transcend the particular modes in which the spiritual dimension has been manifested in the past. Earlier I pointed to a distinction that Marx makes between the "spiritual forces" of human beings on the one hand, and the alienated "religious form" that these forces can have when they involve the projection of an "independent realm in the clouds" from which they seem to stand over human beings as an alien and autonomous power.

The spiritual forces can perhaps best be understood in terms of dynamic energies that have the potentiality to take on different forms in different circumstances. These dynamic energies can be thought of as arising from a diffuse and amorphous unconscious and as crystallizing in consciousness in determinate patterns corresponding to particular ways of addressing existential needs, but as doing so in different ways in different circumstances. A change in the spiritual dimension would involve a reorganization of the dynamic energies of the psychic infrastructure. However, some organizations of the psychic infrastructure are to be seen as more existentially fulfilling than others in given circumstances, while other possible organizations are much less so, or are even existentially meaningless. It all depends on the particular concrete social circumstances, and on the way human life as lived in terms of some particular way of addressing existential needs is actually experienced by real individual human beings.

In Marx's view the spiritual forces have mostly been manifested in the course of human history in modes that he takes to be alienated. However, it is central to his conception of the spiritual dimension that it is possible for spiritual forces to transcend past alienated ways of manifesting themselves, and to become manifested in what he takes to be unalienated ways. We need to take a close look at what this means. And perhaps I can best help with this by giving a sketch that would point to the way in which each of the fundamental existential needs that I have been talking about in the course of this postscript would be manifested, expressed, or addressed in an unalienated way. In doing so I draw primarily from ideas presented in *The Economic and Philosophic Manuscripts of 1844* where Marx had so many important things to say about alienated modes of being (their different dimensions, their dynamics, etc.)—and where he had much to say, both explicitly and by implication, about unalienated modes of being as well. But I have also drawn from material presented in the *Grundrisse*, in *Capital*, and in *The German Ideology*. So then I make some comments about each of the existential needs in turn. But there is no attempt here to be definitive, or to give a complete account.

Unalienated Expression of Existential Needs

In a beautiful passage of the *Paris Manuscripts* where Marx is speaking about the relationship between men and women, he writes: "In this relationship is revealed the extent to which man's need has become a human need; the extent to which, therefore, the other person as a person has become for him a need."[24] Against the background of this passage, I suggest that the existential *need for community* is manifested among other ways as the need to be related to the other person as a person in concrete practice, and also for the other person to be so related to you. For Marx this means a need for people to be so related to one another that there is an experiential recognition of human individuals as social individuals—both the recognition that individuals become the particular kind of social individuals they are by virtue of the particular ways they interact with each other, as well as the recognition that the most positive development of human individuals is dynamically bound up with the most positive development of their social relationships. Such a manifestation of the need for community does not see the connection with others as a hindrance to individual development, but rather as a pathway toward full human development. It is a need for reciprocal, many-sided, life-affirming relations on the part of individuals with many-sided, life-affirming counterparts in order that everyone may become fully human. It is the sort of need for community that involves the concrete practical affirmation of others as ends in themselves as one affirms oneself, as well as the recognition that the freedom of each is tied to the freedom of all.

The existential *need for interconnection with reality* is addressed among other ways by an experiential recognition that the human being is "not an abstract being squatting outside the world," but is essentially a being in the world, a being of nature interacting with nature. It is addressed by a recognition of the internal ontological bonds that obtain between the human individual and the natural environment—ontological bonds that concern not only the actual existence of the human body and its functions, but the existence of the conscious human subject as well, including all the various powers that the human subject comes to acquire. For human beings act in and upon the natural and social environment, and in so doing constitute their powers as real objective powers. Among the things that humans do is that they act on "objects" in the external world. In so doing human beings embody their energies in those objects so that in a sense they become repositories of human subjectivity. Thus there is an internal ontological bond between human subjects and external objects. But whether this ontological connection is experienced in a way that is life-affirming, rather than life-negating, depends on whether human individuals actually comport themselves toward the multiplicity of objects in which human subjective powers have been embodied in ways that are mindful of and respectful of them as embodiments of the energies of social individuals. Thus a need for interconnection with reality that is unalienated requires that, as individuals interrelate with one another through the mediation of objects, they reciprocally affirm each other in concrete social practice as social individuals, and as ends in themselves.

The existential *need for meaning* is addressed by transcending modes of activity that are experienced as meaningless, or that are experienced as an onerous means to some end that is to be realized by the activity—that is, some wished-for goal that lies outside the activity itself. In the kind of unalienated activity that Marx is trying to nurture there is no structural bifurcation between means and ends in the activity. Such activity is not experienced as a means to ends that are external to the activity itself. Rather the activity is experienced as an end in itself, even if it may *also* be activity that is a means to something in fact. In unalienated activity as Marx understands it, one's activity is experienced as intrinsically meaningful. Thus unalienated activity is experienced as spontaneously creative, and as joyful. As Marx puts it, such activity is "a free manifestation of life and an enjoyment of life."[25] But the need for meaning is also manifested and concretely expressed in direct personal relations when people relate to each other as whole persons, and treat each other as ends. Marx highlights the existential importance of such meaningful relations among people when he writes: "Poverty [in the context of genuine socialism] is the passive bond which causes the human being to experience the need of the greatest human wealth—the other human being."[26]

The existential *need for creative expression of one's potentials* is affirmed in Marx's projection of "free conscious activity" as the species character of human beings.[27] In Marx's mind this has the connotation of the need for a many-sided, freely flowing, creative unfolding of individual powers. As he says in *The German Ideology*: "[F]ree activity is . . . the creative manifestation of life arising from the free development of all abilities, of the whole fellow."[28] Elsewhere he writes: "The rich human being is simultaneously the human being in need of a totality of human manifestations of life—the man in whom his own realization exists as an inner necessity."[29] This, of course, is not to be understood as anything like the typical egotism of Western cultures, since for Marx this is all understood as being qualified by the practical recognition of oneself and others as social individuals, and by the recognition that the freedom of each is bound up with the freedom of all. Thus the many-sided, creative unfolding of individual powers is an unfolding that does not seek to dominate the other, but it does not let itself be dominated by the other either. Nor is Marx's affirmation of individual powers to be understood as an affirmation of the kind of possessive individualism that has been so dominant for so long—with all its emphasis on having, and on possessing, whether it be money, things, property, etc. Marx's concern is not with having much, but with being much.

The existential *need for wholeness* has already been suggested in the remarks just made concerning the need for a totality of human manifestations of life, and therewith a many-sided, all-around development. But it is also manifested in the ideal of a harmonious psychic integration of the various dimensions of human being—including the need for the transformation of the cognitive and conative dimensions as they obtain in alienated modes of being (i.e., the transformation of reason and sensuousness) and their dynamic integration in more holistic modes. It also includes the need to overcome the alienated separation of the spiritual dimension and the sensuous dimension that has been characteristic of much of the Western cultural tradition, and the need to dynamically integrate these dimensions in a holistic way. And it includes the transformation of everyday activity into activity that has aesthetic quality to it. Finally the need for wholeness includes the need for people to be interrelated with one another as whole persons, rather than in segmental alienated ways.

The existential *need for a viable value system* is manifested in a practice wherein one treats others, and oneself also, as whole persons—a practice that involves the recognition that the fully developed freedom of each is tied up with the fully developed freedom of all. Some corollaries of this are the categorical imperative to relate to others and oneself in terms of nonviolent, nonracist, nonsexist, nonoppressive, nonexploitative ways of being; as well as the categorical imperative to help transform all those conditions in which human beings are debased, enslaved, exploited, dehumanized, etc. This existential need is also manifested in the need to develop one's potentials. Thus it is manifested in the need to be free. Not just the need to be "free from," however; and not just the need to be "free for"; but the need to be "free at" as well. This connotes an active freedom that involves a need for a many-sided creative activity that constitutes a totality of human manifestations of life—including, of course, the need to be related to the other as a whole person in concrete practice.

The existential *need for a viable worldview* is expressed in the experiential recognition that human beings are natural beings interacting with nature and, further, that human beings are *changing* natural beings interacting with a changing nature. Thus in this worldview human nature is understood historically and in keeping with the notion of a self-evolving process. For it is particular human beings who make themselves to be the particular kind of individuals they are in and through the particular ways they interact with each other and with the environment. And human beings are always more than the particular ways they have made themselves be, inasmuch as they have the potentiality of transcending the ways they have made themselves in the past and of remaking themselves in new ways. Not only that but they have the potential of remaking themselves in keeping with a new spirituality of the sort suggested by the foregoing characterization of an unalienated manifestation of existential needs. Turning to the larger picture this worldview would see nature itself as an evolving process; and, thus, that the smaller world in which we human beings live is interconnected in a vast multiplicity of ways with the process of cosmic becoming—interconnected with a cosmic web of shifting, dynamically interacting energies in which there are no eternal unchanging substances, but in which everything becomes what it is by virtue of the internal dynamic interrelations it has with other things. And it would see that we human beings are not only interconnected with, but are also temporary manifestations of that cosmic process—that all of us are such manifestations, and that perhaps our most fundamental ontological identity lies in that.

Conclusion

In the foregoing presentation I do not take myself as having gone beyond anything that Marx either explicitly said or implicitly presupposed. Let me sum up some of the main points I have addressed. At one level the spiritual dimension was projected to be that dimension of the psyche within which the various existential needs resonate in lived experience. This dimension has to be understood historically, though, since there are different ways of addressing existential needs depending upon the differing sets of specific conditions that obtain in differing historical contexts. Then at another level the spiritual dimension was taken to be that dimension within which diffuse and amorphous dynamic energies containing the wellsprings of human creativity flow below the threshold of consciousness. Spiritual forces were understood in relation to such dynamic energies that have the potentiality to take on different forms in different circumstances. They were construed as arising from a diffuse and amorphous unconscious and as crystallizing in consciousness in determinate patterns corresponding to particular ways of addressing existential needs, and as doing so in different ways in different circumstances.

Then I gave an explanatory sketch that brought out how the spiritual dimension can be understood within the framework of the theory of historical materialism; how it figures in the dynamics of social transformations; and also how changes in modes of spirituality involve reorganizations of the psychic infrastructure. In the immediately preceding discussion I gave a characterization of the various ways in which each of the fundamental existential needs would be addressed in what Marx would consider to be an unalienated mode. Finally I suggested that addressing existential needs in these ways would be constitutive of a mature, unalienated spirituality as understood within a humanistic Marxist perspective; and that this is *the spiritual ideal* that Marx effectively holds up for humankind.

At this juncture I want to suggest that "right understanding" of such a mode of spirituality, and "right effort" guided thereby, hold the best promise in the twenty-first century for dealing in holistic ways with the crisis of the human person that is characteristic of our era. Carrying out such a promise would require *building holistic coalitions* between and among the various specialized groups focused on confronting sexism, racism, economic-class problems, environmental degradation, etc.—and holistic coalitions not only within the capitalist countries themselves, but between those countries and other countries throughout the world wherever oppressed, exploited, marginalized, alienated, and neglected people suffer. In turn, building such transcending holistic coalitions that could nurture developments toward a new plateau of cultural evolution, while acknowledging and even cultivating diversity, would seem to require a nondogmatic, nonsectarian, *this-world oriented* attitude concerning the spiritual dimension. So then, using once again a metaphor used earlier, I project the mode of spirituality presented above as the butterfly whose fluttering wings have the potential to shift cultural evolution in the direction of a stage that *concretely* promotes the genuine well-being of all peoples, and all that this implies concerning nonracist, nonsexist, nonviolent, and nonoppressive modes of being in the world.

As I close perhaps it might be well to mention that the mode of spirituality I have developed above within a humanistic-Marxist perspective is oriented toward many of the same core values that constitute the living heart of the various great world religions, at least the humanistic dimensions of those religions.[30] I especially have in mind the ideals of nonpossessive love and the dignity of the human person, but also the ideal of community with what is taken to be special or sacred. While there are many ontological differences *among* the various great world religions, and *between* them and humanistic Marxism as I have presented it, nonetheless there is an extremely important value convergence as well. I believe this is especially clear in the case of Buddhism—particularly Mahayana Buddhism.[31] But it is also clear in the case of religious perspectives that were developed in the twentieth century within the Christian tradition by various exponents of liberation theology and spirituality. As Machovec has paradoxically put it:

> Twentieth-century theologians have worked out new and more dynamic models for thinking about God [than the models characteristic of the nineteenth century], so that often we Marxists no longer know whether we are still atheists or not in their regard.[32]

Here I take Machovec to be suggesting that humanistic Marxists could readily align themselves with the value orientations espoused by the "more dynamic models for thinking about God" to which he refers, while downplaying whatever ontological discrepancies might obtain. Similarly, once the adherents of the various religions become aware that the living pulsating heart of humanistic Marxism beats with the same rhythm as theirs does, why would not the more open of these adherents be willing to align themselves with humanistic Marxists in building holistic coalitions aimed at addressing the crisis of the human person?

8

Addendum on Buddhism and Marxism[1]

In the addendum that follows I am going to argue that Buddhism and Marxism not only have a great deal in common, but also that they are really quite complementary to one another. Now it may seem strange to some people, I'm sure, to hear the suggestion that Buddhism and Marxism could have much in common. But, in view of the fact that there are many versions of both, my suggestion will seem less strange, hopefully, if I qualify it by indicating that I will be talking about what I take to be the essential core of Buddhism and the essential core of humanistic Marxism.

So I will be arguing that it is the core of Buddhism and the core of humanistic Marxism that have a great deal in common—so much so that they mutually complement one another. This does not mean to say, though, that they have *everything* in common. There are important differences, including differences of a metaphysical sort. For example, presumably all the different schools of Buddhism project some version of reincarnation, while humanistic Marxism does not accept such a notion. Even on this issue, though, perhaps the two perspectives are not so very far apart as they might initially seem. For neither Buddhism nor Marxism accepts the notion of a substantial soul. Thus, Buddhism interprets reincarnation not in terms of a transmigrating soul substance, but in terms of a *continuity of effects from* one life cycle to another.

Some readers might recall an image that Buddha himself presumably employed to help his followers grasp what he meant by reincarnation. Imagine a group of people sitting in a circle, and that each person is holding an unlighted candle. Now imagine that one person in the circle somehow lights her candle, and that she then stretches out to the person sitting next to her who lights his candle from hers; and that, in turn, he reaches out to the next person in the circle who lights her candle from his; and so on, until all the candles held by the people in the circle are lighted. There has been no passage of a substance here, but only a continuity of effects—what amounts to a series of karmic connections. The tradition holds that Buddha himself used this metaphor to suggest that this is what reincarnation is like. Now while a humanistic Marxist would not accept a karmic continuity of effects from incarnation to incarnation in a succession of life cycles in the manner a Buddhist would, the Marxist could readily adopt something like a notion of *social karma*. More about this later though.

The main point here, though, is that the complementary character of Buddhism and Marxism will come out more clearly if we leave aside their different metaphysical stances. There is a well know precedent for this within the Buddhist tradition. An early Buddhist *sutra* tells the story of a follower of Buddha who became more and more distressed with Buddha because he did not address questions such as whether the world is infinite or finite in spatial extent, and whether the world is eternal or not eternal in time, etc. In response Buddha indicated that such metaphysical issues were distractions that pulled one away from the issues that matter most—namely understanding the reality of human suffering, and how it might be alleviated. To insist that metaphysical questions be answered before being concerned about human suffering would be analogous to someone who was hit with a poisoned arrow refusing to let the arrow be extracted, until he knew what caste the one who shot the arrow came from, how tall he was, what kind of wood the arrow was made from, what kind of feathers guided the arrow in its flight, etc. Such a person would die from the poison before such questions could be answered. Similarly, becoming so absorbed in metaphysical issues that one evades a deep probing of human suffering and its causes would only serve to perpetuate such suffering.[2]

In any case, I hold that the primary concern of both Buddhism and humanistic Marxism is indeed a deep concern about human suffering. On the other hand, I take the primary differences between these perspectives to be differences of emphasis concerning the sort of factors involved in human suffering upon which each perspective focuses. Buddhism has traditionally been concerned with the *internal factors* that are involved in the generation of human suffering, and also with various techniques and meditative disciplines it has developed over the centuries in order to deal with those internal factors in a liberating way. On the other hand, humanistic Marxism has been primarily concerned with the *external factors* involved in the generation of human suffering, as well as with a viable understanding of the historicity of such external factors and their development over time (especially those factors summed up in what Marx refers to as the "social relations of production" and the "forces of production").

In order to make a case for Buddhism and humanistic Marxism being mutually complementary, it will be necessary, among other things, to give some sense of how

I construe the humanistic-Marxist perspective. Before taking this up, though, I want to briefly comment on some remarks concerning Marxism made by the Dalai Lama in an interview with him published in the Polish journal *Dialogue and Universalism* in 1997. In this interview the Dalai Lama remarks as follows:

> In spite of the fall of the Moscow communist regime at the end of 1991, I still do not consider it to be a failure or collapse of Marxism. I regard it rather as a collapse of the Marxist totalitarian regime, *not the ideology* [emphasis added]. . . . [W]hat is interesting in the Marxist economics theory is that it puts a big emphasis on how to distribute money, not just on how to make money. So this is for me a moral question in Marxist economy—equal distribution. Because of it I feel that in the Marxist theory of economy there are many more questions about ethics, while in capitalism the only question is how to make more money, and the only thing is how to make a profit. . . . [But between Marxism and Buddhism] there are big differences. Marxists, I think, at least in theory, say that they are concerned about exploited people, the working class people. But in practice they are simply spending their whole energy on destruction of the ruling class. When the destruction has been achieved, for a Marxist there is nothing more to be concerned about with respect to the working class people. Because of a lack of genuine compassion their energy becomes much more destructive than constructive.[3]

Elsewhere the Dalai Lama remarks that "the failure of the regime in the former Soviet Union was, for me, not the failure of Marxism but the failure of totalitarianism. For this reason I still think of myself as half Marxist, half Buddhist."[4] Now I have very high regard for the Dalai Lama, and I share with him the self-characterization of being "half Marxist, half Buddhist." However, I do wonder whether the "half" of myself which is "Marxist" might have quite different contours than the "half" of himself that the Dalai Lama projects to be "Marxist." Let me bring out what I mean by indicating that I take the breakup of the former Soviet Union to be, not just the collapse of a totalitarian Marxist regime, but also an historical refutation of a *totalitarian and dogmatic ideology that radically distorted the authentic Marx.* That is, I take it to be a refutation of a seriously misguided attempt to implement a radically flawed version of Marx's philosophy.

Let me be quite clear here. It was the ideology of orthodox Marxism that was dominant in the former Soviet Union. I hold that this ideology with its economistic and reductionist interpretation of historical materialism, and with its complete detachment from the humanistic dimensions of Marx's thought, actually constitutes a radical distortion of Marx's thought both as a social scientist and as a philosopher.[5] While orthodox Marxism was not fully formulated until long after Marx's death, Marx himself seemed to express his foreboding about such a development. Some readers may be familiar with a lament Marx would often make to Engels in relation to the economistic interpretation of historical materialism that was already beginning to take hold while he was alive. Marx would complain: "All I know is that I am not a Marxist."[6]

Along with the Dalai Lama, I fully acknowledge the kind of brutality to which the former ruling class in Russia (and elsewhere) was subjected by a totalitarian Marxist regime; and along with him I fully acknowledge the wholesale brutality to which millions of peasants and workers were subjected by the Stalinist regime in a program of forced collectivization, etc. Nor should I fail to mention in this context the gruesome brutality to which the people of Tibet, and so many Tibetan Buddhist monks and nuns, were subjected by the Chinese incarnation of orthodox Marxism (if I can use the word "incarnation" here without being offensive). It is most important, though, to acknowledge that it was *orthodox Marxism*, stripped of all the humanistic dimensions of Marx's thought, and construing human beings as puppets in the alleged inevitable march of history, that easily justified such "collateral damage"—all in the name of the glorious future promised by this dogmatic, totalitarian ideology.

Lamentably, the living, pulsating heart of authentic Marxism had been completely excised from this ideology; so it is no wonder that the economic, political, and social practice guided by such an ideology lacked all genuine compassion. Even when the early humanistic writings of Marx were widely disseminated in the 1940s, '50s, '60s—and long after orthodox Marxism had been formulated without any reference to them—orthodox Marxism dismissed these early writings as speculative meanderings that Marx supposedly repudiated in his later work. However, none of this means that Marx himself was without compassion for suffering humanity. Indeed I would argue that it was a deep and profound compassion for suffering humanity that was the abiding motivation which sustained him in his life's work. Nor does any of this mean that humanistic Marxism as a philosophy does not harbor a central place for the primacy of human agency, and for the important role of compassion in human interrelations. With a view toward bringing this out, I turn now to some of the chief features of humanistic Marxism.

Humanistic Marxism (A)

Let me first address the issue of an alleged split between the writings of the early and the late Marx. While orthodox Marxism projects a radical split between the early and late Marx, and while it totally dismisses the humanism of the early Marx, the situation is quite different with respect to humanistic Marxism. Many readers would recognize Polish philosopher Adam Schaff as one of the foremost dissident philosophers struggling in the 1950s and '60s to rescue the humanism of Marx from the straight jacket of Stalinism. In his wonderful book, *Marxism and the Human Individual*, he writes:

> Only when illuminated with the ideas of his youth, the ideas of his philosophical anthropology, does [Marx's] mature thought show all its wealth and its inherent meaning. . . . [For] the key to Marx's economic theory . . . [is to be] found in his anthropology, his theory of man, without which the economics is limited and impotent.[7]

The attempts to contrast the young with the mature Marx—either through acclaiming the former as the only "authentic" one, or making the same exclusive claim for the latter—were bound to provoke the counter-argument that the *work of Karl Marx is an integral whole* which cannot be divided into parts that are not so much different as cut off from each other, or even ideologically opposed. [Emphasis added][8]

Throughout the course of the book from which these citations are taken, Schaff goes on to develop the counterargument that Marx's work is indeed *an integral whole*. Moreover, a significant number of other dissident philosophers—from Poland, Yugoslavia, Czechoslovakia, and many other of those countries caught in the tentacles of Stalinism—struggled collectively to carry this argument all the way through. Together they have powerfully articulated and sustained the case that orthodox Marxism is indeed a gross distortion of Marx's thought; and together they have infused the humanism back into the now breathing, pulsating, living heart of Marxism.

Another of these valiant dissident philosophers was Yugoslavian philosopher Gajo Petrovic, who in his fine book, *Marx in the Mid-Twentieth Century*, provided such a clear exposition of the notion of *praxis* which is so central to Marx's thought. There he writes:

When he rejects the traditional conception of man as a rational animal Marx does not do so simply because this gives reason the primary place, but first of all because he considers that neither reason nor political activity, neither production of tools nor any other special activity or property can be man's essence. Man is not a mechanical sum of his "spheres" (economic, political, moral, artistic, etc). . . . [W]hat makes a man man is not his "main sphere" [or some special sphere] but his whole way of Being, the general structure of his relationship toward the world and toward himself. This way of being, which is peculiar to man, Marx designates by the word "praxis." Man, for Marx, is the being of "praxis."[9]

But what is praxis, one might ask? Praxis is not a thing or a substance; nor is it an attribute of a thing or a substance. *Praxis is an activity!* Praxis is the dynamic interaction through which the human being shapes the environment in some way, and in so doing shapes itself. Praxis is the moving dialectical interface between the human organism and the environment in which the human being is situated. As Petrovic formulates it himself: "Praxis is a universal-creative self-creative activity by which man transforms and creates his world and himself."[10]

If the human being is a being of praxis, then human nature must be understood as a process. If human nature is only properly understood as a process, then one cannot identify human nature as such with the form that it has at some particular stage. For the potentialities of human beings are not exhausted by the particular form and by the particular mode of relations that characterize them at a particular time; no given particular stage embodies the whole truth. Human reality is everything it has been in the past, everything it now is in the present, *and yet is more than it has been in the past and present*. Furthermore, to comprehend human nature one must comprehend this process, and the way in which transitions from one stage to another come about. How to understand this process? Well, as many readers will already realize, Marx understands this process in terms of the interplay between what he refers to as the *"forces of production," the "social relations of production and reproduction,"* and the *"social superstructure."*

Importantly, the "forces of production" and the "social relations of production and reproduction" cannot be understood apart from conscious activity in the world—that is, apart from praxis. They are *two dynamically interacting currents within conscious activity*. And these two interacting currents mutually shape, *and are shaped by*, still another current (or set of currents) of conscious activity in the world—a current which is sometimes misleadingly referred to as the *"social superstructure"*—namely, the modes of consciousness, the predominant ideas, the political and legal institutions, the forms of the family (etc.) that come into being. *The development of the forces of production and the development of the social relations, together with the development of the associated modes of consciousness and predominant ideas—all of this is the development of conscious activity in the world, the development of praxis*. The tensions and conflicts, which obtain within and between these mutually interrelated developments, are tensions and conflicts in human conscious activity in the world. And the development of conscious activity in all these dimensions is the development of human nature in history.

As long as development takes place within the framework of capitalist social reactions, Marx holds that we can expect a structural generation of an increasing dominion of things over human life, and with it *an increasing alienation of people* from one another, from nature, from their own activity, etc. As was indicated above, though, this does not mean that the human being is an economic animal in Marx's view. While on the one hand it is true that conscious activity that is specifically *economic* in character has so far in the course of history been the predominant form of conscious activity for most people, Marx would reject any claim to the effect that economic conscious activity must necessarily predominate always and forever. However, as long as economic conscious activity does in fact predominate, so long will human beings remain alienated from their own activity, from the product of their activity, from nature, and from one another as well.

At the very heart of humanistic Marxism is the recognition of the intensive and extensive scope of human alienation in all its forms, as well as the recognition of the widespread human suffering that attends the many forms of alienation. But side by side with such recognition is a correlated recognition that it is *possible in principle to overcome alienation*. For as Petrović brought out: "[To say] that 'man is praxis' means man is society, freedom, history and future."[11] Moreover: "the interpretation of praxis as a universal-creative self-creative activity contains its determination as a free conscious activity."[12] Among other things, overcoming alienation involves the development of the forces of production to the point where the technological capacity to satisfy material needs exists without necessitating the cultural predominance of economic conscious activity. It involves overcoming types of "social relations of production and reproduction" (whether they be capitalist, or "statist," or "state capitalist" social relations, etc.) that serve to maintain the continued existence of the predominance of economic conscious activity. It involves, further, bringing about transitions in the actual interrelations and forms of association in the context of which men and women produce and reproduce themselves— transitions which will permit the full unfolding of the individual, the realization of the human essence. Moreover, it involves transformation of consciousness on a broad cultural scale. As Petrović and so many others have made clear: "The theory of alienation is not only the central theme of Marx's 'early' writings; it is also the guiding idea of all his 'later' works."[13]

All of this, and more, is required to fully realize the *human essence* as understood by Marx—the ideal of full human development. And what is this then? *"Free conscious activity"* that is formative and transformative of the world and of the self is projected by Marx as the human essence.[14] For Marx this notion has the following implications: Such conscious activity is spontaneous and creative, and is experienced as an end in itself. It is conscious activity that involves joy and pleasure in the very process of the activity, and not just as an aftermath—if that. Thus it is conscious activity that no longer serves merely as a means to ends that are external to it. Moreover, it is conscious activity that is no longer a one-sided development of the individual. Instead it involves the many-sided development of the individual's potentials. However, it is the sort of activity that does not involve or imply the denial or repression of the other as it affirms itself. For it is activity in the world which has adopted for itself a mode of being in the world which can also be universally adopted—a mode of being that is nonoppressive, nonviolent, nonracist, and nonsexist.

Thus, it is conscious activity in the world that has undergone a transformation toward *a new common sense*—a common sense that is sensitive to the dynamic interplay of the social factors which constitute and reconstitute the form of social reality; a common sense that recognizes that the growing dominion of things over human life is grounded in an oppressive and dehumanizing social practice; a common sense that requires the concrete extension of democracy to the workings of the economic process; a common sense that gives full positive recognition to the social nature of human being; a common sense that comprehends that community with other people need not operate as a limitation of individual fulfillment, but rather as a pathway toward individual fulfillment; a common sense that affirms the need for a manifold of human expressions of life, and that affirms as well the need to be related to the other person as a person; a common sense that rejects the oppression and exploitation of women, blacks, etc.—and that rejects their degradation to second-class, semi-persons.

As an index of such humanized social relations, consider this striking passage from Marx's *1844 Manuscripts*:

The relation of man to woman is *the most natural* relation of human being to human being. It therefore reveals the extent to which man's *natural* behavior has become *human*, or the extent to which the *human* essence in him has become a *natural* essence—the extent to which his *human nature* has come to be *nature to him*. In this relationship is revealed also the extent to which man's *need* has become a *human* need; the extent to which, therefore, the *other* person as a person has become for him a need.[15]

Humanistic Marxism (B)

As I continue with these remarks on humanistic Marxism, I will shift the focus to the issue of transitions from one social formation to another—especially the issue of a possible transition from a capitalist social formation to a genuine socialist one. Let me say in this connection that one of the most egregious distortions of Marx's thought has to do with the structural dynamics of such transitions as they are interpreted by orthodox Marxism, and indeed by most of the dominant interpretations of Marx. The central problem with these very misleading interpretations has to do with the way in which they misconstrue "historical materialism"—that is, Marx's general theory of cultural evolution—and also the way in which they misconstrue his mature dialectical method of explanation.

Reacting against the orthodox Marxist view of historical materialism that would "explain away" moral ideals and norms of value "as pure reflexes, as mere camouflage for socio-economic interests," Milan Machovec (a dissident philosopher from Czechoslovakia) argues as follows in his wonderful work, *A Marxist Looks at Jesus.*

Modern [i.e., humanistic] Marxism . . . understands the historico-materialist method as follows: even though it is fully justifiable, indeed necessary, to look to the socio-economic roots of ideas, that does not exhaust the matter. *It is only after the roots have been clearly recognized that the really important task begins* [emphasis added]. One has to ask: which of these ideas offers positive and true knowledge about man's being and existence as well as inspiring ideals, models, and norms of value without which even the best-organized, affluent and technically perfect society would remain impoverished and indeed barbarous. And one has consciously to encourage, develop, and diffuse these norms of value precisely as a materialist who expects no help from on high![16]

Machovec makes it clear that "the greatest distinction between the older Marxists . . . and the so-called 'modern' Marxists," that is, the humanistic Marxists, is that "the latter are already only too aware of the danger of explaining spiritual values away into the indifferent realm of the unreal."[17] In the view of Machovec, it is precisely the value commitments that human beings make in times of social transformations that are most crucial in shaping the unfolding developments.

Against the interpretation of historical materialism characteristic of orthodox

Marxism, I have argued extensively elsewhere[18] that Marx's mature method of dialectical explanation makes clear how there can be *shifts in the relative primacy of the various interrelated factors* operative in a given situation, depending on the changing concrete historical circumstances. Thus, for instance, the economic base would presumably have a *relative primacy* overall in shaping a given social formation when historical conditions are relatively stable—but, even so, *not* in a way that would mechanically determine anything else in the social formation. For elements of the "social superstructure" *always* have a shaping effect as well. On the other hand, when historical conditions change so that social tensions and conflicts build up significantly enough, there can be a shift so that *elements of the superstructure can have a relative primacy* vis-à-vis the economic base itself. Moreover, in Marx's own understanding of a possible transition from a capitalist social formation to a genuine socialist one, various elements in the social superstructure would definitely have a relative primacy in shaping the transition to a new social formation.

Although Marx himself does *not* use such language, I argue that what he projects really amounts to a *relative primacy of the spiritual dimension of human reality* in a transition from capitalism to a genuine socialism. In other words he is implicitly calling for what amounts to a spiritual revolution—and one that I believe is very close in content to the sort of spiritual revolution that the Dalai Lama calls for in his wonderful recent work, *Ethics for the New Millennium*.[19] If I can put it this way, I think one can fairly say that Marx himself is really "half Buddhist." Hopefully this will begin to become clear as I go on to sketch how the spiritual dimension can be understood within the framework of Marx's scientific/philosophical paradigm. To do so I draw from an earlier published paper of mine wherein I gave a developed exposition of the spiritual dimension in Marx.[20]

Now I realize that it can be extremely puzzling for most Westerners to hear any claim that Marx could acknowledge the reality of a spiritual dimension. After all a kind of cultural equation has become embedded in the Western psyche that sees the spiritual as necessarily implying the reality of the supernatural, a substantial soul, and the traditional creator god. However, such a notion will not seem puzzling to those grounded in the Buddhist tradition. For this tradition, like Marx, does not accept the projection of the sort of creator god associated with Christianity and other Western religions; nor does it accept the projection of a substantial and immortal soul. Yet this ancient tradition is renowned for its deep spirituality. For Marx's part, he can readily accept the reality of a spiritual dimension on the basis of the ontological primacy of the kind of biological organisms we human beings are, and of the kind of organic and inorganic world of nature with which we interact all the time. But to take the natural world as ontologically primary vis-à-vis spirituality and the spiritual dimension, to take the natural world as the necessary basis in order for there to be any spirituality at all, does not mean that you can reductively understand spirituality in terms of matter.[21]

How then do we construe the spiritual dimension within Marx's paradigm? Well, in the paper from which I draw, I have explained that Marx's view of human reality, when seen in all its many-sidedness, explicitly and implicitly presupposes an array of existential needs that include the following: the need for meaning, the need for interconnection with reality, the need for community, the need for creative expression of potentials, the need for a viable worldview, the need for a viable value system, and the need for wholeness. I then go on to explain the notion of the spiritual dimension that is at play in Marx's philosophical perspective in relation to such existential needs—and I distinguish various levels of the spiritual dimension in doing so. On one level the spiritual dimension is that dimension of the human psyche within which the fundamental existential needs mentioned above resonate and make themselves felt in lived experience. Moreover, it is a dimension that comes to address these needs in different ways in different concrete circumstances. Since there is a very broad spectrum of possible ways in which human beings can attempt to address these existential needs as historically given conditions vary, this means that the *spiritual dimension is itself historically variable* in some important ways.

What happens within the spiritual dimension during those periods of dramatic transition in human social life, when one sort of social formation is replaced by another, is crucially important. For it is within this dimension that the awareness of a relative satisfaction, or a relative dissatisfaction, of the fundamental existential needs is experienced, as the case may be in given circumstances; and it is within this dimension that older modes of spirituality break down and new modes arise. Furthermore, the breakdown in the existential viability of a given mode of addressing the complex of existential needs within the context of a given social formation is the attendant precursor of such dramatic social transitions.

Moreover, when such a dramatic transition does in fact occur, a new mode of addressing the fundamental existential needs first becomes crystallized because of an interaction between various ideas that have become culturally available and dynamic energies flowing at still deeper levels of the spiritual dimension that are below the threshold of consciousness—levels that contain the wellsprings of human creativity—and once crystallized, the new mode begins to take hold in the community at large. These dynamic energies can be thought of as arising from a diffuse and amorphous unconscious, and as crystallizing in consciousness in determinate patterns corresponding to particular ways of addressing existential needs, but as doing so in different ways in different circumstances. Thus we have to postulate that the spiritual dimension has both conscious and unconscious levels.

A change in the spiritual dimension would involve a reorganization of the dynamic energies of the psychic infrastructure. However, some organizations of the psychic infrastructure are to be seen as more existentially fulfilling than others in given circumstances, while other possible organizations are much less so, or are even existentially meaningless. It all depends on the particular concrete social circumstances, and on the way human life as lived in terms of some particular way of addressing existential needs is actually experienced by real individual human beings. In any case, contrary to the dominant ways of interpreting the theory of historical materialism, I argue that in periods of dramatic social transformation elements of the social superstructure *together with the spiritual dimension as projected here* have a relative primacy over the economic base—and that this is implicit in Marx's own understanding of the theory of historical materialism.

Now Marx himself believed that a transition from the capitalist social reality to a genuine socialism was a real possibility some time close to his own lifetime; for he believed that the intensity of the *combined material and spiritual impoverishment, and the attendant suffering*, of large numbers of people in his era *could* lead to the emergence of a revolutionizing agency that could bring about such a change. It is very important for a comprehension of the theory of historical materialism to recognize that Marx's projection of a possible transition to genuine socialism close to his own lifetime was tied to some very important contingencies. Among the most important were the practical necessity of a widespread transformation of consciousness, as well as a widespread commitment to what amounts to a new spirituality— that is, to a new way of addressing the fundamental existential needs. But, of course, not just *any* transformation of consciousness, or *any* new spirituality.

If I may borrow some phrases from the Buddhist "eightfold path" but with a different meaning than they have there, I would say that in Marx's mind "right effort" and "right understanding" were among the practically necessary prerequisites for any transition to a genuine socialism. Concerning the theme of right effort in this context, it means a collective effort that is guided by the moral commitment to a new ethos, a new spirituality, a new mode of addressing frustrated existential needs—an ethos and a spirituality of the sort that would be at the living, pulsating heart of that unalienated mode of being that Marx associates with what he means by genuine socialism. This mode of being is the very one I tried to capture in the previous section of this addendum when I gave an exposition of what Marx means by "*free conscious activity.*"

Moreover, such right effort must be guided by right understanding. For Marx right understanding in this context means right understanding of the *external causes* of human suffering—i.e., the economic, social, political, and institutional causes of such suffering; especially oppressive and exploitative economic social relations. Furthermore, it means a recognition of the historicity of the various forms that human nature assumes in the course of history; it means an understanding of the possibility of new forms of human being that would be more fulfilling and less alienated than those ways in which human beings have made themselves so far; it means a comprehension of the broad structures of cultural evolution as comprehended by the theory of historical materialism; and it means the recognition that only collective human effort and commitment can actualize such potentialities—for there is nothing predetermined or automatic in the outcome that Marx was trying to nurture.

Buddhist and Marxist Affinities

In this section I will first bring into focus some of the affinities between humanistic Marxism and Buddhism that have already come out, partially at least, in earlier sections of this addendum; and following this I will go on to bring out additional affinities between these two perspectives on human reality. Thus we have already seen that both Buddhism and humanistic Marxism do not accept the notion of a creator god, or the reality of a soul-substance, or any kind of eternal afterlife as an individual substance. Moreover, we have seen that both perspectives are deeply concerned with the reality of human suffering; but also that Buddhism is primarily concerned with the *internal* factors that are generative of human suffering, while Marxism is primarily concerned with the *external* factors generative of the various forms of human suffering. To bring these themes out more fully, let me make some comments concerning the "four noble truths" that stand at the heart of Buddhism as a spiritual outlook.

(a) The first of these "noble truths" is the existential truth that human life is permeated with various types of suffering (i.e., discontent, dis-ease, alienation, etc.); (b) the second truth makes the projection that such suffering is generated by the ceaseless strivings, attachments and aversions of the ego-self; (c) the third truth, in turn, projects that the necessary antidote for such suffering is a "letting go," a transcending of the ego-self; and (d) the fourth noble truth delineates an "eightfold path" to accomplish such a transcendence of the ego-self.[22] (In his classic work on Buddhism, Edward Conze refers to these noble truths as the "common ground" of the various Buddhist traditions.[23])

The central Buddhist concern about human suffering is clearly evident from even this brief indication of the noble truths. But also one can readily surmise that it is primarily the *internal subjective factors* connected with suffering, and its transcendence, that have been the chief focus of Buddhism. In all the various traditions of Buddhism, the suffering human person is construed to be immersed in *samsara*, understood as the empirical life-death cycle, or the flux of becoming in which the ego-self sees itself as immersed, and in which the human being undergoes suffering of various sorts on account of its fixations on, and its aversions and attachments with respect to the various feelings, beliefs, things, people (etc.) that are encountered. Release from suffering as Buddhism understands it requires, first, a recognition of the subjective attachments and aversions of the ego-self as being the cause of one's own suffering; and second, it requires an eventual undoing of all the subjective ego fixations and attachments that lead to the generation of suffering. Furthermore, it is the famous eightfold path with its interrelated regimen of practices that has the potential to bring about release from human suffering through a "letting go" of the ego-self—provided the prescribed practices are faithfully carried out. To be sure, though, it may take many lifetimes for such a "letting go" of the ego-self to be completely carried out.

To exemplify the way that the practices constitutive of the eightfold path are mostly internal subjective practices, let me briefly touch on "right mindfulness"—one of the main dimensions of the eightfold path. In "The Greater Discourse on the Foundations of Mindfulness" we find a classical Buddhist text in which practices are outlined that focus on mindful awareness of breathing, of bodily postures, of feelings, of thoughts, of the four noble truths themselves, etc.[24] Special attention is given to becoming mindfully aware of the array of *subjective* causal factors that lead to the emergence of given feelings such as anger or resentment, to changes in the strength and quality of those feelings, and to the subsiding of those feelings, etc. Moreover, attention is also given to the transformation of the energy of problematic feelings from negative to positive. Likewise special attention is given to mindful awareness of the causal factors associated with given thoughts—when and how they emerge, when and how they disappear, etc. All of this, of course, contrasts markedly with Marx's primary focus on the *external factors* that he sees as being primarily responsible for human suffering in given historical conditions—especially the interrelated factors constitutive of the economic structure of any given social formation, including hierarchical social relations of production involving exploitation and oppression of one class by another class.

Here one might pose the question as to whether Buddha himself, were he alive today, would extend his concern to include the external factors generative of human suffering, as well as the internal factors which he explored so systematically. It seems clear to me that were Buddha alive today, and were he aware of Marx's empirically based understanding of the dynamics of cultural evolution, he would quite definitely extend the practice of mindful awareness to include mindfulness of the external factors involved in the generation of human suffering. That such a suggestion is not amiss will become even clearer if one considers the notion of "*dependent co-origination*" that is an important aspect of another dimension of the eightfold path—namely "right understanding." Before I address this particular issue, though, I mention in passing that there have been recent developments taking place in the Buddhist world that are beginning to explicitly address the external factors associated with suffering. Here I have in mind the development of various movements of "engaged Buddhism," starting in the early twentieth century and reaching right up to the present, that put significant focus on such issues as human rights, social justice, due process, etc.[25]

As I approach the issue of dependent co-origination, let me address it in the context of right understanding. Among other things, *right understanding* in the Buddhist perspective traditionally involves the following: (a) a realization that reality is an ongoing process in which there are no permanent substances—whether soul substances or any other sort of substance; (b) a realization that everything is interconnected directly or indirectly with everything else in a complex network of dependent co-origination; (c) an existential understanding of the four noble truths themselves; and (d) an understanding that full spiritual freedom consists in realizing a mode of enlightened awareness in which the ego-self has been completely transcended.

The Buddhist notion of dependent co-origination, or of "conditioned genesis" as it is sometimes called, is conceptually interwoven with the view that reality is process in character through and through. Among other things, such a view implies that each seemingly separate thing is what it is by virtue of the complex dynamic interactions that it has with all other things—directly or indirectly. Thus, wherever one turns, one finds things to be mutually interconnected with other things so that things are mutually interdependent upon one another for their very being. In a summary formulation, the notion of dependent co-origination projects the following: "With the arising of this, that arises; and with the ceasing of this, that ceases."[26] While this notion is most frequently projected in connection with a chain of twelve conditioned and conditioning links involving internal subjective factors, that range from "ignorance" to "*dukkha*"[27] (suffering), it also has a more general wide-ranging ontological application in Buddhism.

Once again my suggestion is that, were the historical Buddha alive at the present time, and were he fully aware of the humanistic-Marxist perspective on social reality, he would quite naturally extend his notion of dependent co-origination to take account of the various mutually interconnected, and mutually interdependent, external factors operating in a given situation—the sort of factors that generate the various forms of human suffering and of alienation that Marx himself was so concerned to understand. Some people here and there, including myself, even regard Marx as a kind of *bodhisattva*. But in his case he was a sort of "*worldly bodhisattva*"[28] who was concerned with the various external factors that are dynamically associated with human suffering in any given social context. He devoted his life to the theoretical understanding of such factors—not simply with a view toward interpreting the world, but with *a view toward changing it*, so that people could live more completely human lives.[29] Thus if the historical Buddha, with Marx's *bodhisattvic* help, could have identified the specific external factors that functioned to generate and sustain specific forms of suffering and alienation, he would quite naturally have seen that, *when these specific external factors arise, this specific type of suffering and alienation arises; and that if these factors were to cease operating, this suffering would also cease*. Would not the historical Buddha have extended the chain of dependent co-origination so as to mindfully address the external factors dynamically interconnected with human suffering? Would not Buddha himself have recognized that he too was "half Marxist"?

In any case, the classical Buddhist texts recognize that the notion of dependent co-origination applies in all domains of reality, even though its most frequent application in these texts involves the chain of twelve conditioned and conditioning links of internal subjective factors ranging from ignorance to "*dukkha*" (suffering). Contrasting with this is the case of Marx who is also working with a notion of dependent co-origination, although Marx himself does not use this phrase. Consider, for example, the dialectical interplay between the factors constituting the economic base in any given situation, and the factors constituting the social superstructure in that situation. Not only do the interacting factors constituting the economic base mutually shape one another as well as the social superstructure, but also the superstructure and its complex of interrelating factors mutually shape the economic base in their turn—with the base having a relative primacy in periods of stability, and the superstructure having a relative primacy in periods of transition.[30]

Thus the main sphere of application of Marx's own notion of dependent co-origination is the domain with which his theory of historical materialism is concerned—that is, the domain of the ongoing historical process through which human beings make themselves. This is the *domain of praxis* as the moving dialectical interface between human beings and the environment in which they find themselves situated. This is the domain of the dialectical historical process through which human beings make themselves in specific ways on the basis of the specific ways they have made themselves in the past; but also, markedly, the domain in which they make themselves in changing ways when they change the specific ways they interrelate with the environment and with one another. Moreover, just as in the case of Buddhism, this more specific application of Marx's notion of dialectical dependent co-origination is carried out against the ontological background of a more general application of it that views reality all round as a process reality through and through—a reality in which each thing, in any domain whatever, becomes what it is via the dynamic internal relations it has with other things.[31] Just as in the case of Buddhism, this means that nothing has a "self nature" absolutely independent of other things, and that there are no unchanging substances in any absolute sense.

Another one of the striking affinities between Buddhism and Marx concerns the theme of human beings as the makers of themselves. In the preceding sections of this paper I have already given a sketch of the way in which Marx construes human beings to be the makers of themselves. With Marx, though, the focus is clearly on the external conditions in the context of which people make themselves, and remake themselves. But Buddhism also construes human beings as the makers of themselves, although in a different way than Marx does, of course. In the classic *Dhammapada*, for example, we find formulations such as the following: (a) "All that we are is the result of what we have thought: it is founded on our thoughts, it is made up of our thoughts."—(b) "Those who are slaves to passions follow the stream of desires, as a spider runs down the web he has made for himself."—and (c) "Wise people fashion themselves."[32] But once again, with Buddhism the focus in on the internal factors in relation to which human beings make and remake themselves.

Moreover, both perspectives begin their understanding of human beings with a focus on human beings as they are in given conditions that have been shaped by past human action. On Marx's side we find him explicitly indicating that he begins his empirically based understanding of human reality with "the real individuals, their activity and the material conditions under which they live, both those which they find already existing and those produced by their activity."[33] Again the focus is clearly on the *specific* external conditions in the context of which people make themselves, and remake themselves. On the side of Buddhism, in turn, the understanding of human reality begins with mindful awareness of the specific subjective situation in which the human individual finds him- or herself—a subjective situation that has been shaped by the past activity of the individual. Importantly, though, both Buddhism and Marxism agree that, while human beings are shaped by given conditions that have been shaped by human activity in the past, this does *not mean* that they are *completely* shaped by the cumulative results of past activity. For both perspectives agree that present activity is not fatalistically determined by past activity in such a way that human beings are unable to change themselves. Both perspectives hold that, with clear understanding of how human beings have made themselves in specific ways in the past, they can in principle go beyond such past ways of making themselves, and make themselves in significantly new ways. Also both perspectives are concerned to open up horizons for understanding how human beings might make themselves in different ways.

Now let me explicitly address the notion of karma. In the Buddhist tradition the term "karma" has the following connotations: (a) conditioned action; (b) the shaping power of action; as well as (c) the cumulative effects of past actions. Whatever one does in any present moment is partially shaped by the cumulative results of one's past actions—perhaps in most circumstances it is even largely shaped so; but it is *never* completely shaped by one's past action. For one can always begin to change one's karma in any present moment. Moreover, whatever one does in the present shapes one's ongoing future actions. Thus there is a complex cause/effect network at play in the shaping of human activity. It would be well to mention here, in passing, that the Buddhist notion of action is broad enough to include what one might call "mental actions"—such as conditioned feelings, thoughts, etc.—for these too are held to be shaped by karmic energies, and also to shape them. Now if this were all there were to the notion of karma, a humanistic Marxist could well agree to it. However there is a good bit more to it in the Buddhist tradition.

It is well known that Buddhism extends the operation of karma way beyond one's present life. For it projects a succession of lives in the course of which karmic energies that have been shaped over the span of one's many past lives carry over into one's present life, including the present phase of one's present life, and also carry over into one's future life, or lives, depending on the circumstances. This is all associated with a doctrine of rebirth and reincarnation in Buddhism; but, as we have seen earlier, in Buddhism this does not involve any doctrine of a transmigrating substance as it does in Hinduism. In view of the fact that I introduced some citations from the Dalai Lama earlier, it might be well to mention in this context that the present Dalai Lama (the fourteenth) is "held to be the reincarnation of each of the previous thirteen Dalai Lamas of Tibet (the first having been born in 1351 AD), who are in turn considered to be manifestations of Avalokiteshvara, Bodhisattva of Compassion."[34]

To be sure, Marx himself does not adhere to such a doctrine of reincarnation; nor could humanistic Marxism consistently adhere to such a doctrine itself, unless perhaps it were construed in a metaphorical way. That it could be so construed, and has been so construed by some Buddhists seems clear. Thus Alan Watts, a prominent interpreter of Zen Buddhism, writes as follows in his classic work, *The Way of Zen*:

Many Buddhists understand the Round of birth-and-death quite literally as a process of reincarnation. . . . But in Zen, and in other schools of the Mahayana [Buddhism], it is often taken in a more figurative way, as that the process of rebirth is from moment to moment, so that one is being reborn so long as one identifies himself with a continuing ego which reincarnates itself afresh at each moment of time.[35]

A humanistic Marxist could consistently accept such a metaphorical view of rebirth, even though Marx himself does not. Bringing this out fully will involve taking a step beyond Marx himself, but nonetheless a step that is guided by Marx's methodology of dialectical explanation, and a step that extends his paradigm to take account of aspects of the spiritual dimension that Marx himself does not address. Before addressing that issue, though, I want to bring out one of the ways in which humanistic Marxism could quite readily adopt a notion of "social karma"—in fact I would say that such a notion is already at play in Marx's thought even though he does not use the phrase.

So then what could a humanistic Marxist mean by "social karma"? Well, to begin with, let's consider a famous passage from *The German Ideology*, part of which we encountered earlier. Concerning the premises from which he begins his analysis of the human situation, Marx explains:

[They] are not arbitrary ones . . . but the real individuals, their activity and the material conditions under which they live, both those which they find already existing and those produced by their activity. . . . As individuals express their lives, so they are. What they are, therefore, coincides with their production, both with *what* they produce and with *how* they produce. The nature of individuals thus depends on the material conditions determining their production.[36]

Given the context from which this passage is taken, and given so many similar contexts throughout Marx's work, it is clear that in any given situation the "material conditions. . .which they find already existing" is intended to embrace not only some specific pattern of "social relations of production" within the context of which people undertake production in that situation, but also some specific complex of "forces of production" that those people set in motion as they produce.

In both cases such already existing "material conditions" can, for Marx, only be understood as the *summary deposits of the past activity* of those people, who by their very activity in the past constituted them to be those specific material conditions. Such already existing material conditions represent the cumulative results of the past activity of human beings. This holds not only with respect to all the various types of physical equipment, various materials (etc.) that are used in production, but also it holds with respect to those economic structures that have been constituted to be what they are on the basis of the past activity of human beings interacting with one another in all the facets of production and distribution. So then the summary deposits of past human activity embedded in the material conditions that specific individuals find already existing represent one major dimension of what we can refer to as "social karma."

What of other dimensions of such social karma then? Well, for Marx, present activity in production is clearly shaped by the cumulative results of past activity. But depending on circumstances, present activity in production can proceed to "continue things as usual" in the process of production, and simply keep on regenerating the same sort of productive output, and the same sort of social relations of production. So here there would not be any qualitatively new social karma, and human beings would continue to make themselves in the same ways as in the past, so that the cumulative results of their activity were pretty much the same as before. On the other hand, if the present productive activity of people, for whatever set of reasons, involves changes either with respect to "*what* they produce" or with respect to "*how* they produce," then such changes would constitute modifications of their social karma.

A further development of these considerations would also have to take into account the multiplicity of ways in which elements of the so-called social super-structure figure into the shaping of social karma. For example, in any cultural context people are born into situations wherein various socializing agents (including parents, teachers, etc.) transmit the ideas, values, norms, etc. that are predominant in that context—and that are dialectically connected with the economic realities at work in that context. Such ideas, values, and norms can be thought of as dimensions of the collective karmic outcome of the past activity of vast numbers of individuals living in earlier times, and interrelating with one another in specific historically conditioned ways. Such ideas, values, and norms shape, in turn, the ongoing activity of given individuals who have been socialized in that context. But then humanistic Marxism would acknowledge, also, that in certain circumstances it is always possible for some of these given individuals to "let go" of some of the ideas, values, and norms into which they had been socialized, and to gravitate toward new ideas (etc.) and to a modified practice, and thus bring about modifications of their social karma.

Now let me shift focus to some other related affinities between Buddhism and Marxism that have to do with the ego-self. Earlier I mentioned that the various traditions of Buddhism understand the suffering human person to be immersed in *samsara*—that is, the flux of becoming in which the human being undergoes suffering of various sorts on account of its fixations, aversions, and attachments with respect to the various phenomena that are encountered in the flux of becoming. Release from suffering, as Buddhism understands it, requires not only a recognition of the subjective attachments and aversions of the ego-self as being the cause of one's own suffering, but it also requires an eventual complete "letting go" of the ego-self, along with a recognition that the ego-self is really a functional construct of such attachments and aversions. Such "letting go" is carried out via the recommended practices of the eightfold path.

Shortly I will bring Marx back into the picture, but prior to that let me raise the question as to whether Buddhism acknowledges many different forms of the ego-self, or only one form of it. Presumably if there can be many forms of the ego-self, then perhaps they would not all be equally problematic with respect to degrees of suffering, etc. However, if there can only be one form of ego-self, would it be equally problematic for all those not yet spiritually liberated in the Buddhist sense? Well, it seems to me that a plausible resolution of this issue is tied up with the Buddhist notion of karma. I have mentioned the Buddhist view that karmic energies keep carrying over from one lifetime to another, until the ego-self is transcended. If, in the course of a succession of reincarnations, more and more "bad karma" is gradually eliminated from the bundle of karmic energies that carry over from one reincarnation to another, this could presumably mean, implicitly at least, that such a diminution of bad karma is associated with a series of successive forms of the ego-self. Moreover, it could potentially mean a diminution in the degree of suffering undergone in successive life times—especially suffering that is imposed on other people. Such suggestions about the ego-self, though, seem only to be implicit in Buddhism, and not fully explicit—at least in my reading.

Here now I bring Marx back into the picture, especially his theory of human cultural development that interprets human reality as a developing process. The process of human development, including the dynamics of the various stages that characterize its development, is understood in terms of the dialectical interplay between what Marx refers to as the "*forces of production*," the "*social relations of production and reproduction*," and the "*social superstructure*." We saw that the development of all three of these dialectically interrelated dimensions is the development of conscious activity in the world—the development of praxis. For Marx, the development of conscious activity in all these dimensions is the development of human nature in history. Moreover, any particular form of the social superstructure that comes into being at a given stage of human development will involve *some dialectically associated forms of the ego-self*, depending on the particular historically conditioned values, ideas, norms, associated practices (etc.) that obtain in those circumstances.

Furthermore, the specific degree and specific quality of human suffering can vary, and will vary significantly depending on the specific forms of ego-consciousness that are shaped in specific historical conditions. Here it is also important to note that as given social groups approach more and more closely to the ideal of the unalienated mode of being that Marx espouses, the associated forms of ego-self would be less and less egotistical in nature. Thus the *specific form of ego-consciousness* associated with Marx's notion of unalienated spirituality would be quite different than the form associated with the typical capitalists or workers functioning within the capitalist social formation. As the historical conditions shift and change so do the forms of ego-consciousness—all in accordance with Marx's theory of historical materialism. Moreover, some of these forms of ego-consciousness are more pernicious than others; some are more alienated than others, etc.; and in some forms the boundaries of the ego are more rigid and separatist, while in other forms the boundaries of the ego are more open and less rigid. In the case of the form of ego-consciousness associated with Marx's notion of unalienated spirituality, the boundaries of the ego would be quite porous because of the recognition and affirmation in practice of oneself and others as social individuals; and *ego-consciousness here would no longer be egoistic.*

Now it seems clear to me that Marx's theory of historical materialism has a great deal to contribute to the understanding of Buddhist *samsara.* Humanistic Marxism can readily acknowledge the flux of becoming in which human beings undergo suffering of various sorts caused by fixations, aversions, and attachments with respect to the various phenomena that are encountered in the flux of becoming. Importantly though, humanistic Marxism would insist that samsara must be understood as an *"historical materialist samsara."* For samsara is not simply the flux of existence in which the ego-self is pulled this way and that. The flux of samsara has structures—even if they are shifting, changing structures. *Samsara is dominated by economic, social, and political factors.* And the pervasiveness of ego-consciousness in samsara must be understood as the pervasiveness of specific, historically conditioned forms of ego-consciousness. Contrary to the impression one might get from many Buddhist texts, there really are many different empirical forms of samsara. To be sure, all the different forms of samsara are forms in which ego-consciousness is pervasive. But the specific degree and quality of human suffering will vary significantly depending on the specific form of ego-consciousness that is shaped to be what it is in specific historical conditions. This in turn means that clear understanding of the *external* factors involved in the generation of human suffering, and mindful transformations of such factors aimed at alleviating the most egregious types of correctable human suffering, can potentially be of immense help in addressing the suffering of large numbers of people around the world—even if most of them *never* bring about a complete transcendence of the ego-self.

As I bring this addendum to a close, I want to briefly address the issue of how one could view a possible transcendence of the ego-self in a way that would be fully consistent with a humanistic-Marxist perspective. In doing so I draw again from an earlier published paper.[37] In that paper I tried to open up a path on which humanistic Marxism could take some steps beyond Marx himself concerning a level of the spiritual dimension that he himself does not consider. The level to which I refer is that level of the spiritual dimension on which the human being can have direct personal experience of the interconnection with the wider reality in a way that goes beyond the subject/object structure of ordinary consciousness.

To be sure, Marx himself does not speak like this, nor does he implicitly suggest such a position. Nonetheless, in the aforementioned paper I have argued that Marx's theory of historical materialism can only be properly understood when it is comprehended in an open-ended way, and in terms of a succession of dialectically integrated levels of analysis—all of which is implicitly mandated by his mature dialectical method of explanation. In such an explanatory development, each more concretely elaborated level of the explanatory process brings into play more and more complicating factors left out of account on the more abstract levels. When the theory of historical materialism is comprehended in this way, it becomes possible to understand how his philosophical/scientific paradigm can be extended further than Marx himself extended it, by bringing into the picture additional factors left completely out of account by him. Thus I attempt to show how Marx's paradigm can be extended to take account of a deeper level of the spiritual dimension than Marx himself addresses—a level characterised by direct experiential awareness of the interconnection with the wider reality in a way that goes beyond the subject/object structure of ordinary consciousness.

Perhaps this level of the spiritual dimension could, in principle, be approached by "letting go" of any of the historically conditioned forms of the ego-self that historical materialism would recognize—whether this be accomplished via the Buddhist eightfold path, or some other set of such disciplines. However, it could be approached most easily by most people, perhaps, from the mode of ego-self that I associate with Marx's unalienated mode of being—a mode of ego-self that would have *already* let go of much of the egotistical baggage with which most people in most cultures are burdened. Consider this: Most of the baggage that leads people to oppress and exploit one another, as they pursue their private interest in competitive and antagonistic jostling with one another, would have been sloughed off. Thus it would be a fairly short experiential step from the unalienated mode of being that Marx projects—a mode in which people concretely related to one another as whole persons—to a mode of being that had completely transcended the ego-self.

I emphasize right away that in such a mode of awareness one would still be very much in the world, although in a transformed way such that the ego-consciousness of ordinary experience had been transcended, and the various fixations and attachments of ego-consciousness had been undone—at least temporarily. I hasten to add that while ego-consciousness would be transcended, the ego function would not be totally obliterated but would be embraced by, or encompassed by, a more expansive mode of awareness that no longer had the subject/object structure of ordinary consciousness.

Such a mode of awareness is also at the very center of the Buddhist notion of spiritual enlightenment, especially the Mahayana Buddhist notion of *Sunyata*, or *Emptiness*. In the paper I mentioned, I explicitly address the striking similarities between Buddhist Emptiness, and the notion of an unalienated mode of being at play in Marx's thought; and I refer interested readers to that discussion. Here let me conclude with a metaphor. I can imagine Marx and Buddha facing one another, each standing close to a sort of threshold that separates Marx's notion of an unalienated mode of being and Buddha's notion of spiritual enlightenment; and both of them reaching across this threshold and embracing one another as brothers—two compassionate *bodhisattvas* embracing across thousands of years.

Notes

Introduction

1. Alvin Gouldner, *The Two Marxisms* (New York: Seabury Press, 1980).
2. For example, see Albrecht Wellmer's chapter on "The Latent Positivism in Marx's Philosophy of History" in his work *Critical Theory of Society*, trans. John Cumming (New York: Seabury Press, 1974). Wellmer's basic thesis is that "[t]he union of historical materialism and the criticism of political economy in Marx's social theory is inherently contradictory" (p. 74). And this, because the "basic assumptions of Marx's interpretation of history" supposedly imply a positivist theory of social development, "in contrast to the ideology-critical approach of the theory" (ibid). Wellmer's discussion is explicitly tied back to the interpretation of Marx given by Jürgen Habermas. See Chaps. 2 and 3 of his work, *Knowledge and Human Interests*, trans. Jeremy J. Shapiro (Boston: Beacon Press, 1971). The basic assumption of Habermas' interpretation is Marx's supposed *"reduction of the self-generative act of the human species* to labor" (p. 42); *but,* important to add, labor in the sense of "instrumental action" from which the dimensions of social interaction and linguistic "communicative action" have been stripped away. Similarly, in his interpretation of Marx's concept of a materialistic synthesis between man and nature, Habermas construes "objective activity," which simultaneously shapes man and nature, as constitutive of the "objectivity of possible objects of experience," but *not* as constitutive of the objectivity of possible social relations between and among social individuals. Habermas sees "labor" and "objective activity," *as thus denuded,* as the philosophical basis of Marx's understanding of history, and his program to build a natural science of man. Follow Habermas in such assumptions, and it is simple to make Marx out to be a positivist. To be sure, Habermas recognizes the critical dimension of Marx's social theory, but he does so in a way that injects a theoretical schizophrenia between Marx's "philosophical frame of reference" and his "empirical analyses"—between what Habermas sometimes calls Marx's "categorial level" and "the level of his material investigations" (pp. 52-53). Habermas writes: "Alongside the forces of production in which

instrumental action is sedimented, Marx's social theory also incorporates into its approach the institutional framework, the relations of production. It does not eliminate from practice the structure of symbolic interaction and the role of cultural tradition, which are the only bases on which power . . . and ideology can be comprehended. But this aspect of practice is not made part of the philosophical frame of reference. . . . Thus in Marx's works a peculiar disproportion arises between the practice of inquiry and the limited philosophical self-understanding of this inquiry. In his empirical analyses Marx comprehends the history of the species under categories of material activity *and* the critical abolition of ideologies, of instrumental action *and* revolutionary practice, of labor *and* reflection at once. But Marx interprets what he does in the more restricted conception of the species' self reflection through work alone" (p. 42). Rather than interpret Marx's philosophical category "labor" as a concrete universal that has to be understood in relation to its more concrete elaborations, which more adequately disclose its intended meaning (including the dimension of social interaction, etc.), Habermas reduces the meaning of Marx's philosophical category "labor" to a common language meaning of "labor," summed up in his notion of "instrumental action," and he goes on to operate with this reduced meaning as an *abstract universal* (after the fashion of the now traditional positivist distortions of Marx) in his discussion and interpretation of the scientific dimension of Marx's thought. We maintain against Habermas that an understanding of Marx's dialectical movement from abstract to concrete (which requires that more abstract concepts be interpreted in relation to their more concrete elaborations) would overcome the theoretical schizophrenia that Habermas sees in Marx. And it would also bring out the philosophical harmony of the critical and scientific dimensions of Marx's social theory. For we have a "critical science" in the mature Marx. Once one sees the way the critical dimension is integrated with the scientific dimension in Marx's "science of man," then one would understand that the program of "one science," which the early Marx called for, does not imply positivism as Habermas and others contend. It implies rather that each of the special theoretical sciences must also be seen as having its critical dimension, which (when made explicit) would bring out the social shaping of specific scientific theories in the different scientific domains.

Chapter 1

1. See, for example, the chapter on "Being-in-the-World in General as the Basic State of Dasein," in Martin Heidegger, *Being and Time*, trans. J. Macquarrie and E. Robinson (New York: Harper & Row, 1962). Earlier in this work Heidegger writes: "Thus 'phenomenology' means . . . to let that which shows itself be seen from itself in the very way in which it shows itself from itself. . . . But here we are expressing nothing else than the maxim formulated above: 'To the things themselves!'" (ibid., p. 58). In the same context he writes: "Phenomenology is our way of access to what is to be the theme of ontology, and it is our way of giving it demonstrative precision. *Only as phenomenology is ontology possible.* In the phenomenological conception

of 'phenomenon,' what one has in mind as that which shows itself is the Being of entities, its meaning, its modifications and derivatives" (ibid., p. 60).

For some trenchant criticism of Heideggerian themes, see Karel Kosík's profound work on the *Dialectics of the Concrete*, trans. Karel Kovanda with James Schmidt, ed. Robert S. Cohen and Marx W. Wartofsky (Dordrecht: D. Reidel Publishing Co., 1976). Among other things, Kosík argues that "[t]he method of the 'philosophy of care' is at once mystifying and demystifying in that it presents the everyday in a *particular* reality as though it were the everyday as such. It does not distinguish between the everyday and the 'religion' of the workaday, i.e. the alienated everyday" (ibid., p. 45).

2. The ontological structure referred to here must be understood in terms of internal relations. For the concept of being-in-the-world abstractly indicates concrete internal relations that obtain between the world and human existence.

3. In this connection, note this passage: "Nature is man's *inorganic body*—nature, that is, in so far as it is not itself the human body. Man *lives* on nature—means that nature is his *body*, with which he must remain in continuous interchange if he is not to die. That man's physical and spiritual life is linked to nature means simply that nature is linked to itself, for man is a part of nature." K. Marx, *Economic and Philosophic Manuscripts of 1844*, trans. M. Milligan and ed. D. J. Struik (New York: International Publishers, 1964), p. 112. For some discussion of the "biology of dialectical materialism," consult Venable's chapter on "Man as an Organism," in Vernon Venable, *Human Nature: The Marxian View* (Cleveland: World Publishing, 1966), pp. 56–73.

4. Fromm notes that in the state of alienation the awareness of the internal connection between subject and object is obliterated. "Alienation is essentially experiencing the world and oneself passively, receptively, *as the subject separated from the object*." E. Fromm, *Marx's Concept of Man* (New York: Ungar Publishing Co., 1967), p. 44 (italics added).

5. As used in this context the notion of the "general form" of being-in-the-world is meant to refer to the *broad structures* that characterize human being wherever it is found.

6. The particular formulation of the general form of being-in-the-world as given here is an adaptation of Petrovic's formulation of "praxis as a universal-creative self-creative activity... by which man transforms and creates his world and himself." G. Petrovic, *Marx in the Mid-Twentieth Century* (Garden City, N.Y.: Doubleday & Co., 1967), pp. 78–79.

7. K. Marx, "Theses on Feuerbach," in K. Marx and F. Engels, *The German Ideology*, ed. S. Ryazanskaya (Moscow: Progress Publishers, 1968), p. 665.

8. At one point Marx speaks of such objects as "repositories of subjective activity." K. Marx, *Pre-Capitalist Economic Formations*, trans. J. Cohen, ed. and with intro. by E. J. Hobsbawm (New York: International Publishers, 1965), p. 86.

9. In this connection we refer to Heidegger's notion of "readiness-to-hand," which parallels Marx's view on this theme. Against the background of the notion of "presence-at-hand" in terms of which things are understood as

just occurring among other things, just filling space, so to speak (see Heidegger's *Being and Time*, p. 54), Heidegger explains that the "equipment" which we use in our "concernful dealings with the world" (ibid., p. 96-97) does not just occur in space; but has a kind of being that essentially involves "an *assignment* or *reference* of something to something" (ibid., p. 97). "The kind of Being which equipment possesses—in which it manifests itself in its own right—we call 'readiness-to-hand'" (ibid., p. 98).

10. In his important early essay (written in 1932) on the *Economic and Philosophic Manuscripts*, Marcuse brings this out clearly, making a contrast between alienation and objectification. He writes:

> Objectification—the definition of man as an "objective being"—is not simply a further point appended to the definition of the unity of man and nature, but is the closer and deeper foundation of this unity. (Objectification as such belongs—like his participation in nature—to the essence of man, and can thus not be "superseded"; according to revolutionary theory only a particular form of objectification—reification, "estrangement"—can and must be superseded.) H. Marcuse, "The Foundations of Historical Materialism" in *Studies in Critical Philosophy*, trans. J. De Bres (Boston: Beacon Press, 1973), pp. 17-18.

11. In the *Economic and Philosophic Manuscripts*, p. 180, Marx refers to human activity as "the subjectivity of *objective* essential powers, whose action, therefore, must also be something *objective*."

12. Ibid., p. 181.

13. In connection with the position taken by Marx and Engels on man as the maker of himself, we should also note that, in their view, man has not yet made himself with full practical consciousness of himself as a social individual. For some good commentary on this, see Venable, *Human Nature: The Marxian View*, pp. 74-81. Also see some of Engels' formulations that bear directly on man's failure to make history consciously so far, and his capacity to make it consciously in the future. One place these formulations are given is in *Reader in Marxist Philosophy*, ed. H. Selsam and H. Martel (New York: International Publishers, 1963), pp. 191-96, 203, 211-12, and 223.

14. As Marx says: "[A]ll history is nothing but a continuous transformation of human nature." *The Poverty of Philosophy* (New York: International Publishers, 1963), p. 147. For a good discussion of changing human nature, see Venable's chapters on "Human Change in Fact" and "Human Change in Theory," in *Human Nature: The Marxian View*, pp. 13-45.

15. In relation to the distinction between relatively fixed needs and changing needs, see *The German Ideology* by Karl Marx and F. Engels, ed. S. Ryazanskaya (Moscow: Progress Publishers, 1968), p. 282. In this context we also note that Erich Fromm associates a distinction made by Marx in *Capital* between human nature in general, and the specific historical expressions of human nature, with the distinction between relatively fixed and changing needs. Marx writes: "To know what is useful for a dog, one must study dog-nature. This nature itself is not to be deduced from the principle of utility. Applying this to man, he that would criticise all human acts, movements, relations, etc., by the principle of utility, must first deal with

human nature in general, and then with human nature as modified in each historical epoch." Marx, *Capital*, vol. 1, p. 668. Fromm writes: "In line with this distinction between a general human nature and the specific expression of human nature in each culture, Marx distinguishes . . . two types of human drives and appetites: the *constant* or fixed ones, such as hunger and the sexual urge, which are an integral part of human nature, and which can be changed only in their form and the direction they take in various cultures, and the *'relative' appetites*, which are not an integral part of human nature." Fromm, *Marx's Concept of Man*, p. 25.

16. For some good discussion concerning the place of human needs in the development of production, and the relation of needs to the other factors determining production, see Venable's chapter on "The Condition of Being Human: Production," in *Human Nature: The Marxian View*, especially pp. 82–83.

17. As *The German Ideology* puts it: "Life involves before everything else eating and drinking, a habitation, clothing and many other things. The first historical act is thus the production of the means to satisfy these needs, the production of material life itself. . . . The satisfaction of the first need (the action of satisfying, and the instrument of satisfaction which has been acquired) leads to new needs; and this *production of new needs* is the first historical act." (italics added) Marx and Engels, *The German Ideology*, pp. 39–40.

18. Ibid., p. 31.

19. Ibid., pp. 31–32.

20. For some good secondary material on this development see M. Cornforth, *Historical Materialism* (New York: International Publishers, 1954), especially the second part on "How Society Develops," pp. 49–132. In addition, see Venable's chapter on "The Condition of Being Human: Production," in *Human Nature: The Marxian View*, especially pp. 81–97.

21. We point out that the determination of which factors might be predominant in given situations is a matter of empirical research. On this theme see Venable, *Human Nature: The Marxian View*, pp. 90f.

22. See Cornforth's discussion in *Historical Materialism*, pp. 104–5. We stress here that, although the theory of historical materialism does indeed maintain that some kind of social superstructure will arise on a given basis and will correspond to that basis, no suggestion is made that the social superstructure can be deduced from the base. The social structure cannot be determined *a priori*, even if the base is given. For telling formulations on this issue see *The German Ideology*, p. 36, and *Capital*, vol. 3, pp. 791–92. Also see formulations from Engels aimed at correcting the mistaken impression that the superstructure is a mechanical by-product of the base, in *Selected Correspondence*, pp. 475 and 517; "Letter to J. Bloch (1890)" and "Letter to H. Starkenburg (1894)."

23. For good discussion on these themes, see Cornforth, *Historical Materialism*, pp. 41–42 and 105–9.

24. Marx and Engels, *The German Ideology*, p. 40.

25. In this and the following chapters, the particular alienated mode of being-in-the-world with which we shall be concerned is the one associated with

the antagonistic social structures of capitalism. Strictly speaking, i.e., in comparison with what Marx means by an unalienated mode of being-in-the-world, the entire history of man up to now has been the history of the alienated development of human powers. (On this theme see, for example, Marx, *Economic and Philosophic Manuscripts*, pp. 136, 142–43.) This means that there have been many specific forms of the alienated mode of being-in-the-world. In any case, our treatment of the alienated mode of being-in-the-world will be confined to the mode associated with capitalism.

26. See Marx's essay "Estranged Labor," in the *Economic and Philosophic Manuscripts*, especially pp. 114–19.

27. Ibid., p. 113.

28. Hegel is Marx's mentor on this issue, as on so many others. We refer especially to the section on "The Doctrine of Essence," in G. W. F. Hegel, *Science of Logic*, trans. W. H. Johnston and L. G. Struthers (2 vols.; London: Allen & Unwin, 1961), vol. 2, especially pp. 15–18. But also consult Herbert Marcuse's discussion of Hegel's conception of essence in *Reason and Revolution* (Boston: Beacon Press, 1960), pp. 142ff.

29. For discussion on the notion of real possibility see Marcuse's *Reason and Revolution*, pp. 151ff. Also consult Gustav Wetter's *Dialectical Materialism*, trans. Peter Heath (New York: Frederick A. Praeger, 1958), especially pp. 396–401. And for primary discussion in Hegel on this theme see the *Science of Logic*, vol. 2, pp. 173–86.

30. Marx, *Economic and Philosophic Manuscripts*, p. 114.

31. *The Writings of the Young Marx on Philosophy and Society*, ed. Lloyd D. Easton and Kurt H. Guddat (Garden City, N.Y.: Doubleday, 1967), p. 240.

32. K. Marx and F. Engels, *The Holy Family* (Moscow: Foreign Languages Publishing House, 1956), pp. 162–63.

33. Easton and Guddat, eds., *The Writings of the Young Marx*, p. 237.

34. Marx, *Economic and Philosophic Manuscripts*, p. 159.

35. For a striking formulation by Marx along these lines made in connection with his analysis of the process of "simple exchange," see K. Marx, *Grundrisse*, trans. and with a Foreword by Martin Nicolaus (Middlesex, England: Penguin Books, 1973), pp. 241–42.

36. Fritz Pappenheim, *The Alienation of Modern Man* (New York: Modern Reader Paperbacks, 1968), p. 81.

37. In the *Economic and Philosophic Manuscripts*, p. 116, Marx writes: "Every self-estrangement of man, from himself and from nature, appears in the relation in which he places himself and nature to men other than and differentiated from himself. . . . In the real practical world self-estrangement can only become manifest through the real practical relationship to other men. The medium through which estrangement takes place is itself *practical*."

38. Hegel's analysis of the dialectic of "Lordship and Bondage" was a key influence that shaped Marx's thinking on this interconnection. See G. W. F. Hegel, *The Phenomenology of Mind*, trans. J. B. Baillie (New York: Harper & Row, 1967), pp. 228–40. Marx's analysis of the relation between worker and capitalist can be understood as a more concretely specified elaboration of the dialectical relationship between Lordship and Bondage

which is given by Hegel. For some helpful commentary on the Lordship-Bondage relation see Bernstein, *Praxis and Action* (Philadelphia: University of Pennsylvania Press, 1971), pp. 25-28.

39. For formulations by Marx on the "forced" character of work in capitalism, see the *Economic and Philosophic Manuscripts*, pp. 110-11; and *Capital*, vol. 1, pp. 297, 632-33, and 673.

40. Marx, "Excerpt Notes of 1844," in Easton and Guddat, eds., *The Writings of the Young Marx*, p. 281.

41. Marx, *Economic and Philosophic Manuscripts*, p. 116.

42. Ibid., p. 155.

43. The appropriative activity of the capitalist becomes crystallized in the power of money. In this connection see Marx's discussion of money as "the alienated ability of mankind" in the *Economic and Philosophic Manuscripts*, pp. 167-68.

44. Ibid., p. 115.

45. On this theme see the *Economic and Philosophic Manuscripts*, pp. 119-32.

46. Perhaps no single aspect of Marx's thought has been more misunderstood than the position that he takes on the supersession of private property. In any case, if one is to understand what Marx means when he speaks of the supersession of private property, it is necessary to understand what Marx means by "private property." First of all, a distinction must be made between *personal* property and *private* property. In contrast to nonexploitative personal property, private property refers to private ownership in the *means of production*, including materials and instruments of production, natural resources, etc. Here we might mention that private property, for Marx, does not always refer to the capitalist form of private property. Thus in *Capital*, vol. 1, p. 834, Marx writes: "Private property, as the antithesis to social, collective property, exists only where the means of labour and the external conditions of labour belong to private individuals. But according as these private individuals are labourers or not labourers, private property has a different character." Later Marx goes on to write: "Political economy confuses on principle two very different kinds of private property, of which one rests on the producers' own labour, the other on the employment of the labour of others. It forgets that the latter not only is the direct antithesis of the former, but absolutely grows on its tomb only" (ibid., p. 838). When Marx advocates the supersession of private property, it is only that kind of private property that rests on the exploitative "employment of the labour of others" that Marx has in mind. If Marx does not advocate a return to private property in the means of production of a sort "which rests on the producers' own labour," it is only because this form of private property in the means of production is based on "the fusing together of the isolated independent labouring individual with the conditions of his labour" (ibid., p. 836). With the development of the forces of production in capitalism, and especially with the development of machines and factories, production became *social* production, rather than production by independent individuals. However the reality of *social* production was not accompanied by *social* appropriation. Rather, private property in the means of production took on a new form.

47. Marx, *Economic and Philosophic Manuscripts*, p. 119.
48. Ibid., p. 135.
49. Easton and Guddat, eds., *The Writings of the Young Marx*, p. 281.
50. Karl Jaspers, *Man in the Modern Age*, trans. Eden and Cedar Paul (Garden City, N.Y.: Doubleday & Co., 1957), p. 159.

Chapter 2

1. There are now many works that deal with various aspects of Marx's method. A number of these are listed in a helpful bibliography that accompanies Robert S. Cohen's long article "Karl Marx" in *Dictionary of Scientific Biography*, vol. 15 (New York: Scribners, 1978).
2. K. Marx, *Grundrisse* (trans. Nicolaus), p. 101. (The sentence order in the text is altered.) Also compare Hegel's formulation of his version of the "dialectical movement from the abstract to the concrete" as cited by Lenin in his *Philosophical Notebooks* in a section focused on Hegel's *Science of Logic*. V. I. Lenin, *Philosophical Notebooks, Collected Works*, vol. 38 (Moscow: Foreign Languages Publishing House, 1961), p. 231.
3. Louis Althusser, *For Marx*, trans. Ben Brewster (New York: Vintage Books, 1970), pp. 186. For further discussion by Althusser along these lines, consult L. Althusser and E. Balibar, *Reading Capital*, trans. Ben Brewster (New York: Pantheon Books, 1970), pp. 40–41 and 189–90.
4. Marx, *Grundrisse*, p. 101. Consult the famous "Fruit" passage that elaborates on this theme and sets Marx apart from Hegel and "speculative philosophy." See K. Marx and F. Engels, *The Holy Family* (Moscow: Foreign Languages Publishing House, 1956), pp. 78–82.
5. Althusser, *For Marx*, p. 185.
6. Marx, *Grundrisse*, p. 101.
7. The general way of thinking within which empirical research has been undertaken for the most part, since the early days of modern science, is a nondialectical way of thinking. This means that empirical research has been, for the most part, nondialectical empirical research. Engels explores the contrast between these different modes of empirical research in the first chapter of *Anti-Dühring*, among other places. See F. Engels, *Anti-Dühring*, trans. Emile Burns, ed. C. P. Dutt (New York: International Publishers, 1966), pp. 27ff.
8. In this connection, Marx even projects the economic categories, which figure in his analysis, as forms of existence of the concrete-real under investigation. See *Grundrisse*, p. 106.
9. See, e.g., F. Engels' chapter on "Dialectical Materialism," in his work *Ludwig Feuerbach and the Outcome of Classical German Philosophy*, ed. C. P. Dutt (New York: International Publishers, 1941).
10. Hegel, quoted by Lenin in his *Philosophical Notebooks*, p. 106.
11. Bertell Ollman, *Alienation: Marx's Conception of Man in Capitalist Society* (Cambridge: Cambridge University Press, 1971), p. 15.
12. Ibid., p. 62.
13. Lenin, *Philosophical Notebooks*, p. 99.

14. Carol C. Gould, *Marx's Social Ontology: Individuality and Community in Marx's Theory of Social Reality* (Cambridge: MIT Press, 1978), see chap. 1.
15. Brand Blanshard, *The Nature of Thought*, 2 vols. (London: Allen & Unwin, 1939).
16. Blanshard explains that there is "the most intimate connection between the doctrine of abstract universals and the doctrine that things may be related externally. . . . And it is evident that just as the abstract universal and external relations are natural allies, so are the concrete universal and internal relations" (ibid., vol. 2, pp. 459-60).
17. Ibid., p. 452.
18. See ibid., pp. 453, 484, and 488.
19. One clear example of this is the criticism advanced against Blanshard's formulation of internal relations by Ernst Nagel in *Sovereign Reason* (Glencoe, Ill.: The Free Press, 1954), especially in pp. 266-95. Whereas Blanshard projects his own view of internal relations as having both a linguistic and an ontological emphasis, Nagel attempts to critically overthrow Blanshard by effectively refusing Blanshard the right to adopt linguistic conventions suitable to the explanation of his own ontology of internal relations, and in a way that seems to amount to the authoritarian projection of his own linguistic conventions as the prescriptive conventions for thinking and talking about reality. And when Nagel (pp. 271ff.) discusses Blanshard's key phrase, i.e., "the nature of a term," Nagel mistakenly assumes that Blanshard means only the nature of an individual as grasped in language and thought. At the core of his criticism Nagel writes: "[I]t is quite clear that just what characters are included in an individual, and just where the boundaries of an individual are drawn, depend on decisions as to the use of language" (*Sovereign Reason*, p. 275). Nagel suggests that linguistic conventions can and do set the boundaries of the nature of individuals as they are grasped in thought. But when Blanshard speaks about "the nature of a term," he refers both to the nature of an individual as grasped in thought and language and to the nature of an individual as it exists concretely. At issue is the extent to which the nature of an individual as grasped in thought, and as established by *particular* linguistic conventions, reflects the nature of the individual as it exists in the concrete-real. As against Nagel, it would seem that empirical investigation *must* come into play in attempting to assess the adequacy with which the nature of an individual as grasped in thought, through *particular* linguistic conventions, reveals the nature of an individual as it exists in the concrete-real.
20. A later passage makes this clear. Blanshard writes: "The terms we are discussing are not abstractions, but terms in the concrete" (*The Nature of Thought*, vol. 2, p. 484).
21. For some passages that disclose the conceptual setting within which Blanshard's formulation of the theory of internal relations functions, see *The Nature of Thought*, vol. 2, pp. 260-64, 276, and 449, and vol. 1, pp. 632-33.
22. Ibid., pp. 488-89.
23. One might interpret him to be advancing the weaker thesis that "nothing is unknowable," rather than the thesis that "everything could be known at once"—in principle at least.

24. On the theme of structure, see Althusser's long essay "On the Materialist Dialectic," in *For Marx* and the essay on "Marx's Immense Theoretical Revolution," in *Reading Capital.*

25. Althusser, *For Marx*, p. 199.

26. Ibid., p. 202.

27. The phrase "each essential articulation of the structure" recurs throughout Althusser's analysis. Here we must also deal with Ollman's claim to the effect that Althusser views as impossible the existence of structures in a framework of internal relations. Ollman writes: "It is because of the supposed inability of this relational view to house structures that Althusser rejects the conclusion to which so much of his work points. Instead, after clearly demonstrating the impossiblity of isolating social factors in Marxism he argues that Marx instigates a revolution in philosophy by making the 'structure of the whole' . . . ultimately responsible for the character and development of any part. . . . Althusser's fundamental error lies in misusing the concept of structure in much the same way that Hegel misused the concept of idea; that is, a generalization based on examining many particular instances (in this case, various particular structures of the whole) is treated as an independent entity, which is then used to determine the very parts that give rise to it" (Ollman, *Alienation: Marx's Conception of Man in Capitalist Society*, pp. 266–67). In sharp contrast to Ollman's interpretation of Althusser's misuse of the concept of structure, which supposedly projects a structure as standing outside the parts it determines "as an independent entity," listen to Althusser's own words. "The structure is not an essence *outside* the economic phenomena which comes and alters their aspect, forms and relations and which is effective on them as an absent cause, *absent because it is outside them*. . . . This implies therefore that the effects are not outside the structure, are not a pre-existing object, element or space in which the structure arrives to *imprint its mark*: on the contrary, it implies that the structure is immanent in its effects, a cause immanent in its effects in the Spinozist sense of the term, that *the whole existence of the structure consists of its effects*, in short that the structure, which is merely a specific combination of its peculiar elements, is nothing outside its effects" (Althusser, *Reading Capital*, pp. 188–89).

28. In this context, a few words concerning the way in which Althusser's failure to take account of the difference between the abstract universal and the concrete universal constitutes a major flaw, which (apart from the evidence of the *Grundrisse*, and other mature works of Marx) undermines an argument he gives in *For Marx*. He claims that Marx "radically broke" with the positions he has taken in his early works on alienation, humanism, etc. According to Althusser, Marx supposedly adopted a "theoretical antihumanism" in 1845, with what he calls the "works of the break," *The German Ideology*, and "The Theses on Feuerbach" (see *For Marx*, pp. 34 and 229). In these works, Althusser rightly sees Marx as theoretically pitted against philosophical positions which hold that there is a "universal essence of man," such that "this essence is the attribute of *each single individual*"—that is, against philosophical positions which hold that "it is essential that each carries in himself the whole human essence, if not in fact,

at least in principle" (see *For Marx*, p. 228). In these formulations we have the *abstract universal* in play. Although it is true that with *The German Ideology* Marx wanted to dissociate himself from the language of essences, so as to prevent misunderstanding of his own position, his own early humanism was never committed to abstract essences of the traditional sort. Contrary to the assumption at play in Althusser's claims about a "radical break" between the early and late Marx, Marx's *early and later* humanism, and the notion of essence associated with it, was always projected in terms of the concrete universal and not in terms of the abstract universal. The difference is crucial.

29. Ollman, *Alienation*, p. 40.
30. Kosík, *Dialectics of the Concrete*, pp. 1-6.
31. On the theme of "reflection," consult Lenin in his *Philosophical Notebooks*, p. 182.
32. Melvin Rader, *Marx's Interpretation of History* (New York: Oxford University Press, 1979), pp. 150-51.
33. Ibid., p. 159.
34. Marx, *Capital*, vol. 1, pp. 24-25. Concerning this distinction between the method of inquiry and the method of presentation, we cite Robert S. Cohen's essay "Karl Marx" in the *Dictionary of Scientific Biography*, vol. 15, p. 410. Cohen writes: "Marx distinguishes the method of inquiry from the method of exposition. Inquiry *(Forschung)* is factually realistic, beginning with initially uninterpreted data that are subjected to analysis in stages of complexity that demand insightful abstraction, simplification, and subtlety. The factual data *(Tatsache)* are the concrete entities, or wholes; and the results of analysis are abstract principles, analyzed into theoretically formulated 'parts,' hypothetically guided by theories that have been based upon, and more or less tested by, previous empirical investigations. Inquiry is a complex stage of empiricism and of inductive and hypothetical analysis.

Presentation *(Darstellung)* gives the results their necessary development, which aims to be a conceptual return to the concrete and brings the component parts or qualities of any subject matter together in their 'organic' interrelatedness and their evolutionary or historical movements. The return will be mediated by expository as well as theoretical demands so as to clarify the separate qualities and the various relations among them and with their environment. . . . As he [Marx] understood the problem of knowledge, scientific thought must be completed by a careful conceptual process of synthesis, by removal of the [simplifying] assumptions stage by stage, and by the asymptotic approximation to the concrete complexity of the real world."
35. Ollman, *Alienation*, p. 62.
36. Ibid., p. 64.
37. Ibid., pp. 67-68.
38. Ibid., p. 68.
39. Ibid., p. 266.
40. Ibid., p. 267.
41. On Ollman's view of Marx's use of language, and of the meaning of his terms, see the chapter "With Words That Appear Like Bats," in *Alienation*.

42. Paul M. Sweezy, *The Theory of Capitalist Development* (New York: Monthly Review Press, 1970), pp. 18–19. Also, Melvin Rader in *Marx's Interpretation of History* brings out the critical importance of "levels of abstraction" for the understanding of Marx's thought. In the course of his discussion, which emphasizes the model of organic development as the proper model for understanding Marx, Rader comes to penetrating critical grips with interpretations of Marx which stress the base-superstructure model in ways that tend to be mechanistic or reductionist. Rader concludes that Marx "apparently never thought of the base-superstructure and organic models as alternatives. The explanation may be that he regarded the former as the more abstract and the latter as the more concrete. The difference is in the level of abstraction rather than in flat contradiction" (ibid., p. 119).

43. Blanshard, *The Nature of Thought*, vol. 1, pp. 581–82.

44. Ibid., p. 585.

45. In this context consider also the way in which Wittgenstein dissociates himself from the traditional view of the abstract essence that inheres in, and is common to, its various species. See Ludwig Wittgenstein, *The Blue and Brown Books* (New York: Harper & Row, 1965), p. 17; and also his *Philosophical Investigations*, trans. G. E. M. Anscombe (New York: Macmillan, 1953), especially sections 65–77 and 139–41. With his notion of "family resemblances," Wittgenstein comes close to a stance on the problem of universals which, in all essential respects, is the same as the position referred to in other quarters as the concrete-universal.

46. Blanshard, *The Nature of Thought*, vol. 1, pp. 583–84.

47. See ibid., especially pp. 581–627.

48. Ibid., pp. 588–90.

49. For a striking formulation of what is at issue here, see ibid., p. 589.

50. In the Preface to *Capital*, Marx writes: "In the analysis of economic forms, moreover, neither microscopes nor chemical reagents are of use. The *force of abstraction* must replace both. But in bourgeois society the commodity-form of the product labor—or the value-form of the commodity—is the *economic cell form*" (Marx, *Capital*, vol. 1, p. 12). (emphasis added)

51. In dialectical cognition, as Lenin puts it in his *Philosophical Notebooks* (p. 253), "Human thought goes endlessly deeper from appearance to essence, from essence of the first order, as it were, to essence of the second order, and so on *without end*" (Lenin's emphasis). Here, of course, Lenin is speaking about "essence" as interpreted in terms of the concrete universal and not in terms of the abstract universal of traditional Western philosophy. "Essence of the first order" is the first approximation to the essential structures of the concrete totality; and "essence of the second order" is the more concretely developed version of the essential structures developed within the projected structures of the first approximation, etc.

52. Marx, *Capital*, vol. 3, pp. 212–13.

53. Marx, *Capital*, vol. 1, p. 707.

54. Marx, *Capital*, vol. 3, p. 232.

55. See *Capital*, vol. 3, pp. 232–40. The factors that Marx explores here are as follows: "Increasing Intensity of Exploitation," "Depression of Wages Below the Value of Labour-Power," "Relative Over-Population," "Foreign Trade," "The Increase of Stock Capital," and "The Cheapening of Elements of

Constant Capital." It is important to note here that, as capitalism develops, additional factors that Marx does not point to may also come into play and serve to counteract the tendency of the rate of profit to fall, e.g., the "market replacing" functions of the state in the monopoly phase of capitalism.

56. For some now classic formulations of the deductive–nomological model of explanation, see Carl Hempel's *Aspects of Scientific Explanation: And Other Essays* (New York: Free Press, 1965).

57. In his work on *Conceptual Foundations of Scientific Thought* (New York: Macmillan, 1968), Marx W. Wartofsky brings out that "the deductive model of explanation is incomplete as an account of scientific explanation," because it leaves out the conceptual framework within the context of which specific laws are projected (see p. 278).

58. Marx, *Grundrisse*, pp. 100.

59. Ibid., p. 108.

60. Nicolaus writes in the Foreword to his translation of the *Grundrisse*: "That the start of the *Grundrisse* Introduction had been a false one, Marx acknowledged about a year and a half later, in 1859, after he had twice rewritten the Chapter on Money to ready it for print. The notion that the path of investigation must proceed from simple, general, abstract relations towards complex particular wholes no longer appeared to him, then, as 'obviously the scientifically correct procedure.' In his justly famous Preface to the *Critique of Political Economy*, written to replace the *Grundrisse* Introduction, he writes as follows: 'I am suppressing a general Introduction which I had thrown on paper, because on closer consideration any anticipation of yet-to-be-proved results seems to me a distraction, and the reader who wishes to follow me at all must resolve to climb from the particular up to the general!'" (Nicolaus, Foreword to Marx, *Grundrisse*, p. 38).

It is important to note that Nicolaus fails to make a distinction between the "dialectic as inquiry" and the "dialectic as exposition." At no time does Marx project the "path of investigation" as one that leads from the abstract to the concrete. In the text ahead we provide an alternate interpretation of what motivated Marx to withhold his Introduction as a "proper introduction" to his work *A Contribution to the Critique of Political Economy*. See the translation by S. W. Ryazanskaya, ed. with intro. by Maurice Dobb (New York: International Publishers, 1970).

61. Nicolaus, Foreword to the *Grundrisse*, p. 37.

62. Marx writes: "In all forms of society there is one specific kind of production which predominates over the rest, whose relations thus assign rank and influence to the others. It is a general illumination which bathes all the other colours and modifies their particularity. It is a particular ether which determines the specific gravity of every being which has materialized within it. . . . Capital is the all-dominating economic power of bourgeois society. It must form the starting point as well as the finishing point" (*Grundrisse*, pp. 106–7).

63. Marx, *Grundrisse*, p. 85.

64. The first chapter of *Capital* is concerned with the analysis of the commodity. The opening sentences read as follows: "The wealth of those societies in which the capitalist mode of production prevails, presents itself as 'an immense accumulation of commodities,' its unit being a single commodity.

Our investigation must therefore begin with the analysis of the commodity"
(Marx, *Capital*, vol. 1, p. 41). Commenting on the commodity as a starting
point for analysis, Nicolaus maintains that such a starting point is "superior
as dialectics to the previous starts, because it *contains* contradiction from the
outset, in embryo; whereas the 'pure' (indeterminate, eternal, absolute and
universal) beginning starts, falsely, by *excluding* an opposite (else it would
not be pure!), and hence has to pull its antithesis in by the hairs, out of
'nothing'" (Nicolaus, Foreword to Marx, *Grundrisse*, p. 38). From the
context of Nicolaus' comment it is clear that the "previous starts" to which
Nicolaus refers when he says that starting with the commodity is "superior *as
dialectics* to the previous starts," it is clear that the reference is to the "general, abstract determinants which obtain in all forms of society" and from
which the movement from abstract to concrete is to begin. The fact that
Nicolaus views the commodity as a beginning superior as dialectics to a beginning from such "abstract determinants" seems to rest on lumping Hegel and
Marx together on just the very issue in relation to which Marx was careful to
dissociate himself from Hegel. One might agree with Nicolaus that Hegel
starts his own analysis (in his *Science of Logic*) with an abstraction that
excludes its opposite and then goes on "to pull its antithesis in by the hairs."
But the abstract relations from which the movement from abstract to concrete is to begin do not *for Marx* exclude their opposites. For example,
shortly after discussing production-in-general—one of the abstract relations
obtaining for all societies—Marx writes: "Production, then, is also immediately consumption, consumption is also immediately production. Each
is immediately its opposite" (Marx, *Grundrisse*, p. 91). Moreover, in the
movement from abstract to concrete as understood by Marx, there is no
pulling of antitheses in by the hairs. Marx's movement is an explanatory
movement, not a generative one.

65. For example, after a preliminary distinction between "use value" and "exchange value," Marx goes on to specify progressively the concept of exchange value more and more fully, with the introduction of more and more
factors into his analysis, namely, the principle that exchange value "must
be capable of being expressed in terms of something common" to all
commodities; the principle that "the exchange of commodities is evidently
an act characterized by a total abstraction from use value"; the notion of
"human labor in the abstract" as that which is common to all commodities,
etc. (see *Capital*, vol. 1, pp. 41–45).

66. K. Marx, *A Contribution to the Critique of Political Economy*, p. 20.

67. Ibid., p. 19.

68. That this was not peculiar coming from Marx is attested to in a letter written
to Engels in 1865, two years prior to the publication of the first volume of
Capital, where Marx speaks of holding back the publication of *Capital* for
similar reasons. Marx writes: "But I cannot bring myself to send off anything
until I have the whole before me. Whatever shortcomings they may have,
the merit of my writings is that they are an artistic whole, and that can only
be attained by my method of never having them printed until they lie before
me as a *whole*." (In *Marx and Engels: Selected Correspondence*, trans. Dona
Torr [New York: International Publishers, 1942], p. 204). Given the scope

of Marx's project it is no wonder that he had to struggle for so many years before he felt he was at the point where he could undertake his scientific presentation in *Capital*. And as important as the main text of the *Grundrisse* is, it should be kept in mind that it did not constitute *for Marx himself* an adequate working out of what he projected in its Introduction as a scientific method of explanation. Not only does the main text of the *Grundrisse* begin with an analysis of money, rather than the commodity, but it is sprinkled with stage directions which Marx gives himself for developing the later presentation in *Capital*. (For example, "to be brought forward," p. 235; "all this belongs already in the first chapter," p. 362; "the anticipated material is to be put here," p. 746; "this section is to be brought forward," p. 881.) Moreover, Marx himself projected the *Grundrisse* as a "rough draft." None of this is meant, though, to deny that the *Grundrisse* is part of Marx's scientific work. For we see the distinction between the "dialectic as inquiry" and the "dialectic as presentation" as a distinction that Marx makes *within* the domain of his scientific work; and see the *Grundrisse* as belonging to his scientific work. Also see Kosik's *Dialectics of the Concrete* (p. 109) on the theme of the commodity as the proper starting point for *Capital*.

Chapter 3

1. This is the translation given in Marx and Engels, *Selected Works*, pp. 182–83.
2. Helmut Fleischer's book, *Marxism and History*, trans. E. Mosbacher (New York: Harper & Row, 1973), is very largely a critique of his view of the Soviet Marxist interpretation of historical materialism.
3. Engels, "Letter to Joseph Bloch" (Sept. 21, 1890), in Marx and Engels, *Selected Correspondence*, pp. 475–77.
4. V. I. Lenin, "A Talk With Defenders of Economism," in V. I. Lenin, *Selected Works*, one-vol. ed. (New York: International Publishers, 1971).
5. Ibid., p. 44.
6. Ibid., p. 46.
7. V. I. Lenin, *What Is to Be Done?* (New York: International Publishers, 1929). See especially pp. 31–54.
8. Fleischer, *Marxism and History*, p. 38.
9. Ibid., p. 43.
10. The first Russian edition of this textbook, *Osnovy Marksistskoj Filosofi*, appeared in 1958. Fleischer quotes from a 1960 German edition.
11. See, for example, *Fundamentals of Marxism-Leninism*, ed. C. Dutt (Moscow: Foreign Languages Publishing House, 1961), especially the section on "Laws of History and Man's Conscious Activity" in chap. 4. Therein we read: "The laws according to which society develops do not operate automatically, of their own accord. Formed as a result of man's activity, these laws determine in their turn the general direction of human activity. There can be no social laws without people, outside their activity. . . . In fact, historical laws of themselves, without people, do not make history. They determine the course of history only through the actions, the struggle and the consciously directed efforts of millions of people" (pp. 165–66).

12. J. Stalin, *Dialectical and Historical Materialism* (New York: International Publishers, 1940); and J. Stalin, *Economic Problems of Socialism in the U.S.S.R.* (New York: International Publishers, 1952).

13. Stalin, *Dialectical and Historical Materialism*, p. 20.

14. Ibid.

15. Stalin, *Economic Problems*, p. 63.

16. Ibid.

17. Ibid., p. 9.

18. Fleischer, *Marxism and History*, p. 35.

19. Ibid., p. 90.

20. Ibid., p. 35.

21. Marx, Preface to *Capital*, vol. 1, p. 13.

22. For a discussion of the Laplacian view of causality, see Milič Čapek, *The Philosophical Impact of Contemporary Physics* (Princeton: D. Van Nostrand, 1961), especially chap. 8.

23. Marx and Engels, *The Communist Manifesto*, p. 42.

24. Marx, *Capital*, vol. 1, p. 15.

25. One of Popper's works which has had wide influence in confusing Marx's position is *The Open Society and its Enemies*, rev. ed., 2 vols. (New York: Harper & Row, 1963). An extended "Reply to Dr. Karl Popper's Refutations of Marxism" is given by Maurice Cornforth in *The Open Philosophy and the Open Society* (New York: International Publishers, 1968). Although Cornforth's response to Popper is quite significant in many respects, a tighter and more effective critique of Popper on a philosophical level could be given if the critique of Popper were carried on in a way that brought Marx's method of explanation into explicit play.

26. With the sense that he has a crucial argument undermining any contention that there could be a law of social development, Popper writes: "Although we may assume that any actual succession of phenomena proceeds according to the laws of nature, it is important to realize that practically *no sequence of, say, three or more causally connected concrete events proceeds according to any single law of nature....* The idea that any concrete sequence or succession of events (apart from such examples as the movement of a pendulum or a solar system) can be described or explained by any one law, or by any one definite set of laws, is simply mistaken. There are neither laws of succession, nor laws of evolution" (Karl Popper, *The Poverty of Historicism* [New York: Harper & Row, 1964], p. 117). Contrary to what Popper suggests, a proposed law of social development need not involve any suggestion that it can explain all the concrete detail of social development. As for Marx, the law of social development which he proposes indicates only the broad structures *within the framework of which* the concrete developments can be comprehended. Such laws do not purport to explain the concrete reality in all its detail.

27. Popper, *The Poverty of Historicism*, p. 128.

28. Ibid., p. 115.

29. Ibid., pp. 115–16.

30. Ibid., p. 128.

31. Marx and Engels, *The German Ideology*, p. 51.

32. Ibid., p. 63.

33. For some good discussion concerning the dependence of political and ideological developments on economic developments refer to F. Engels, *Ludwig Feuerbach and the Outcome of Classical German Philosophy*, ed. C. P. Dutt (New York: International Publishers, 1941), pp. 47–61. And for some good discussion concerning the relation between scientific development and economic development, see Robert S. Cohen's long essay "Friedrich Engels" in the *Dictionary of Scientific Biography*, vol. 15 (New York: Scribners, 1978).

34. Concerning this theme, see Marx's case study in *The Eighteenth Brumaire of Louis Bonaparte*, ed. C. P. Dutt (New York: International Publishers, 1935).

35. Engels, "Letter to Mehring," July 14, 1893, in *On Historical Materialism*, p. 305.

36. The phrase is borrowed from Svetozar Stojanović. See his work, *Between Ideals and Reality*, tran. Gerson S. Sher (New York: Oxford University Press, 1973). Among other things, he gives an analysis of the social relations that currently prevail in the Soviet Union.

37. A significant discussion of this theme is undertaken by Venable in *Human Nature: The Marxian View*; see especially pp. 171–213.

38. Along these lines refer to Engels' discussion of socialized production versus private appropriation in *Socialism: Utopian and Scientific*, in Marx and Engels, *Selected Works*, pp. 417–34.

39. Engels writes: "[W]hile the material mode of existence is the *primum agens* this does not preclude the ideological spheres from reacting upon it in their turn, though with a secondary effect" ("Letter to Schmidt," Aug. 5, 1890, in *On Historical Materialism*, p. 290).

40. Mao Tse-Tung, "On Contradiction," in *Mao Tse-Tung: Selected Works*, vol. 2 (New York: International Publishers, 1954); see especially pp. 35–41. Mao's suggestions about the "unevenness" of dialectical development have been further developed by L. Althusser in *For Marx*; see pp. 193–218.

41. Mao, "On Contradiction," p. 41.

42. Among the works of Fromm which are especially significant for the themes which are taken up in this section are the following: *The Anatomy of Human Destructiveness* (New York: Holt, Rinehart and Winston, 1973), especially chap. 10; *Escape from Freedom* (New York: Avon Books, 1965), especially the Appendix; *Beyond the Chains of Illusion* (New York: Simon & Schuster, 1962), especially chaps. 8 and 9; and "The Application of Humanist Psychoanalysis to Marx's Thought," in *Socialist Humanism: An International Symposium*, ed. Erich Fromm (Garden City, N.Y.: Doubleday & Co., 1965).

43. Fromm, *Escape from Freedom*, p. 305.

44. Fromm, "The Application of Humanist Psychoanalysis to Marx's Thought" in *Socialist Humanism*, pp. 231–32. For complementary formulations, see *Escape from Freedom*, pp. 304–5; and *Beyond the Chains of Illusion*, pp. 78–79.

45. Fromm, *Escape from Freedom*, pp. 305–7.

46. Ibid., p. 305.

47. Fromm, *Socialist Humanism*, p. 234.
48. Ibid.
49. See Marx and Engels, *The German Ideology*, p. 61.
50. Fromm writes: "Protestantism was the answer to the human needs of the frightened, uprooted, and isolated individual who had to orient and to relate himself to a new world. The *new character structure, resulting from economic and social changes* and intensified by religious doctrines, became in its turn an important factor in shaping the further social and economic development" (italics added) (Fromm, *Escape from Freedom*, pp. 121-22). But also see the extended discussion that Fromm gives in the same work in the chapter on "Freedom in the Age of the Reformation."
51. The phrase "existential vacuum" is borrowed from Victor Frankl. According to Frankl the "will to meaning" is the most fundamental factor in understanding human motivation. When the "will to meaning" is not fulfilled there ensues an "existential vacuum" that tends to be filled by the development of the "will to power" or the "will to pleasure." See Victor Frankl, *From Death-Camp to Existentialism* (Boston: Beacon Press, 1959).
52. See Max Weber, *The Protestant Ethic and the Spirit of Capitalism*, trans. T. Parsons (New York: Charles Scribner's Sons, 1958).
53. Ibid., p. 90.
54. Ibid., p. 55.
55. Ibid., p. 91.
56. Ibid., p. 183.
57. Ibid., p. 90.
58. Karl Marx, "Contribution to the Critique of Hegel's Philosophy of Right," in K. Marx and F. Engels, *On Religion* (Moscow: Foreign Languages Publishing House, 1957), p. 42.
59. See Albert Einstein, *Ideas and Opinions*, ed. Carl Seelig (New York: Dell Publishing, 1973), p. 57.
60. Ibid., p. 50.
61. Ibid., p. 49.
62. See Paul Tillich, *The Courage to Be* (New Haven: Yale University Press, 1952).
63. Ibid., p. 155.
64. In this connection, see especially Daisetz Teitaro Suzuki's *Essays in Zen Buddhism*, 1st ser. (London: Luzac and Co., 1927); as well as his work, *Zen and Japanese Culture* (Princeton: Princeton University Press, 1959).
65. See Suzuki's essay "On Satori," in *Essays in Zen Buddhism*.
66. Ibid., p. 249.
67. Ibid., p. 216.
68. Ibid.
69. Ibid., p. 242.
70. Ibid., p. 249.
71. Karl Marx, *Economic Manuscripts*, in David McLellan, ed., *Karl Marx: Selected Writings* (Oxford: Oxford University Press, 1977).
72. Marx, *Grundrisse*, p. 490.
73. In this connection see Engels' chapter, "The Part Played by Labour in the

Transition from Ape to Man," in *Dialectics of Nature*, trans. and ed. by Clemens Dutt, with Preface and Notes by J. B. S. Haldane (New York: International Publishers, 1940).

74. We see these two particular existential needs as having something like the status of "archetypes of the collective unconscious"—if we may use the language of Carl Jung, but without adopting the specific archetypes that he postulates. See Carl G. Jung, *The Archetypes and the Collective Unconscious*, trans. R. F. C. Hull (Princeton: Princeton University Press, 1968). Although Jung has sometimes been dismissed as a "fascist" by some Marxists, we hold that there is much in Jung's work that is important; and that a "critical appropriation" of his work, similar to Marcuse's critical appropriation of Freud in *Eros and Civilization*, needs to be made.

75. Marx, *Grundrisse*, p. 489.

76. Fromm, *The Anatomy of Human Destructiveness*, p. 230.

77. Ibid., p. 231.

78. Ibid., p. 251.

79. Ibid., p. 226.

80. Rader, *Marx's Interpretation of History*, pp. 98–99.

81. Marx, *Capital*, vol. 1, p. 709.

82. Ibid., pp. 836–37.

83. This is the translation from *Selected Works* of Marx and Engels, p. 182.

84. Marx, "Theses on Feuerbach," in *The German Ideology*, p. 660. In another place, Marx writes: "In revolutionary activity the changing of oneself coincides with the changing of circumstances" (*The German Ideology*, p. 234).

85. As Rader remarks in *Marx's Interpretation of History*: Marx "conceived the typology of historical development as little more than a heuristic device, not as a Procrustean bed to which history must be fitted by violent foreshortening" (p. 132). One of the best single sources for primary material on the issue of stages of historical development is Karl Marx, *Pre-Capitalist Economic Formations*, trans. J. Cohen, ed. and with intro. by E. J. Hobsbawm (New York: International Publishers, 1965). The introduction by Hobsbawm is especially significant.

86. On the issue of Lassalle, see Franz Mehring, *Karl Marx*, trans. Edward Fitzgerald (Ann Arbor: University of Michigan Press, 1962), pp. 305–15. Marx's argument against Lassalle is important in view of the fact that Lassalle founded the "General Association of German Workers," but then led this association into theoretical and practical compromise with the Prussian state in a way that betrayed the principles of socialism as understood by Marx. This argument against Lassalle is made by Marx in extensive correspondence as well as in the *Critique of the Gotha Programme*. For some of this correspondence, see letters 80, 81, and 113 in Marx and Engels, *Selected Correspondence*.

87. See Svetozar Stojanović, *Between Ideals and Reality*, trans. G. S. Sher (New York: Oxford University Press, 1973).

88. Ibid., pp. 48–49.

89. In this connection see Fromm's *Anatomy of Human Destructiveness*, pp. 218ff.

Chapter 4

1. Shulamith Firestone, *The Dialectic of Sex: The Case for Feminist Revolution* (New York: Bantam Books, 1971).
2. Ibid., p. 8.
3. Ibid.
4. Ibid., pp. 11–12.
5. For material on this theme, see the chapter on "The Family," in F. Engels' work, *The Origin of the Family, Private Property and the State* (New York: International Publishers, 1942). The term "group marriage" is borrowed by Engels from Lewis Morgan's *Ancient Society.* Evelyn Reed addresses the confusion which has developed in relation to this term in *Woman's Evolution: From Matriarchal Clan to Patriarchal Family* (New York: Pathfinder Press, 1975), where she writes: "Morgan's term 'group marriage' refers to a system of mating by which the brothers and sisters of one group mated. with the sisters and brothers of another group. The term led to certain misunderstandings. It was construed by some to mean that a man had a 'group' of wives in the manner of a polygamous setup. . . . [However, the] system called 'group marriage' was simply an intermating agreement or alliance made between two groups, i.e., two clans, to effect a new kind of fraternal relationship between them, one that included the interchange of sisters and brothers as mates. Within this collective agreement every match was made on a voluntary, individual basis. Far from monopolizing or controlling the sexual activities of any woman, a man had to wait until the desired partner gave him the signal that she was available as a mate" (p. 186).
6. Firestone, *The Dialectic of Sex*, p. 9.
7. Karl Marx, *The Ethnological Notebooks of Karl Marx*, ed. and transcribed, with an Introduction by Lawrence Krader (Assen: Van Gorcum & Comp. B. V., 1972).
8. The full title of Lewis H. Morgan's work is *Ancient Society: Or Researches in the Lines of Human Progress from Savagery, through Barbarism to Civilization.* It was originally published in 1877 by H. Holt of New York.
9. Marx, *Ethnological Notebooks*, p. 116. (emphasis deleted)
10. Engels, *The Origin of the Family*, p. 61.
11. See the *Grundrisse*, pp. 471ff, where Marx discusses pre-capitalist social formations. In these pages Marx speaks recurrently about "the naturally arisen clan community," which he projects as the "presupposition" for communal appropriation and utilization of the land, etc., on the part of those human beings who lived prior to the advent of class societies. Moreover, Marx is quite clear in indicating that "the naturally arisen clan community" is the historical predecessor of social formations based on slavery, serfdom, etc., which social formations are "always secondary, derivative, never original" (p. 496). Just after indicating that slavery, serfdom, etc., are derivative, and not historically original social formations, Marx writes, as if to bring out that the historically original clan communities were not based on relations of domination of one person, or social group, over another: "It is of course very simple to imagine that some

powerful, physically dominant individual, after first having caught the animal, then catches humans in order to have them catch animals; in a word, uses human beings as another naturally occurring condition for his reproduction (whereby his own labor reduces itself to ruling) like any other natural creature. But such a notion is stupid—correct as it may be from the standpoint of some particular given clan or commune—because it proceeds from the development of *isolated individuals*. But human beings become individuals only through the process of history. He appears originally as a *species-being [Gattungswesen], clan being, herd animal*, although in no way whatever as a ζῷον πολιτικόν in the political sense" (p. 496). "The original unity between a particular form of community (clan) and the corresponding property in nature, or relation to the objective conditions of production as a natural being, as an objective being of the individual mediated by the commune—this unity, which appears in one respect as the particular form of property—has its living reality in a specific *mode of production* itself, a mode which appears both as a relation between the individuals, and as their specific active relation to inorganic nature, a specific mode of working (which is always family labour, often communal labour). The community itself appears as the first great force of production" (p. 495). There is no suggestion from Marx that "family labor" in these earliest clan communities had involved the social domination of one class, or sex, over another. In another place, Marx writes: "The only barrier which the community can encounter in relating to the natural conditions of production—the earth—as to *its own property* (if we jump ahead to the settled peoples) is *another community*, which already claims it as its own inorganic body. *Warfare* is therefore one of the earliest occupations of each of these naturally arisen communities, both for the defence of their property and for obtaining new property. . . . If human beings themselves are conquered along with the land and soil as its organic accessories, then they are equally conquered as one of the conditions of production, and in this way arises slavery and serfdom, which soon corrupts and modifies the original forms of all communities, and then itself becomes their basis" (p. 491).

12. Evelyn Reed, *Woman's Evolution*, p. 97.
13. See Marx's *Ethnological Notebooks*, p. 120; and Engels' *The Origin of the Family*, p. 51.
14. For a description of these stages, see Engels' chapter on "Stages of Pre-historic Culture," in *The Origin of the Family*. Engels' discussion is based on Morgan's analysis in *Ancient Society*. For a critical reformulation of Morgan's stages, see Reed's discussion in *Woman's Evolution*, p. 340.
15. Engels, *The Origin of the Family*, p. 51.
16. Ibid.
17. Firestone, *The Dialectic of Sex*, pp. 12-13.
18. Marx and Engels, *The German Ideology*, p. 40.
19. Reed, *Woman's Evolution*, p. 131. Concerning the issues raised in this context, we cite the Introduction to Reed's work where she writes: "The resurgence of the women's liberation movement has thrown the spotlight on certain dubious assumptions and disputed questions regarding the past.

Foremost among these is the subject of the matriarchy. Was there a period in human history when women held a highly esteemed and influential place? If so, how did they lose their social eminence, and become the subordinate sex in patriarchal society? Or is the matriarchy, as some say, a myth that has no historical basis? . . . The question of the matriarchy is decisive in establishing whether or not the modern father-family has always existed. The very structure of the maternal clan system precluded it. Instead of being the basic social unit from time immemorial, as most anthropologists contend, it is a late arrival in history, appearing only at the beginning of the civilized epoch" (pp. xiii–xviii). Reed's whole work, which is rooted in the tradition of evolutionary anthropology for which Lewis Morgan is one of the founding fathers, sustains these claims.

20. Althusser, *For Marx*, p. 199.
21. For some good essays dealing with various philosophical aspects of male-female social relations, see *Women and Philosophy: Toward a Theory of Liberation*, ed. Carol C. Gould and Marx W. Wartofsky (New York: Putnam, 1976).
22. Sandra Harding, "What Is the Real Material Base of Patriarchy and Capital?" in *Women and Revolution*, ed. Lydia Sargent (Boston: South End Press, 1981), p. 144. We mention that Harding's essay presupposes the economic determinist interpretation of Marx, which we have found to be so problematic.
23. Ibid., pp. 146 and 152.
24. Nancy Chodorow, *The Reproduction of Mothering: Psychoanalysis and the Sociology of Gender* (Berkeley: University of California Press, 1978).
25. See especially chaps. 11 and 12 of Chodorow's work.
26. Harding, "What Is the Real Material Base?" p. 157.
27. Engels, *The Origin of the Family*, p. 16.
28. Ibid., p. 79. See Engels' chapter on "The Iroquois Gens" for a full account.
29. Ibid., p. 77.
30. Ibid.
31. Ibid., p. 79.
32. Reed, *Woman's Evolution*, p. 417.
33. Engels, *The Origin of the Family*, p. 50.
34. Ibid.
35. Ibid., p. 58.
36. Ibid., p. 66. Emphasis added.
37. Ibid., p. 67. Emphasis added.
38. Marx, *Capital*, vol. 1, p. 536.
39. Iris Young, "Beyond the Unhappy Marriage: A Critique of Dual Systems Theory," in *Women and Revolution*. Among other things, Young's essay is a critique of Heidi Hartmann's essay "The Unhappy Marriage of Marxism and Feminism: Towards a More Progressive Union," which appears as the lead essay in *Women and Revolution*. Hartmann's essay presents a version of the dual systems theory.
40. Ibid., p. 45.
41. Ibid., p. 50.
42. Ibid., p. 51. Emphasis added.

43. Ibid., p. 52.
44. Ibid., p. 58.
45. Ibid.
46. Ibid.
47. Ibid., p. 61.
48. On this theme see, for example, Jean Baker Miller's chapter on "Subordinates and Dominants," in *Toward a New Psychology of Women* (Boston: Beacon Press, 1977). Miller writes: "A subordinate group has to concentrate on basic survival. Subordinates, then, know much more about the dominants than vice versa. They have to. They become highly attuned to the dominants, able to predict their reactions of pleasure and displeasure. Here, I think, is where the long story of 'feminine intuition' and 'feminine wiles' begins. It seems clear that these 'mysterious' gifts are in fact skills, developed through long practice, in reading many small signals, both verbal and non-verbal" (p. 10).
49. Evelyn Reed, *Problems of Women's Liberation* (New York: Pathfinder Press, 1970), p. 73.
50. Betty Friedan, *The Feminine Mystique* (New York: W. W. Norton, 1963).
51. The first chapter of Friedan's book bears this title.
52. Paul A. Baran and Paul M. Sweezy, *Monopoly Capital: An Essay on the American Economic and Social Order* (New York: Monthly Review Press, 1966).
53. Ibid., p. 72.
54. Ibid., p. 113.
55. Marx, *Capital*, vol. 3, pp. 216–23.
56. Concerning this theme, Marx writes: "We know . . . that the labour–process may continue beyond the time necessary to reproduce and incorporate in the product a mere equivalent for the value of the labour-power. Instead of the six hours that are sufficient for the latter purpose, the process may continue for twelve hours. The action of labour-power, therefore, not only reproduces its own value, but produces value over and above it. This surplus-value is the difference between the value of the product and the value of the elements consumed in the formation of that product, in other words, of the means of production and the labour-power" (*Capital*, vol. 1, p. 232).
57. As Marx brings out: "The wage-form thus extinguishes every trace of the division of the working day into necessary labour and surplus–labour, into paid and unpaid labour. All labour appears as paid labour. . . . In slave-labour, even that part of the working day in which the slave is only replacing the value of his own means of existence, in which, therefore, in fact, he works for himself alone, appears as labour for his master. All the slave's labour appears as unpaid labour. In wage-labour, on the contrary, even surplus-labour, or unpaid labour, appears as paid. There the property-relation conceals the labour of the slave for himself; here the money-relation conceals the unrequited labour of the wage-labourer" (*Capital*, vol. 1, p. 591).
58. See Marx's chapter on "The Rate of Profit," in *Capital*, vol. 3.
59. Marx, *Capital*, vol. 3, p. 216.

60. In *Monopoly Capital*, Baran and Sweezy have separate chapters on these themes. See chaps. 5 and 7.
61. Most of the relevant material is indicated by Martin Nicolaus in his Foreword to his full translation of the *Grundrisse*; see pp. 52ff.
62. On this issue, see the letter from Marx to Engels April 2, 1858, in *Selected Correspondence*, pp. 105-9.
63. Marx, *Capital*, vol. 3, p. 110.
64. V. I. Lenin, *Imperialism: The Highest Stage of Capitalism*, in *Lenin: Selected Works*, one-vol. ed. (New York: International Publishers, 1971).
65. Baran and Sweezy, *Monopoly Capital*, p. 4.
66. Ibid., pp. 53-54.
67. Marx, *Capital*, vol. 3, pp. 208-9.
68. Ibid., p. 177.
69. Marx, *Capital*, vol. 1, p. 558.
70. Baran and Sweezy, *Monopoly Capital*, p. 60.
71. Marx, *Capital*, vol. 3, pp. 208-9.
72. Ibid., p. 210.
73. Ibid.
74. Marx W. Wartofsky delivered his paper, "Karl Marx and the Outcome of Classical Marxism," at a symposium on Marx and Science held February 11-12, 1983, under the auspices of the Boston Colloquium for the Philosophy and History of Science at Boston University.
75. Ibid., pp. 5-7.
76. Ibid., p. 4.
77. Ibid., p. 18.
78. Ibid., p. 14.
79. Kosik, *Dialectics of the Concrete*, p. 109.
80. Marx, *Capital*, vol. 1, p. 709.
81. Marx, *Capital*, vol. 3, p. 213.
82. Ibid., pp. 249-50.
83. Ibid., p. 258.
84. Jürgen Habermas, *Legitimation Crisis*, trans. and with an Introduction by Thomas McCarthy (Boston: Beacon Press, 1975), p. 46.
85. Ibid., pp. 86-93.
86. Ibid., p. 72.
87. Marx, *Capital*, vol. 3, p. 238.
88. For some good material on this theme, see the chapter on "The Absorption of Surplus: Militarism and Imperialism," in *Monopoly Capital* by Baran and Sweezy.
89. Ibid., p. 108.
90. Ibid.
91. Marx, *Capital*, vol. 1, p. 684.
92. Ibid., p. 673.
93. Ibid., pp. 677-80.
94. Ibid., p. 707.
95. Ibid., pp. 691-93.
96. Ibid., p. 809.
97. Ibid., p. 709.

98. Ibid., p. 625.
99. Refer to the chapter on "The Structure of the Working Class and its Reserve Armies," in Harry Braverman, *Labor and Monopoly Capital* (New York: Monthly Review Press, 1974).
100. This contrasts, say, with the earliest period of capitalism, during which structurally generated (relatively) short-term tendencies toward such an increase in physical misery did exist. The period referred to is the period of the so-called primitive accumulation, which "is nothing else than the historical process of divorcing the producer from the means of production" (*Capital*, vol. 1, p. 786).
101. Marx, *Capital*, vol. 1, pp. 708-9.
102. On this theme see Braverman's *Labor and Monopoly Capital*, chap. 15, "Clerical Workers," chap. 16, "Service Occupations and Retail Trade," chap. 17, "The Structure of the Working Class and its Reserve Armies."
103. Friedrich Nietzsche, *The Will to Power*, trans. Walter Kaufmann and R. J. Hollingdale, and ed. with Commentary by Walter Kaufmann (New York: Vintage Books, 1968), p. 3.
104. Rader, *Marx's Interpretation of History*, p. 205.
105. Ibid.
106. We speak here especially about the *Economic and Philosophic Manuscripts*, and the *Grundrisse*. In *Marx's Interpretation of History*, Rader notes that these two works, along with others, "did not appear in print until 1927 or later, and the *Grundrisse* as a whole was not published until 1939"—and not in English until 1973. In the same context Rader notes: "The fundamentalist characterization of the base-superstructure doctrine reflects 'scientific socialism,' the 'Marxism' formulated by theoreticians of German Social Democracy between 1875 and 1914. This 'scientific' version was promulgated when less than half of what Marx had written was published" (pp. 5-6).
107. See for example, Friedrich Nietzsche, *Thus Spoke Zarathustra*, in *The Portable Nietzsche*, selected and trans., with an Introduction, Prefaces, and Notes by Walter Kaufmann (New York: Viking Press, 1968), pp. 370-75.
108. See Søren Kierkegaard, *The Attack upon "Christendom,"* in *A Kierkegaard Anthology*, ed. Robert Bretall (Princeton: Princeton University Press, 1946).
109. We borrow the phrase "legitimation crisis" from Habermas, but extend the meaning of the phrase to cover the kind of existential anxiety that arises when an individual begins to radically question given beliefs that had hitherto been accepted unquestioningly.
110. Rader, *Marx's Interpretation of History*, pp. 205-6.
111. Marx, *Economic and Philosophic Manuscripts*, in McLellan, ed., *Karl Marx: Selected Writings*, p. 88.

Chapter 5

1. This analysis is given in Marx's well-known essay on "Estranged Labor," in the *Economic Manuscripts*, pp. 106-19.
2. Ibid., p. 116.
3. Ibid., pp. 114-15.

4. István Mészáros takes important note of this in *Marx's Theory of Alienation* (New York: Harper & Row, 1972), p. 258. Also see Adam Schaff's discussion of the social individual in his chapter on "The Marxist Concept of the Individual," in *Marxism and the Human Individual*, ed. Robert S. Cohen, trans. O. Wojtasiewicz (New York: McGraw-Hill Book Co., 1970). And see Carol Gould's *Marx's Social Ontology* for some fine discussion on the social individual in Marx.

5. K. Marx, *The Grundrisse*, selections ed. and trans. David McLellan (New York: Harper & Row, 1972), p. 72.

6. K. Marx and F. Engels, *The Holy Family*, trans. R. Dixon (Moscow: Foreign Languages Publishing House, 1956), p. 163.

7. See, for example, one of Marx's critics who in speaking of freedom claims that there is only one "genuine article," which is "the right of the individual to do what he chooses." H. B. Parkes, *Marxism: An Autopsy* (Chicago: University of Chicago Press, 1964), pp. 113-14.

8. I. Kant, *Foundations of the Metaphysics of Morals*, trans. Lewis White Beck (Indianapolis: Bobbs-Merrill Co., 1959).

9. Ibid., p. 47.

10. Ibid., p. 54.

11. Ibid., p. 39.

12. Ibid., p. 49.

13. Ibid., p. 28.

14. Ibid., p. 47.

15. Ibid., p. 51.

16. This is not to say that Kant himself was not concerned about the rights of individuals. On this theme we agree with Hans Reiss when he writes in his Introduction to *Kant's Political Writings*, trans. H. B. Nisbet (Cambridge: Cambridge University Press, 1970): Kant "wanted to provide a philosophical vindication of representative government, a vindication which would guarantee respect for the political rights of all individuals" (p. 4).

17. See Kant's *Foundations of the Metaphysics of Morals*, pp. 39-41.

18. Marx, *Grundrisse* (trans. Nicolaus), pp. 244-45. (emphasis added) For a companion formulation, see p. 156 in the Nicolaus translation of the *Grundrisse*.

19. In this connection see *The German Ideology*, pp. 44-45.

20. Marx, "On the Jewish Question," in *Writings of the Young Marx*, p. 225.

21. Easton and Guddat, eds., *Writings of the Young Marx*, p. 272.

22. On these themes see G. W. F. Hegel, *Philosophy of Right*, trans. T. M. Knox (Oxford: The Clarendon Press, 1965), especially paras. 260 and 187.

23. Marx, "On the Jewish Question," in *Writings of the Young Marx*, p. 241. Toward a more complete understanding of what Marx means when he characterizes human emancipation as a condition in which man's "social force is no longer separated from him as political power," see Avineri's chapter on "The New Society," in *The Social and Political Thought of Karl Marx*. Among other things, Avineri gives special attention to the problem of understanding the meaning of the "abolition of the state" in socialism. See especially pp. 202-4.

24. Marx, *Economic and Philosophic Manuscripts*, pp. 143-44.

25. Marx, *Capital*, vol. 3, p. 820.
26. F. Engels, *Anti-Dühring*, ed. C. P. Dutt & trans. E. Burns (New York: International Publishers, 1966), p. 125.
27. Petrovic, *Marx in the Mid-Twentieth Century*, p. 123.
28. Ibid., p. 124.
29. Ibid., p. 123.
30. F. Engels, *Dialectics of Nature*, ed. and trans. C. Dutt (New York: International Publishers, 1940). See Engels' discussion of "Chance and Necessity" in the notes, pp. 230–35.
31. Ibid., p. 232 (italics added).
32. Ibid.
33. Ibid., p. 233. For Hegel's formulations bearing on this issue, see G. W. F. Hegel, *Science of Logic*, trans. W. H. Johnston and L. G. Struthers, 2 vols. (London: Allen & Unwin, 1961), vol. 2, pp. 182–83. Also see Marcuse's commentary on Hegel's conception of necessity in *Reason and Revolution*, pp. 153ff.
34. Engels, *Dialectics of Nature*, p. 224.
35. Ibid., p. 234.
36. In this connection, consult the section on "Necessity and Contingency," in Gustav A. Wetter's *Dialectical Materialism: A Historical and Systematic Survey of Philosophy in the Soviet Union*, trans. Peter Heath (New York: Frederick A. Praeger, 1958), pp. 381–96.
37. Marx, *Capital*, vol. 1, pp. 82–83.
38. Ibid., p. 83.
39. Marx, *The Grundrisse* (tr. McLellan), pp. 142–43.
40. For one formulation of this, see Marx, *Capital*, vol. 1, p. 208.
41. Concerning this distinction, see Marx, *Capital*, vol. 1, pp. 240–41, *Capital*, vol. 3, pp. 833–34, and *The Grundrisse* (tr. McLellan) pp. 141–43.
42. "Surplus-value is the difference between the value of the product and the value of the elements consumed in the formation of that product, in other words, of the means of production and the labour-power" (Marx, *Capital*, vol. 1, p. 232). Surplus-value is created by labor-power. "[T]he value of labour-power, and the value which that labour-power creates in the labour process are two entirely different magnitudes. . . . The specific use–value which this commodity possesses [is that] of being *a source not only of value, but of more value than it has itself*" (Marx, *Capital*, vol. 1, pp. 215–16).
43. "All surplus-value, whatever particular form (profit, interest, or rent) it may subsequently crystallize into, is in substance the materialization of unpaid labour. The secret of the self-expansion of capital resolves itself into having the disposal of a definite quantity of other people's unpaid labour" (Marx, *Capital*, vol. 1, p. 585).
44. The exploitative character of surplus-value is masked by the wage-form. On this theme see *Capital*, vol. 1, pp. 591 and 639.
45. Marx, *The Grundrisse*, p. 141.
46. Ibid., p. 136.
47. For a discussion of the meaning of "artificial" in Marx, see Mészáros, *Marx's Theory of Alienation*, pp. 175ff.
48. See *Capital*, vol. 3, p. 250, for one formulation of this contradiction.

49. *Capital*, vol. 1, p. 423.
50. As Marx writes: "As soon as labour in the direct form has ceased to be the great well-spring of wealth, labour time ceases and must cease to be its measure, and hence exchange value (must cease to be the measure) of use value" (Marx, *Grundrisse* [tr. Nicolaus], p. 705).
51. Marx, *Capital*, vol. 1, p. 43.
52. Marx, *The Grundrisse* (tr. McLellan), p. 141.
53. Ibid., p. 145.
54. Marx and Engels, *The Communist Manifesto* (ed. Ryazanoff), p. 45.
55. Marx, *The Grundrisse*, p. 145.
56. Ibid., pp. 144–45.
57. Ibid., p. 142.
58. In the *Grundrisse* Marx writes that, once the associated individuals appropriate their own surplus labor, "and *disposable time* thereby ceases to have an *antithetical* existence—then, on the one side, necessary labour time will be measured by the needs of the social individual, and, on the other, the development of the power of social production will grow so rapidly that, even though production is now calculated for the wealth of all, *disposable* time will grow for all. For real wealth is the developed productive power of all individuals. The measure of wealth is then not any longer, in any way, labour time, but rather disposable time. *Labour time as the measure of value* posits wealth itself as founded on poverty, and disposable time as existing *in and because of the antithesis to surplus labour time*; or, the positing of an individual's entire time as labour time, and his degradation therefore to mere worker, subsumption under labour" (*Grundrisse* [tr. Nicolaus], p. 708).
59. For a formulation that Marx gives on the contrast between necessary time and nonworking time, see Marx, *The Grundrisse* (tr. McLellan), pp. 144–49; and *Capital*, vol. 3, pp. 819–20.
60. See the *The Grundrisse*, pp. 142–45, on this theme.
61. Marx, *Wages, Price and Profit*, in Marx and Engels, *Selected Works*, p. 225.
62. On this theme, see *The Grundrisse*, p. 144, for example.
63. Marx, *Capital*, vol. 1, p. 256.
64. Ernest Mandel, *Marxist Economic Theory*, trans. B. Pearce (New York: Monthly Review Press, 1968), vol. 2, p. 674.
65. E. Fromm, *The Sane Society* (Greenwich: Fawcett Publications, 1955), p. 124.
66. Marx, *Economic and Philosophic Manuscripts*, p. 113.
67. K. Marx, *Pre-Capitalist Economic Formations*, trans. J. Cohen, ed. and with intro. by E. Hobsbawm (New York: International Publishers, 1965), p. 84.
68. Marx, *Capital*, vol. 1, p. 326.
69. Ibid., p. 187.
70. Ibid., p. 297.
71. Ibid., p. 633. For further formulations along these same lines, see especially pp. 625, 639–40, and 673 in *Capital*, vol. 1.
72. Marx, *The Grundrisse*, p. 134.
73. It might be well to point out here that talk about the continuing predominance of economic conscious activity should not be taken as

denying that there has been some decrease in the length of the working day as capitalism has developed. However, the potential impact of this decrease on the creation of a qualitatively better society is largely undercut by other factors.

74. Marx, *Capital*, vol. 1, p. 260.

75. This is not to say that social relations play no role at all in the quantitative predominance of economic conscious activity in feudalism. This predominance is primarily grounded on the level of development of productivity, but is secondarily grounded on the social relations of feudalism; but these social relations do not in their very structure operate to extend working time as much as possible.

76. On this, see *The German Ideology*, pp. 67-68.

77. Marx, *The Grundrisse*, p. 144.

78. Ibid.

79. Ibid., p. 142.

80. Marx, *Economic and Philosophic Manuscripts*, p. 136.

81. This comes out clearly in *The Grundrisse*, pp. 70-71.

82. Ibid., p. 119.

83. Marx, *Capital*, vol. 1, p. 649.

84. *Capital*, vol. 3, p. 820.

85. H. Marcuse, *Five Lectures*, trans. J. J. Shapiro and S. M. Weber (Boston: Beacon Press, 1970), p. 62.

86. H. Marcuse, *An Essay on Liberation* (Boston: Beacon Press, 1969), p. 21.

87. Marx, *The Grundrisse*, p. 124.

88. Ibid., pp. 148-49.

89. For a discussion of the place of the *Grundrisse* in Marx's work as a whole, and especially its relation to *Capital*, see McLellan's introductory essay to_ his translation of selections from *The Grundrisse* and the Foreword, by Nicolaus, to his translation of the complete text.

90. Marx, *Capital*, vol. 1, p. 241.

91. *Capital*, vol. 3, p. 819.

92. See *The Grundrisse* (tr. McLellan), pp. 142 and 148.

93. For some telling discussion on this issue, see Iring Fetscher's article on "The Young and the Old Marx" together with Marx W. Wartofsky's Comment on it in *Marx and the Western World*, ed. N. Lobkowicz (Notre Dame: University of Notre Dame Press, 1967). Wartofsky writes: "[I]t seems a perverse and narrow 'dialectic' which insists that the young and the old Marx are dichotomous because they are different, as if the integrity and continuity of Marx's philosophical framework could have been preserved only if he had spent the rest of his life endlessly repeating what he had said in his earliest works. On such a perverse view, Marx's *development*, in the sense that his later works are transformations of earlier ideas, is taken to be evidence that his later work is opposed to, or even contradictory to, his earlier work. A profounder view of the integrity of Marx's views from 'young' to 'old' is to see in Marx the fundamental continuity of certain root-concepts—in particular, the central ones of alienation and objectivication" (*Marx and the Western World*, p. 40). In this same connection see discussions in Mészáros, *Marx's Theory of Alienation*, pp. 217-32; and Fromm, *Marx's Concept of Man*, pp. 69-79.

94. For Mandel's discussion of Marx's retention of the theory of alienation in his later work, see *The Formation of the Economic Thought of Karl Marx*, pp. 174–80.
95. Ibid., p. 160.
96. Ibid., pp. 161–62.
97. Ibid., p. 162.
98. Marx and Engels, *The German Ideology*, p. 550.
99. Ibid., p. 324.
100. Ibid., p. 338.
101. Ibid., p. 257.
102. Ibid., p. 86.
103. This is from the introduction to a *Contribution to the Critique of Hegel's Philosophy of Right* (written in 1843) in *Karl Marx: Early Writings*, trans. and ed. T. B. Bottomore (New York: McGraw-Hill, 1964), p. 43.
104. Marx, *Economic and Philosophic Manuscripts*, p. 112.
105. Ibid., p. 138.
106. Ibid., pp. 37–38.
107. Marx, "On the Jewish Question" in Easton and Guddat, eds., *The Writings of the Young Marx*, p. 231.
108. Ibid., p. 241.
109. Marx, *Economic and Philosophic Manuscripts*, p. 177.
110. Ibid., p. 113.
111. Marx and Engels, *The German Ideology*, p. 246.
112. See *The German Ideology*, p. 524; and *The Grundrisse* (tr. McLellan), p. 67.
113. However, we note that there are two very rare occurrences of Marx's word for "species being" (*Gattungswesen*) in the *Grundrisse* (tr. Nicolaus), pp. 243 and 496.
114. Marx, *Economic and Philosophic Manuscripts*, pp. 138–39.
115. Ibid., p. 138.
116. *The German Ideology*, p. 290.
117. Ibid., p. 45. For other formulations of this theme, see *The German Ideology*, p. 283; and *Capital*, vol. 1, p. 396.
118. In close connection with this, see Mészáros' discussion of "having" in *Marx's Theory of Alienation*, pp. 210–11.
119. This description is given in "Excerpt Notes of 1844," in *Writings of the Young Marx*, p. 281.
120. Marx, *Economic and Philosophic Manuscripts*, pp. 138–39.
121. Ibid., p. 144.
122. See the well-known passage in the *Economic and Philosophic Manuscripts*, in which Marx speaks about the "rich human being," p. 144.
123. Ibid., p. 134.
124. Marx, *The Grundrisse* (tr. McLellan), pp. 70–71.
125. *The German Ideology*, p. 495.
126. Mészáros, *Marx's Theory of Alienation*, pp. 212–13.
127. This is Marcuse's formulation. See *Eros and Civilization*, p. 164.
128. For an elaboration of this theme by Marcuse, see pp. 47 and 182 of *Eros and Civilization*.

129. Marx, *Economic and Philosophic Manuscripts*, pp. 110-11.
130. But also see Marcuse's discussion of "technological rationality" in *One-Dimensional Man*, pp. 144-69.
131. Marcuse, *Eros and Civilization*, p. 101.
132. Ibid., pp. 99-100.
133. In this connection, see the formulation in *The German Ideology*, pp. 37-38.
134. In this connection, we refer to a set of unpublished lectures by Marx W. Wartofsky called "Towards an Historical Epistemology." In explaining his view that "our modes of cognitive praxis change and develop historically with changes in the modes of social and practical activity," Wartofsky proposes "as the foundation for an historical epistemology . . . that the genesis, and the historical development of cognitive praxis involves representation; that our pre-cognitive or non-cognitive praxis, our ordinary outward action in the world, becomes distinctively human when it is mediated by representation; and that it is in the construction or production and use of such representative artifacts that human action becomes teleological and rational." Wartofsky explains further that the notion of representation he has in mind "has to do with the representation not of the world as it is, but of the world as we come to know it in our practical interaction with it, or as we conceive or imagine it to be, in our *prospective* or future action in it. Thus, it is the world made, reproduced, reformed by human action that becomes both the genesis and the object of our representation. In a profound sense, this *imago mundi* is what Aristotle chracterized, in his definition of tragedy, as an *imitation of an action*."
135. Concerning Kant's conception of reason, as well as Hegel's conception of the history of reason, see K. Brien, *Human Freedom in Marx*, pp. 265-68.
136. In his lectures "Towards an Historical Epistemology," Wartofsky points out that the most traditional approach to epistemology is one "which characterizes the problems of perception, belief and knowledge as timeless and ahistorical *analytical* questions, and attempts an essentialist definition or characterization of human knowing. . . . The essentialist character of this model lies precisely in its unconscious universalization of a particular, limited, historical view of cognition."
137. For this discussion, see Marcuse's chapter on "The Aesthetic Dimension," in *Eros and Civilization*.
138. Ibid., pp. 157-58.
139. On this theme, see Marcuse, *An Essay on Liberation*, pp. 30-31.
140. Marx, *Economic and Philosophic Manuscripts*, pp. 139-41. The sentence order is modified.
141. In relation to the theme that human sensuousness must be considered in historical terms, see Marcuse, *An Essay on Liberation*, p. 32; and *Studies in Critical Philosophy*, p. 218.
142. In *Eros and Civilization*, p. 166, Marcuse points to the importance of this distinction for aesthetic philosophy.
143. See *The German Ideology*, pp. 291-92, on this theme; also Marcuse's *Eros and Civilization*, pp. 184-85.
144. In a chapter on "The Transformation of Sexuality into Eros," in *Eros and Civilization*, Marcuse speculates about the nonrepressive, nondestructive

transformation of the conative-libidinal forces beyond the established social reality. Instinctual liberation in a nonrepressive context "involves not simply a release but a *transformation* of the libido: from sexuality constrained under genital supremacy to erotization of the entire personality. It is a spread rather than explosion of libido—a spread over private and societal relations which bridges the gap maintained between them by a repressive reality principle" (p. 184). "The free development of transformed libido within transformed institutions, while eroticizing previously tabooed zones, time, and relations, would *minimize* the manifestations of *mere* sexuality by integrating them into a far larger order, including the order of work" (p. 185). "The organism in its entirety becomes the substratum of sexuality, while at the same time the instinct's objective is no longer absorbed by a specialized function—namely, that of bringing 'one's own genitals into contact with those of someone of the opposite sex.' Thus enlarged, the field and objective of the instinct becomes the life of the organism itself. This process almost naturally, by its inner logic, suggests the conceptual transformation of sexuality into Eros" (p. 187). "Moreover, nothing in the nature of Eros justifies the notion that the 'extension' of the impulse is confined to the corporeal sphere. If the antagonistic separation of the physical from the spiritual part of the organism is itself the historical result of repression, the overcoming of this antagonism would open the spiritual sphere to the impulse" (p. 192).

Chapter 6

1. For example, Marx writes: "The mode of production in material life determines the general character of the social, political, and spiritual processes of life." Preface to *Critique of Political Economy*, in *Reader in Marxist Philosophy*, p. 186.

2. The first complete English translation of Marx's doctoral dissertation, *The Difference Between the Democritean and Epicurean Philosophy of Nature*, appears as an Appendix to Norman Livergood's *Activity in Marx's Philosophy*, with him as the translator of Marx's text (The Hague: Martinus Hijhoff, 1967). The citations in our text come from pp. 79-81.

3. In this connection, we indicate our agreement with Livergood's position developed in *Activity in Marx's Philosophy*, where he writes (p. ix): "It is in Epicurus' concept of the declination of the atoms that Marx finds the most fruitful grounds for the development of his own thought. The atom with its activity of declination became a symbol of the active self for Marx. Whereas Democritus had remained in the realm of external determinism, Epicurus offers a more fruitful conception of *self*-determination. If the atom can be viewed as inwardly active, then we can escape mechanistic determinism."

4. Paul Oppenheim and Hilary Putnam, "Unity of Science as a Working Hypothesis," in H. Feigl, M. Scriven, and G. Maxwell, eds., *Minnesota Studies in the Philosophy of Science* (Minneapolis: University of Minnesota Press, 1958), vol. 2. Putnam has long since abandoned the position he took in this early essay with Oppenheim. See, e.g., Putnam's paper on "Reduc-

tionism and the Nature of Psychology," in *Cognition*, International Journal of Psychology (Amsterdam: Elsevier, 1973), vol. 3, pp. 131-46. We still use the early essay since it represents an exceptionally clear formulation of the classic view of the unity of science.

5. Oppenheim and Putnam, "Unity of Science," p. 4.
6. Ibid., p. 15.
7. Ibid., p. 6.
8. Ibid., p. 15.
9. Ibid., p. 16. In connection with this theme, we refer to Meyerson's view that "the principle of causality is none other than the principle of identity applied to the existence of objects in time." Emile Meyerson, *Identity and Reality*, trans. K. Loewenberg (New York: Dover Publications, 1962), p. 43.
10. Oppenheim and Putnam, "Unity of Science," p. 6.
11. Ibid., p. 15.
12. David Bohm, *Causality and Chance in Modern Physics* (Princeton: D. Van Nostrand, 1957).
13. For explanation and discussion of this principle, see Bohm, *Causality and Chance*, especially chap. 3. Also see Werner Heisenberg, *Physics and Philosophy: The Revolution in Modern Science* (New York: Harper & Row, 1962), especially chaps. 1-4. And see Milič Čapek, *The Philosophical Impact of Contemporary Physics* (Princeton: D. Van Nostrand, 1961), especially chap. 16.
14. In reference to the indeterminacy relations that he formulated, Heisenberg writes that the "lower limit to the accuracy with which certain variables can be known simultaneously may be postulated as a law of nature." Werner Heisenberg, *The Physical Principles of the Quantum Theory*, trans. C. Eckart and F. C. Hoyt (Chicago: University of Chicago Press, 1930), p. 3.
15. Bohm, *Causality and Chance*, p. 85.
16. Ibid., p. 86.
17. See Bohm, *Causality and Chance*, p. 88; and also Čapek, *The Philosophical Impact of Contemporary Physics*, pp. 307ff.
18. Bohm, *Causality and Chance*, p. 87.
19. See chap. 4 of *Causality and Chance*, especially pp. 104-16, for Bohm's alternative interpretation of the quantum theory.
20. Bohm writes that his alternative interpretation of the quantum theory would "permit the representation of quantum-mechanical effects as arising out of an objectively real sub-stratum of continuous motion, existing at a lower level, and satisfying new laws which are such as to lead to those of the current quantum theory as approximations that are good only in what we shall call the quantum-mechanical level" (*Causality and Chance*, p. 104). Also see pp. 69 and 94.
21. Ibid., p. 106.
22. Ibid., p. 116.
23. Ibid., p. 141.
24. Ibid., pp. 1-2.
25. Ibid., p. 2.
26. Ibid., p. 141. For additional material on the very rich discussion that Bohm provides on the interconnections between the concepts of causality and

chance, see especially pp. 2-3, 20-25, 28-32, and 140-43 of *Causality and Chance*.

27. In this connection we note a comment that Bohm makes on the "integration of substructure and background." He writes: "[T]he next step in physics may well show the inadequacy of the simple procedure of just going through level after level of smaller and smaller particles, connected perhaps by fields which interact with these particles. Instead, we may find that the background enters in a very fundamental way even into the definition of the conditions for the existence of the new kinds of basic entities to which we will eventually come, whatever they may turn out to be. Thus, we may be led to a theory in which appears a much closer integration of substructure and background into a well-knit whole than is characteristic of current theories" (*Causality and Chance*, pp. 138-39).

28. Concerning the mechanistic philosophy Bohm writes: "At bottom, the only changes that are regarded as possible within this scheme are quantitative changes in the parameters or functions defining the state of the system . . . while fundamental qualitative changes in the modes of being of the basic entities and in the forms in which the basic laws are to be expressed are not regarded as possible. Thus, the essence of the mechanistic position lies in its assumption of fixed basic qualities, which means that the laws themselves will finally reduce to purely quantitative relationships" (ibid., p. 131).

29. Ibid., p. 133.

30. Ibid., p. 135.

31. Ibid. The sentence order is slightly modified here.

32. On the assumption of the qualitative infinity in nature see chap. 5 of *Causality and Chance*, especially pp. 132-40.

33. Alfred Schmidt, *The Concept of Nature in Marx*, trans. Ben Fowkes (London: New Left Books, 1971), p. 195.

34. Ibid., p. 59.

35. Ibid., p. 52.

36. Robert S. Cohen, "Friedrich Engels," in the *Dictionary of Scientific Biography*, vol. 15 (New York: Charles Scribner's Sons, 1978), pp. 141-42. Also see Cohen's coordinate article "Karl Marx" in the same volume.

37. Engels, *Anti-Dühring*, p. 51.

38. Schmidt, *The Concept of Nature in Marx*, pp. 183-84.

39. To bring this out in connection with the theme of matter, we cite the *Dialectics of Nature* (p. 328), in which Engels writes that "matter as such and motion as such have not yet been seen or otherwise experienced by anyone, but only the various, actually existing material things and forms of motion. Matter is nothing but the totality of material things from which this concept is abstracted, and motion as such nothing but the totality of all sensuously perceptible forms of motion; words like matter and motion are nothing but *abbreviations* in which we comprehend many different sensuously perceptible things according to their common properties. Hence matter and motion *cannot* be known in any other way than by investigation of the separate material things and forms of motion, and by knowing these, we also, *pro tanto* know matter and motion as such."

40. R. S. Cohen, "Friedrich Engels," p. 135.
41. See *Dialectics of Nature*, pp. 24-25, for Engels' formulations along these lines.
42. Ibid., p. 26.
43. Ollman, *Alienation*, p. 58.
44. Ibid.
45. Engels, *Dialectics of Nature*, p. 27.
46. See, for example, *Capital*, vol. 1, pp. 26 and 338.
47. Lenin, *Philosophical Notebooks*, p. 117.
48. Schmidt, *The Concept of Nature in Marx*, p. 59.
49. Ibid., pp. 184-85.
50. For example, Schmidt speaks of "that incompatibility between dialectic and materialism which has been repeatedly emphasized by a number of critics" (ibid., p. 59). He spells out what he means by this in a footnote where he approvingly cites Maurice Merleau-Ponty who wrote: "'It has often been asked, and with reason, how a materialism could be dialectical, how matter, if one applies this word strictly, could contain the principle of productivity and novelty which is called a dialectic'" (ibid., p. 210).
51. Thomas S. Kuhn, *The Structure of Scientific Revolutions*, 2d ed. (Chicago: University of Chicago Press, 1970). See especially pp. 182-87 of Kuhn's 1969 Postscript. In the same connection, see Kuhn's essays, "Second Thoughts on Paradigms" and "Objectivity, Value Judgment, and Theory Choice," which appear in Thomas S. Kuhn, *The Essential Tension: Selected Studies in Scientific Tradition and Change* (Chicago: University of Chicago Press, 1977).
52. Harold I. Brown, *Perception, Theory, and Commitment: The New Philosophy of Science* (Chicago: University of Chicago Press, 1977), p. 111.
53. In this association we contend that the discipline of evolutionary biology is especially ripe for such a dialectical reconstruction. Much of the critical work for a dialectical reconstruction in this field has already been done collectively by the thinkers who forged the "synthetic theory of evolution," e.g., Ernst Mayr, Bernhard Rensch, and Theodosius Dobzhansky.
54. See the section on "Freedom as the Recognition of Necessity" in Chapter 5.

Postscript to Second Edition

1. Chris Sciabarra, "Marx on the Precipice of Utopia," *Critical Review* 2, no. 4 (1988): 76-81.
2. Marilyn Nissim-Sabat, "Review of *Marx, Reason, and the Art of Freedom*," *Ethics* 99, no. 3 (1989): 647-648.
3. Daniel Little, "Review of *Marx, Reason, and the Art of Freedom*," *Review of Radical Political Economics* 21, nos. 1 & 2 (1989): 163-164. Also see my reply to Daniel Little's review in the same issue, pp. 166-168.
4. Daniel Little, *The Scientific Marx* (Minneapolis: University of Minnesota Press, 1986).
5. See my "Review of *The Scientific Marx*" in *Review of Radical Political Economics* 21, nos. 1& 2 (1989): 159-163. Also see Daniel Little's reply to my review in the same issue, pp. 164-165.
6. Little, *The Scientific Marx*, p. 129.
7. Ibid., p. 131.
8. Ibid., pp. 146-7.
9. Ibid., pp. 40-67.
10. Karl Marx, "Preface to Second Edition," *Capital*, Vol. 1, ed. Frederick Engels & trans. Samuel Moore and Edward Aveling (New York: Modern Library, 1906), p. 26.
11. See my discussion of the concrete universal in Chapter 2 of *Marx, Reason, and the Art of Freedom*, pp. 30-44.
12. Marx, "Preface to Second Edition," p. 25.
13. Sean Sayers, "Review of *Marx, Reason, and the Art of Freedom*," *Science & Society* 54, no. 2 (1990): 235-38.
14. See, for example, Karl Marx, *Grundrisse*, trans. and with a Foreword by Martin Nicolaus (Middlesex, England: Penguin Books, 1973), pp. 539-543.
15. Nissim-Sabat, "Review," p. 648.
16. Much of the material in *Part Two* is adapted from my previously published article on "Marx and the Spiritual Dimension" in *Topoi: An International Review of Philosophy* 15, no. 2 (1996): 211-223. I gratefully acknowledge the kind permission of Kluwer Academic Publishers to adapt some sections of this previously published article for use in this *Postscript*.
17. Karl Marx, *Karl Marx: Selected Writings*, ed. David McLellan (Oxford: Oxford University Press, 1977), p. 509.
18. Karl Marx, *Writings of the Young Marx on Philosophy and Society*, trans. and ed. Loyd D. Easton and Kurt H. Guddat (Garden City, N.Y.: Doubleday, 1967), p. 250.
19. See Chapter 6 of *Marx, Reason, and the Art of Freedom* for further discussion of these themes.
20. Marx, *Writings of the Young Marx*, p. 250.
21. This listing of existential needs has been adapted from Erich Fromm, *The Anatomy of Human Destructiveness* (New York: Holt, Rinehart, and Winston, 1973), pp. 230-31.
22. Milan Machovec, *A Marxist Looks At Jesus* (Philadelphia: Fortress Press, 1976), p. 21. [Original German title: *Jesus Für Atheisten*, 1972.]
23. See *Marx, Reason, and the Art of Freedom*, p. 3.
24. Karl Marx, *Economic and Philosophic Manuscripts of 1844*, ed. with an Introduction by Dirk J. Struik, trans. Martin Mulligan (New York: International Publishers, 1964), p. 134.
25. Marx, *Writings of Young Marx*, p. 281.

26. Marx, *Manuscripts of 1844*, p.144.

27. Ibid., p.113.

28. Karl Marx and Frederick Engels, *The German Ideology*, ed. S. Ryazanskaya (Moscow: Progress Publishers, 1968), p. 246.

29. Marx, *Manuscripts of 1844*, p.144.

30. For an important elaboration of the contrast between "authoritarian religion" and "humanistic religion," see Erich Fromm's *Psychoanalysis and Religion* (New Haven: Yale University Press, 1979), pp. 34-45.

31. For a developed exposition of the convergence between humanistic Marxism and Buddhism see Kevin M. Brien, *"Logos* and *Mythos:* Humanistic Marxism and Buddhism," *Dialogue and Universalism* 12, no. 3 (2002): 77-100; and also note no. 1 for the "Addendum on Buddhism and Marxism."

32. Machovec, *A Marxist Looks At Jesus*, p. 21.

Addendum on Buddhism and Marxism

1. Much of the material in this addendum is adapted from my paper "Buddhism and Marxism: Ironic Affinities" published in *Dialogue and Universalism* 14, no. 1-2 (2004). I gratefully acknowledge the kind permission of the Editors of *Dialogue and Universalism* to adapt materials from this previously published article for use in this addendum.

2. See *The Middle Length Discourses of the Buddha* [a translation of the *Majjhima Nikaya*], trans. Bhikkhu Nanamoli and Bhikkhu Bodhi (Boston: Wisdom Publications, 1995), pp. 533-36.

3. His Holiness The Dalai Lama, "An Interview" conducted by Andrew N. Woznicki, *Dialogue and Universalism* 7, no. 11-12 (1997): 16.

4. His Holiness The Dalai Lama, *Beyond Dogma: Dialogues and Discourses,* trans. Alison Anderson and Marianne Dresser (Berkeley: North Atlantic Books, 1996), p. 110.

5. For a sustained analysis and argument along these lines, consult the main text of *Marx, Reason, and the Art of Freedom*—especially Chapter 3.

6. Karl Marx and Frederick Engels, *The Selected Correspondence of Marx and Engels*, trans. Dona Torr (New York: International Publishers, 1942), p. 472.

7. Adam Schaff, *Marxism and the Human Individual,* ed. Robert S. Cohen, trans. Olgierd Wojtasiewicz (New York: McGraw Hill, 1970), pp. 18-25.

8. Ibid., pp. 21-22.

9. Gajo Petrovic, *Marx in the Mid-Twentieth Century* (Garden City, NY: Doubleday & Co., 1967), pp. 77-78.

10. Ibid., pp. 78-79.

11. Ibid., p. 23.

12. Ibid., p. 79.

13. Ibid., p. 32.

14. Karl Marx, *Economic and Philosophic Manuscripts of 1844,* ed. with an Introduction by Dirk J. Struik, trans. Martin Mulligan (New York: International Publishers, 1964), p. 113.

15. Ibid., p. 134.

16. Milan Machovec, *A Marxist Looks at Jesus* [1st American edition], Introduction by Peter Hebblethwaite (Philadelphia: Fortress Press, 1976), p. 35.

17. Ibid., p. 34-35.

18. See *Marx, Reason, and the Art of Freedom*, especially Chapters 2, 3 & 4.
19. His Holiness The Dalai Lama, *Ethics for the New Millennium* (New York: Riverhead Books, 1999).
20. Kevin M. Brien, "*Logos* and *Mythos*: Humanistic Marxism and Buddhism," *Dialogue and Universalism* 12, no. 3 (2002): 76-100.
21. For discussion of this theme see *Marx, Reason, and the Art of Freedom*, Chapter 6.
22. For a classic presentation of these noble truths, see *The Long Discourses of the Buddha* [a translation of the *Digha Nikaya*], trans. Maurice Walshe (Boston: Wisdom Publications, 1995), pp. 344-49.
23. Edward Conze, *Buddhism: Its Essence and Development* (New York: Harper & Row Publishers, 1975), pp. 27-52.
24. See *The Long Discourses of the Buddha*, pp. 335-50.
25. See *Engaged Buddhism: Buddhist Liberation Movements in Asia*, ed. Christopher Queen and Sallie King (Albany: State University of New York Press, 1996); and also *Engaged Buddhism in the West*, ed. Christopher Queen (Boston: Wisdom Publications, 2000).
26. This is an abbreviation of a classical formulation from the *Samyutta Nikaya* that can be found in *Buddhist Texts Through the Ages*, trans. & ed. E. Conze, *et al* (Boston: Shambhala,1990), p. 66.
27. See *Buddhist Texts Through the Ages,* pp. 65-82 for a classical presentation of these "twelve links."
28. See the essay on "Worldly Bodhisattvas" in *The Gethsemani Encounter: A Dialogue on the Spiritual Life by Buddhist and Christian Monastics,* ed. Donald W. Mitchell and James Wiseman, O.S.B. (New York: Continuum Publishing Co., 2003), pp. 140-46.
29. See Marx's famous "Theses on Feuerbach" in *Writings of the Young Marx on Philosophy and Society*, trans. & ed. Loyd D. Easton and Kurt H. Guddat (Garden City, N.Y.: Doubleday, 1967), pp. 400-02.
30. See *Marx, Reason, and the Art of Freedom*, Chapters 3 and 4.
31. Ibid., Chapter 6.
32. From the *Dhammapada*, published in *The Teachings of the Compassionate Buddha*, ed. E. A. Burtt (New York: New American Library, 2000), pp. 28, 45, 33.
33. Karl Marx and Frederick Engels, *The German Ideology*, trans. & ed. S. Ryazanskaya (Moscow: Progress Publishers, 1968), p. 31.
34. This information can be found at the following website maintained by the Office of Tibet and the Tibetan Government-in-Exile: http://www.dalailama.com/ (accessed January 2004).
35. Alan Watts, *The Way of Zen* (New York: Vintage Books, 1957).
36. Marx, *The German Ideology*, p. 31.
37. See note no. 20.

Bibliography

Althusser, Louis. *For Marx*. Translated by Ben Brewster. New York: Vintage Books, 1970.
Althusser, Louis, and E. Balibar. *Reading Capital*. Translated by Ben Brewster. New York: Pantheon Books, 1970.
Avineri, Sholomo. *The Social and Political Thought of Karl Marx*. Cambridge: Cambridge University Press, 1968.
Baran, Paul A. *The Political Economy of Growth*. New York: Monthly Review Press, 1957.
Baran, Paul A., and Paul M. Sweezy. *Monopoly Capital: An Essay on the American Economic and Social Order*. New York: Monthly Review Press, 1966.
Benedict, Ruth. *Patterns of Culture*. Preface by Margaret Mead. Boston: Houghton Mifflin, 1959.
Bergson, Henri. *Creative Evolution*. Translated by Arthur Mitchell. New York: Henry Holt & Co., 1931.
Bernal, J. D. *Science in History*. 4 vols. Cambridge: MIT Press, 1971.
Bernstein, Richard J. *Praxis and Action*. Philadelphia: University of Pennsylvania Press, 1971.
Blanshard, Brand. *The Nature of Thought*. 2 vols. London: Allen & Unwin, 1939.
Bohm, David. *Causality and Chance in Modern Physics*. Foreword by Louis de Broglie. Princeton: D. Van Nostrand, 1957.
Bradley, F. H. *Appearance and Reality*. Oxford: Oxford University Press, 1966.
Braverman, Harry. *Labor and Monopoly Capital*. New York: Monthly Review Press, 1974.
Brien, Kevin M. "Buddhism and Marxism: Ironic Affinities." *Dialogue and Universalism* 14, no. 1-2 (2004).
————. *Human Freedom in Marx*. Ann Arbor: University Microfilms International, 1978.
————. "*Logos* and *Mythos*: Humanistic Marxism and Buddhism." *Dialogue and Universalism* 12, no. 3 (2002): 77-100.
————. *Marx, Reason, and the Art of Freedom*. Philadelphia: Temple University Press, 1987.
————. "Marx and the Spiritual Dimension." *Topoi: An International Review of Philosophy* 15, no. 2 (1996): 211-223.
————. "Review of *The Scientific Marx*." *Review of Radical Political Economics* 21, nos. 1& 2 (1989): 159-163.
Brown, Harold I. *Perception, Theory and Commitment: The New Philosophy of Science*. Chicago: University of Chicago Press, 1977.
Brown, Norman O. *Life Against Death*. New York: Random House, 1959.

Bunge, Mario. *Causality: The Place of the Causal Principle in Modern Science.* Cambridge: Harvard University Press, 1959.

Burtt, E. A., ed. *The Teachings of the Compassionate Buddha.* New York: New American Library, 2000.

Capek, Milic. *The Philosophical Impact of Contemporary Physics.* Princeton: D. Van Nostrand, 1961.

Chodorow, Nancy. *The Reproduction of Mothering: Psychoanalysis and the Sociology of Gender.* Berkeley: University of California Press, 1978.

Cohen, Robert S. "Dialectical Materialism and Carnap's Logical Empiricism," in *The Philosophy of Rudolf Carnap.* Edited by Paul A. Schilpp. La Salle, Ill.: Open Court Publishing Co., 1963.

————. "Friedrich Engels" in the *Dictionary of Scientific Biography*, Vol. 15. New York: Charles Scribner's Sons, 1978.

————. "Karl Marx" in the *Dictionary of Scientific Biography*, Vol. 15. New York: Charles Scribner's Sons, 1978.

————. "Marxism and Democracy," in *Marxism and Democracy.* Edited by Herbert Aptheker. New York: Humanities Press, 1965.

————, ed. *Marxism and the Human Individual* by Adam Schaff. See Schaff.

Cohen, Robert S., and Marx W. Wartofsky, eds. *Dialectics of the Concrete* by Karel Kosik. See Kosik.

Cornforth, Maurice. *Historical Materialism.* New York: International Publishers, 1954.

————. *Marxism and the Linguistic Philosophy.* New York: International Publishers, 1967.

————. *The Open Philosophy and the Open Society.* New York: International Publishers, 1968.

Conze, Edward. *Buddhism: Its Essence and Development.* New York: Harper & Row Publishers, 1975.

Conze, Edward *et al*, trans. & ed. *Buddhist Texts Through the Ages.* Boston: Shambhala,1990.

de Beauvoir, Simone. *The Second Sex.* Translated and edited by H. M. Parshley. New York: Alfred A. Knopf, 1952.

Desan, Wilfrid. *The Marxism of Jean-Paul Sartre.* Garden City, N.Y.: Doubleday & Co., 1966.

————. *The Tragic Finale.* New York: Harper Bros., 1960.

Dewey, John. *Art as Experience.* New York: Capricorn Books, 1958 (orig. ed., 1934).

Dobzhansky, Theodosius. *Mankind Evolving: The Evolution of the Human Species.* New Haven: Yale University Press, 1962.

Dunham, Barrows. *Giant in Chains.* New York: Hill and Wang, 1965.

————. *Man Against Myth.* New York: Hill and Wang, 1962.

Dutt, Clemens, ed. *Fundamentals of Marxism-Leninism.* Moscow: Foreign Languages Publishing House, 1961.

Einstein, Albert. *Ideas and Opinions.* Edited by Carl Seelig. With translations by Sonja Bargmann. New York: Dell Publishing, 1973.

Einstein, Albert, and Leopold Infeld. *The Evolution of Physics.* New York: Simon & Schuster, 1961 (orig. ed., 1938).

Engels, Frederick. *Anti-Dühring.* Translated by Emile Burns. Edited by C. P. Dutt. New York: International Publishers, 1966 (orig. ed., 1878).

————. *The Condition of the Working Class in England.* Translated by Florence Kelley Wischnewetzky. London: Allen & Unwin, 1950 (orig. ed., 1845).

————. *Dialectics of Nature.* Translated and edited by Clemens Dutt. Preface and Notes by J. B. S. Haldane. New York: International Publishers, 1940 (orig. ed., 1925).

————. *Ludwig Feuerbach and the Outcome of Classical German Philosophy.* Edited by C. P. Dutt. New York: International Publishers, 1941 (orig. ed., 1888).

————. *The Origin of the Family, Private Property, and the State.* New York: International Publishers, 1942 (orig. ed., 1884).

————. *The Peasant War in Germany.* Translated by Moissaye J. Olgin. Introduction and Notes by D. Riazanov. New York: International Publishers, 1966 (orig. ed., 1850).

————. *Socialism: Utopian and Scientific.* Translated by Edward Aveling. Introduction by the author. London: Allen & Unwin, 1950 (orig. ed., 1880).

Engels, Frederick, and Karl Marx. See Marx and Engels.

Fanon, Frantz. *The Wretched of the Earth.* Translated by Constance Farrington. Preface by Jean-Paul Sartre. New York: Grove Press, 1968.

Fetscher, Irving. "The Young and the Old Marx," with Comment by Marx W. Wartofsky, in *Marx and the Western World.* Edited by Nicholas Lobkowicz. Notre Dame, Ind.: University of Notre Dame Press, 1967.

Feuerbach, Ludwig. *The Essence of Christianity.* Translated by George Eliot. Introduction by Karl Barth. Foreword by H. Richard Niebuhr. New York: Harper Bros., 1957 (orig. ed., 1841).

Firestone, Shulamith. *The Dialectic of Sex: The Case for Feminist Revolution.* New York: Bantam Books, 1971.

Fischer, Ernst. *Art Against Ideology.* Translated by Anna Bostock. New York: George Braziller, 1969.

————. *The Necessity of Art.* Translated by Anna Bostock. New York: Penguin Books, 1964.

Fleischer, Helmut. *Marxism and History.* Translated by Eric Mosbacher. New York: Harper & Row, 1973.

Ford, Kenneth W. *The World of Elementary Particles.* New York: Blaisdell Publishing Co., 1963.

Frankl, Victor. *From Death-Camp to Existentialism.* Boston: Beacon Press, 1959.

Freud, Sigmund. *Civilization and Its Discontents.* Translated and edited by James Strachey. New York: W. W. Norton, 1962.

Friedan, Betty. *The Feminine Mystique.* New York: W. W. Norton, 1963.

Fromm, Erich. *The Anatomy of Human Destructiveness.* New York: Holt, Rinehart and Winston, 1973.

————. *The Art of Loving.* New York: Harper Bros., 1956.

————. *Beyond the Chains of Illusion.* New York: Simon & Schuster, 1962.

————. *Escape from Freedom.* New York: Avon Books, 1965 (orig. ed., 1941).

————. *Man for Himself: An Inquiry into the Psychology of Ethics.* Greenwich, Conn.: Fawcett Publications, 1968.

————. *Marx's Concept of Man.* With a translation from Marx's *Economic and Philosophic Manuscripts* by T. B. Bottomore. New York: Frederick Ungar, 1967.

————. *The Revolution of Hope.* New York: Bantam Books, 1968.

————. *The Sane Society.* Greenwich, Conn.: Fawcett Publications, 1955.

————, ed. *Socialist Humanism: An International Symposium.* Garden City, N.Y.: Doubleday, 1965.

————. *Psychoanalysis and Religion.* New Haven: Yale University Press, 1979.

Garaudy, Roger. *Karl Marx: The Evolution of His Thought.* Translated by Nan Apotheker. New York: International Publishers, 1967.

Gessen, B. *The Social and Economic Roots of Newton's "Principia."* With an Introduction by Robert S. Cohen. New York: Howard Fertig, 1971 (orig. ed., 1931).

Gould, Carol C. *Marx's Social Ontology: Individuality and Community in Marx's Theory of Social Reality.* Cambridge: MIT Press, 1978.

Gould, Carol C., and Marx W. Wartofsky, eds. *Women and Philosophy: Toward a Theory of Liberation.* New York: Putnam, 1976.

Gouldner, Alvin. *The Two Marxisms.* New York: Seabury Press, 1980.

Habermas, Jürgen. *Knowledge and Human Interests.* Translated by Jeremy Shapiro. Boston: Beacon Press, 1971.

———. *Legitimation Crisis.* Translated and Introduced by Thomas McCarthy. Boston: Beacon Press, 1975.

Harding, Sandra. "What is the Real Material Base of Patriarchy and Capital?" in *Women and Revolution.* Edited by Lydia Sargent. Boston: South End Press, 1981.

Harrington, Michael. *Socialism.* New York: Saturday Review Press, 1972.

Hegel, G. W. F. *The Phenomenology of Mind.* Translated with an Introduction and Notes by J. B. Baillie. With an Introduction to the Torchbook Edition by George Lichtheim. New York: Harper & Row, 1967 (orig. ed., 1807).

———. *Philosophy of Right.* Translated by T. M. Knox. Oxford: Clarendon Press, 1965 (orig. ed., 1821).

———. *Reason in History.* Translated by Robert S. Hartman. Indianapolis: Bobbs-Merrill Co., 1953 (orig. ed., 1837).

———. *Science of Logic.* 2 vols. Translated by W. H. Johnston and L. G. Struthers. London: Allen & Unwin, 1961 (orig. ed., 1812-16).

Heidegger, Martin. *Being and Time.* Translated by John Macquarrie and Edward Robinson. New York: Harper & Row, 1962 (orig. ed., 1927).

Heisenberg, Werner. *The Physical Principles of the Quantum Theory.* Translated by C. Eckart and F. C. Hoyt. Chicago: University of Chicago Press, 1930.

———. *Physics and Philosophy: The Revolution in Modern Science.* New York: Harper & Row, 1962.

Hempel, Carl G. *Aspects of Scientific Explanation and Other Essays in the Philosophy of Science.* New York: Free Press, 1965.

His Holiness The Dalai Lama. *Beyond Dogma: Dialogues and Discourses,* trans. Alison Anderson and Marianne Dresser. Berkeley: North Atlantic Books, 1996.

———. *Ethics for the New Millennium.* New York: Riverhead Books, 1999.

———. "An Interview" conducted by Andrew N. Woznicki. *Dialogue and Universalism* 7, no. 11-12 (1997).

History of the Communist Party of the Soviet Union (Bolsheviks). Edited by a Commission of the Central Committee of the C.P.S.U.(B.). San Francisco: Proletarian Publishers, 1976 (orig. ed., 1938).

Hodges, Donald Clark. "The Method of Capital" in *Science & Society.* Vol. 31, no. 4 (Fall 1967).

Hook, Sidney. *From Hegel to Marx.* Ann Arbor: University of Michigan Press, 1962 (orig. ed., 1936).

———, ed. *Determinism and Freedom in the Age of Modern Science.* New York: Collier Books, 1961.

Jaspers, Karl. *Man in the Modern Age.* Translated by Eden and Cedar Paul. Garden City, N.Y.: Doubleday, 1957.

Jung, Carl G. *The Archetypes and the Collective Unconscious.* 2d ed. Translated by R. F. C. Hull. Princeton: Princeton University Press, 1968 (orig eds., 1934-55).

———. *Memories, Dreams, Reflections.* Recorded and Edited by Aniela Jaffe. Translated by Richard and Clara Winston. New York: Vintage Books, 1965 (orig. ed., 1961).

———. *On the Nature of the Psyche.* Translated by R. F. C. Hull. Princeton: Princeton University Press, 1969 (orig. ed., 1947).

———. *Two Essays on Analytical Psychology.* Translated by R. F. C. Hull. Princeton: Princeton University Press, 1972 (orig. eds., 1917 and 1928).

———. *The Undiscovered Self.* Translated by R. F. C. Hull. New York: New American Library, 1958 (orig. ed., 1957).

Kant, Immanuel. *Critique of Judgement.* Translated and with an Introduction by J. H. Bernard. New York: Hafner Publishing Co., 1951 (orig. ed., 1790).

———. *Critique of Practical Reason.* Translated and with an Introduction by Lewis White Beck. Indianapolis: Bobbs-Merrill Co., 1956 (orig ed., 1788).

———. *Critique of Pure Reason.* Translated by Norman Kemp Smith. New York: St. Martin's Press, 1965 (orig. ed., 1781).

———. *Foundations of the Metaphysics of Morals.* Translated and with an Introduction by Lewis White Beck. Indianapolis: Bobbs-Merrill Co., 1959 (orig. ed., 1785).

———. *Kant's Political Writings.* Edited with an Introduction and Notes by Hans Reiss. Translated by H. B. Nisbet. Cambridge: Cambridge University Press, 1970.

———. *Perpetual Peace.* Edited with an Introduction by Lewis White Beck. Indianapolis: Bobbs-Merrill Co., 1957 (orig. ed., 1795).

Kaufmann, Walter. *Nietzsche.* New York: Vintage Books, 1968.

Kierkegaard, Søren. *The Attack upon "Christendom."* Translated by Walter Lowrie. In *A Kierkegaard Anthology.* Edited by Robert Bretall. Princeton: Princeton University Press, 1946.

Kolakowski, Leszek. *Toward a Marxist Humanism.* Translated by Jane Zielonko Peel. New York: Grove Press, 1968.

Kosik, Karel. *Dialectics of the Concrete.* Edited by Robert S. Cohen and Marx W. Wartofsky. Translated by Karel Kovanda with James Schmidt. Dordrecht: D. Reidel Publishing Co., 1976.

Kuhn, Thomas S. *The Essential Tension: Selected Studies in Scientific Tradition and Change.* Chicago: University of Chicago Press, 1977.

———. *The Structure of Scientific Revolutions.* 2d ed. Chicago: University of Chicago Press, 1970 (orig. ed., 1963).

Lenin, V. I. *Imperialism: The Highest Stage of Capitalism.* In *Lenin: Selected Works.* One-vol. ed. New York: International Publishers, 1971 (orig. ed., 1917).

———. *Philosophical Notebooks.* Translated by Clemens Dutt. Edited by Stewart Smith. Vol. 38 in *Collected Works.* Moscow: Foreign Languages Publishing House, 1961 (orig. ed., 1933).

———. *Selected Works.* One-vol. ed. New York: International Publishers, 1971.

———. *What Is to Be Done?* New York: International Publishers, 1929 (orig. ed., 1902).

Lewis, John. *The Life and Teaching of Karl Marx.* New York: International Publishers, 1965.

Little, Daniel. "Review of *Marx, Reason, and the Art of Freedom.*" *Review of Radical Political Economics* 21, nos. 1 & 2 (1989): 163-164.

———. *The Scientific Marx.* Minneapolis: University of Minnesota Press, 1986.

Livergood, Norman D. *Activity in Marx's Philosophy.* With the first complete English translation by N. Livergood of Marx's Doctoral Dissertation, *The Difference Between the*

Democritean and Epicurean Philosophy of Nature, as an Appendix. The Hague: Martinus Nijhoff, 1967.

Lobkowicz, Nicholas, ed. *Marx and the Western World*. Notre Dame, Ind.: University of Notre Dame Press, 1967.

The Long Discourses of the Buddha [a translation of the *Digha Nikaya*], trans. Maurice Walshe. Boston: Wisdom Publications, 1995.

Lukacs, Georg. *History and Class Consciousness*. Translated by Rodney Livingstone. Cambridge: MIT Press, 1971 (orig. ed., 1923).

Machovec, Milan. *A Marxist Looks At Jesus*. Philadelphia: Fortress Press, 1976. [Original German title: *Jesus Für Atheisten*, 1972.]

Malcolm X, and Alex Haley. *The Autobiography of Malcolm X*. New York: Grove Press, 1966.

Mandel, Ernest. *The Formation of the Economic Thought of Karl Marx*. Translated by B. Pearce. New York: Monthly Review Press, 1971.

————. *Marxist Economic Theory*. 2 vols. Translated by B. Pearce. New York: Monthly Review Press, 1968.

Mao Tse-Tung. "On Contradiction," in *Mao Tse-Tung: Selected Works*. vol. 2. New York: International Publishers, 1954.

Marcuse, Herbert. *Eros and Civilization*. New York: Vintage Books, 1955.

————. *An Essay on Liberation*. Boston: Beacon Press, 1969.

————. *Five Lectures*. Translated by Jeremy J. Shapiro and Shierry M. Weber. Boston: Beacon Press, 1970.

————. *Negations*. Translated by Jeremy J. Shapiro. Boston: Beacon Press, 1968.

————. *One-Dimensional Man*. Boston: Beacon Press, 1968.

————. *Reason and Revolution*. Boston: Beacon Press, 1960 (orig. ed., 1941).

————. *Soviet Marxism*. New York: Vintage Books, 1961.

————. *Studies in Critical Philosophy*. Translated by Joris De Bres. Boston: Beacon Press, 1973.

Markovic, Mihailo, *From Affluence to Praxis*. Ann Arbor: University of Michigan Press, 1974.

Marx, Karl. *Capital*. vol. 1. Edited by Frederick Engels. Translated by Samuel Moore and Edward Aveling. Revised and amplified by Ernest Untermann. New York: Modern Library, 1906 (orig. ed., 1867).

————. *Capital*. vol. 2. Edited by Frederick Engels. New York: International Publishers, 1967 (orig. ed., 1885).

————. *Capital*. vol. 3. Edited by Frederick Engels. New York: International Publishers, 1967 (orig. ed., 1894).

————. *The Class Struggles in France*. Introduction by F. Engels. New York: International Publishers, 1964 (orig. ed., 1850).

————. *A Contribution to the Critique of Political Economy*. Translated by S. W. Ryazanskaya. Edited with an Introduction by Maurice Dobb. New York: International Publishers, 1970 (orig. ed., 1859).

————. *Critique of Hegel's "Philosophy of Right."* Translated by Annette Jolin and Joseph O'Malley. Edited with an Introduction and Notes by Joseph O'Malley. Cambridge: Cambridge University Press, 1970 (orig. ed., 1927).

————. *Critique of the Gotha Programme*. With appendices by Marx, Engels, and Lenin. Edited by C. P. Dutt. New York: International Publishers, 1938 (orig. ed., 1891).

————. *The Difference Between the Democritean and Epicurean Philosophy of Nature*.

Marx's Doctoral Dissertation appears as an Appendix to Norman Livergood's *Activity in Marx's Philosophy*. See Livergood (orig. ed., 1902).

————. *Early Texts*. Translated and edited by David McLellan. New York: Barnes & Noble, 1971.

————. *Early Writings*. Translated and edited by T. B. Bottomore. Foreword by Erich Fromm. New York: McGraw-Hill, 1964.

————. *Economic and Philosophic Manuscripts of 1844*. Edited with an Introduction by Dirk J. Struik. Translated by Martin Milligan. New York: International Publishers, 1964 (orig. ed., 1932).

————. *The Eighteenth Brumaire of Louis Bonaparte*. Edited by C. P. Dutt. New York: International Publishers, 1935 (orig, ed., 1852).

————. *The Ethnological Notebooks of Karl Marx*. Transcribed and edited, with an introduction by Lawrence Krader. Assen, The Netherlands: Van Gorcum, 1972.

————. *Grundrisse*. Translated with a Foreword by Martin Nicolaus. Middlesex, England: Penguin Books, 1973 (orig. ed., 1939).

————. *The Grundrisse*. Selections from the full text. Edited and translated by David McLellan. New York: Harper & Row, 1972 (orig. ed., 1939).

————. *Karl Marx: Selected Writings*. Edited by David McLellan. Oxford: Oxford University Press, 1977.

————. *Karl Marx: Texts on Method*. Translated and edited by Terrell Carver. With Prefaces to Marx's "Introduction" to the *Grundrisse*, and to Marx's "Notes on Adolph Wagner," and Commentary on Marx's "Introduction," by Terrell Carver. New York: Harper & Row, 1975.

————. *The Poverty of Philosophy*. With an Introduction by Frederick Engels. New York: International Publishers, 1963 (orig. ed., 1847).

————. *Pre-Capitalist Economic Formations*. Selected from the *Grundrisse*. Edited and with an Introduction by E. J. Hobsbawm. Translated by Jack Cohen. New York: International Publishers, 1965.

————. *Selected Writings in Sociology and Social Philosophy*. Translated by T. B. Bottomore. Edited with an Introduction and Notes by T. B. Bottomore and Maximilien Rubel. Foreword by Erich Fromm. New York: McGraw-Hill, 1964.

————. *Theories of Surplus Value*. Part I. Translated by Emile Burns. Edited by S. Ryazanskaya. Moscow: Progress Publishers, 1968 (orig. ed., 1905-10).

————. *Theories of Surplus Value*. Part II. Translated and Edited by S. Ryazanskaya. Moscow: Progress Publishers, 1968 (orig. ed., 1905-10).

————. *Theories of Surplus Value*. Part III. Translated by Jack Cohen and S. W. Ryazanskaya. Edited by S. W. Ryazanskaya and Richard Dixon. Moscow: Progress Publishers, 1971 (orig. ed., 1905-10).

————. *Writings of the Young Marx on Philosophy and Society*. Translated and Edited by Lloyd D. Easton and Kurt H. Guddat. Garden City, N.Y.: Doubleday, 1967.

Marx, Karl, and Frederick Engels. *Basic Writings on Politics and Philosophy*. Edited by Lewis S. Feuer. Garden City, N.Y.: Doubleday, 1959.

————. *The Communist Manifesto*. Translated by Eden and Cedar Paul. Edited with an Introduction and Notes by D. Ryazanoff. New York: Russell & Russell, 1963 (orig. ed., 1848).

————. *The German Ideology*. Edited by S. Ryazanskaya. Moscow: Progress Publishers, 1968 (orig. ed., 1932).

————. *The Holy Family*. Translated by R. Dixon. Moscow: Foreign Languages Publishing House, 1956 (orig. ed., 1845).

————. *On Religion*. Moscow: Foreign Languages Publishing House, 1957.

————. *Selected Correspondence*. Translated by Dona Torr. New York: International Publishers, 1942 (orig. ed., 1934).

————. *Selected Works*. In one volume. New York: International Publishers, 1968.

Marx, Karl, Frederick Engels, and V. I. Lenin. *On Historical Materialism*. New York: International Publishers, 1974.

————. *Reader in Marxist Philosophy*. Edited with an Introduction and Notes by Howard Selsam and Harry Martel. New York: International Publishers, 1963.

Maslow, Abraham H. *The Farther Reaches of Human Nature*. New York: Viking Press, 1972.

————. *Toward a Psychology of Being*. New York: D. Van Nostrand, 1968.

Mayr, Ernst. *The Growth of Biological Thought: Diversity, Evolution, and Inheritance*. Cambridge: Harvard University Press, 1982.

————. *Populations, Species, and Evolution*. An Abridgment of *Animal Species, and Evolution*. Cambridge: Harvard University Press, 1970.

Mehring, Franz. *Karl Marx*. Translated by Edward Fitzgerald. Introduction by Max Shachtman. Ann Arbor: University of Michigan Press, 1962.

Menninger, Karl. *Man Against Himself*. New York: Harcourt, Brace & World, 1938.

Mészáros, István. *Marx's Theory of Alienation*. New York: Harper & Row, 1972.

Meyerson, Emile. *Identity and Reality*. Translated by Kate Loewenberg. New York: Dover Publications, Inc., 1962 (orig. ed., 1908).

Miller, Jean Baker. *Toward a New Psychology of Women*. Boston: Beacon Press, 1977.

The Middle Length Discourses of the Buddha [a translation of the *Majjhima Nikaya*], trans. Bhikkhu Nanamoli and Bhikkhu Bodhi. Boston: Wisdom Publications, 1995.

Moore, Barrington, Jr. *Social Origins of Dictatorship and Democracy*. Boston: Beacon Press, 1967.

Moore, G. E. *Philosophical Studies*. London: Routledge & Kegan Paul, 1922.

Morgan, Lewis Henry. *Ancient Society: Or Researches in the Lines of Human Progress from Savagery, through Barbarism to Civilization*. New York: H. Holt, 1877.

Mumford, Lewis. *The Condition of Man*. New York: Harcourt Brace Jovanovich, 1973.

————. *Technics and Civilization*. New York: Harcourt, Brace & World, 1963 (orig. ed., 1938).

————. *Technics and Human Development*. New York: Harcourt Brace Jovanovich, 1967.

Nagel, Ernst. *Sovereign Reason*. Glencoe, Ill.: Free Press, 1954.

Nietzsche, Friedrich. *The Birth of Tragedy*. Translated and with Commentary by Walter Kaufmann. New York: Vintage Books, 1967.

————. *On the Genealogy of Morals*. Translated by Walter Kaufmann and R. J. Hollingdale. Edited with Commentary by Walter Kaufmann. New York: Vintage Books, 1969.

————. *The Portable Nietzsche*. Selected and translated, with an Introduction, Prefaces, and Notes, by Walter Kaufmann. New York: Viking Press, 1968.

————. *The Will to Power*. Translated by Walter Kaufmann and R. J. Hollingdale. Edited with Commentary by Walter Kaufmann. New York: Vintage Books, 1968.

Nissim-Sabat, Marilyn. "Review of *Marx, Reason, and the Art of Freedom*." *Ethics* 99, no. 3 (1989): 647-648.

Ollman, Bertell. *Alienation: Marx's Conception of Man in Capitalist Society*. Cambridge: Cambridge University Press, 1971.

Oppenheim, Paul, and Hilary Putnam. "Unity of Science as a Working Hypothesis," in *Minnesota Studies in the Philosophy of Science*. Vol. 2. Edited by H. Feigl, M. Scriven, and G. Maxwell. Minneapolis: University of Minnesota Press, 1958.

Pappenheim, Fritz. *The Alienation of Modern Man.* New York: Modern Reader Paperbacks, 1968 (orig. ed., 1959).

Parkes, Henry Bamford. *Marxism: An Autopsy.* Chicago: University of Chicago Press, 1964.

Paton, H. J. *Kant's Metaphysics of Experience.* 2 vols. London: Allen & Unwin, 1965.

Pepper, Stephen C. *World Hypotheses.* Berkeley: University of California Press, 1970.

Petrovic, Gajo. *Marx in the Mid-Twentieth Century.* Garden City, N.Y.: Doubleday, 1967.

Popper, Karl R. *The Logic of Scientific Discovery.* New York: Basic Books, 1959.

——. *The Open Society and Its Enemies.* rev. ed. 2 vols. New York: Harper & Row, 1963 (orig. ed., 1945).

——. *The Poverty of Historicism.* New York: Harper & Row, 1964.

Progoff, Ira. *Jung's Psychology and Its Social Meaning.* Garden City, N.Y.: Anchor Books, 1973.

Putnam, Hilary. "Reductionism and the Nature of Psychology," in *Cognition,* International Journal of Psychology, vol. 3. Amsterdam: Elsevier, 1973.

Putnam, Hilary, and Paul Oppenheim. "Unity of Science as a Working Hypothesis." See Oppenheim.

Queen, Christopher, ed. *Engaged Buddhism in the West.* Boston: Wisdom Publications, 2000.

Queen Christopher, and Sallie King, eds. *Engaged Buddhism: Buddhist Liberation Movements in Asia.* Albany: State University of New York Press, 1996.

Rader, Melvin. *Marx's Interpretation of History.* New York: Oxford University Press, 1979.

Reed, Evelyn. *Problems of Women's Liberation.* New York: Pathfinder Press, 1970.

——. *Woman's Evolution: From Matriarchal Clan to Patriarchal Family.* New York: Pathfinder Press, 1975.

Reich, Wilhelm. *Character Analysis.* (3d ed., rev. and enl.) Translated by Vincent R. Carfagno. New York: Simon & Schuster, 1972.

——. *The Mass Psychology of Fascism.* (3d ed., rev. and enl.) Translated by Vincent R. Carfagno. New York: Simon & Schuster, 1970.

Rensch, Bernhard. *Evolution above the Species Level,* trans. Dr. Altevogt. New York: Columbia University Press, 1960.

Rorty, Richard M. "Relations, Internal and External" in *The Encyclopedia of Philosophy.* Vol. 7. Edited by Paul Edwards. New York: Macmillan & Free Press, 1967.

Sargent, Lydia, ed. *Women and Revolution.* Boston: South End Press, 1981.

Sartre, Jean-Paul. *Being and Nothingness.* Translated and with an Introduction by Hazel E. Barnes. New York: Washington Square Press, 1966.

——. *Search for a Method.* Translated and with an Introduction by Hazel E. Barnes. New York: Vintage Books, 1968.

Sayers, Sean. "Review of *Marx, Reason, and the Art of Freedom.*" *Science & Society* 54, no. 2 (1990): 235-38.

Schaff, Adam. *Marxism and the Human Individual.* Edited by Robert S. Cohen. Introduction by Erich Fromm. Based on a translation by Olgierd Wojtasiewicz. New York: McGraw-Hill, 1970.

Schmidt, Alfred. *The Concept of Nature in Marx.* Translated by Ben Fowkes. London: New Left Books, 1973.

Schumpeter, Joseph A. *Capitalism, Socialism and Democracy.* New York: Harper & Row, 1962.

Sciabarra, Chris. "Marx on the Precipice of Utopia," *Critical Review* 2, no. 4 (1988): 76-81.

Shapere, Dudley. "Meaning and Scientific Change," in *Mind and Cosmos: Essays in Contem-*

porary Science and Philosophy. The University of Pittsburgh Series in the Philosophy of Science, vol. 3. Pittsburgh: University of Pittsburgh Press, 1966.

———. *Reason and the Search for Knowledge: Investigations in the Philosophy of Science.* Boston: Reidel, 1984.

Stalin, Joseph. *Dialectical and Historical Materialism.* New York: International Publishers, 1940.

———. *Economic Problems of Socialism in the U.S.S.R.* New York: International Publishers, 1952.

Stojanovic, Svetozar. *Between Ideals and Reality.* Translated by Gerson S. Sher. New York: Oxford University Press, 1973.

Suppe, Frederick, ed. *The Structure of Scientific Theories.* 2d ed. Edited with a Critical Introduction and an Afterword by Frederick Suppe. Urbana: University of Illinois Press, 1977.

Suzuki, Daisetz T. *Essays in Zen Buddhism.* 1st ser. London: Luzac and Co., 1927.

———. *Zen and Japanese Culture.* Princeton: Princeton University Press, 1959.

Sweezy, Paul M. *Modern Capitalism and Other Essays.* New York: Monthly Review Press, 1972.

———. *The Theory of Capitalist Development.* New York: Monthly Review Press, 1970 (orig. ed., 1942).

Sweezy, Paul M., and Paul A. Baran. *Monopoly Capital.* New York: Monthly Review Press, 1966.

Sweezy, Paul M., and Charles Bettelheim. *On the Transition to Socialism.* New York: Monthly Review Press, 1971.

Tillich, Paul. *The Courage to Be.* New Haven: Yale University Press, 1952.

Tucker, Robert. *Philosophy and Myth in Karl Marx.* Cambridge: Cambridge University Press, 1965.

Vazquez, Adolfo Sanchez. *Art and Society.* Translated by M. Riofrancos. New York: Monthly Review Press, 1973.

Venable, Vernon. *Human Nature: The Marxian View.* Cleveland: World Publishing, 1966 (orig. ed., 1945).

Walsh, W. H. *Metaphysics.* New York: Harcourt, Brace & World, 1963.

———. *Philosophy of History.* New York: Harper & Row, 1960.

Wartofsky, Marx W. *Conceptual Foundations of Scientific Thought.* New York: Macmillan, 1968.

———. "Karl Marx and the Outcome of Classical Marxism." Paper delivered at a symposium on Marx and Science held Feb. 11-12, 1983, under the auspices of the *Boston Colloquium for the Philosophy and History of Science,* at Boston University.

———. "Perception, Representation and the Forms of Action: Towards an Historical Epistemology" in *Ajatus* 36, 1976 (originally read in 1973).

———. "Towards an Historical Epistemology." Unpublished Lectures.

Wartofsky, Marx W., and Robert S. Cohen, eds. *Dialectics of the Concrete* by Karel Kosik. See Kosik.

Wartofsky, Marx W., and Carol C. Gould, eds. *Women and Philosophy: Toward a Theory of Liberation.* New York: Putnam, 1976.

Watts, Alan. *The Way of Zen.* New York: Vintage Books, 1957.

Website maintained by the Office of Tibet and the Tibetan Government-in-Exile: http://www.dalailama.com/ (accessed January 2004).

Weber, Max. *The Protestant Ethic and the Spirit of Capitalism.* Translated by Talcott Parsons. Foreword by R. H. Tawney. New York: Charles Scribner's Sons, 1958.

Weizenbaum, Joseph. *Computer Power and Human Reason*. San Francisco: W. H. Freeman & Co., 1976.

Wellmer, Albrecht. *Critical Theory of Society*. Translated by John Cumming. New York: Seabury Press, 1974.

Wetter, Gustav A. *Dialectical Materialism: A Historical and Systematic Survey of Philosophy in the Soviet Union*. Translated by Peter Heath. New York: Frederick A. Praeger, 1958.

Wittgenstein, Ludwig. *The Blue and Brown Books*. New York: Harper & Row, 1965.

———. *Philosophical Investigations*. Translated by G. E. M. Anscombe. New York: Macmillan, 1953.

Young, Iris. "Beyond the Unhappy Marriage: A Critique of Dual Systems Theory," in *Women and Revolution*. See Sargent.

Index

abstract universals: Blanshard on, 30–31, 269n16; and concrete universals, 30–33; and distortions of Marx, 50–51, 162, 200, 262n2, 270–71n28; and external relations, 269n16; and Marx's universe of discourse, 31, 42–43; and Wittgenstein, 272n45

alienated activity: and activity as a means, 11–12, 149–50, 165–66; and alienated production vs. unalienated, 141–60; and alienated reason, 173–75; and alienated vs. unalienated modes of being, 8–14, 127–80; as antisensuous, 173, 177; and characteristic activity of capitalist and worker, 12–13; and dichotomy between reason and sensuousness, 172–74; and domination by productive apparatus, 12–13, 136, 141–42; and "having," 165–69; and internal contradictions of capitalism, 142–144; and predominance of economic conscious activity, 148–51; and rationality of domination, 173, 175. *See also* alienation; unalienated activity

alienation: and capitalism, 220–21; and characteristic activity of capitalist and worker, 12–13; and contrast with objectification, 264n10; and crisis of human person, 119–26; in early and late Marx, 160–61, 289n93; and existential mean-inglessness, 59, 119–23; four aspects of, 127–28; Fromm on, 263n4; and "lordship-bondage" relation in Hegel, 266–67n38; and male-female social relations, 98, 125; and Petrovic, 244–45; and "primitive accumulation" in early capitalism, 285n100; and private property, 13; and self-alienation, 12, 266n37; and social relations, 10–14, 128–36; and species essence, 9–10, 161–65; structural generation of, in capitalism, 98, 114–19, 125; and world history, 266n25. *See also* alienated activity; unalienated activity

Althusser, Louis: and the bifurcated Marx, 23, 270–71n28; on complex unity, 22–23, 87; on concrete-real vs. concrete-in-thought, 18; critique of, 23, 28–29; and internal relations, 23, 270n27; and movement from abstract to concrete, 17; vs. Ollman, 23, 28–29, 270n27; and structure, 22–23, 28–29, 270n27

Baran, Paul, and Paul Sweezy: on contrast between monopoly and pre-monopoly capitalism, 100–5; critique of, 101–6; on fall in rate of profit, 100–1; on price determination, 104; on rising surplus, 100–1; on stagnation, 113

311

73; on publication dates of Marx's
works, 285n106; on traditional
Marxism, 120-21
reason: an alienated activity, 172–73; as antisensuous, 173, 177; and being-in-the-
world, 1; as changing and historical,
174, 176–80; and dialectical theory of
unity of science as extension of theoretical reason in Marx, 186–95; extralogical content of, 174–75; "laws" of
dialectics as regulative principles of,
198–200; Marcuse on, 173; Marx's
logic of explanation as an instrument of
theoretical reason, 17–41, 199; as metaphysical, 175; and metaphysics,
181–82; practical reason in Kant,
130–31, 174–75; practical reason in
Marx, 131, 135–36; and "praxis," 174;
and rationality of domination, 173; and
sensuousness, 172–80; theoretical
reason in Kant, 130, 174; and traditional
separation of, from "lower faculties,"
172–73; transformation of theoretical
and practical modes of, 177–80; as
unchanging, 174–75
Reed, Evelyn: on ancient matriarchy, 83, 87,
282n19; and "group marriage," 280n5;
and origins of private wealth, 94; on
social relations of capitalism and complicity of women, 98
Reiss, Hans: on Kant and political rights of
individuals, 286n16
religion: Einstein on, 69; and existential
needs, 69–71; Marx on, 69; a positive
view of, 69–71; and Protestant ideology, 67–68; spiritual forces vs.,
222–224; Suzuki on, 71; Tillich on,
69–70; and Weber, 67–68. *See also*
Buddhism
revolutionizing agency, a: as anticipated by
Marx, 116, 118–19; in contemporary
stage of capitalism, 119–26; and crisis
of human person, 119–26; and male-
female social relations, 124–26; and
transformation of consciousness,
123–26

Sayers, Sean: on Brien's interpretation of
Marx, 218–21
Schaff, Adam: and social individuals,
242–43, 286n4
Sciabarra, Chris: on Brien's interpretation of
Marx, 209–10
Schmidt, Alfred: on "abstract matter" and
Engels, 197; critique of, 196–97, 200–1;
on dialectics of a "world mind," 200; on
Engels' dialectics of nature, 195–96; on
alleged "incompatibility between
dialectic and materialism," 295n50
scientific revolution: Brown on, 204; and
Kuhn's notion of a "disciplinary
matrix," 202–3; and the heuristic potential of Marx's "logic of explanation" for
science, 202–4; and Marx's "disciplinary matrix," 203–4
sensuousness: and alienated activity, 172–74;
conative-libidinal aspect of, 178–79,
292n144; as historically conditioned,
177–78; and rationality of domination,
173–74; and reason, 172–80; sense-perceptive aspect of, 178–79; and "transformation of sexuality into Eros,"
291–92n144; in unalienated activity,
172, 176–80
social individuals: and Gould, 286n4; and
nature of social relations, 128–35; and
Schaff, 286n4
social relations: and abstract vs. concrete
community, 133–36; and activity as end
in itself in socialism, 153–54; alienated
mode of, 10–14, 128–29, 132–35,
141–42; alienated vs. unalienated,
128–36; concrete vs. abstract, 47–48;
and dualism of abstract citizen and private individual, 133–34, 286n23; and
Hegel, 134; and the "human interest,"
134–36; and Kant, 130–31; and "the
naturally arisen clan community,"
280–81n11; and nature of individual
development, 128–29, 135, 166–72;
and a new common sense, 135–36; and
practical reason in Marx, 131–32,
135–36; and private vs. general interest,
132–33; and specific nature of social